The Restoration

# *A History of Early Modern England*

General Editor: John Morrill

This series provides a detailed and vivid account of the history of early modern England. One of its principal aims is to capture the spirit of the time from the point of view of the people living through it. Each volume will be broad in scope covering the political, religious, social and cultural dimensions of the period.

**Published**

The Birth of the Elizabethan Age
England in the 1560s
*Norman Jones*

The Restoration
England in the 1660s
*N. H. Keeble*

England in the 1670s
*John Spurr*

England in the 1690s
*Craig Rose*

The Birth of Britain*
A New Nation 1700–10
*W. A. Speck*

* denotes out of print

**In Preparation**

England in the 1590s
*David Dean*

England in the 1650s
*Ann Hughes*

# The Restoration

*England in the 1660s*

N. H. Keeble

Blackwell Publishing

350 Main Street, Malden, MA 02148-5018, USA
108 Cowley Road, Oxford OX4 1JF, UK
550 Swanston Street, Carlton South, Melbourne, Victoria 3053, Australia
Kurfürstendamm 57, 10707 Berlin, Germany



First published 2002 by Blackwell Publishers Ltd, a Blackwell Publishing company

*Library of Congress Cataloging-in-Publication Data*

Keeble, N. H.
The Restoration: England in the 1660s / N. H. Keeble.
p. cm. – (A history of early modern England)
Includes bibliographical references and index.
ISBN 0-631-19574-2 (alk. paper) – ISBN 0-631-23617-1 (pbk.: alk. paper)
1. Great Britain–History–Charles II, 1660–1685. 2. Great Britain–History–Restoration, 1660–1688. 3. England–Civilization–17th century. I. Title. II. Series.
DA445. K44 2002
941.06′6–dc21

2002001980

A catalogue record for this title is available from the British Library.

Typeset in 10 on 12pt Baskerville
by Kolam Information Services Pvt. Ltd, Pondicherry, India
Printed and bound in the United Kingdom by TJ International, Padstow, Cornwall

For further information on
Blackwell Publishing, visit our website:
www.blackwellpublishing.com

To Jen

# *Contents*

# *Preface*

I must first express my gratitude to Professor John Morrill, FBA, for giving me the opportunity to write this book. I count myself privileged to have been asked to contribute to the History of Early Modern England series of which he is the general editor and I especially appreciate his taking a chance on one who is not a historian by training or profession.

I owe a considerable debt to the following friends and colleagues for giving their time to read through, and to comment upon, parts of this study: David Bebbington, Professor of History at the University of Stirling; Gordon Campbell, Professor of Renaissance Studies at the University of Leicester; Thomas N. Corns, Professor of English and Head of the School of Arts and Humanities at the University of Wales, Bangor; Mark Goldie, Fellow of Churchill College, Cambridge; Richard L. Greaves, Robert O. Lawton Distinguished Professor of History at Florida State University. They have rescued me from many errors and infelicities. For those which remain, I alone am responsible.

I must acknowledge, too, how very much I owe to those whose work in the last twenty years has restored scholarly excitement to the 1660s (and to the later seventeenth century in general). In addition to the colleagues I have mentioned, among historians I think particularly of Tim Harris, Michael Hunter, Ronald Hutton, Steven Pincus, Paul Seaward, Jonathan Scott, John Spurr and Blair Worden; and among literary scholars, of Paul Hammond, Michael McKeon, David Norbrook, Annabel Patterson and Steven Zwicker. The many references to them in my notes to this book do not adequately record the extent of my indebtedness to their work. In one respect, however, I have not followed them. Repudiating anglo-centrism, the best current writing on the early modern period is alive to the complex interactions between the nations of the British isles. I, though, make no mention of Scotland, Wales or Ireland. This is not because I have forgotten the Celtic nations, but simply because the title of the series in which my book appears confines its attention to England.

Since, many years ago now, Dr Geoffrey F. Nuttall, FBA, acted as the external examiner of my D. Phil. thesis, he has been for me a model of scholarly accuracy, clarity and integrity. Although in the course of preparing this book I have (unusually) not troubled him with drafts and queries, I should not like something of mine to appear in print without my acknowledging how much in all I write I owe to his inspiration.

I am much indebted to Blackwell Publishers for the understanding and courtesy with which they responded to what became my annual letter explaining that the project was not yet completed. They (and Professor Morrill) have patiently tolerated the inordinate length of time which, because of administrative commitments, it has taken me to finish this book.

I am grateful to the British Academy for an award under its Research Leave Scheme which extended a period of research leave granted by the University of Stirling. To Stirling I am additionally grateful for a second sabbatical in which to finish the book. The Carnegie Trust for the Universities of Scotland generously provided a grant to fund travel to libraries.

Some passages derive from previously published material: in chapter 2 from '"When civil fury first grew high, / And men fell out they knew not why...": *Hudibras* and the Making of History', *Literature and History*, 7 (1998), 70–87; in chapter 6 from '"Till one greater man / Restore us...": Restoration Images in Bunyan and Milton', which appeared in *Bunyan Studies*, 6 (1995/96), 6–33, and, in revised form, in David Gay, James G. Randall and Arlette Zinck (eds), *Awakening Words: Bunyan and the Language of Community* (Newark: University of Delaware Press, and London: Associated University Presses, 2000), pp. 27–50; in chapter 6 from my *The Literary Culture of Nonconformity in Later Seventeenth-century England* (Leicester: Leicester University Press, and Athens, GA: University of Georgia Press, 1987); and in chapter 8 from introductions to the chapters in my *The Cultural Identity of Seventeenth Century Woman: A Reader* (London: Routledge, 1994). I gratefully acknowledge the permission of the copyright holders to re-use this material.

I dedicate this book to my wife. It is because her life is so firmly rooted in the present that I am able to abscond to the seventeenth century sure of a safe return.

NHK

# *Abbreviations*

| | |
|---|---|
| Abernathy | George R. Abernathy, 'The English Presbyterians and the Stuart Restoration', *Transactions of the American Philosophical Society*, ns 55, 2 (1965), 5–101 |
| Ailesbury | [Thomas Bruce], *Memoirs of Thomas, Earl of Ailesbury*, The Roxburghe Club, 2 vols (1890) |
| Baker | Sir Richard Baker, *A Chronicle of the Kings of England... Whereunto is Added the Reign of King Charles the First, and the First Thirteen Years of his Sacred Majesty King Charles the Second... in which are... the most remarkable occurrences relating to his Majesties most happy and wonderful Restauration, by the prudent conduct, under God, of George late duke of Albemarle... as they were extracted out of his Excellencies own papers* [cont. by Edward Phillips], 5th edn (1670) |
| Baxter *CCRB* | N. H. Keeble and Geoffrey F. Nuttall, *Calendar of the Correspondence of Richard Baxter*, 2 vols (Oxford, 1991) |
| Baxter *RB* | Richard Baxter, *Reliquiae Baxterianae*, ed. Matthew Sylvester (1696); reference is to part, page and numbered section |
| *BJRL* | *Bulletin of the John Rylands Library* |
| Bosher | Robert S. Bosher, *The Making of the Restoration Settlement: The Influence of the Laudians, 1649–1662* (1951) |
| Browning | Andrew Browning (ed.), *English Historical Documents, 1660–1714* (1966) |
| Bulstrode | Sir Richard Bulstrode, *Memoirs and Reflections upon the Reign and Government of King Charles the Ist., and K. Charles the IId.* (1721) |
| Bunyan *GA* | John Bunyan, *Grace Abounding to the Chief of Sinners*, ed. Roger Sharrock (Oxford, 1962) |

| | |
|---|---|
| Bunyan *MW* | *The Miscellaneous Works of John Bunyan*, gen. ed. Roger Sharrock, 13 vols (Oxford, 1976–94) |
| Bunyan *PP* | John Bunyan, *The Pilgrim's Progress*, ed. James Blanton Wharey, revd Roger Sharrock, 2nd edn (Oxford, 1960) |
| Burnet *OT* | *Burnet's History of My Own Time, part I: the Reign of Charles the Second*, ed. Osmund Airy, 2 vols (Oxford, 1897–1900) |
| Burnet *SOT* | *A Supplement to Burnet's History of My Own Time*, ed. H. C. Foxcroft (Oxford, 1902) |
| *CH* | *Church History* |
| *CHJ* | *Cambridge Historical Journal* |
| *CJ* | *The Journals of the House of Commons*, vol. 7: *1651–59*, vol. 8: *1660–67*, vol. 9: *1667–87* (n.d.) |
| Clarendon *HR* | Edward, Earl of Clarendon, *The History of the Rebellion and Civil Wars in England*, ed. W. Dunn Macray, 6 vols (1888; rptd Oxford, 1992) |
| Clarendon *LC* | Edward, Earl of Clarendon, *The Life of Edward, Earl of Clarendon . . . in which is included A Continuation of his History of the Grand Rebellion, from the Restoration in 1660 to his Banishment in 1667*, 2 vols (Oxford, 1857) |
| *CSPD* | Mary Ann Everett Green (ed.), *Calendar of State Papers, Domestic Series, 1658–1670*, 12 vols (1860–95) |
| *CTB* | William A. Shaw (ed.), *Calendar of Treasury Books*, 32 vols, vols 1–3: *1660–1672* (1904–8) |
| Davies | Godfrey Davies, *The Restoration of Charles II, 1658–1660* (1955; rptd Oxford, 1969) |
| Dryden | Paul Hammond (ed.), *The Poems of John Dryden*, 4 vols in progress, vol. 1: *1649–1681* (1995) |
| *EcHR* | *Economic History Review* |
| *EHR* | *English Historical Review* |
| Evelyn | *The Diary of John Evelyn*, ed. E. S. de Beer, 6 vols (Oxford, 1955) |
| Grey | Anchitell Grey (ed.), *Debates of the House of Commons, from the year 1667 to the year 1694*, 10 vols (1763); reference is to volume 1 |
| *H* | *History* |
| Hamilton | Anthony Hamilton, *Memoirs of Count Grammont*, trans. Sir Walter Scott, ed. Gordon Goodwin, 2 vols (Edinburgh, 1908) |
| *Harl. Misc.* | *The Harleian Miscellany: or, a Collection of Scarce, Curious and Entertaining Pamphlets and Tracts . . . found in the late Earl of Oxford's Library*, 8 vols (1744–6) |

| | |
|---|---|
| Harris | Tim Harris, *Politics under the Later Stuarts: Party Conflict in a Divided Society, 1660–1715* (1993) |
| Henning | Basil Duke Henning (ed.), *History of Parliament: The House of Commons, 1660–1690*, 3 vols (1983) |
| *HJ* | *Historical Journal* |
| *HLB* | *Huntington Library Bulletin* |
| *HLQ* | *Huntington Library Quarterly* |
| Holmes | Geoffrey Holmes, *The Making of a Great Power: Late Stuart and Early Georgian Britain, 1660–1722* (1993) |
| *HR* | *Historical Review* |
| Hutchinson | Lucy Hutchinson, *Memoirs of the Life of Colonel Hutchinson*, ed. N. H. Keeble (1995) |
| Hutton *CII* | Ronald Hutton, *Charles II: King of England, Scotland and Ireland* (Oxford, 1989) |
| Hutton *R* | Ronald Hutton, *The Restoration: A Political and Religious History of England and Wales, 1658–1667* (Oxford, 1985) |
| *JBS* | *Journal of British Studies* |
| *JEH* | *Journal of Ecclesiastical History* |
| *JHI* | *Journal of the History of Ideas* |
| Keeble | N. H. Keeble, *The Literary Culture of Nonconformity in Later Seventeenth-century England* (Leicester, 1987) |
| Lacey | Douglas R. Lacy, *Dissent and Parliamentary Politics in England, 1660–1689* (Rutgers, NJ, 1969) |
| Lister | T. H. Lister, *Life and Administration of Edward, First Earl of Clarendon; with original correspondence*, 3 vols (1837–8) |
| *LJ* | *The Journals of the House of Lords*, vol. 11: *1660–66*, vol. 12: *1666–75* (n.d.) |
| Ludlow | Edmund Ludlow, *A Voyce from the Watch Tower*, ed. A. B. Worden, Camden Society 4th ser. 21 (1978) |
| McKeon | Michael McKeon, *Politics and Poetry in Restoration England: The Case of Dryden's 'Annus Mirabilis'* (Cambridge, MA, 1975) |
| Marvell *CP* | Andrew Marvell, *Complete Poetry*, ed. George de F. Lord (1984) |
| Marvell *LI* | [Andrew Marvell], *Last Instructions to a Painter* |
| Marvell *P&L* | *The Poems and Letters of Andrew Marvell*, ed. H. M. Margoliouth, revd Pierre Legouis and E. E. Duncan-Jones, 2 vols, 3rd edn (Oxford, 1971) |
| Milton *CPW* | *Complete Prose Works of John Milton*, gen. ed. Don M. Wolfe, 8 vols (New Haven, CT, 1953–83) |

| | |
|---|---|
| Milton *PJM* | *The Poems of John Milton*, ed. John Carey and Alastair Fowler, 2nd corrected impression (1968) |
| Milton *PL* | John Milton, *Paradise Lost* |
| Milton *PR* | John Milton, *Paradise Regained* |
| Milton *SA* | John Milton, *Samson Agonistes* |
| Milward | *The Diary of John Milward, Esq., Member of Parliament for Derbyshire, September 1664 to May 1668*, ed. Caroline Robbins (Cambridge, 1938) |
| Ogg | David Ogg, *England in the Reign of Charles II* (2nd edn 1956; rpt. in one volume, Oxford, 1967) |
| *Old Parl. Hist.* | *The Parliamentary or Constitutional History of England, from the earliest times to the Restoration . . . by several hands*, 24 vols, 2nd edn of vols 14–22 (1751–63) |
| Pepys | *The Diary of Samuel Pepys*, ed. Robert Latham and William Matthews, 11 vols (1970–83) |
| Reresby | *Memoirs of Sir John Reresby*, ed. Andrew Browing, 2nd edn (1991) |
| Rochester | John Wilmot, Earl of Rochester, *The Complete Works*, ed. Frank H. Ellis (Harmondsworth, 1994) |
| Rugg | *The Diurnall of Thomas Rugg, 1659–1661*, ed. William L. Sachse, Camden Society, 3rd ser. 91 (1961) |
| Scott | Jonathan Scott, *England's Troubles: Seventeenth-century English Political Instability in European Context* (Cambridge, 2000) |
| Seaward | Paul Seaward, *The Cavalier Parliament and the Reconstruction of the Old Regime, 1661–1667* (Cambridge, 1989) |
| *Somers Tracts* | John Somers, *A Collection of Scarce and Valuable Tracts*, ed. Walter Scott, 12 vols, 2nd edn (1809–14) |
| Spurr | John Spurr, *The Restoration Church of England, 1646–1689* (New Haven, CT, 1991) |
| *State Trials* | *A Complete Collection of State Trials and Proceedings for High Treason and Other Crimes and Misdemeanours*, ed. William Cobbett, cont. F. B. and T. J. Howell, 28 vols (1809–20) |
| *Statutes* | *The Statutes of the Realm . . . 1101–1713, printed by command of His Majesty King George the Third*, [ed. A. Luders, T. E. Tomlins et al.], 11 vols (1810–28), vol. 5: *1625–80* (1819) |
| Steele | Robert Steele, *A Bibliography of Royal Proclamations of the Tudor and Stuart Sovereigns . . . 1485–1714*, Bibliotheca Lindesiana 5, 2 vols (Oxford, 1910); reference is to item number in vol. 1 |

| | |
|---|---|
| Thomason | G. K. Forstescue (ed.), *Catalogue of the Pamphlets, Books, Newspapers and other Manuscripts . . . collected by George Thomason, 1640–1661*, 2 vols (1908) |
| *TRHS* | *Transactions of the Royal Historical Society* |
| Whitelocke | [Bulstrode Whitelocke], *Memorials of the English Affairs . . . or, An Historical Account of what passed from the beginning of the reign of King Charles the First, to King Charles the Second his Happy Restauration* (1682) |
| Wing | Donald Wing (ed.), *Short-Title Catalogue of Books Printed in England, Scotland, Ireland and Wales and British America . . . 1641–1700*, 4 vols, 2nd revd edn (New York, 1994–8) |

# *A Note on Conventions, Procedures and Dates*

Full details of works referred to by author's surname and short title are given in an earlier note to the chapter in which the reference occurs. The place of publication of all works cited is London unless otherwise stated. The original spelling of seventeenth-century titles is reproduced, but not their capitalization or punctuation. In quotations from seventeenth-century texts, the spelling and punctuation of the original are reproduced. All dates, following seventeenth-century English usage, are Old Style. The year is taken as beginning on 1 January.

# *Introduction*

No decade in English history opens so decisively as the 1660s. None so dramatically or emphatically announces itself with such splendid public affirmations of security and stability, of right order restored on the ruins of the past; none so loudly heralds a new age. The very date itself, *1660*, has a euphonious harmony which, if it no longer has quite the numerological significance or millennial suggestiveness it had for some seventeenth-century witnesses, yet rings in English memory as resonantly as 1066. 'Great joy all yesterday at London; and at night more bonefires then ever and ringing of bells and drinking of the King's health upon their knees in the streets' wrote Pepys in his diary on 2 May 1660, the day after the Convention's vote that according to 'fundamental laws' the government of England was by King, Lords and Commons.[1] Those bonfires have burned bright in many a subsequent account of 1660 and of the 1660s. Though there is increasing historiographical awareness that joy was by no means universal or unalloyed in May 1660 (Pepys himself added that it was 'a little too much'), the ringing of church bells and the fountains flowing with wine continue to provide the key images of the moment of the Restoration: it remains a 'watershed'.[2]

With the benefit of hindsight, 1660 does indeed appear to mark a turning-point in history: the end of one story and the beginning of another. There is no denying that Charles II did come back in 1660, nor that monarchy and episcopacy were restored, nor that the republican experiment was never again attempted in England. Some such sense of finality has shaped many accounts of the period, sometimes to the point of taking 1660 to mark the end of the seventeenth century and the beginning of the 'long eighteenth century'. At the time, panegyrists, anxious to recommend themselves to the new regime or to secure a patron, developed just this conception of the events of 1660, speaking of a new dawn, a new age, akin to the settling of Rome by Augustus after its civil wars, if not to the universal peace promised by the birth of Christ. In the experience of those who lived through those events, however, 1660 carried with it no assurance of finality. Though the return of Charles II had long been both plotted and resisted, its achievement in 1660 was virtually unforeseen. Contemporaries found only providential explanations sufficient to accommodate an occurrence so swiftly and unexpectedly accomplished, apparently without human contrivance – even, indeed, contrary to human contrivance, 'without', as Evelyn put it in his diary, 'one drop of bloud, & by that very Army which rebell'd against [the King]: but it was the Lords doing'.[3] The Restoration was consequently as startling to its beneficiaries as to its victims; disorientation and apprehension were common to both.

In this predicament, neither tradition nor history offered any guidance. The Restoration was not only unplanned but unique, an event without precedents by which to interpret or understand it. Neither those who relinquished nor those who gained power in 1660 quite knew what had been won and lost, nor how far they might trust to what, contemplating in Samson an image of victorious heroism reduced to powerlessness, Milton called 'the change of times'.[4] Nor could they have confidence that yet another 'revolution' (in the seventeenth-century sense of that term)[5] did not lie in store. No one who had lived through the unprecedented turmoil of the previous twenty years, and particularly through the bewildering eighteen months since Cromwell's death, had any reason to be confident that this settlement in the affairs of the state would prove more durable than the succession of constitutional contrivances which had succeeded each other with increasing rapidity, accelerating in 1659 to intervals of a few weeks in the increasingly frantic 'maygame of fortune' in the 'braine-sick' state'.[6] Despite the public acclamations which greeted Charles, both he and his Chancellor, Edward Hyde, afterwards Earl of Clarendon, were well aware that there could be no guarantee what the enduring loyalty of English people might prove to be.[7] The pamphleteer Marchamont Nedham opined in 1659 that 'A Great part of the Nation may be said to be *Neuters* . . . not addicted to any one Party'.[8] Perhaps a good many shared Pepys's private opinion (after the event) that the Puritans 'at last will be found the wisest' and his apprehension (as late as 1668) that the fanatics (as he styled them) and nonconformists might 'get the upperhand'.[9] Certainly, from the moment Charles landed at Dover, the restored authorities lived in constant fear of plots and uprisings. London's experience of plague and fire further unsteadied nerves, for these were providences more readily interpreted as divine punishments than as blessings in accord with the great mercy (as the royalists had it) of the Restoration.

And by 1665 there was good reason to suppose there might indeed be divine dismay at the way things were going. If no decade began more confidently, none so quickly slipped into disappointment, disillusionment and resentment. Long before 1670 it was clear that the victors in 1660 were making no better a job, and in many ways rather a worse job, of running the country than had Oliver Cromwell, if not the Republic. From the middle of the decade what begins to assume the characteristics of a political opposition increasingly challenges the restored regime, drawing its inspiration at least in part from the supposedly discredited 1640s and 1650s. The experience of defeat in the Dutch war unleashed a satirical campaign which demonstrated that the revolutionary aspirations of the Interregnum had not simply vanished overnight and that the clamant vociferousness of the dominant public voice in 1660 had drowned out, but not finally silenced, many other discordant voices. In the end, the 1660s proved inconclusive; they brought back the King, but settled nothing.

'Restoration' is, then, better understood as process than as an event, and as a process which never achieves the closure its public propaganda so vehemently claimed. Something certainly happened in 1660, and of momentous importance, dominating the consciousness of everyone who lived through the ensuing decade. What had occurred, however, and what it might mean for the future, were questions which admitted of answers only as the decade developed, and, even then, the answers were neither single nor simple: save in the narrowest political sense, there was not one Restoration but many. This diversity of experience and expectation is the subject of this book. Its interest is in the anxieties and tensions, insecurities and bewilderments through which the decade represented itself in personal terms; in the rival models of the past and the future, and the competing efforts to vindicate the one and to secure the other, which shaped political and religious life; in the reactionary and the innovative in a cultural sensibility poised between the medieval and the modern, between Renaissance and Enlightenment; and in the interactions through which notions of personal, church and state identity were received from the 1650s and passed to the 1670s. The Restoration it sets out to describe is not a tidy affair and certainly not a finished affair. For this reason, there are very few conclusions in this study.

Consequently, though it aspires to coherence and accuracy, this is not primarily a narrative account of the events of the 1660s. Its progress is in the main chronological, but it is structured around a series of topics which are explored largely through the versions of their experience compiled by those who lived through the decade. From this point of view, it matters less whether or not they constitute accurate historical records (if we may still suppose there are any such documents) than that they reveal the aspirations and fears of their writers. This book is interested in the construction of identities, in roles and role-playing, in culturally supportive or subversive myths, in perceptions, claims and counter-claims. It therefore depends heavily upon diaries, journals and memoirs, upon contemporary chronicles, polemical tracts, pamphlets and newspapers. It is no wonder that anyone writing on the 1660s with this kind of bias should call Pepys in evidence, but here he is accompanied not only by Evelyn but by Lucy Hutchinson, by Clarendon, Baxter, Burnet and a host of others. Milton, Dryden, Marvell, Bunyan and Rochester are also among those called in evidence, for, though they may take up genres and conventions which derive from literary precedent and tradition (often, ultimately, classical or biblical), their matter is immediate and to hand in the 1660s. *Paradise Lost* may very well be an epic for all time, but it is also emphatically a poem of and for its age. As a result, this study has a more literary side to it than is perhaps usual, or to be expected, in a study which appears in a History of Early Modern England series. It does, however, also take up with acts of parliament, though again with as much interest in the preconceptions and assumptions they articulate as in the details of their legislation: despite the implicit claim to a kind of omniscient and impartial justness in their formulaic and legalistic language, their sense of the significance of the past, the duty of the present, and the shape of the future is no less specific or partisan than that of the republican Edmund Ludlow, let us say, or the Quaker George Fox.

These various names might give us pause. An extraordinary thing about the decade is that it is quite the richest yet in our cultural history in diaries, memoirs and other kinds of autobiographical writing. There are a host of particular motives for these – apologetic, confessional, memorial, exculpatory, polemical, laudatory and so on – but inescapably an unprecedented number and variety of individuals felt compelled to get their experiences down on paper. Literary scholars are much exercised by the history of subjectivity, which they tend to find especially interesting in the Renaissance, that is, in England, in the sixteenth century and in Elizabethan drama. In truth, however, it is the 1660s which are the decade of 'what I felt, what I smartingly did feel'.[10] We are now all well schooled in the irrecoverability of history, in its textuality, if not fictionality; yet there remains the incontestable fact that, with all the qualifications we might wish to enter about the shaping effect of the circumstances of their production, here are texts which had authors compelled into words by what they felt, and authors for whom we are the readers addressed: posterity is their intended audience. No previous decade had been so determined to have its voice heard by subsequent decades. This study tries to listen.

# *1*

# *The Return of the King (1658–1660)*

## 1 The Fall of the Protectorate (September 1658–April 1659)[1]

'All Men wondred to see all so quiet, in so dangerous a time' wrote the Puritan minister Richard Baxter of the autumn of 1658. The death of Oliver Cromwell on 3 September signalled no discernible quickening of either royalist or republican pulses. There was no sudden or general upsurge of public opinion either against the Protectorate or for a return to monarchy: 'Contrary to all expectation both at home and abroad, this earthquake was attended with no signal alteration', recalled Charles II's Chancellor, Edward Hyde, afterwards Earl of Clarendon.[2] Nor, though 'all the commonwealth party' may have 'cried out upon [Richard's] assuming the protectorship, as a high usurpation', was there any concerted attempt by republicans to undo what they saw as the perversion of the Good Old Cause into the tyranny of rule by a single person: 'There is not a dogge that waggs his tongue, soe great a calm are wee in', observed John Thurloe, Oliver's, and now Richard's, Secretary of State.[3] *The Humble Petition and Advice*, the Protectorate's constitution since 1657, empowered Cromwell to name his successor, but this was managed 'so sleightly, as some doubt whether he did it at all' reported John Barwick, future Dean of St Paul's, in a letter to Charles II. Nevertheless, despite the want of any formal or written nomination, Richard Cromwell's succession was generally accepted not only without opposition but with signs of positive relief. The proclamation of his succession was acclaimed in London and provincial cities, and a hundred or more loyal addresses were received in which 'the Counties, Cities, and Corporations of *England* sen[t] up their Congratulations, to own him as Protector'. National stability and civic welcome marked the inauguration of the second Protectorate.[4] The experiment of the major-generals had caused resentment, and there was no escaping the ultimate sanction of military power which legitimized Cromwellian rule, but in its later years the increasingly traditional and conservative manner, court and constitution of the Protectorate had begun to win confidence in what was beginning to appear to be a settled form of government. Many were impressed that Cromwell's foreign policy was more to the credit of a Protestant nation than that of the Stuarts, and many were coming to recognize that in significant respects the experience of Cromwellian rule was more liberal and humane than that of Charles I, particularly in its quite exceptionally generous policy of religious toleration, its allowance of an unusual degree of freedom to the press, and its aspiration to reform the law. All the indications were that the Protectorate would survive.

The welcome in the country at large was not, however, matched in the estate upon which the Protectorate depended, the Army. As Protector, Richard Cromwell was constitutionally its commander-in-chief. It was in this role that his father had been supremely successful, demonstrating superlative qualities as a military leader and forging bonds of loyalty through war. This exceptional achievement only accentuated Richard's complete lack of military experience. His younger brother Henry, or any one of a number of senior officers, were better qualified to exercise high command. The unfavourable comparison with his father and the estimate of his character which became current was succinctly put by the fiercely republican Lucy Hutchinson in her memoir of her regicide husband, Colonel John Hutchinson: Oliver's 'son Richard was a peasant in his nature, yet gentle and virtuous, but became not greatness'; he 'had not a spirit fit to succeed his father, or to manage such a perplexed government'.[5] Upon Richard Cromwell's succession, Charles Fleetwood, as lieutenant-general of all the army the highest ranking officer, did secure the signatures of the senior officers of the armies of England, Scotland and Wales to a loyal address, presented to Richard two weeks after his father's death, to which he responded with undertakings to promote only 'Men of known Godliness and sober Principles', to maintain 'an equal and just Liberty to all Persons that profess Godliness' and to improve Army pay, as the address desired.[6] This was reassuring, but the Army wished supreme command to be vested in Fleetwood and, as he himself wrote in October to Henry Cromwell, had 'a great desire, that the good old spirit may still be kept alive'. That spirit, more republican in politics, more enthusiastic in religion and more extreme in temper than Richard Cromwell's, led to confrontations between him and Army officers in October and November, but Richard's appeals for unity and loyalty reassured his critics, at least sufficiently to permit Oliver's state funeral on 23 November to pass without incident and to allow the issuing of writs in December for a new parliament.[7]

Tension between 'Commonwealthsmen', or republicans, who resented rule by a single person, and Cromwellians ('the Court Party' to its opponents), Presbyterians and crypto-royalists sympathetic to such rule, doomed the parliament which met on 27 January 1659. The former shared a deep-rooted suspicion of the constitution of the Protectorate and of Richard as inadequate defenders of the republican ideal. They feared, wrote one contemporary chronicler, 'that the Protector did intend to cast them out of their Places, and put the Army into the hands of the Nobility and Gentry of the Nation, thereby to bring in the King'. The traditional inclinations of the latter preferred the Protectorate to a Republic and disrelished the Army's role in government. The shape of things to come was intimated by the House's inability to agree to a bill in recognition of Richard's right and title as Lord Protector and Chief Magistrate, and this despite every member having sworn on taking his seat to 'be true and faithful to the Lord Protector of the Commonwealth'.[8] However, though coherent and committed as a group, republicans had no clear majority in the Commons. While they could delay business and prolong debates, members of a more conservative temper continued to recognize Richard as the chief magistrate and to co-operate with the House of Lords, whose constitutional identity republicans did not accept. The result was stalemate: 'The proceedings at Westminster', wrote Barwick in February to Hyde, 'are so full of distraction, that it is probable they will end in confusion. For the one party thinks the protectorists cannot stand, and the other that the commonwealth cannot rise.'[9] While the Protectorate's legislative arm was thus being effectively crippled by republican filibustering, the republican campaign was being conducted still more vigorously outside parliament. *The Humble Petition of Many Thousand Citizens to the Parliament*, presented on 15 February, called for the restoration to parliament of supreme authority and a succession of tracts promoted the Good Old Cause by presenting the Protectorate as a threat to Army power, to civil liberty and to religious toleration. Their heady and inflammatory mix of biblical oracles, apocalyptic imagery, millenarian expectancy and Fifth Monarchist fervour incited agitation and civil disobedience.[10]

This fervour outside the House served only to stiffen resolve within not to yield to military, republican or enthusiastic demands. Although republican members such as Sir Arthur Haslerig, Sir Henry Vane and Thomas Scot spoke in its favour, the Commons rejected the *Humble Petition*. It appeared increasingly willing to criticize all that had been done by the Rump Parliament, to circumscribe the national church more narrowly, to limit toleration, to favour the peers and, in the case of some members, even to contemplate monarchy. Nor was anything done to meet the Army's pressing pay arrears. Both it and Richard came increasingly to be seen as more sympathetic to moderates and to Presbyterians than to the Army and to religious radicals. Certainly, men like Baxter, politically conservative and deeply opposed to Oliver Cormwell, invested in Richard Cromwell great hopes of religious and political recovery for the nation. What to his Army critics might appear Richard's lamentable want of military experience was to Baxter his strength: since he 'never had any hand in the War', he might 'be used in the healing of the Land':

> Many sober Men that called his Father no better than a Trayterous Hypocrite, did begin to think that they *owed him Subjection.* They knew that the King was by Birth their Rightful Sovereign... But they were astonished at the marvellous Providences of God, which had been against that Family all along, and they thought that there was no rational probability of his Restoration, having seen so many Armies and Risings and Designs overthrown, which were raised or undertaken for it: They thought that it is not left to our liberty, whether we will have a Government, or not; but that *Government* is of Divine Appointment; and the Family, Person or Species is but of a subservient, less necessary determination: And that if we cannot have him that we would have, it followeth not that we may be without...[11]

As Army grandees and Commonwealthsmen alike found themselves increasingly dissatisfied with the direction Richard and his parliament appeared to be taking, approaches were made in late March by the Wallingford House party (so known from Fleetwood's London residence where the senior officers met) to the republican Edmund Ludlow, and through him to Vane and Haslerig, to attempt to forge a joint policy. This new resolve produced a challenge to the civil authority and to Richard in *The Humble Representation and Petition of the General Council of the Officers of the Armies of England, Scotland and Ireland* of 6 April, which called upon Richard to support and promote the Good Old Cause, to act against royalists now prominent in London, and to meet the Army's arrears of pay. It was an ominous flexing of military muscle. To it Bulstrode Whitelocke, at this time one of the Keepers of the Great Seal, traced 'the beginning of *Richard*'s fall... set on foot by his relations; [John] *Desborough* who married his Aunt, and *Fleetwood* who married his sister, and others of their party'. Baxter was implacably hostile to the 'Firebrands of the Army', to 'the Sectarian party' and to those he called 'the Vanists', but he understood well enough the power struggle that was taking place:

> when they saw that he [Richard] began to favour the sober People of the Land, to honour Parliaments, and to respect the Ministers, whom they called Presbyterians, they presently resolved to make him know his Masters, and that it was *they* and not *he*, that were called by God to be the chief Protectors of the Interest of the Nation'.[12]

The Commons, however, was unresponsive when Richard forwarded this petition to them two days later and the rift with the Army became unbridgeable when, on 18 April, the House resolved that commissioned officers should subscribe an undertaking not to disrupt its proceedings and, by the overwhelming majority of 163 votes to 87, that the General Council of Army Officers should not meet except with the approval of the Protector and both houses of parliament. Even as this motion was before the Commons, Richard attempted to assert his authority by dissolving the General Council and ordering officers in London back to their regiments. On 21 April the Army in return demanded the dissolution of parliament. In this contest, troop loyalty was to their senior officers rather than to their notional commander-in-chief, Richard. Bereft of military support, Richard had to submit. The compliance of the Commons was secured on 23 April by the simple expedient of locking and guarding the doors to the House.[13]

Following this coup, 'All matters were at a stand', observed Whitelock.[14] This was to be the first of four Army interventions in public affairs within the next year. In each case, again in October, through Lambert, in December, through Fleetwood, and in February 1660, through Monck, the result was constitutional uncertainty and administrative disorder while political thinking strove to catch up with events. On this occasion, in the absence of a parliament, the Council of Officers (a smaller body than the all-inclusive General Council), sitting at Fleetwood's residence, Wallingford House, assumed the constitutional authority to govern. The inclination of these grandees, bound to Oliver and his legacy by personal, familial and professional ties, was to preserve the Protectorate, with or without Richard as its head. However, the body of Army opinion, as expressed by junior officers, was religiously enthusiastic and politically republican and this carried the day. On 6 May the General Council issued a declaration in which, observing that 'the good Spirit, which formerly appeared among us, in the Carrying on of this Great Work, did daily decline, so as the Good Old Cause itself became a Reproach', it invited the return to government of those former 'eminent Assertors' of the Cause who had sat as members of the purged Long Parliament between December 1648 and 20 April 1653. In its reply, the restored Rump readily accepted the Army's contention that there had been a 'special Providence of God' with the members of that assembly and resolved 'not to neglect this opportunity... for the Prosecution of what yet remains of their great Trust'. Prudently, but ominously, neither they nor the Army chose to recall that it was their failure in that trust which had led the Army itself forcibly to turn them out in 1653.[15]

## 2 The Rump Restored (May–September 1659)[16]

Some 42 MPs assembled on Saturday 7 May out of what the House itself took to be a total of eligible survivors of the purged Long Parliament of 78.[17] This rump of a rump comprised the core of radical, enthusiastic and republican opinion in England, to its supporters the essence of the revolution; but it had less show of legitimate authority than any regime since the execution of Charles I. Though ultimately dependent upon the military might of Cromwell, Barebone's Parliament and the Protectorate parliaments could lay claim to some constitutional legitimacy. This body sat solely by the authority of the Army, to which it was twice indebted, for its original formation in 1648 and for this second opportunity to exercise power.[18] Most obviously, its authority was compromised by the 'secluded' members surviving from Pride's Purge, over two hundred of them. The most vociferous of these, the veteran Presbyterian campaigner William Prynne, led a deputation to demand admission to the House at its first sitting. It was turned away by the Army guards. When, two days later, Prynne contrived to enter the chamber only to find himself prevented from returning in the afternoon, he embarked upon a sustained pamphlet campaign for the next six months, denying the legitimacy of the regime and calling for a return of the full Long Parliament.[19] In this, he could appeal to a widespread sentiment. The restored Rump enjoyed far less general support than had its predecessor, the Second Protectorate Parliament; its promoters and apologists were intense and committed, but by the majority of the political nation – Presbyterian, Cromwellian, royalist, episcopalian – they were derided as 'a mean and schismatical party', supported by 'fanatic spirits'.[20]

While Prynne fulminated, the restored Rump recommended itself to radical opinion as the likeliest authority to realize its aspirations. There was no mistaking the disposition of the 31-member Council of State appointed on 13 May: it included 15 senior Army officers (Lambert, Desborough, Fleetwood and Ludlow among them) and 16 civilians, prominent among whom were Haslerig, Vane, Scot, James Harrington and Henry Neville. The Commons soon found itself the target of papers, petitions and tracts on the three perennially contentious topics of the revolution: legal reform, the abolition of tithes and full religious toleration. National toleration for all save episcopalians and Roman Catholics was an aspiration of the Army's *Humble Petition and Address of the Officers* presented to the Rump on 13 May 1659, as was a republican constitutional settlement and provision for an elected legislature to succeed the Rump, which should not 'by their long sitting become burthensome or inconvenient'.[21] These petitioners were curiously unmindful of the fact that during its previous term the Rump had failed to legislate on these very issues and had disappointed this very constituency. It should, then, have occasioned no surprise that, despite serious-minded endeavour, this Rump no more abolished tithes than had its previous incarnation or its successor, the Barebone's Parliament; it no more favoured Quakers than had Oliver's or Richard's parliaments; it made no headway with legal reform; it could not agree on a form of republican constitution for its successor; and it was no more able to manage its fiscal affairs to allow a reduction in Army arrears than had any Interregnum parliament.

By mid summer, neither the Army nor radical religious opinion any longer had much regard for the restored Rump. The House did not, however, correspondingly rise in the estimate of conservatives. By virtue of its dependence upon the Army it was regarded as complicit in the forcible abolition of the Protectorate. Its resumption of power might so disenchant former Cromwellians that, like the Admiral of the Fleet, Edward Mountague, and the regicide Colonel Richard Ingoldsby, they were in the summer of 1659 prepared to entertain approaches from Charles II. This disaffection of those whom, with a republican's scorn, Lucy Hutchinson called 'the Protectorean faction', might have been foreseen, but not, perhaps, that dismay at the Army coup and the re-establishment of the Commonwealth shared by Presbyterians, royalists, and uncommitted local leaders of a traditional temper now encouraged them to consider actively working together for a restoration of monarchy as the only way to prevent either military dictatorship or anarchy. Baxter, for example, was approached in the summer of 1659.[22] For royalists themselves, the Rump was damned not only as an illegitimate regime but as a government republican in its politics and apparently radical in its religious sympathies. It may not have legislated to satisfy radical demands, but it quite failed to curb, and by this very failure exacerbated, what, with increasing dismay, royalist opinion saw as the anarchic insurgency of enthusiastic religious sects (especially the Quakers). On 1 August a royalist uprising broke out, contrived largely by John Mordaunt, in the spring of 1659 created Viscount for his energetic pursuit of the royalist cause, but known to history as Booth's Uprising after Sir George Booth, its most notable leader. It was a conspicuous failure. The Council of State had gained advance warning of the rebellion and Booth's followers were routed on 19 August by John Lambert at Winnington Bridge and Booth himself was committed to the Tower.[23]

This was apparently the final end of royalist hopes. The Republic had shown itself able efficiently and speedily to neutralize and overcome the best the royalists could hope to put in the field against it. Both the old Sealed Knot and the newer royalist confederacy established in 1658 around the figure of Mordaunt were utterly discredited. The Rump was restrained in its reaction, but it pursued royalist fugitives, sequestrated some estates and set about purging the commissions of peace.[24] The victory of the Republic did tend to strengthen the movement towards an alliance between its conservative opponents, as the only hope of securing its demise. Presbyterians, royalists and even some Independents, began to correspond and to make common cause. Nevertheless, the standing of Charles and his court in Europe was lamentable. He would, it appeared, be a permanent exile, dependent upon the charity of European monarchs while Lambert and the Army enjoyed unchallenged supremacy. With a new confidence the form of a permanent constitution for the commonwealth was debated by religious radicals, Fifth Monarchists and republicans in a fine display of optimistic ingenuity. This was not a development viewed sympathetically by MPs at Westminster, jealous of their recently resumed authority.[25]

## 3 Don Juan Lamberto[26] (October–December 1659)

Given the Rump's vulnerability to conservative criticism on the one hand and to pressing radical demands on the other, members of the House might have been expected judiciously to cultivate those to whom they owed their power, the Army and its officers. The Rumpers could sit as the sole legislative authority only as long as the military guard at the door of the House admitted them and denied access to the secluded members, and they knew full well that this Army was as capable of ejecting them as it was of restoring them; it had done both once already. Although, as desired in the 13 May petition, Fleetwood was appointed commander-in-chief, the man of whom they had most cause to be wary was the officer who had presented that petition, John Lambert. Promoted to major-general at the age of only 28, he had had an outstanding military career as a cavalry officer, taking a decisive part in the parliamentarian victories in the Second Civil War and in the Scottish campaign. He was Cromwell's closest ally in forging the Protectorate, whose first constitution, the *Instrument of Government*, he drafted in late 1653, and, until he was deprived of his commission when he fell out with Cromwell over the offer of the crown in 1657, his most likely successor. Despite being no regicide, an opponent of the initiatives of the Fifth Monarchist Thomas Harrison and of the Barebone's Parliament, and despite being a gentleman of whom the royalists had some hopes, he enjoyed a unique standing with the ordinary soldiery of the Army and he was the only one of its officers who had had some expectation of holding supreme power. He was thus the most dangerous of the restored Rump's potential enemies. Not surprisingly, republicans held him in even less esteem than Cromwell. Lucy Hutchinson dismissed Winnington Bridge as 'a very cheap victory' and in her opinion 'his ambition . . . had this difference from the Protector's: the one was gallant and great, the other had nothing but an unworthy pride, most insolent in prosperity, and as abject and base in adversity'.[27]

In September, at Derby, Lambert's victorious officers addressed to parliament *The Humble Petition and Proposals of the Officers under the Command of the . . . Lord Lambert* for effecting the reforms requested in the Army petition of May which, they charged, the Commons had neglected. At the end of that month, Mordaunt opined that 'Lambert is so put to it, by Sir. Ar[thur] H[aslerig] and [Thomas] Scot that he is either lost, or must loose them. And the House will either be dissolved or purged unlesse by a common consent, new writs be issued out.' It was a shrewd forecast. The attempt of the Commons, led by Haslerig, to admonish those responsible for the Army's petition led to an even fiercer *Humble Representation and Petition of the Officers* (5 October), which defended Lambert's soldiers, demanded the censure of MPs who criticized the Army and the payment of arrears, and reiterated the demand for reform to secure civil and religious liberties.[28] In response, 'The parliament carried it very high against the Army', revoking the commissions of nine officers who had signed a letter soliciting support for this petition (including Lambert and Desborough), annulling Fleetwood's commission as commander-in-chief and placing the Army under the joint control of Fleetwood, Ludlow, Haslerig and four other commissioners answerable to parliament. There could be no mistaking the determination of members that the Army should be subordinate to their will. By 8 October the royalist Sir Edward Nicholas could write to Mordaunt that 'All our letters from England this week say the Army and parliament cannot agree long, and its beleeved that before Christmas the Army will dissolve, or (at least) purge the parliament'. They did not wait till Christmas. 'The string is like to break with skrewing too high', wrote the royalist Barwick, in a letter of 13 October, 'for the Army hereabouts incline to Lambert and his party', and so it proved. That day 'the late principal Officers of the Army whose Commissions were vacated, drew up Forces in and about *Westminster*, obstructed all Passages both by Land and Water, stopped the Speaker in his Way, and placed and continued Guards upon and about the doors of the Parliament-House'. In Whitelocke's account of this incident we catch a glimpse of the courage and authority which so recommended Lambert. Confronting the parliamentary guard, Lambert commanded them to dismount, 'and though *Lambert* were on foot, and none with him, yet *Evelyn* at the head of his Troop, dismounted at his command, and his Troop also obeyed *Lambert*'. The Rump was once more locked out.[29]

For nearly two weeks there was such a constitutional vacuum as had followed the forcible dissolution of Richard Cromwell's parliament in April: 'now no Government in the Nation, all in confusion; no Magistrate either own'd or pretended, but the souldiers & they not agreed' wrote John Evelyn in his diary under 16 October. 'We are', observed Barwick, 'yet at gaze, what government we shall have.' It was not even clear whether parliament had been dissolved, or merely suspended. There was, though, no doubt who wielded power. Within a few days attendance at meetings of the Council of State had become so thin that there was no alternative to the Army's Council of Officers, acting under Fleetwood, whom it declared to be commander-in-chief. On 26 October the Army's General Council finally replaced the Council of State with a 23-member Committee of Safety. Civilians formed a majority on this committee, but this did not impress those hostile to the Army. In the words of one contemporary royalist chronicler, after 17 years deprived of just government, the nation 'groaned under a fatal *Anarchy*; which to supply, a Tumultuary *Juncto* was set up, called a *Committee of Safety*'. It is true that, despite the apprehension of some that 'the success [of Winnington Bridge] inspired him with the ambition of imitating Cromwell, in dissolving the parliament, and making himself protector', and the judgement of others that, as 'a Person of great Parts and good Courage', he was 'as fit for a *Protectorship* as *Oliver*, and some think fitter', Lambert had not instituted a third protectorate.[30] Nevertheless, the country had effectively reverted to a military dictatorship under a ruler seemingly as invincible as Cromwell himself had been.

Lambert's reign was, however, to prove the briefest of the several hegemonies of 1659. Looking back, Lucy Hutchinson blamed Lambert's 'insolent usurpation' for the final collapse of the Republic, for it 'so turned the hearts of all men, that the whole nation began to set their eyes upon the King beyond the sea, and think a bad settlement under him better than none at all but to be still under the arbitrary power of such proud rebels as Lambert'. From the opposite side of the political divide, Mordaunt, believing in 'the firme resolution of some of the most considerable persons in England... to hazzard all by rising to restore the King', saw in Lambert's ejection of the Rump a royalist opportunity. Royalists such as Sir John Grenville were convinced that 'it is now most apparant to all men living, there can never be any happy setlement without his Majesties establishment'. However, when it came, the challenge to Lambert was issued from quite another, and unforeseen, quarter. It was made by the one force which had hitherto never opposed the Army and the only one, with the power to do so effectively: the Army itself.[31]

The commander responsible had hardly impinged upon the English political consciousness. George Monck had been a professional soldier since 1625 and had fought for many masters, including both Charles I and the Long Parliament. Under Cromwell he had served as general-at-sea (1652–3) and as commander-in-chief in Scotland since 1654. He was apparently of Presbyterian persuasion, but 'He had', wrote Hyde, 'no fumes of religion which turned his head, nor any credit with, or dependence upon, any who were swayed by those trances'. He had played no part in public life, and, resident in Scotland, he was all but unknown to both the government and the public in London. He had sworn allegiance to Richard Cromwell, but since the restoration of the Rump he had conducted himself in public as its loyal servant, taking no part in the Army's increasing criticism of, and opposition to, its proceedings. Like other moderate leaders, he received an approach from Charles II in the summer of 1659, when he was believed to be 'more inclinable to the parliament then the Army but yet more inclinable to a free [parliament], then either'. There were, however, no signs that he was inclined to go beyond this: as Hyde remarked in November 1659, if Monck had 'any designe to serve the King' it was 'very strange' that he did not let the royalists know of it.[32] What he did declare was commitment to national stability, to a clear separation of military and civil power, and to the subordination of military authority to civil. That obedience is 'the greatest virtue which is required in a Souldier' had long been one of his maxims. Back in February, when tension was growing between Richard Cromwell's parliament and the Army grandees, he had written to Thurloe from Dalkeith: 'I am sorry some officers of the Army should trouble themselves with thinges they have nothing to do withall; but you need not doubt for the officers here'. In view of these sentiments the Army commanders had cause to be 'in some fear' how Monck would react to their dissolution of Richard Cromwell's parliament, but on 12 May he had written a dutiful letter of acquiescence and congratulation to Fleetwood and the Council of Officers. However, the letter's desire that 'honourable provision' be made for Richard Cromwell, that no 'particular partie' in religion be preferred, and that 'the freedome and priviledges of [the people's] representatives' be asserted were foreign to the inclinations of Wallingford House. That same moderate disposition appears in a letter Monck wrote to the Speaker in June 1659: 'Obedience is my greate principle and I have alwaise, and ever shall, reverence the Parliament's resolutions in civill things as infallible and sacred'.[33] It is consonant with this that in September he ordered his officers not to subscribe the Derby petition when it was circulated in Scotland. Consonant too, that when he heard of Lambert's coup, he wrote from Edinburgh to Fleetwood, to Lambert and to Lenthall on 20 October declaring his opposition to the Army's action and his support for the excluded MPs. His letter was received in London on the 25th; on the 28th the Committee of Safety decided to send Lambert with a force of some 12,000 men against Monck and he left London on 3 November.[34]

In the event, no military action took place: Lambert's final campaign proved a lamentable anti-climax to his career. With the October coup he had overreached himself; power began ineluctably to slip from him the moment he appeared to have seized it completely. Rather than invade and risk alienating English opinion by an apparently hostile, and certainly burdensome, incursion, Monck had the prudence 'to be on the defensive, so that Lambert must march into Scotland to seeke him and the season being now so severe, t'will incommode his men extreamly; t'will be near a monthes march to the frontiers of Scotland from hence'. While Lambert was gathering his force and making his way to Newcastle, which he reached on 23 November, Monck secured his own Army's loyalty through judicious promotions, transferrals and dismissals and entered into negotiations with the Committee of Safety, thereby minimizing the likelihood of hostilities, even should the opposing armies finally find themselves in the same vicinity. Delay and prevarication were his shrewdest tactics. The Committee of Safety had to govern without any semblance of constitutional legitimacy, under threat of civil war, and in the face of a London populace among whom opinion began to run decisively against the Army. Monck's stand against Lambert received ever increasing support in the capital, where he was in correspondence with the largely sympathetic Common Council of the City. As Baxter put it, 'while *Monk* held them Treating, his Reputation increased, and theirs abated, and their Hearts failed them, and their Soldiers fell off'. Tracts berating the Army for the illegality of its proceedings began to appear, orchestrated by the republicans, who had now regrouped under Haslerig and were agitating for the return of the Rump. Other pamphleteers argued in support of Monck, and for a free parliament. The radical alliance forged during the Civil War and cemented by Pride's Purge was finally cracking: 'The thing most to be wondered at is, that the Congregationall men are many of them disgusted at the Army' wrote Barwick.[35] Increasing unrest on the streets of London boded ill. By late November the law-courts were closed, the judges' commissions having expired, and trade in the city was seriously disrupted. There was friction between civilians and soldiers and the behaviour of the apprentices of the city grew increasingly riotous, especially after their presentation to the City's Common Council on 5 December of a petition calling for a free parliament. 'Many of the apprentices doe boldly say that as their predecessors did help to drive out the father, so they are resolved to bring home the sonne', wrote Nicholas.[36] There was evidence, too, of growing opposition to the Army's action in the provinces and throughout the country at large. In Yorkshire, no less a figure than Thomas, Lord Fairfax, declared for Monck and against Lambert. On 13 December the fleet under Vice-Admiral John Lawson, declared for the purged parliament and, on the 16th, sailed to Gravesend and blocked the Thames. In Ireland, whence Ludlow had returned to London on hearing of Lambert's action, the commanders Sir Charles Coote and Sir Hardress Waller declared for the Rump. Meanwhile, Haslerig, Scot, Ashley Cooper and five other members of the superseded Council of State continued to meet in secret, working against the Committee of Safety and the Wallingford House group. They entered into negotiations with Monck, issued pamphlets, and hatched a plot to seize the Tower of London. On 3 December Haslerig established a base at Portsmouth where the military governor, Colonel Nathaniel Whetham, a friend of Ashley Cooper, and his garrison, declared for the Rump and threatened a march on London.[37]

In this extremity, the inability of the Committee of Safety and the General Council of Officers to agree upon a constitutional settlement was fatal. While they, and their subcommittees, wrangled through November and December over toleration, tithes, qualifications for parliamentary candidature and the franchise, any residual entitlement they may have had to the respect due to governors was frittered away. By December Bulstrode Whitelocke, a member of the Committee of Safety, had become convinced that 'Monk's *design was to bring in the King, and that without terms for the Parliament party*'. He told the despairing Fleetwood that he had only two choices: to declare for a free parliament or to offer his support to Charles II. By Whitelocke's own account, Fleetwood was willing to anticipate Monck and adopt the royalist solution, but he was inhibited by his inability to consult Lambert and overruled by Vane, Desborough and Major-General James Berry. There was a third course, which Whitelocke had not mentioned, and Fleetwood's inaction forced him into it. With the disorder in London approaching uncontrollable proportions, on 24 December he surrendered the keys of the House to the Speaker with the observation 'that the Lord had blasted them and spitt in their faces, and witnessed against their perfidiousnesse'. On 26 December about forty MPs were readmitted to the House.[38]

All this while, Lambert had been marooned in the north of England, unable to risk leaving the road south open to Monck and unable to influence events in London while his situation grew ever more desperate. Spread thinly throughout Northumberland in search of shelter, afflicted by bitterly cold weather and heavy snow, ill-provisioned and unpaid, morale in his Army steadily declined. Public opinion in the north grew increasingly hostile since his troops were 'forced to take free quarter'. Lambert's forces had not the commitment to tolerate these appalling conditions, and his Army gradually melted away. Monck's Coldstreamers, meanwhile, were benefiting from their general's belief that troop morale, regular supplies and pay were crucially a commander's concern. On 27 December, when the die had been cast, Lambert finally turned south, but, unable to preserve under his command a sufficient force to pose any threat, he was reduced to submitting himself to the clemency of the restored MPs on 4 January, who ordered him 'to one of his dwelling-houses most remote for the City of London, in order to the quiet and peace of this Commonwealth'. 'All things here at present in so great a cloud', wrote Hartgill Baron to Mordaunt on 29 December, 'that the most quick sighted or wisest man living is not able to make a judgement what may be the issue.'[39]

## 4 The Long Parliament Restored (January–March 1660)[40]

Since early December the Scottish Army had maintained from Coldstream, on the border, 'that famous Leaguer, where the General encamped and besieged (as it were) *England* and *Ireland*'. Finally, on 1 January, Monck ordered his infantry to cross the Tweed, and the next day he himself followed with the cavalry. His purpose, however, was very far from clear, for he had already achieved his declared aim: Lambert had submitted and the Rump had been restored. The pretext for an invasion had by now passed. When Monck came 'out of *Scotland*... no man knew what he would do, or declare'.[41] There were many possibilities: his plan might be to establish military rule under his own leadership, for, after the flight of Lambert, he was by far the most powerful military figure in Britain; it might be to restore Richard Cromwell and the Protectorate; it might be to shore-up the Rump and republican government; it might be to secure the return of the members of the Commons secluded by Pride's Purge in 1648, and so re-establish a Presbyterian regime; it might be to insist on dissolution and the election of a new and free parliament; and it might be to work for the restoration of the Stuarts. To further confuse prognostication, any one of these ends might prove a means to another. Monck's biographers would claim that it was his 'full and constant purpose to Restore his Majesty' and that he '*did all along with a direct Eye aim at the Kings* Restauration', but, after the event no other version of the (now) Duke of Albemarle's intentions would be tolerable. Whether he saw things so clearly at the time is doubtful.

In himself and his manner, Monck gave nothing away. He was, in the words of Milton's nephew Edward Phillips, 'the most reserved man then living'; he could 'keep his reserves with Men' and 'kept himself in a cloud' agreed John Price, one of his chaplains; another chaplain, Thomas Gumble, described him as 'of a silent reserved nature, one that thought much, but spoke little'.[42] Because of this 'reservednesse' royalists, who had been making unsuccessful attempts to convey to him Charles's assurances 'of the kindnesse and good opinion wee have ever had of him', could not make out whether he might be for them or not; his actions were a 'mistery'; 'Monck no flesh understands' exclaimed Mordaunt in exasperation in early January; it is 'too difficult to make any warrantable conclusion of Monck's intentions', 'what he really is none knows'. The general did not even impress: 'a dull heavy man' says Pepys, with some disappointment, when he finally saw Monck in London. Pepys's 'lord', Edward Mountagu, formerly a Cromwellian general but in 1661 created Earl of Sandwich for his part in effecting the Restoration, similarly judged Monck 'a thick-skulled fellow'. 'All the world is now at a loss to think what Monke will do' wrote Pepys under 18 January. Two months later, in mid March, even though the dissolution of the Long Parliament was then assured, the London barber Thomas Rugg could write in his journal that Monck had 'not fully declared his minde'.[43]

As a result, an air both of expectancy and of apprehension marks comments on public affairs during the first three months of 1660. History seemed to have lost its momentum. Far from an inevitable rush towards the restoration of monarchy, public life seemed almost suspended. At the start of the year, a Church of England observer remarked of public affairs that 'Never was more said, and less known'. Three months later, in late April, he was still as bemused: 'It is yet standing water with us, we neither flow nor ebbe; how farr the near approaching Parlament may ether [*sic*] advance or drive us back, I know not'. In January the country was reported to be 'full of confusion', the city of London 'in suspence' awaiting Monck's arrival. As he moved slowly south (he was at York on 11 January), the addresses, petitions and messages of welcome he received did not merely applaud his stand against the Army coup and for the purged parliament; they welcomed his action as preparatory to further constitutional movement. Private and public letters, petitions and declarations, from individuals and from local authorities, circulated in favour both of the secluded members and of a free parliament (that is, elected without restriction of franchise or candidature). To the addressees, Monck's response was studiously non-committal: 'The *Generals* Return consisting in a Nod, a Frown, or the Rubbing of his Fore-head, if the Speech were long'. He issued a statement that the Army would not accept the return of the secluded members, that any attempt to restore them would lead to public disorder, and that, by holding elections to fill its vacancies, the House would anyway become free and representative.[44] Even so, when he arrived in London on 3

February, 'he had many cry to him for a free parliament', but some days later Pepys was still 'at a great stand to think what will become of things, whether Monke will stand to the Parliament or no'. On 3 March he heard 'from many, that things are in a very doubtful posture', with rumours that Monck himself might assume supreme power, that the parliament might endeavour 'to keep the power in their hands', or that 'my Lord Protector would come in place again'. In one respect, at least, the rumours were not idle. In March the republican Edmund Ludlow was approached with a design 'for the setting up of Richard againe', but he responded with contempt (and good sense) that he would 'durst not adventure to scratch my finger for the promoting thereof, knowing that confusion, and consequently the bringing in of Charles Steward, would be the product of it'.[45] During March, Monck was feted and dined 'by most of the companyes of London' in order, as the hostile witness of Ludlow has it, 'to ratify and confirme the bargaine they had made with him, and to express their desires of having the King brought in'. He was not far wide of the mark, for Monck was now in touch with Charles through an intermediary and the 'bringing in of Charles Steward' had been actively in hand since January, when Charles had authorized royalist agents to offer pardon to all save regicides and issued instructions how to win soldiers and Londoners to the royalist cause. A glimpse of the kind of activity now being undertaken is afforded by Evelyn's note that in January he spoke to Colonel Herbert Morley, Lieutenant of the Tower, 'concerning delivering it to the King, and the bringing of him in, to the greate hazard of my life'. Nevertheless, when Monck was asked by the republican colonel John Okey for an assurance that he was 'against Charles Steward', Monck 'gave him his hand before all the officers, that he would oppose his comming in to the utmost', and, in April, Monck still 'continued his sollemne protestations that he would be true to the interest of the Commonwealth, against a King and Howse of Lords'. 'Things seem very doubtful what will be the end of all', wrote Pepys on 13 March, remembering the Army's role in recent history, 'for the Parliament seems to be strong for the King, which the soldiers do all talk against'; 'Monck is so dark a man, no perspective can looke through him, and it will be like the last scean of some excellent play, which the most judicious cannot positively say how it will end', wrote Mordaunt to Henrietta Maria in late January.[46]

As Monck continued his inexorable march towards London (he left York on 16 January and was in Market Harborough on the 23rd, Northampton on the 25th) the restored Rump, under the leadership of Haslerig, now 'very jocund and high' at having through Lambert's capitulation finally (as it seemed) overcome the Army, applauded and approved all Monck had done and rewarded him with estates and honours. It assured him that parliament would meet all his expenses and pay his soldiers, and desired him 'speedily' to come to London. The Rump also sought to distance itself from the radicalism of the Army and to recommend itself to its new patron by moves of studied moderation. It set about purging those hostile to its authority and it reinstated men who had opposed the events of 1648–9 and others who had been supporters of the Protectorate. Lambert, Desborough and other officers 'who had acted against Parliament in the late Interruption' were placed under house arrest. The Army's chief champion in the Commons, and the man most identified with religious radicalism, Sir Henry Vane, was expelled and placed under house arrest. In a similar vein, a proposal that members should be required to renounce the house of Stuart was not adopted. The pamphlet literature shows a similar reaction against religious and political extremism, berating the Quakers in particular.[47] However, though its actions and pronouncements appeared to mark a turning away from its radical heritage, the Rump showed no inclination to yield to the pressure for its dissolution. It did not agree to permit the return of the secluded members, who, never having taken the Engagement to the Commonwealth, could be expected to vote to end the term of the republican Rump; nor did it decide on dissolution in favour of a general election to a new parliament, which might be expected to show a Presbyterian, if not a royalist majority. Instead, it resolved on by-elections to fill its seats, but by-elections hedged with restrictions on candidature and franchise designed to ensure the participation only of the politically sympathetic.[48]

This determination to perpetuate itself was scant recommendation. The Rump's history was too graphically present to allow many to be persuaded by its new moderate image. 'The most sober here conclude, without their [the secluded members'] admission or a free parliament, the Rump will not sit long', wrote the royalist Hartgill Baron from London on 29 December. Four days later, Pepys reports 'Great talk that many places have declared for a free Parliament; and it is believed that they will be forced to fill up the House with the old members' excluded since Pride's Purge of 1648. Rugg similarly records under January that 'the [Rump] parliament did not please the people in regard they ware so few in number, not above 60 or 70, and they were hated the more because they would not permitt the secluded members to sitt with them. All cryes out for a free Parliment.' When, on 23 January, the Rump endeavoured to secure its authority and future as a republican government by issuing a declaration committing itself to a permanent constitutional settlement, to the impartial administration of justice, to support for the ministry and the universities, and to the maintenance of tithes, 'I do not find people apt to believe them' wrote Pepys.[49] In particular, the City of London was quite unpersuaded by these undertakings. Its Common Council became a centre of opposition to the payment of taxes levied by the Rump and the focus of the movement (both Presbyterian and royalist) for a more representative legislative assembly. Its demand that the secluded members should be readmitted prompted Prynne once more to lead a delegation of them to seek admittance to the House, which, predictably, was turned away by soldiers. In

November Prynne's pamphleteering had earned him a letter of recognition and appreciation from no less a person than Charles himself, and Prynne's reaction to being once more excluded was to renew his literary campaign with his usual indefatigability and ferocity.[50] It was at this time, in this mood of hostile reaction after its second restoration and in part through Prynne's efforts, that the royalists' sobriquet *Rump* for the purged parliament became general, and that the vilificatory, denigratory and scatological possibilities of the term began to be deployed by controversialists and satirists.[51]

By the second week of February this hostility had so provoked the Rump that it turned to its new-found champion to assert its authority. On 28 January Monck was at St Albans; on 3 February, with some 6,000 troops, he had finally reached London, having ensured a peaceful entry and secured his own authority through the Rump's agreement that regiments stationed in London should be dispersed and quartered outside the city. On Monday 6 February Monck attended the House to receive its thanks and had spoken, not entirely to its satisfaction, against extremism, either royalist or radical, and had requested that it proceed to elections to fill its vacancies.[52] Three days later this alliance between the studiously moderate Monck and the beleaguered Rumpers was put to the test. Over a month before, on 23 December, London's Common Council had resolved to call out six regiments of trained bands, reorganized under officers of a predominantly royalist disposition, and on the 24th it had ordered that chains, gates and other defences be set up to bar access to city streets if need be. Although the Council's declared aim was to counter growing public disorder in the city, these measures were easily construed as provocative and defiant by the Rump. This interpretation was further encouraged when, on 8 February, the Common Council received sympathetically a petition effectively calling upon it not to co-operate with the Rump or to recognize either its tax-raising or legislative authority. If the Rump could not command the loyalty of the capital there were scant hopes for its writ beyond; steps were consequently taken 'for reducing of the City to the Obedience of Parliament'. The Commons readily approved when the Council of State ordered Monck to enter the City to restore public order, to arrest prominent members of the Common Council, to break down the City's defences and to station troops in the city. They also declared null and void the recent elections to the Common Council and resolved on an act to appoint a new Council 'with such Qualifications as the Parliament shall think fit'.[53] When, on 9 February, Monck entered the city and, the next day, took down 'all the gates of the Citty, and portcullises, posts and chaines', his action so disappointed the hopes vested in him that it 'made the poore cittizans look very bigg on him, and for the present, [thinking] that all theire expectations in him [ware] lost, many did that night curse and sweare att him like divells': 'All the City indeed seem'd as People confounded with wonder and Anxiety'. 'The City look mighty blank and cannot tell what in the world to do', wrote

Pepys.[54] The next day, however, the decision was finally taken to curb the Rump's overweening exercise of its power. On the morning of the 11th, Monck and 14 of his officers signed and despatched to parliament a letter of protest at its recent order, which, it expostulated, had dismayed the many who clamoured for legal government and a full and free parliament. There was disquiet, too, that parliament had not proceeded decisively against Lambert or Vane, or finalized a constitutional settlement, and that it had received kindly a vehemently anti-royalist petition. The letter required the House to issue writs to fill its vacancies by the following Friday, 17 February, to dissolve by 6 May, and to arrange for the election of a full and free parliament as its successor. This letter was read in the House that same day, 11 February.[55]

The effect of this 'brisk and smart Letter' was instantaneous: hearing 'the news of a letter from Monke, who was now gone into the City again and did resolve to stand for the sudden filling up of the House', Pepys found it 'very strange how the counteneance of men in the Hall was all changed with joy in half an hour's time'; when Monck himself appeared in public there was 'such a shout I never heard in all my life, crying out "God bless your Excellence"', while his soldiers were hailed with 'extraordinary good words' by the London citizenry who were so 'open-handed' with them that 'they are most of them drunk all day, and have money given them'. Opposition to the republican regime and jubilant anticipation of its demise now knew no restraint. 'Never was joy so Universall', wrote the royalist pamphleteer Roger L'Estrange, '*wise* men grew mad upon't, and *mad* men *sober*. The cryes, the Bonfires, and the fume of Rosted Rumps, did quite take down the *Legislative Stomack*'. That night,

> news rane like wild fier... that now his Excellency would put in the sceluded [*sic*] members that Oliver put out because they would not consent to the death of the Kinge, that hee would stand by them, and they should have a free Parliment, made boonefiers very thick in every street and bells ringing in every church and the greatest acclamations of joy that could posiably be expresed, and many drunk for joy... Also in the suburbs boonefiers, and as they hard the newes quit through England, Scotland and Ireland.

Thomas Rugg's account is corroborated by Pepys, who, late on the evening of 11 February, counted 14 bonfires 'between St Dunstan's and Temple-bar', and 'could at one view tell 31 fires' from the Strand bridge. In King Street there were seven or eight fires, 'and all along burning and roasting and drinking for rumps – there being rumps tied upon sticks and carried up and down. The butchers at the maypole in the Strand rang a peal with their knifes when they were going to sacrifice their rump. On Ludgate-hill there was one turning of the spit, that had a rump tied upon it, and another basting of it': 'the common joy that was everywhere to be seen!... it was past imagination, both the greatness and the suddenness of it'.[56]

There was 'now a State of War between the *Scotish* [*sic*] *Army*, and the *Parliament*' such as might seem wearisomely familiar to those who had lived through the Commonwealth and Protectorate, but Monck did not attempt any such forcible ejection of MPs as had been effected by Cromwell in 1653 and in 1659 by Fleetwood and by Lambert. Remaining true to his 'principle' he required the legislature to act on its own behalf: members were to 'be their own *Excecutioners* within their walls of Empire'. Ten days after this 'signal day' Monck suddenly and dramatically impelled parliament further down this road. Despite his declared opposition to the readmission of the secluded members and despite the fact that the House had proceeded, as he wished, with arrangements for elections, he and his officers decided on the readmission of the secluded MPs. On condition that they preserved the Republic, safeguarded the Presbyterian church and permitted toleration of sects, that they raised a tax to meet the Army's arrears, and that they proceeded to a speedy dissolution of the House, issuing writs for a new parliament to meet on 20 April, on 21 February Monck's soldiers permitted them to enter the House, to the astonishment of the sitting MPs. It may be that his discussions and negotiations with all the competing factions had persuaded him that they were irreconcilable; it may be that he was finally persuaded that readmission was the swiftest and simplest way to ensure the final dissolution of the House; perhaps the volubility of the public outcry persuaded him it had to be heeded; and it may be that this had been his intention all along and that the opportunity had finally presented itself.[57] What further he intended cannot be known. In an address to the now fully restored Long Parliament he still maintained a studiously moderate position, insisting that the national interest 'must lye in a Commonwealth' and that, 'after so long and bloody a War against the King for breaking in upon their Liberties', people would not tolerate the restoration of monarchy. Furthermore, monarchy in the state would mean prelacy in the church, 'which these Nations, I know, cannot bear, and against which they have so solemnly sworn: And indeed moderate, not rigid, Presbyterian Government, with a sufficient Liberty for Consciences truly tender, appears at present to be the most indifferent and acceptable Way to the Church's Settlement'. Perhaps this did represent the limit of Monck's aspirations at this stage, but, whatever his thinking, the history of the purged parliament, created by the Army in 1648, twice restored by it and now three times rejected, was finally brought to a close, and brought to a close amidst general rejoicing. Evelyn, Pepys and Thomas Rugg all report great jubilation when the secluded members were readmitted on 21 February: 'out of the window it was a most pleasant sight to see the City from [one] end to the other with a glory about it, so high was the light of the Bonefires and so thick around the City, and the bells rang everywhere'.[58]

Some 90 secluded members resumed their seats on 21 February. Republican commitment was not obliterated. Rumpers such as Haslerig and Scot continued to sit, and, though they were now in a minority, it was by no means an insignificant one; average attendance rose from 44 before the return of the secluded members to 111 after.[59] For Commonwealthsmen, for whom the purged parliament had been the glory of the revolution and the true repository of the Good Old Cause which Cromwell had betrayed, parliament was now so far from being restored to a more truly representative body that it was all but defiled by the presence of those they regarded as temporizing Presbyterians, men who had been prepared in 1647–8 to do a deal with Charles I. It was to attempt to placate such republican feeling in the Army that, on that same day, 21 February, *A Letter from General Monck and the Officers Here*... was despatched to troops stationed outside London reassuring them that 'since the Providence of God hath made Us free at the cost of so much Bloud' its signatories would never 'return to our old Bondage' or 'lose so glorious a Cause' as their liberty, but such protestations carried little weight with men of the stamp of Edmund Ludlow, convinced that the secluded members had been excluded by 'a lawfull authority' – namely, the vote of 'a quorum of the House of Commons' – and that they were now no better than 'Monck's journeymen', brought back by 'treachery and force' to overthrow 'the privilege of parlament'. He refused to sit in the House once they returned and was prepared to engage in a plot to assassinate Monck.[60]

Had he remained, Ludlow would have found its proceedings intolerable for, despite the persistence of republican sentiment, the return of the Presbyterian members decisively changed the temper of the Commons. After all, it had been their royalism in 1648 that had led to their original exclusion. In June 1659 Barwick had written to Hyde that 'If they can get in all the members that sate in 48, it is thought there will be a great alteration; for then those, that were immediately guilty of the king's blood, will be much the lesser party', and this, he added, would 'most advance his majesty's interest'. This had now come about. The majority in the fully restored Long Parliament promptly turned on the Rump and all its works. On 21 February, the day of the secluded members' readmission, they voted to erase from the record all decisions surrounding Pride's Purge. This was more than a simple act of revenge. The Purge on 6 December 1648 had been precipitated by the Army's determination to frustrate the Long Parliament's vote of 5 December to proceed to a settlement with Charles I. On 18 December 1648 the purged parliament agreed that members might register their dissent from that earlier vote for settlement with Charles I. That decision was among those which the restored Long Parliament now erased from the record, but the decision to treat with Charles I still stood. The implication was that this parliament was prepared to treat with Charles II. The restored Long Parliament also set about reversing more recent history. In the next few days it reinstated London's Common Council; it ordered the City's gates, posts and chains to be repaired at public cost; it abolished the Army Commission and appointed Monck commander-in-chief; it discharged from his post as Dean of Christ Church the leading Independent minister John Owen, who had been warmly thanked by the Rump for his sermon at its restoration in May; and it freed from their imprisonments Booth, the leader of the royalist uprising of the previous summer, the Presbyterian Earl of Lauderdale and Bishop Matthew Wren, imprisoned since 1651 and 1641 respectively. Lambert was sent to the Tower and, with the Army's leaders arrested or discredited, 'great care was taken' also to disable the troops by, in Burnet's words, scattering them

> in wide quarters, and not to suffer too many of those who were still for the old cause to lie near one another. The well and the ill affected were so mixed, that in case of any insurrection some might be ready at hand to resist them . . . above all they took care to have no more troops than was necessary about the city.[61]

The new Council of State was predominantly of a Presbyterian and covertly royalist temper; only 7 of its 31 members were Rumpers. Despite the efforts of the Commonwealthsmen, and some agitation among Army officers, the enlarged House proceeded to enact the Presbyterian and moderate legislation which Monck had required: the Westminster Confession of Faith was agreed to be 'the Publick Confession of Faith of the Church of *England*' and the Solemn League and Covenant was republished and displayed in churches, where it was to be read annually. The Covenant included a promise to defend the King, and, led by Prynne and despite Monck's caution, Presbyterian members began to express pro-monarchical sentiments in the House. Indeed, Presbyterians were now so determined upon a restoration that, Denzil Holles later told Burnet, they 'pressed the royalists to be quiet, and to leave the game in their hands; for their appearing would give jealousy, and hurt that which they meant to promote'. And, finally, the Commons did agree on its own dissolution by 15 March and that a new parliament should meet on 25 April.[62]

With such tendencies evident in its members, and its term thus set, the restoration of the full Long Parliament was so far from calming the constitutional uncertainty that it only encouraged speculation about what might succeed it. At the beginning of March Pepys found that 'Great is the talk of a single person', though at this stage there were still several candidates: Charles, Monck or even 'Richard [Cromwell] again'. Vilification of the Rump continued unabated, but Milton's *Readie and Easie Way to Establish a Free Commonwealth*, first issued in the last week of February and re-issued in an enlarged second edition in early April, was still arguing the increasingly forlorn republican case, while his friend Marchamont Nedham was discrediting the Stuart cause in *News from Brussels*, which appeared in March. However, the pro-monarchical case was now also being publicly heard. In November 1659 it had been 'capital to speake or write in favour' of Charles Stuart when, in response to the justification of Lambert's coup in *The Armies Plea for their Present*

*Practice*, Evelyn's anonymous *Apology for the Royal Party* had responded by rehearsing the 'wretched *Interludes, Fancies and Fantasms*' of government since Charles I's execution to argue that only the restoration of monarchy could secure a stable settlement. There was no such risk when, in late February, Pepys read 'a pamphlet, well-writ and directed to Generall Monke in praise of the form of Monarchy which was settled before the Warrs', and Evelyn, that same month, published a pamphlet in defence of Charles against the attempt of Nedham's 'wicked forged paper' *News from Brussels* 'to render him odious, now when every body were in hopes & expectation of the Gen: & Parliaments recalling him, & stablishing the Government on its antient and right basis'.[63] Prynne, moving the bill for dissolution of the Long Parliament, had on 1 March openly stated in the House that the writs for the next parliament should be moved 'In King Charles' name', and a few days later Pepys was hearing talk that 'the King would come in'. It was about this time that Rugg, too, first heard people in London calling for the return of Charles II. By 5 March Pepys could write 'Great hopes of the King's coming again' and on the 6th he noted that 'Everybody now drinks the King's health without fear, whereas before it was very private that a man dare do it'. When, a day late on 16 March, the Long Parliament finally dissolved 'very cheerfully', in Pepys's words, people began 'to talk loud of the King': there was, wrote Rugg, 'heare in London great expectation that the King of England will be brought [in] by the Parliament that is to sit in Aprille next'. By 19 March Pepys could finally write that 'All the discourse nowadays is that the King will come again; and for all I see, it is the wishes of all and all do believe that it will be so'. The movement had become so irresistible that by 4 April Pepys's friend Robert Blackborne, Secretary to the Admiralty under the Commonwealth and Protectorate and a convinced Puritan, was not only persuaded 'that the King must of necessity come' but, to Pepys's surprise, commended Charles 'for a sober man' and professed 'how quiet he would be under his government'. In April Rugg saw pictures of Charles II 'sett up in houses without the least molestation' which formerly 'was almost a hanging matter so to doe'. That same month he saw Thames watermen wearing 'those badges that they wore in the time of Kinge Charles the Firsts dayes'. By the time the Convention met, people, in Pepys's experience, had begun to speak 'very freely' of the King's coming.[64]

## 5 Monarchy Restored (April–May 1660)[65]

Some spoke too freely. When, on 25 March, Matthew Griffith preached in Mercers' Chapel on his own pointedly extended version of Proverbs 24.21 ('My son, fear God and the King, and meddle not with them that be *seditious or* desirous of change'), the intemperance and virulence of his support for the return of Charles II threatened to dismay waverers rather than to win converts to the royalist cause. A few days later the printed sermon appeared with an appended historical survey of the last 20 years which concluded that 'without the restitution of *King CHARLES* to his native rights, we can in reason look for no solid settlement of Religion, or Law, Liberty or Property, Peace or Plenty, Honour or Safety'. Its dedication to Monck urged him, now that we are '*upon the point of recovery*', to continue '*what you have already so happily begun . . . till you have finish'd this great and good work, and brought it to perfection*'. For such enthusiastically public promotion of what was still, technically, treason, Griffith found himself committed to Newgate by the Council of State on 5 April. There was, though, very little likelihood that anything could now stay the monarchist movement, as no less a committed figure than Milton conceded when, in his final defence of the Good Old Cause, his *Brief Notes upon a late Sermon Titl'd The Fear of God and the King*, he forlornly proposed that, if there must be a monarchy, then let it be elective and let us choose 'out of our own number one who hath best aided the people, and best merited against tyrannie', that is (presumably), Monck. Roger L'Estrange's anonymous reply, *No Blinde Guides*, impatiently dismissed Milton's claim that, as England is no longer a monarchy, there is no one with an hereditary claim to the title of its king.[66]

At just the time Milton's tract was published there was more dramatic evidence that the cause was lost. On 10 April, Lambert escaped from the Tower, where he had been confined since 4 March for having refused to leave London. It 'was supposed he would draw a considerable body of the Army together speedily' but in the event only a few hundred gathered at the muster arranged, with a nice sense of history, at Edgehill on 22 April. With his customary style, Lambert 'was mounted on a Barb' but 'on ploughed land' its speed was useless and, when his supporters fled, Lambert had ignominiously to yield to Richard Ingoldsby. That it should have been a regicide who returned him to the Tower was a sign of the times which Ludlow, who had declined to become involved in the attempted uprising, would have understood. Keeping himself out of public view in a house in Somerset in April, he found that the royalist Colonel Robert Phillips had lately visited the same house, equally privately: 'It was twielight (as we call it) with us both: with me it was as that of the evening, when it darkens by reason of the departure of the sunne, but with him as that of the morning, when it vanisheth by reason of its rising'.[67]

With the close of the Long Parliament's 20-year term, both its members, even its Speaker William Lenthall, and its military servants, such as Mountague, set about making their individual peace with the Stuarts.[68] And, at last, royalist perplexity over Monck was resolved. Hitherto he 'would hold no conference' with royalists and had not been drawn to do so when, in the summer of 1659, his brother Nicholas, a Presbyterian minister, afterwards Bishop of Hereford, conveyed a letter from Charles brought to England by

Monck's cousin Sir John Grenville, afterwards Earl of Bath. Monck had then refused to accept the letter, but, a day or two after the dissolution of the Long Parliament, he not only received Grenville and accepted the King's letter but professed that the restoration of monarchy had all along been his intent. At a private meeting, arranged by another kinsman, Sir William Morice, afterwards Secretary of State, Monck finally and unequivocally declared that 'As to the Kings Majesty... None wish'd him greater felicity than he, nor desired his Restauration with more passion'. He was ready 'not only... to obey his [Majesty's] Commands, but to sacrifice my Life and Fortune in his Service'. Perhaps he was not being disingenuous. Certainly, there is no doubt that his profession of loyalty was now in tune with the public mood, leading Hyde to suppose that Monck realized that when the members of the Convention met, 'there would be a warmth amongst them that could not be restrained or controlled, and they might take the business so much into their own hand that they might leave no part to him to merit of the King'. Once declared, however, there was nothing half-hearted about his allegiance. Just as he had done the royalists' work for them by opposing Lambert, and so rendering a foreign invasion unnecessary, so his readiness to promote the restoration was conditional only upon the payment of Army arrears and indemnity; he expressed no opinion about the institution of monarchy or its constitutional role. He did, however, offer advice which, unless the report of it is coloured by subsequent events, earned his dukedom, for upon it the success of the Restoration would depend. Cautious as ever, he refused to reply to Charles in writing lest the letter be intercepted, but he had Grenville commit to memory three pieces of advice. First, to prevent anxiety and fear, the King should declare 'a free and general pardon to all his Subjects, and engage himself to give it under the Great Seal, to all that should submit to his Authority, except such as should be exempted by the *Parliament*'; secondly, that sales of public lands should be confirmed and the soldiers' arrears paid; thirdly, that the king should express his willingness to consent to an act 'for toleration of Liberty of Conscience to all his Subjects'. Monck also recommended that Charles remove from the Roman Catholic Spanish Netherlands to the Protestant United Provinces, a domicile more congenial to Puritan sentiment.[69]

In his unconcern about conditions Monck, despite his Presbyterian background, differed from such Presbyterian lords and MPs as Denzil Holles, one of those whom Charles I had attempted to arrest in 1642, William Pierrepont, son of the 1st Earl of Kingston and a secluded member, and William Russell, 5th Earl (and afterwards 1st Duke) of Bedford. They continued consistently to maintain the Presbyterians' Civil War negotiating position with Charles I, namely, that the Army and Navy should be under parliamentary control, and monarchy and church established on the clearly defined constitutional and Presbyterian principles enunciated by the Long Parliament in the Newcastle

Propositions of 1646 and in the Treaty of Newport put to Charles I in September 1648 when he was a prisoner on the Isle of Wight.[70] Though very willing to support a restoration, they were accordingly determined that it should depend upon Charles II's acquiescence to such terms: 'there must be strict conditions to which he must be bound, which it should not be in his power to break', in Hyde's words. Though unwilling, Hyde anticipated such a negotiated settlement with the Presbyterians if ever the restoration became a possibility. More ardent spirits, though they recognized in the Presbyterians 'the chief wheele of this motion' towards restoration, were less ready to pay their price. Writing to Charles in November 1659 of 'a close correspondence between some of the presbiterian lords and Monck', Mordaunt had reported that 'the best wee can hope for... will be the articles of the Isle of Wight, and the parliament of 48, and those I doubt not will restore you, but not so restore you, as your faithfull servants desirte. For Sir, tis a great and glorious prince we hope to see you, not what they please to make you'. Although there was now no possibility that Presbyterian demands would founder, as they had in 1648, on Army and Independent disquiet, yet founder they would, this time on opposition from the opposite quarter.[71]

That opposition could be foreseen from the elections to the Commons House of the Convention. In the debates in March calling for a new parliament, Prynne's proposal that the writs should be moved in the King's name was defeated and it was agreed they would be issued in the name of the Keepers of the Liberties of England. The decision to forbid Catholics and unrepentant royalists and their sons to stand for election was consonant with this republicanism. However, a different temper declared itself when, on 13 March, the Engagement (or oath of allegiance) to the Commonwealth (that is, to government without a king or House of Lords), hitherto required of new members, was abolished and all orders concerning it were expunged from the Commons' journals. In this mood, the House rejected a proposal to deprive all royalists of the franchise. Since, as Ludlow observed, 'they had given liberty to cavaleers to choose, it was not like that they would choose any of other principles': and the prohibition on royalists standing was consequently 'no more regarded than dead men's Shoes; the Countrey hastening to their Election'. When it met on 25 April, the Convention was dominated by members who were, in Hyde's words, 'of singular affection to the King', with 'very few' members 'who did not heartily abhor the murder of his father and detest the government that succeeded'.[72] Of the 300 or so members whose family allegiances in the Civil War can be determined, 158 came from royalist families, 150 from parliamentarian, but these 150 were almost all Presbyterian. A total of 108 members had actually been in arms for Charles I. The ranks of Commonwealthsmen, of Army officers and of Independents and Cromwellians, were very thin. Although, as Burnet put it, 'The republicans went about as madmen, to rouse up their party... their time was past. All were either as men amazed or asleep . . . The elections of parliament men run all the other way.' The parliamentary careers of the Army grandees, of Fifth Monarchists such as Thomas Harrison, of Vane, Haslerig and other republicans, of parliamentarian lawyers like Oliver St John, and of the Speaker of the Long Parliament, William Lenthall, were over. No member of the Committee of Safety set up after Lambert's coup was elected and only 15 of those who had sat in the restored Rump in 1659 were returned to the new House, of whom one was declared not duly elected and three were expelled.[73] The expulsions were of the regicide John Hutchinson, and of Robert Wallop and Francis Lascelles, both nominated as judges of Charles I but neither a signatory of the death warrant (Lascelles, it seems, never sat). Altogether five regicides or judges were returned, but the election of Ludlow was disputed and the House found against him, which, of the five, left only Ingoldsby, whose capture of Lambert had sufficiently redeemed him.[74] No wonder that for republicans of Ludlow's stamp, for whom, since the Long Parliament was not legally dissolved, the Convention could only ever be 'a nominall Howse of Commons', the elections to the Convention were little more than a royalist subterfuge, conducted under cover of Monck's feigned impartiality.[75]

However, although, in Lucy Hutchinson's scornful phrase, the Presbyterians were now 'the white boys' and there was a large group of over a hundred former members of the Long Parliament, it was outnumbered by members who had never sat before (208 MPs). Furthermore, the Presbyterians lacked coherence and leadership as a group and their parliamentary effectiveness was severely compromised by the virulence with which Prynne pursued former Cromwellians and Independents. His vindictiveness not only played into royalist hands by delaying votes and prolonging debates, it dissipated the force of the Presbyterian position since it dismayed many more moderate Presbyterians. Heneage Finch, afterwards Lord Chancellor and 1st Earl of Nottingham, Edward Turner, afterwards knighted and Speaker of the Cavalier Parliament, Job Charlton, afterwards Justice of the Common Pleas, and Roger Palmer, afterwards Attorney-General, proved far more adept at managing debates in the royalist cause. The Presbyterians did secure the election of a sympathetic Speaker, Harbottle Grimston, but they found themselves unable to command an outright majority in either the Lords or Commons. Furthermore, now that the return of Charles was all but certain, for any Presbyterian member to make a stand for a conditional restoration was to jeopardize his position once the King had been restored.[76] 'The Cavaliers', as Mountagu reported to Pepys, 'have now the upper hand clear of the Presbyterians.' When (on 8 May) Sir Matthew Hale proposed a subcommittee be constituted to consider which of the clauses of the 1648 Treaty of Newport should be presented to the King, he was opposed by Monck and the motion was withdrawn. The possibility of making terms with Charles, of offering a conditional restoration, simply never arose. His return was to be, as Andrew Marvell later remarked, neither 'soiled with the blood of Victory, nor lessened by any capitulations of Treaty'.[77]

The one person who might have been expected to support the Presbyterian position studiously declined to do so, even, as in the case of Hale's proposal, opposing it. With his usual taciturnity Monck, in the main, simply 'now sat still'. He made no opening address to the parliament which he had called into being and offered that assembly no advice or guidance. However, and again as usual, he had a hand to play. Following his meeting with Grenville in mid-March he had received from Charles five letters dated from Breda on 4 April to be communicated to the President and Council of State and to Army officers, to the fleet, to the Speakers of the Commons and the Lords, and to the Lord Mayor, Aldermen and Common Council of London; these letters were accompanied by a public *Declaration*. On 1 May, '*Monk*'s Hood' was finally 'take off': he revealed to the House that Grenville had these letters and *Declaration*, as yet unopened, from Charles, and the House, 'with a general acclamation', called for Grenville and had the documents read; 'And from this time Charles Steward was no more heard of, and so universal a joy was never seen within those walls'. Following motions of thanks and gratitude and resolutions to print the *Declaration* and to send £50,000 to the King, the Commons, on what Pepys called the 'happiest May-day that hath been many a year in England', unanimously approved a motion put by Morice concurring with the Lords that 'according to the antient and fundamental Laws of this Kingdom, the Government is, and ought to be, by King, Lords, and Commons' and that ways should be sought 'to obtain the King's Return to his People'.[78]

# 2

# *The Restoration Year (1660–1661)*

## 1 'Past all humane policy'

> And all this without one drop of bloud, & by that very Army, which rebell'd against him: but it was the Lords doing, *et mirabile in oculis nostris*: for such a Restauration was never seene in the mention of any history, antient or modern, since the returne of the *Babylonian* Captivity, nor so joyfull a day & so bright, ever seene in this nation: this hapning when to expect or effect it, was past all humane policy.[1]

The diarist John Evelyn was at a loss to explain how the restoration of monarchy and the return of Charles II came about in May 1660. It appeared to be an event not simply without human agency, but contrary to human contrivance, rendering impotent political and military power, as the very Army which had warred on Charles II, defeated and executed him, and abolished monarchy, effected the return of his son to his throne. In his astonishment and incredulity, Evelyn is representative. When, as Mordaunt wrote to Henrietta Maria in January 1660, there was no precedent of 'three kingdoms lost and recovered without some hazzard', how could their recovery have been achieved so swiftly, so unexpectedly and without any loss of blood? The Restoration was, announced the title of John Price's account of it, a *Mystery*, though one which, in his letter to Monck from Breda, Charles turned to his advantage by arguing that his return without an invasion or foreign aid, when (implicitly) he could have had either, was evidence of his love towards and tender care of his people.[2] In fact, despite having been long plotted, the change of regime in May 1660 took the monarch as much by surprise as it did everyone else. It occurred, in Clarendon's words, 'with miraculous expedition', 'in a trice', as Baxter put it, when it was thought 'next impossible' and the royalists, in the poet Abraham Cowley's view, 'had not the least glympse of Hope' of it. In his sermon at the coronation on 23 April 1661, George Morley, then Bishop of Worcester and afterwards of Winchester, was incredulous: who, he asked, 'would have Believed a little above a year agoe, that ever he should have lived to see *this Day*', 'so great, so sudden, so wonderful a *Change* from what we *were of late*, to what *we are now*' that it 'is like the *Resurrection* from the *Dead*'.[3]

Contemporaries found only providential explanations adequate for so unfathomable an event. Baxter is typical:

> It seemed wonderful to me, that an Army that had got so many great and marvellous Victories, and thought themselves so unconquerable, and talkt of nothing but Dominion at home, and marching up to the Walls of *Rome*, should all be broken and brought into Subjection, and finally Disbanded, without one blow stricken, or one drop of Blood shed! and that by so small a power as *Monk*'s Army in the beginning was: So Eminent was the hand of God in all this Change!

Though, as the man responsible for ending Baxter's ministry at Kidderminster, Morley was frequently at odds with Baxter, with this he agreed. In his coronation sermon he found the 'immediate hand' of God in both the preservation of Charles after his defeat by Cromwell at Worcester in 1651 and in the Restoration, but 'more signally and more remarkably in the latter', for there was no precedent for a king so long exiled, after so many changes of government, being 'so solemnly Invited, so magnificently Conducted, so triumphantly Received and so joyfully and universally Acknowledged and Welcomed by all the Subjects; And all this, without *blood*, without *blows*, without *bargain*, and without any *obligation* at all to any *Foreign* Prince or State for it'. Preaching at Whitehall on 28 June 1660, a day of thanksgiving for the Restoration, Gilbert Sheldon, afterwards successively Bishop of London and Archbishop of Canterbury, developed the same theme:

> all we did, or could do, toward a settlement proved nothing worth, all attempts vain, no *Treaties*, no *Armies*, no *Endeavors* by ourselves or to others that wished well to our Peace did us good, though never so probable, never so hopeful; they were all lost and frustrate, all vanished into nothing. How visible was Gods hand in it . . .[4]

Even Monck himself declared, 'It was not I that did this; you know the Jealousies that were had of me, and the oppositions against me; It was God alone who did it'. It was not merely the fashion for biblical typology which sent Evelyn back two thousand years for a precedent. The Restoration so effectively, so painlessly and so quickly frustrated the whole range of Puritan aspiration that its beneficiaries could not but see it as a divine mercy: 'it was the Lord's doing'. 'Never was there so miraculous a change as this, nor so great things done in so short a time', wrote the 72-year-old Bishop of Salisbury, Brian Duppa, 'But *A Domino Factum est istud*: no humane wisdom can claime a share in it'.[5] Those who lost power were as bewildered as those who gained it. As Milton's Chorus in *Samson Agonistes* was to observe despairingly of the predicament of God's champion: 'God of our fathers, what is man! / That thou towards him with hand so various, / Or might I say contrarious, / Temper'st thy providence through his short course'.[6]

It is true that ever since the death of Cromwell on 3 September 1658 increasing anarchy had induced at best a weariness with, at worst an appalled dismay at, the incompetencies, rivalries and disorders into which the Protectorate and the Commonwealth successively collapsed. However, there is an element of wisdom after the event in Sir John Reresby's reflection in his memoirs, written up after the Restoration, that in the summer of 1659, 'by the disputes beween our new governours, the ambition of some and jealosies of others, the dislike of the Parlaments proceeding on one hand and the haughty and insolent demeanour of the officers of the Army on the other, it was easy to decern that a door was oponing for the Kings return into England'.[7] When he was lamenting the country's 'unsettlement and division' in July 1659 it had not occurred to Edward, 3rd Viscount Conway, that this afforded any opportunity to the royalists; he thought 'the whole game is like to be played between the 5th Monarchy men . . . and between [*sic*] Commonwealth men'. In the letters exchanged between the Northamptonshire royalist Sir Justinian Isham and Brian Duppa, Bishop of Worcester, the cleric who had been closest to Charles I in his final months and tutor to his son till the Prince of Wales left England in 1646, there is no hint throughout 1659 or early 1660 that either correspondent thought their political fortunes might improve. That this was not simply prudent wariness for fear their letters should be intercepted is indicated by the pronounced and resigned tenor of what they did commit to paper. 'The folly and madness' of a world in which 'we have seen so many revolutions, and so suddaine, that it was never better instanc'd unto us then now how all sublunary things are *tenui pendentia filo*' was what bore on Sir Justinian as late as January 1660. In February the Bishop confessed that the times 'toss, and tumble me', so that, though his trust is in God, 'there is still left a *motus trepidationis*, such as that of the needle in the compass, which though it looks towards the north, yet hath its quiverings and shakings'. 'Parlaments and Armies, changes and revolutions' so dominate the scene that when, at last, on 27 March, Duppa acknowledges that 'our spring of hopes' may be about to break, it is yet very tentatively: 'we have been so often deluded with expectations . . . that every sunshine is suspected by me'. No wonder that when, in May, he was finally convinced, it was by nothing less than the 'miraculous'.[8]

This is the burden of Clarendon's account in his *History of the Rebellion* of the 18 months preceding the Restoration. He insists repeatedly on the forlorn predicament of the royalists. When the Second Protectorate of Richard ensued smoothly, 'the King's condition never appeared so hopeless, so desperate', 'for a more favourable conjuncture they could never expect than this, that had blasted all their hopes, and confirmed their utmost despair'. When, in

April 1659, the 'simplicity' of Richard Cromwell, as Pepys put it, lost him 'all that his father had left him', 'the return of the government' into military hands seemed, wrote Clarendon, 'to be the most dismal change that could happen, and to pull up all hopes of the King by the roots'. By July 'there appeared as great a calm as ever, and the government as well settled to the general content of the people'. It was not in the least disturbed by the royalist uprising that summer, whose swift suppression by Lambert left the Rump apparently 'in as absolute possession of the government of the three nations as ever Cromwell had been'. There seemed to Clarendon to be some hopes of Spanish military aid in the autumn, when the country's stability was put in jeopardy by Lambert's coup, but with the restoration of the Rump on 24 December 'all those contentions and raging animosities [were] composed or suppressed without one broken head' and the opportunity was lost since to the Spanish, as to everyone else, the government of England appeared 'more securely settled against domestic disturbances, than it had been under Cromwell himself'. Charles is credited with 'some faint hope' that Monck's march south 'might yet produce some alteration', but, Clarendon adds parenthetically, 'God knows it was very faint', and, early in 1660, it faded. Monck's peaceful entry into London and his apparent submission to parliament augured so well for political stability and continuity in England that 'all the little remainder of [Charles's] hopes was extinguished, and he had nothing left before his eyes but a perpetual exile . . . a greater consternation and dejection of mind cannot be imagined than at that time covered the whole Court of the King'.[9]

There is, of course, a deliberate rhetorical strategy at work here. Clarendon is preparing the ground for the climax of his history, and for a particular understanding of the nature and import of that climax. The helplessness of the royalists demonstrates that it was not human but divine agency which was at work: at the end of March 1660 all those around the King despaired of his prospects 'till they were awakened and confounded by such a prodigious act of Providence as [God] hath scarce vouchsafed to any nation, since he led his own chosen people through the Red Sea'.[10] Like Evelyn, Clarendon can find only in God's dealings with Israel a comparable case of such pronounced divine favour to a nation. It was, opined Edward Phillips, 'one of the most extraordinary actions, that has ever been mentioned in Story'. Rugg was equally hard put to it to find an historical precedent: 'I question not but the memory herof will be as deare to us as ever Brutus was to Roome, Deborah or Judith to Israll, or other more famous, if more famous ever were any. Vivet le Roy.' Reresby could instance no precedent: it was 'a thing never read of in story, that when monarchy was laid aside at the expence of soe much blood it should return again without the shedding of blood'. From the inexplicable ease with which the Restoration was effected Cowley drew just Clarendon's inference: 'Here, here we see th' Almighty's hand indeed, / Both by the beauty of the work we see't and by the speed'.[11]

## 2 The Royal Martyr

> At the later end of the year 1648 I had leave given mee to goe to london to see my Father, & during my stay there at that time at Whitehal it was that I saw the Beheading of King Charles the first... On the day of his execution, which was Tuesday, Jan. 30, I stood amongst the crowd in the street before Whitehal gate, where the scaffold was erected, and saw what was done, but was not so near as to hear any thing. The Blow I saw given, & can truly say with a sad heart; at the instant whereof, I remember wel, there was such a Grone by the Thousands then present, as I never heard before & desire I may never hear again.[12]

History did offer one interpretative key to May 1660. To many, the decisive event in the history of the 1660s had occurred eleven years before the Restoration, on 30 January 1649. In the view of Gilbert Burnet, no friend to the Stuarts, it was Charles I's 'serious and Christian deportment' on the scaffold which 'made all his former errors be quite forgot, and raised a compassionate regard to him, that drew a lasting hatred on the actors, and was the true cause of the great turn of the nation in the year 1660'.[13] What had happened to Charles I, and his bearing as he sustained it, offered one way of understanding the unprecedented event with which the 1660s began. At the Restoration there were those for whom Charles I remained a Man of Blood justly condemned to death on such scriptural authority as Genesis 9.6, Numbers 35.33 and Proverbs 24.23, 28.17. In the debate on the dissolution of the Long Parliament the regicide Thomas Scott ringingly declared that 'he should desire no greater honour in this world, after the Lord should call him out of it, then to have this epitaph written on his tombe, Heere lyes one who had a hand and a heart in the execution of Charles Steward, late King of England'. For persons of this cast of mind, such as Ludlow, in May 1660 'tyranny and oppression... was coming like a flood upon us',[14] but the 'grone' heard by the young Philip Henry, afterwards the exemplary nonconformist minister of Board Oak, Cheshire, expresses quite another interpretation of the proceedings. It was one Charles I himself had fostered. At his trial on 20–27 January 1649 the '*Royal Actor*', in Marvell's phrase, cast himself as the victim of arbitrary power, defying what he characterized as the 'usurped authority' of the court with the claim that 'I do stand more for the liberty of my people, than any here that come to be my pretended judges': 'For if power without law may make laws, may alter the fundamental laws of the Kingdom, I do not know what subject he is in England, that can be sure of his life, or anything that he calls his own'.[15]

This self-construction was promoted with extraordinary success by *Eikon Basilike: The Pourtraicture of his Sacred Maiestie in his Solitudes and Sufferings* (1648, that is, 1649). Its essential rhetorical strategy is signalled by the famous frontispiece engraving by William Marshall which depicts Charles surrounded by symbols of constancy and grace, regally attired but kneeling in a devotional pose as, with his kingly crown at his feet and grasping a crown of thorns, he gazes heavenwards to an eternal crown of glory.[16] In the first-person text, apparently excerpted from private papers, journals and meditations, Charles is motivated neither by a desire for power nor by the wish to enslave his people but by the determination to follow his conscience in the defence of their liberties and of the episcopal church, no matter the cost: 'I know no resolutions more worthy a Christian King, then to prefer his Conscience before his Kingdoms'. It is his preferring 'the inward peace of My Conscience, before any outward tranquility' which fortifies him in the adversities which he bears with exemplary patience, confident that, in his sufferings, 'the Rock of *Israel* will be an everlasting stay and defence' and that, like Job, his steadfastness will be rewarded. He appears as an innocent victim and a martyr, his trials and death not deserved but a temporal agony through which he earns eternal bliss: 'They knew My chiefest Armes left Me, were those only, which the ancient Christians were wont to use against their Persecutors, Praiers and Tears. These may serve a good mans turn, if not to conquer as a souldier, yet to suffer as a Martyr.' Throughout, the words and gestures of Christ are echoed by this sainted king: 'As Christ did sometime over *Jerusalem*' so he weeps over the agonies of his country and its capital London; he 'will rather chuse to wear a Crown of Thorns with my Saviour'; his sufferings recall the agony in the garden of Gethsemane: 'I pray not so much, that this bitter cup of a violent death may passe from me, as that of his wrath may passe from all those, whose hands by deserting me, are sprinkled, or by acting and consenting to my death are embrued with my blood'. In his death, neither vengeful nor resentful, but grieved, he prophesies that that those who 'build [*Babel*] with the bones, and cement it with the blood of their Kings' will not be suffered to prosper and that he will be vindicated.[17]

This conception of Charles I and his fate offered a way to construe the astonishing events of the spring of 1660. Although structured as an autobiographical and confessional work, *Eikon Basilike* was apologetic in purpose and almost certainly in great, if not entire, part the work of John Gauden, after the Restoration successively Bishop of Exeter and of Worcester. After repeated reprintings during the Interregnum it was triumphantly included in the sumptuous *Workes of King Charles the Martyr* of 1662.[18] By then, the cult of King Charles the Martyr had been given official status by the proclamation that 30 January would henceforth be observed as a 'Solemn Fast & day of humiliation to deplore the sinns which so long had provoked God against this Afflicted Church & people ... [and] to expiate the Gilt of the Execrable Murder of the late *King Char*: I'. A special commemorative service, almost certainly composed by Duppa, was published in January 1661 and included, in revised form, in the 1662 Book of Common Prayer; its second lesson was from Matthew 27 on Christ's trial and crucifixion. Annually that service, and the accompanying sermons, extolling the royal martyr as 'A royall Gemme, a religious mirrour, the *Lands Ornament*, the Churches Phenix', 'as great a Saint as a King', berated the sin of rebellion, inculcated obedience to his son and promoted the Church of England as the only true guardian of kingship.[19] Charles I was almost as forceful a presence in the early Restoration years as his son: within two days of the vote for the Restoration, steps were taken for the re-erection of dismantled statues of Charles I and for the erection of new statues of him throughout the kingdom; it was his portrait, derived from the Marshall frontispiece, which was displayed by local authorities in May 1660.[20]

The return of Charles II thus came to vindicate the stand taken by his father: Charles I's sacrifice was not in vain. The year 1660 turned his defeat and death into victory and rebirth as Providence restored Charles I in the person of his son. On his way to his coronation, Charles II rode beneath a depiction of himself on horseback which was strongly reminiscent of Van Dyke's images of his father. Panegyrists made rhetorical play on the coincidence of the name of father and son – 'But CHARLES more bright appeares since CHARLES is gone' – and ambiguously hailed April as the month which had given 'CHARLES his second Birth'.[21] The translation of William Juxon, who had accompanied Charles I to the scaffold, to Canterbury in September 1660, forged a direct link between the execution of the father and the coronation of the son (though, because of the Primate's infirmity, Sheldon had actually to officiate). The Restoration thus both confirmed the sanctified status of Charles I, and derived its own significance and meaning from his death. From its third edition, the *Eikon Basilike* included, as well as the frontispiece, a portrait of the prince, now Charles II, the *eikon* of his father. In the words of Abraham Cowley,

> The martyr's blood was said of old to be
> The seed from whence the church did grow.
> The royal blood which dying Charles did sow
> Becomes no less the seed of royalty.
> 'Twas in dishonour sown,
> We find it now in glory grown:
> The grave could but the dross of it devour;
> 'Twas sown in weakness, and 'tis raised in power.[22]

This notion that Charles I was restored in the figure of his son led to representations of Charles II in terms similar to those used of his father. He too became a man tested by trial, even a martyr, of exemplary patience and of refined religious sensibility, 'precious in God's sight, and as Gold out of the Fire', as the royalist Sir Richard Bulstrode put it. This concentration upon Charles's deprivations and trials became a way of according to him the victory which had eluded him militarily. The poet Alexander Brome transformed a decade of incapacity into a moral triumph: by choosing 'patient suffering' rather than 'to *Retort* / Their injuries', Charles 'did subdue / The *Traytors* fury, and the *Traytors* too', and so 'grew *Victorious*'.[23] Writing in late March 1660 in reply to Milton's *Readie and Easie Way*, the author of *The Dignity of Kingship* dedicated his apologia for monarchy to 'Charles the Good', since he is 'the most *Illustrious* for *Vertue*, *Constancy* in *Religion*, and *Heroick Patience*, under the most sharp *Tryals*, and extraordinary *Afflictions*, wherein (in imitation of his trule *Magnanimous Royall Father*) he hath appeared *more then Conqueror*'.[24]

This was a construction of Charles which inflated his sufferings through references to Israel's wilderness wanderings and to the Babylonian exile. In his speech at the close of the Convention, Clarendon observed that God would not have led Charles 'through so many Wildernesses of Afflictions of all Kinds' and preserved him against all enemies 'but for a Servant whom He will always preserve as the Apple of His own Eye'. Old Testament history furnished other parallels: like Moses, in the eyes of royalist interpreters Israel's first king, Charles had taken refuge in flight to be providentially returned from a foreign land to save his people; like David, he was delivered from his enemies.[25] In his *Sermon Preached at Hampton-Court* on the anniversary of the Restoration in 1662 Richard Allestree developed the parallel with David into a sustained exposition of the divine plan and of the election of Charles to kingship:

> We cannot look upon his life but as the issue of prodigious bounty, snatch'd by immediate Providence out of the gaping jaws of tyrannous, usurping, murtherous malice, merely to *keep* him for *our needs*, and for *this day*: One whom God had train'd up and manag'd for us, just as he did prepare *David their King*, at *thirty* years of age to take possession of that *Crown* which God had given him by *Samuel* about *twelve* years before; and in those years to prepare him for *Canaan* by a *Wilderness*, to *harden* him with discipline, that so the luxuries and the effeminacies of a Court might not *emasculate* and *melt* him; by constant Watches, cares and business, to make him equal for, habituated to, careful of, and affected with the business of a Kingdome; and by *constraining* him to *dwell in Mesech*, with Aliens to his Religion, to teach him to be constant to his *own*, and to *love Sion*. And hath he not prepared *our David* so for us?[26]

Since typologically David represented Christ, the association with David might introduce an even more exalted strain of eulogy. The Christ-like associations of the Charles I cult were transferred to Charles II, notably by Dryden in *Astraea Redux: a Poem on the Happy Restoration of his Sacred Majesty* (1660).[27] Charles himself underscored the sanctity of kings by touching for the 'King's Evil' during his exile and by doing so within three weeks of his return in a ceremony which recalled Jesus's healing touch.[28]

These conventions of representation thus served both to reawaken a traditional sense of the majesty of kingship, to justify Charles I and the Stuarts, to explain the Restoration and to reassure disillusioned subjects that this time there was a revolution in national affairs which was divinely managed. This, however, was a line of panegyric which hardly outlasted the Restoration year, for the realization that Charles II was a man very different to his father very quickly rendered belief in its exalted ideals impossible.[29] The abandonment of its inappropriate imagery marked the beginning of that loss of confidence in the restored regime which was to grow steadily more pronounced as the decade progressed.

## 3 'A time of universal festivity & joy'

On 8 May 1660 a procession of soldiers, heralds and trumpeters, with the speakers of the Lords and Commons, other members of both Houses and Monck, riding in a hundred or so coaches, proclaimed Charles king successively in Westminster Palace Yard, in Whitehall and at Temple Bar, 'with a great deal of pomp' and 'with an universal Testification of Loyalty from all degrees'. 'The remainder of the day and night', writes Clarendon, 'was spent in those acclamations, festivals, bells, and bonfires, as are the natural attendants upon such solemnities.' Rugg was more forthcoming: 'All the bells in the Citty range . . . numberless of bonfiers, great gunes playing from the Tower, great store of wine give[n] by many and at every bonefier beere, where they dranke his Majesties health, plentifull. Many of the bonefiers abided all night; many poore harts was sadly belated to their beds.'[30] Similar scenes were played out in provincial towns throughout the country.[31] This jubilation spilled over the Channel. Even before the vote on 1 May it was Pepys's impresssion that the gentry – the 'looser gentry' in Ludlow's view – 'flocked' to the King at Breda, whither he had arrived from Brussels on 4 April. This stream now turned into a flood of well-wishers as suppliants and petitioners began to cross to Holland, ambitious to be 'amongst the first of those who made the first demonstrations of their affections . . . to his majesty by supplying his necessities' with 'good presents in English gold', so that, by the middle of May, 'Breda swarmed with English'. Such was the exodus that the poet Katherine Philips could exhort Charles to 'Hasten (great prince) unto thy British Isles, / Or all thy subjects will become exiles', for, 'if thou dost stay, thy gasping land / Will itself empty on the Belgique strand' and the country formerly 'unmonarch'd' will now 'unpeopled be'.[32] When Charles sailed into the Hague from Breda on 15 May it was to an 'incredibly splendid and noble reception . . . All the ambassadors and public ministers of kings, princes, and states, repaired to his majesty, and professed the joy of their masters on his majesty's behalf.' After 'eight or ten days' of 'triumphs and festivals, which could not have been more splendid if all the monarchs of Europe had met there', Charles boarded ship on 22 May. The English fleet, anchored in the Downs, had on 3 May received the vote of 1 May and the *Declaration of Breda* with a pledge of loyalty by its commanders and, according to Pepys, who was an eye-witness from Mountagu's flagship, 'the greatest joy imaginable' among the seamen. Without waiting for parliament's authority, Mountagu, as Clarendon reports, sailed for Holland on 11 May, 'carried by his own affection and duty', arriving off the Dutch coast at Scheveningen on 14 May. A delegation of six peers and twelve members of the Commons was received on the 16th to present the 'invitation and supplication of the Parliament, that his majesty would be pleased to return, and take the government of the kingdom into his hands', presenting Charles with £50,000 to settle any debts he might have incurred. They were followed by a delegation of 16 representatives of the City of London, and a group of Presbyterian ministers (whom Pepys had seen 'sadly dipped' upon their arrival at Scheveningen, when their landing craft was overturned by rough surf). From each of these groups Charles received assurances not only of their own joy and loyalty, but of 'all possible affection, duty, and obedience from all his subjects'. For some days rough sea prevented any boats leaving the shore and James, Duke of York was not able to take command of the fleet until 22 May. He was joined the next day by Charles who, accompanied by an 'Extraordinary press of Noble company and great mirth', sailed for England from Scheveningen on 23 May, landing at Dover at 1.00 p.m. on Friday, the 25th.[33]

It was, then, in an already well-established spirit of festival and triumph that Charles landed at Dover. There was no less a carnival air among those who greeted him. Since the beginning of the month there had been a frenzy of civic activity, both to express appropriately royalist sentiments and to prepare to receive the King. In London, when everyone was 'full of expectations of his Majesty[s] cominge',

> The cittizans are very buissey in fittinge of there severall Halls, the masters of eatch Hall makinge liveres, eatch Hall severall liveres for theire footmen, streamers and pendents, new gildinge and fixinge, all in a readness against that day [of the King's return]; eatch Hall strivinge to outbrave the other; in severall streets grat bonfiers made att the corners, tow or three stories high, with pitched barrells, and on the tope of some a streamer with a crowne of Charles the Second pictured theron. These stood neere a weeke before they were fired; they needed not watches to looke to them, for the boyes of eatch street was night and day playing by them. Theire was a bone fier erected in Southwark higher then any house, made with a grat deale of art and skill; in the liberty [of] Westminster there wer many statly ones made; in the Covent Garden one made with a mast of a ship standing and a barrell one the top of it. Almost att evry taverne where roome was were sett up one, and evry privett house laid in some provisions or other to express their joy that day of his Majesty[s] cominge.

At Dover Charles landed with his brothers James and Henry, Duke of Gloucester where, received by Monck 'with all imaginable love and respect', they responded by 'kissing and imbracing him, that all Parties were satisfied, to admiration'. All four, with George Villiers, 2nd Duke of Buckingham 'in the boote', then took coach for Canterbury, with jubilant crowds, 'as if the whole kingdom had been gathered', and cheering onlookers, 'The Shouting and joy expressed by all... past imagination'. 'Never were seen such numbers of people of all Degrees and Conditions, thronging all the Road from *Dover* to *London*; many Women and Children came many miles, and placed themselves upon hillocks in the way, and many men upon trees (like *Zachaeus*) to see this blessed sight, and all with the greatest joy'.[34] On 29 May, his thirtieth birthday, Charles entered the capital, to unparalleled rejoicing:

> This day came in his Majestie *Charles* the 2d to London after a sad, & long Exile, and Calamitous Suffering both of the King & Church: being 17 yeares: This was also his Birthday, and with a Triumph of above 20000 horse & foote, brandishing their swords and shouting with unexpressable joy: The wayes straw'd with flowers, the bells ringing, the streetes hung with Tapissry, fountaines running with wine: The Mayor, Aldermen, all the Companies in their liver<ie>s, Chaines of Gold, banners; Lords and nobles, Cloth of Silver, gold & velvett every body clad in, the windos & balconies all set with Ladys, Trumpets, Musick, & <myriads> of people flocking the streetes & was as far as *Rochester*, so as they were 7 houres in passing the Citty, even from 2 in the afternoone 'til nine at night: I stoode in the strand, & beheld it, & blessed God.[35]

Evelyn's account is corroborated by other observers: 'of spectators, if I shold say fifteen hundred thousand I shold not much ere, accompting from Blackheath to Whitehall, the feilds, highwaies and hedges, covered waies, covered with people; the trees laden with boies, the streets thronged, the stages, stales, windowes, full (some even on the roofes)' to watch the King's 'princely march' in procession with 'all the gentry in theire bravery and gallant splendour', peers 'in great atendance' on his majesty, 'foot men in rich liveryes', maidens in 'white wastcoats and crimson petecoats', trumpeters and banner bearers, and troop upon troop of retainers and soldiers dressed in scarlet, blue and green tunics and doublets, with lace trimmings and edged in silver and gold, set off with coloured scarves, the streets through which they passed 'richly hanged with tapstry' and lined by the London militia and trained bands, guildsmen and liverymen, and the crowd responding with 'such shouting as the oldest man alive never heard the like'. *The Parliamentary Intelligencer* reported that 'The solemnity of this day was concluded by an infinite number of Bonfires, it being observable, that as if all the houses had turned out their chimnies into the street (the weather being very warm) there were almost as many fires in the streets, as houses, throughout *London* and *Westminster*'.[36]

This spirit of carnival was to last for another year. There were processions and lavish dining, 'with great pomp', when, on 5 July, Charles, his brothers, the Privy Council and both Houses of Parliament were entertained at Guildhall by the Lord Mayor and Aldermen of London 'with as much pompe

& splendor as any Earthly prince could do', 'the streetes adorn'd with Pageants &c. at immense cost'. On 25 September, when Mary of Orange, the Princess Royal, came to London, there were bonfires and bells ringing. On 29 October, Lord Mayor's Day, there was a procession with allegorical tableaux which included a representation of 'a greate Wood, with the royal Oake, & historie of his Majesties miraculous escape at *Bosco-bell* &c.' (though these did not impress Pepys, who found them 'poor and absurd'). And 5 November was celebrated with more than usual fervour. At the popular level, drunkenness and disorder, involving the harassment of Puritan ministers, attacks on Quakers and the theft of goods allegedly previously taken from royalist houses, threatened to get out of hand, but the restored regime had a very deliberate interest in maintaining this spirit of carnival.[37] The forms of popular celebration – eating, drinking, dancing, bonfires – affirmed the legitimacy of kinds of entertainment which had been embargoed under the Republic and Protectorate. Mayday celebrations had been forbidden during the Interregnum, but on 1 May 1660 maypoles were again erected with, at Deal at least, the 'setting up the Kings flag . . . and drinking his health upon their knees in the streets and firing the guns'. Old England returned with the King. The massive cedar maypole, allegedly the highest in Europe at 134 feet, paraded through London and erected in the Strand on 14 April 1661 to the accompaniment of drums and pipes and trumpets, decorated with streamers, lanterns, crowns and the royal arms, was not only the centre for morris dancing and festivity but, in its very nature, declared that this was no longer a Puritan age.[38]

The more formal pageantry of these events similarly signalled the new monarchical age. Oliver Cromwell had received a magnificent funeral, but, on the whole, the previous regime had been uneasy about excessive displays of ceremony. In deliberate contrast, the splendour of Restoration ceremonial announced that the King (and not merely another regime) was indeed come. The theatricality of the proceedings surrounding the Restoration manifested the glory of monarchy and situated onlookers in the position of subjects, spectators to be overawed by the lavish excess and magnificence of royalty. Unlike the sober egalitarianism of republican formality, these celebrations insisted upon the difference between the ruled and their rulers.[39] This was most splendidly realized in Charles's pre-coronation progress from the Tower of London to Whitehall on Monday 22 April 1661. In Reresby's judgement, 'The triomphall arches, pagiants, musick, made to receive and entertain [Charles] and the whole Court and other attendants as he passed, were finer and richer then was ever known upon the like occasions in England' – and not only England; Conway was in no doubt that the 'sumptuousness' of the proceedings were 'much admired . . . as exceeding the glory of what hath passed of the like kind in France'.[40] At the centre of the celebration was a procession of peers and royalty, but it embraced also music, drama, song and architecture, turning, for that day, London itself into a stage for the spectacle. The elaborate preparations for the pageant and procession, 'much thought upon and talked of' in London early in 1661,[41] were in the hands of a Committee of Entertainment, of which Sir John Ogilby, formerly Master of the Revels for Ireland, was a member, responsible for 'the poetical part . . . consisting of speeches, emblems, mottoes, inscriptions &c.' He was also licensed to publish the official account of the proceedings, *The Relation of His Majesty's Entertainment Passing through the City of London to his Coronation* (1661), on sale on the day of the royal progress. It was followed by the fuller *The Entertainment of His most Excellent Majestie Charles II in his Passage through the City of London* (1662) which, with plates by Wenceslaus Hollar, describes in detail, as its title page advertises, *the Whole Solemnity: the Triumphal Arches, and Cavalcade, Delineated in Sculptures; the Speeches and Impresses Illustrated from Antiquity . . . his Majesties Solemn Coronation: with his Magnificent proceeding; and Royal Feast in Westminster Hall.*[42]

For the occasion the streets were freshly gravelled and decorated with streamers and banners, tapestries hanging from the windows, the 'cundits runinge wine'. Four wooden triumphal arches, each nearly 100 feet high and decorated with pictorial images from English history and classical antiquity, with emblems and literary mottoes, were constructed at the Lime Street end of Leadenhall Street, at the Royal Exchange in Cornhill, near the Wood Street end of Cheapside and in Fleet Street. At each of these the procession of peers, Privy Councillors and officers of state preceding the royal family and King, amounting to over 1,000 horse and a greater number of foot, halted for a ceremony of welcome, before passing through.[43] These four triumphal arches, inspired by earlier Renaissance spectacles and royal progresses (themselves modelled on Roman triumphs), both commemorated and interpreted recent history by drawing upon well-established patterns of symbolic representation. Charles was imaged as the triumphant emperor Augustus, his return to London paralleled by Octavius's return to Rome after the civil wars of the second triumvirate. He came as the fulfilment of imperial prophecy restoring the golden age. The motto of the first arch was *Adventus Augusti*, the second depicted Charles as the British Neptune, the third was dedicated to Concord and the fourth celebrated '*Uberity*, or *Plenty*'. Through aggressive images of England's dominion of the seas, with the figures of Asia, Africa and America supporting the arms of the English trading companies, a future of maritime imperialism and of mercantile profit was augured, while the arches' depictions of rebellion associated with decapitated heads and of monarchy associated with concord and plenty left no doubt of the dominant them: *felix temporum reparatio.*[44]

As the King approached each of these arches, a scene was played out linking Charles with his father, with the King of Peace and with the golden age, with stability and prosperity. At the first arch the figure of Rebellion was banished by the figure of Monarchy; at the second the figure of Thames hailed Charles as 'our *Neptune*, every Port, and Bay / Your Chambers: the whole Sea is Your High-way / Though sev'ral Nations boast their Strength on Land, / Yet You alone the Wat'ry World command'. This address was followed by a seamen's song which less decorously urged Charles '*Thy Royal Navy rig / And We'll not care a Fig / For* France, *for* France, *the* Netherlands, *nor* Spain. / *The* Turk, *who looks so big / W'll whip him like a Gig / About the* Mediterrane . . .'. At the third arch, the figures of Concord, Love and Truth saluted Charles in song as the 'Prince confirm'd by Heav'nly Signs' who 'Brings healing Balm' and so 'Convert[s] Iron-times to Gold'. The point is given a messianic and an apocalyptic resonance:

> Comes not here the King of Peace,
>   Who, the Stars so long fore-told,
> From all Woes should us release,
>   Converting Iron-times to Gold?

At the fourth a woman representing Plenty insisted again on the transformation of human history: 'the Star, which at Your Happy Birth / Joy'd with his Beams (at Noon) the wond'ring Earth, / Did with auspicious lustre, then, presage / The glitt'ring Plenty of this Golden Age'. Unhappily, there was some discord in the presentation of these images of harmony: the loudness of the music spooked the horses – 'the Duke of York's horse threw him twice' and 'The King was in great danger till he commanded the music to cease'.[45]

Throughout the proceedings the emphasis was upon magnificence and luxurious opulence to reflect the innate glory of kingship in a manner which would have recommended itself at the court of the Sun King. The restored regime legitimated itself through a dazzling visual impact which routed all opposition, prevented all demur. Splendour is the keynote in the account written by Sir Edward Walker, Garter King of Arms of an event 'The Magnificence of which . . . for the richenesse & beauty of the Habitts both of his Ma*jestie*, the Nobility, & all others, with their Horses and furniture, being so great, as no age hath seene the like in this, or any other Kingdome'.[46] Spectators were amazed at the succession of 'glorious personages' in the 'splendid *Cavalcade*', 'many of their cloathes embridred with pearls and dimonds. The Lord Whorton [Wharton?] exceeded all for dimonds; his horse was set with dimons and pearls and other costly ornaments'. Another witness supposed that the 'furnitures' for Wharton's horse cost £8,000, but this was far exceeded by the £30,000 Buckingham was reputed to have laid out on his coronation robes. 'So glorious was the show with gold and silver', wrote Pepys, who watched from near the second arch (dedicated to the Navy), 'that we were not able to look at it – our eyes at last being so much overcome with it'; he found it 'impossible to relate the glory of . . . this day'. After the coronation itself in Westminster Abbey and the ensuing banquet in Westminster Hall, on St George's Day, 23 April, Pepys opined that 'besides the pleasure of the sight of these glorious things, I may now shut my eyes against any other objects, or for the future trouble myself to see things of state and shewe, as being sure never to see the like again in this world'.[47]

## 4 Restoration or Revolution?

There were, however, other ways to view the celebrations of 1660–1:

> Mean while our primitive great sire, to meet
> His godlike guest, walks forth, without more train
> Accompanied than with his own complete
> Perfections, in himself was all his state,
> More solemn than the tedious pomp that waits
> On princes, when their rich retinue long
> Of horses led, and grooms besmeared with gold
> Dazzles the crowd, and sets them all agape.[48]

Milton's description of Adam walking to meet the archangel Raphael in prelapsarian Eden expresses a deep dissatisfaction, Puritan and republican, with the excess, the hypocrisy and the political manipulativeness of royal pageantry. The clamorous volume of the Restoration festivities sought to drown out such dissenting voices, and it does so very effectively in royalist accounts of the occasion.[49] This is Sir Richard Bulstrode:

> Upon this King's most happy Restoration, there was seen from all Parts his loyal Subjects contending how to express their Gratitude to Heaven for its glorious Favour, and the King's no less than miraculous Return . . . every Man striving who should first pay the humble Oblation of their Duties, which really proceeded from hearts full of Reverence and Obedience to his sacred Person; being possessed with a deep Sense of the Honour and good Fortune they had to be born his Subjects.

The uniformity and generality of the joy so much insisted on in such memoirs gives the impression that it was entirely spontaneous and universally genuine. The people welcomed Charles with 'an unanimous consent', they proclaimed him with 'universal alacrity' and they 'exhausted themselves in festivals and rejoicings for his return'.[50] Perhaps, but while there is no doubt that a good deal of the celebration was genuine enough, unanimous consent is not the only possible explanation for general jubilation. The assertive confidence of the celebratory pageantry in fact disguised the fragility of the Restoration, the vociferous acclaim with which it was welcomed the very uncertainty of its popular support, the confidence of its monarchical imagery the doubtfulness of the monarchy's durability.

People might have a variety of motives for striving to outdo each other in expressions of loyalty. In a hierarchical and parochial society, local circumstances counted for a good deal. There is some evidence that celebration in 1660, like public agitation in 1659, was encouraged and supported, if not engineered, by local leaders and gentry, though it is not always easy to tell how far they were fomenting, and how far reacting to, popular agitation.[51] Less questionably, self-interest and self-preservation were powerful arguments to declare oneself of the dominant side and to distance oneself from those overthrown. It would take courage to stand against the pressure of family and neighbours caught up in the spirit of reaction. Material security dictated that, 'though fully in their affections and principles' against the Restoration, some 'thought it prudence to swim with the streame'.[52] In these circumstances, the country's unanimous conversion to royalism merited a degree of scepticism. Hyde no more trusted the 'universal joy' in the Commons when the *Declaration of Breda* was read on 1 May than he did the mood of the capital where, on 29 May, 'the joy was universal' because 'whosoever was not pleased at heart, took the more care to appear as if he was'. He notes the same phenomenon as Bulstrode, but with rather a different gloss:

> And from this time [1 May 1660] there was such an emulation and impatience in Lords and Commons and city, and generally over the kingdom, who should make the most lively expressions of their duty and of their joy, that a man could not but wonder where those people dwelt who had done all the mischieve, and kept the King so many years from enjoying the comfort and the support of such excellent subjects.

This wry sentiment received more famous form in the observation Clarendon records that Charles himself made 'smilingly' as he entered London, 'that he doubted it had been his own fault that he had been absent so long, for he saw nobody that did not protest he had ever wished for his return'. The thought was given a considerably more bitter turn by Lucy Hutchinson: Charles entered London

> with an universal joy and triumph, even to his own amazement; who, when he saw all the nobility and gentry of the land flowing into him, asked, where were all his enemies? For he saw nothing but prostrates, expressing all the love that could make a prince happy. And indeed it was a wonder in that day to see the mutability of some, and the hypocrisy of others, and the servile flattery of all. Monck, like his better genius, conducted him, and was adored like one that had brought all the glory and felicity of mankind home with this prince.[53]

While the dominant ideology everywhere controlled public manifestations of sentiment there could, then, be no certainty what the true and enduring loyalty of the majority of English people might be, or even of what it was in

1660. Principled opponents, commited to the Good Old Cause, might think 'complying for the present... the most probable way to be serviceable to honest men and their interest for the future'. Milton was not the only one for whom to decide to recall Charles II was to choose 'a captain back for *Egypt*'. Ludlow used the same phrase, and was equally scornful of the 'ceremony and outward pompe' of majesty. The imagery of sun and light so prevalent in public discourse was deployed quite differently by the republican and Independent Lucy Hutchinson in her then-unpublished memoir of her regicide husband written in the 1660s: in March 1660 'that glorious Parliament [came] to a period, not so fatal to itself as to the three nations, whose sun of liberty then set, and all their glory gave place to the foulest mists that ever overspread a miserable people'. Similarly, Ludlow records in his unpublished memoir that, at the time of the elections to the Convention, he and his sister spoke of 'the thick clowd of confusion that was comming not only upon us but on all that feared God'. Rather than cleansing the Rump's foulness the Restoration defiles the Republic's splendour. Puritans of a less extreme persuasion were still far from comfortable with the proceedings of 1660–1. In his diary Philip Henry recorded with laconic brevity: 'King crowned, great joy, much sin, the Lord pardon. 'Twas a very wett evening, which prevented something of God's Dishonour.'[54]

Occasionally, there were more public indications of such scepticism. Ludlow would have it that on the first 30 January anniversary 'the publique meetings were very thinne', and he instanced, as evidence of continuing 'affection to the good old cause', the collection of £104 to relieve the regicides imprisoned in the Tower taken at a single meeting of the congregation of the Presbyterian Henry Wilkinson, lecturer at All Hallow's, Lombard Street, 'the reporte of which gave a great allarum to the Court'. In the elections to what would be known as the Cavalier Parliament in March 1661 the City of London returned two Presbyterian and two Independent members, 'all of them such as had adheared to the Parlament party', with loud acclaim and cries of '"noe bishops, noe Lord Bishops"'. Ludlow maintains that, 'least the choyce of the Citty should influence the country to doe the like', the royalists 'seize the common pacquet to prevent the publication thereof'. A few days later the eminent Presbyterian Zachary Crofton was imprisoned to silence the anti-episcopalian rhetoric of his preaching, which, says Pepys pointedly, 'doth please some and displease others exceedingly'.[55] The public burning in May 1661 of what the Commons now described as 'a traiterous Writing, in Parchment, called, An Act declaring and constituting the People of *England* to be a Commonwealth, or free State' of 1649 made Pepys 'think of the greatness of this late turne and what people will do tomorrow against what they all, through profit or fear, did promise and practise this day'. Surveying the London scene at the end of August he could 'see no content or satisfaccion anywhere in any one sort of people'. When, in September 1661, Henry More wished for the happiness of peace for all three kingdoms, it was because he was apprehensive they might not have it.[56]

The behaviour of the disbanded officers and soldiers of the New Model Army was a particular cause for concern. At his death, Cromwell had commanded 25 regiments in England alone, amounting to some 40,000 men; in January 1660 there were still 34,000 regular soldiers in arms. In a total English population of perhaps 5 million, this was a huge body of men, and one which had shown itself not only militarily invincible but equally irresistible when it chose to exercise its political will.[57] In late February 1660 officers and regiments had been ordered out of the capital as a precaution. A month later the Council of State issued a proclamation forbidding political agitators to incite the troops and in early April 1660, in the tense period between the dissolution of the Long Parliament and the meeting of the Convention, Monck, on the advice of his brother-in-law Thomas Clarges, took the precaution of securing from Army officers in London and the provinces an engagement to hold no meetings to discuss matters of state and to accept whatever was decided by the new parliament.[58] The *Declaration of Breda* prudently promised to pay 'all arrears' due to officers and soldiers, but quite how to carry this out was a matter which much exercised the Convention during the spring and summer months of 1660. This was a matter of urgency, for many feared what Ludlow applauded, that 'the Army who had fought against [Charles I] were in their affections still the same' when Charles landed in May, and consequently might 'make head against' the restored regime. There was great relief when, though some soldiers refused the oath of allegiance upon which arrears were conditional, the Army was paid off and disbanded without serious incident by early 1661. 'The court was at great quiet when they got rid of so uneasy a burden as lay on them from the fear of such a body of men.'[59] Once disbanded, however, the soldiers of the New Model were still the occasion of disquiet. A large body of men was released into the country, politicized and former republicans, often radical, with their swords, which they had been allowed to keep, and, in the main, without employment. They were inevitably a source of anxiety and suspicion, especially in times of tension over plots, and were hence the subject of a succession of proclamations forbidding them the capital. In December 1660, following the committal of Thomas White for suspected plotting,

> for almost a fortnight togeather all the talke was a plot or what persons was taken prisoners, and the more because the most part of the Army was disbanded, and for the most part of them they came up to London to endeovre a livelyhood and the like, so that some reported as if they had a designe to band againe if posiable, but that jelesoue was by degrees taken of when nothing but report was the things.

A proclamation was issued on 17 December banishing all cashiered officers and soldiers 20 miles from London unless they had legitimate business there.

They were again ordered to leave London just prior to the coronation. A more positive step was taken to deal with the situation when the Convention passed an act permitting disbanded soldiers to take up a trade even though they had not competed an apprenticeship. Nevertheless, the common view, reported by Pepys in October 1660, remained that disbanded soldiers were responsible for lawlessness and robbery in London.[60]

Such worries were fuelled by repeated scares of plots. On 29 March, on shipboard at Gravesend, Pepys heard 'a great whispering of some of the Vice-admiralls captains that they were dissatisfied and did intend to fight themselves to oppose the Generall: but it was soon hushed'. In the weeks between the dissolution of the Long Parliament and the Restoration, care was taken by Pepys's 'Lord' Edward Mountagu, appointed general-at-sea by the Rump but now in touch with Charles and working actively for the Restoration, 'to put by as much of the Anabaptists' who served in the Navy as possible, and to 'keep things quiet', but just how quiet they really were was a moot point.[61] The escape of Lambert from the Tower in April 1660 threatened 'to obstruct the expected settlement' and dismayed those apprehensive of a return to military or republican rule, for after it 'the Phanatiques have held up their heads high'. With his recapture near Daventry, Northants, on 22 April, 'their whole design is broke and things now very open and safe', but, though to Pepys's mind 'every man begins to be merry and full of hopes', in late April, just before the Convention met, Duppa feared 'the hott brethings of vindictive spirits': 'Many machinations ther ar, plots under ground and above, to praevent any settling at all'. A suspected plot was reported the very day Charles landed. Six months after the Restoration, Duppa, now Bishop of Winchester, yet prayed that 'our publick sores' do not break out again. Despite the execution of 'pernicious flies and waspes' (that is, the regicides), his correspondent Isham yet agreed that 'Scorpions yet remaine' who might undo all.[62] How securely Charles was settled on his throne was called in question again by Overton's 'great plot' of mid-December 1660, and still more by Venner's Fifth Monarchist uprising in London on 6–9 January 1661, which, though it was never more than a localized revolt, 'yet did it much dampe the spirit of the prophane Court party to observe such high courradge and resolution amongst those they thought wholy subdued and trodden under foote'. The fear was that there were 500 of them, when they in fact numbered only 40–60: 'A thing that never was heard of, that so few men should dare and do so much mischief. Their word was "King Jesus, and the heads upon the gates" ' (that is, the heads of the regicides). The reason they could spread such terror was precisely that fear of instability ran so deep; it was expected.[63]

Anxiety, insecurity and apprehension were, then, as much a part of the Restoration experience as were celebration and relief. Official and loyalist accounts of the Restoration were in no doubt that events had been divinely impelled to march purposefully on to their proper conclusion, but the experience of the time was of contingency, insecurity and doubt rather than of Providential inevitability. 1660 carried with it no assurance of finality. Bewildering constitutional instability had followed the collapse of the Protectorate, with governments, and forms of government, succeeding each other within a few weeks. To Bulstrode it was as if, subject to 'so many Changes and Revolutions', the nation was 'mad'. These dizzying transitions are contemptuously recounted in a briskly dismissive summary in Hobbes's *Behemoth*: having traced the exchanges of power up to Cromwell's death, he goes on

> Sixthly, from September the 3rd 1658 to April the 25th 1659, Richard Cromwell had it as successor to his father. Seventhly, from April the 25th 1659 to May the 7th of the same year, it was nowhere. Eighthly, from May the 7th 1659, the Rump, which was turned out of doors in 1653, recoverd it again; and shall lose it again to a Committee of Safety, and again recover it, and again lose it to the right owner.[64]

1660 offered no guarantee that power would not change hands again. Throughout that year, and intermittently for the remainder of the decade, there was private fear and occasional public panic that the pattern of 1659 would reassert itself. For all its apologists' insistence, monarchy did not appear the inevitable order of things. The Restoration, it has been well said, 'was not a *fait accompli* but an aspiration'.[65] Uncertainty about Monck's intentions is hardly a sufficient explanation for the very late manifestation of pronounced royalist sentiment. At the collapse of the Second Protectorate the royalists had been in no position to marshall mass support; quite the contrary, as Booth discovered. Only a few weeks before it occurred, Monck was still saying that the nation would not tolerate the restoration of monarchy, professing, in late February 1660, his preference for a moderate Presbyterianism.[66] Royalism hence had barely two months to gather itself for its grand occasion. So long coming and so tentatively contrived, the Restoration might be thought a solution of last resort, adopted only when a succession of ever more desperate attempts to secure a non-monarchical solution had failed. The rapture which greeted it might express relief that a solution had been found as much as positive delight in this particular solution. If Charles was the answer to people's prayers, they were perhaps prayers that anarchy should end rather than that the King should enter into his own again.[67]

This apprehension explains why contemporaries characteristically spoke of their experience not in linear and progressive terms but through cyclical and recursive imagery. After the experience of the previous 20 years, and especially of the previous 18 months, there could be no confidence that yet another 'revolution' (in the seventeenth-century sense of that word)[68] did not lie in store. 'The Nation . . . seemed to have bin made the maygame of fortune' wrote the royalist Sir Philip Warwick of the 'giddy and braine-sick temper' of the state after Cromwell's death. Baxter used the same image, writing of 'the

Insolencies of *Vane* and *Lambert* [in late 1659], and the Fanaticks in *England* and *Ireland*, who set up and pull'd down governments as boldly as if they were making a Lord of a Maygame'. The cyclical nature of recent history was similarly remarked by Sir Justinian Isham writing to Duppa after the return of the secluded members to the Long Parliament: 'We read of *texti doctrinarum*, we have lately had as many several doctrines as there are points on the compass, that they having now gon around they begin Presbiterian againe, and who knowes not wither this dance may not like others end in the same measure they began'. It was 'that after ages may learne constancie from these our inconstant revoluctions that have so long had the prodominicy in the[se] nations' that Rugg began his journal in 1659. Following the vote of 1 May, Ludlow found 'the wheele to goe round soe fast' that he could not tell 'where it might rest'.[69]

It was perhaps to signal a break in this cycle that, on the royalist side, the word *restoration* was so insisted upon. Though *revolution* was occasionally used of the events of 1660, for the King's supporters *restoration* (initially more usually in the form *restauration*) instantly became the usual term to denote what had occurred.[70] It is what Mordaunt anticipated throughout his plottings; it is Charles's own word in the *Declaration of Breda*; it is the word used in the *Journals of the House of Commons* under 30 May 1660; it is Clarendon's word at the end of his *History*; it is Evelyn's (though not Pepys's) in his *Diary* under 29 May 1660; it is Sir John Reresby's in his *Memoirs* under 25 April; it is Cowley's for the title of his *Ode* and Dryden's for *Astraea Redux: a poem, on the happy restoration and return of his sacred majesty.*[71] On the other hand, the word was shunned by dissidents and sceptics. Lucy Hutchinson, hoping that 1660 would not prove final, refers to it merely as a *change*, not a *restoration*, as does Ludlow, who uses *change* in his own voice and when quoting the regicide Thomas Harrison, but *restauration* when paraphrasing Hyde. Marvell speaks of 'His Majesties happy Return', and Milton similarly never uses the substantival form *restoration*, because, we may conjecture, it had become so characteristic of royalist discourse.[72] It implied the recovery of a settled state of things. *Revolution* implied no such closure, which is why, in the comments cited above, Bulstrode distinguishes Charles's *restoration* from the *revolutions* of 1659. For the same reason, *revolutions* is the *Declaration of Breda*'s word for the 'the continued distractions' of the previous years and Clarendon's word for the changes of 1659–60, each, in its way, a restoration of a former constitutional mode which its supporters hoped would be final, but, from Clarendon's point of view, merely another change: '*This sudden* Revolution' of 1660, and it alone, should be '*best known by the name of the* Restauration'.[73]

To this way of thinking the Restoration marked both an end and a beginning. Edward Phillips concluded his continuation of Richard Baker's *Chronicle of the Kings of England*, and so the *Chronicle* itself, with the Restoration and coronation, since no 'more happy Period', promising an end to the 'Capricious Revolutions' of the past and 'a long continued Calm and Peaceful Government' for the future, could be imagined. It was, indeed, the end of history: 'the Intricate Turns and Labyrinths of Fortune being now at length run out', Phillips was confident that public events would hencforth 'run more smooth and clear'.[74] To ensure that 1660 was indeed just such a *restoration* and not merely a *revolution* was the purpose of the public celebrations surrounding the events of Charles's recovery of power. In contrast to the recurrent anxieties and disturbing contingencies of the private experience of 1659–60, the public Restoration year was deliberately designed to run in an orderly and symbolically suggestive fashion from one potently significant date, Charles's birthday, to another, St George's Day. It did not take four days to travel from Dover to London; Charles waited for two days in Canterbury and passed a night in Rochester to contrive the entry into London on 29 May, for a reason clearly understood by the Convention when, the very next day, it proposed a bill which became the *Act for a Perpetuall Anniversary Thanksgiving on the nine and twentyeth date of May* (12 Car.II c.14): the date marked 'the most memorable Birth day not onely of his Majesty both as a man and Prince but likewise as an actual King, and of this and other His Majesties Kingdomes all in a great measure new borne and raised from the dead on this most joyfull day'. The date of 29 May became a 're-birth day'.[75] Similarly, the significance of changing the coronation date from 6 February 1660 to 23 April was underlined by the largest single investiture of Garter knights (that is, of the Order of St George) and, a few days before the coronation, of over sixty Knights of the Bath, both with appropriate pageantry. On the central table of Ogilby's first arch the depiction of Charles on horseback recalls not only Charles I but also St George.[76]

And yet, the doubts persisted. Though the day of Charles's coronation was 'very serene and fair', immediately following the ceremony 'there was very terrible Thunders, when none expected it'. This severe storm reminded Richard Baxter of Charles's 'Father's Coronation, on which, being a Boy at School, and having leave to play for the Solemnity, an Earthquake .... did affright the Boys, and all the Neighbourhood'. His disclaimer that 'I intend no Commentary on these, but only to relate the Matter of Fact' may be thought not entirely ingenuous. Certainly, the 'Brief Narrative' of the coronation appended to Ogilby's *Entertainment* was sufficiently concerned that 'some sort of People were apt to interpret as *ominous*, and *ill-boding*' the fact that during the coronation feast in Westminster Hall 'it began to *Thunder* and *Lighten* very smartly' to devote its final two pages to countering this interpretation. Its accumulation of classical instances of such phenomena being of '*prosperous*, and *happy presage*' and its insistence that 'the Heavens, with Vollies of *Thunder*, and nimble flashes of *Lightning*, seemed to give a *Plaudite*, and Acclamation, to this Grand and Sacred *Solemnity*', implies its sensitivity to the threat posed by the rival discourse.[77]

## 5 Executions and Exhumations

While the present and future were being celebrated in pageant and festival, the security of the new regime depended upon the obliteration of the recent past. This process was underway even before the Convention voted the restoration of monarchy and the recall of the King. History was reversed as the symbols of republican power were replaced by royalist icons.[78] This reversal was epitomized by an incident on 15 March, the day before the dissolution of the Long Parliament, when, 'about 5 a-clock in the afternoon', 'the wrighting in golden letters that was ingraved under the stature of Charles the First, Kinge of England, in the Royall Exchange, London (the writinge was thus: Exit Tyrannus, Regum Ultimmus, Anno Libertatis Angliea, Anno Domini 1648, Jan. 30th) was washed out by a kind of a painter'. The onlookers, adds Pepys, 'cried out "God bless King Charles the Second"'.[79] On 29 March, well before the Convention met, Pepys records hearing that 'the King's Effigies was new-making, to be set up in the Exchange again' and, a month later, he heard 'how in many churches in London and upon many signs there and upon merchants' ships in the river they have set up the King's arms'. On 3 May, before Charles II had been publicly proclaimed, the Lords ordered that statues of Charles I be re-erected, that 'the Arms of a Commonwealth be demolished and taken away, wherever they are, and the King's Arms set up in their Rooms; and that the King's Majesty be publicly prayed for, by all Ministers, in their Churches; and that some Place be considered of where Genral *Monck*'s Statue may be set up'. On 7 May the statue of Charles I was erected again in Guildhall yard, and that same day orders were made for the King's arms to be set up in courts of justice in place of those of the Commonwealth and for the Navy's standards to be changed. The next day the King's arms replaced those of the Commonwealth over the Speaker's chair in the Commons and on 9 May the House ordered that 'the Arms of this Commonwealth, where-ever they are standing, be forthwith taken down; and that the King's Majesty's Arms be set up instead thereof'.[80] Anchored in the Downs on the morning of 11 May, about to set sail for Scheveningen, 'we begun to pull down all the State's arms in the fleet – having first sent to Dover for painters and others to come to set up the King's'. Once on board, on 23 May, Charles and the Duke of York set about renaming the ships of the fleet, so that they sailed to Dover not in the *Naseby* but in the *Charles*, in company not with the *Richard* but the *James*, thereby, as Dryden put it, obliterating England's shame. And, as Charles entered London, effigies of Cromwell were hanged in windows and burned on the celebratory bonfires by enthusiastic citizens, as were, Ludlow remarked, 'the armes of the Commonwealth, the badges of their owne freedome'. The face of the state was changing before people's eyes. By September 1660 Rugg could write that in Westminster 'all statuters or figuers or inscriptions that was sett up either by the

Portector [*sic*], or in his dayes or before since these troubles, or any that was of the Portectors own effigis, or tokens of signes of him, was quite washed out and in the places of them as if they had never been'.[81]

The forms of popular reaction caught the mood through mockery of the past. *The Parliamentary Intelligencer* for 21–28 May 1660 reported:

> The Solemnization of the Funeral of a certain Monster they called *The Commonwealth*, represented by an ugly misshapen body without an Head, but with an huge insatiable belly, and a prodigious Rump. The deformed Corps attended by Friends in Vizards, instead of mourners, was carried to the grave, and buried without expectation of Resurrection.[82]

The sobriquet *Rump* invited scatalogical merriment: Rugg records, under April 1660, that 'Att this time came forth jeeringe books about the Rump Parliment: one booke called The Rump Brought a Bedd, another called The Rumps Arse Scalled... another called The Buriall of Mother Rump... another called The Rumps Fart, and another called Mother Rumps Be—of Hir Selfe, and twenty more'. This is the Rabelesian underside of the formal pageantry: 'the Rump Parliment was so hated and jeered that butchers boyes would say, Will you buy any Parliment rumps and kidneys? and it was a very ordnary thing to see littl children to make a fier in the streets and burne rumps'. 'Boys do now cry "Kiss my Parliament" instead of "Kiss my arse", so great and general a contempt is the Rump come to among all men, good and bad', wrote Pepys, who in February heard of 'a picture hung up at the Exchange, of a great pair of buttocks shitting of a turd into [John] Lawsons mouth, and over it was writ "The thanks of the House"'.[83]

And, finally, the present had to be cleansed of those survivors who had created the now discredited past. Twenty-nine regicides were indicted before a Grand Jury of Middlesex at Hick's Hall on 9 October 1660 and their two-day trial opened on 10 October at the Old Bailey. Ten were immediately executed between 13 and 19 October.[84] On 17 October, Evelyn, though he had not witnessed the executions that day, 'met their quarters mangld & cutt & reaking as they were brought from the Gallows in baskets on the hurdle: o miraculous providence of God'. Peter Mundy did witness the executions that day:

> They hang near half quarter of an houre while the hangman strips them starcke naked and cutts them downe, and then presently, while they are hott, (I say not alive), cutts of their privityies, casts them first into the fire, the[n] opens them, dissembowells them, casting their entraills into the fire allsoe, lastly holding up their hearts in hand one after another, cries to the people – 'See the heart of a traitor'. It is don alike to all.

There were some additional ghastly touches to these proceedings. As he was taken to the place of execution, Hugh Peters, who had been prey to fears about how courageously he would meet death, 'On the sledge with him was carryed, with the face bare towards him, the head of Major Generall Harrison; notwithstanding which dismall sight, and barbarous usuadge, he passed rejoycingly through the streetes'. Pepys was sensitive to the cycle of justice, reflecting on the execution of Harrison: 'Thus it was my chance to see the King beheaded at White-hall and to see the first blood shed in revenge for the blood of the King at Charing-cross'. (He also, perhaps like many another, had occasion to be apprehensive lest anyone now should remember that on 'the day the King was beheaded' he had declared that, were he then to preach to Charles I, his text should be 'The memory of the wicked shall rot'.)[85]

The admonitory burden of this exemplary justice was not confined to the gruesome ritual of the executions themselves. The severed heads were displayed on the Tower of London and on London Bridge, where, in the summer of 1661, they were among the first sights viewed by the Dutchman William Schellinks on a visit to Britain. The quartered parts of the condemned were posted on city gates, with two exceptions. John Carew, though he had not surrendered but was captured, had been only narrowly excepted from the Act of Oblivion when an earlier decision not to except him for life was reversed. His 'Quarters by a great favour are not to be hanged up', and his brother was permitted to receive his body for burial. Francis Hacker was not quartered, out of consideration to his royalist family.[86] We should not suppose familiarity led to indifference to such spectacles, nor to insensitivity to the suffering involved: the 'limbs of some of our new Traytors set upon Aldersgate' was to Pepys 'a sad sight to see' which made him reflect 'a bloody week this and the last have been'.[87] It was not to be the last bloody week: between 19 and 21 January 1661 fifteen of those involved in Thomas Venner's Fifth Monarchist uprising were executed, Venner himself and Roger Hodgkin with the full ritual of drawing and quartering. Later still, in March 1662, the regicides John Barkstead, John Okey and Miles Corbet were arrested in the Hague and hanged, drawn and quartered at Tyburn on 19 April.[88]

In January 1661 the past was undone in another grim spectacle. On 4 December the Lords and Commons ordered that the 'carcasses' of Oliver Cromwell, Henry Ireton, Thomas Pride and John Bradshaw 'be with all Expedition, taken up, and drawn upon a Hurdle to Tiburne, and there hanged up in their Coffins for some time; and after that buried under the said Gallows'.[89] The exhumations took place on 26 January – Rugg records that when Cromwell's vault was 'broke open, the people crowded very much to see him, who gave sixpence a peece for to see him'. On 30 January, that awesome anniversary now for the first time observed, the bodies were drawn to Tyburn, hanged, decapitated and buried. This was the mirror image of the entry and coronation processions, and, like them, it met, so reports claim, with universal approbation:

> On Monday night, *Cromwel* and *Ireton*, in two several Carts, were drawn to Holborn from Westminster, where they were digged up on Saturday last, and the next morning *Bradshaw*. To day they were drawn upon sledges to *Tyburne*, all the way (as before from *Westminster*) the universal out-cry and curses of the people went along with them. When these three carcasses were at *Tyburne*, they were pull'd out of their Coffins, and hang'd at the several angles of that Triple Tree, where they hung till the Sun was set; after they were taken down, their Heads cut off, and their loathsome Trunks thrown into a deep hole under the Gallows.

The heads (of which the Order makes no mention) were 'set upon poles on the top of *Westminster Hall*, by the common Hangman. *Bradshaw* is placed in the middle (over that part where that monstrous High Court of Justice sate), *Cromwell* and his Son-in-Law *Ireton* on both sides of *Bradshaw*'.[90] Reflecting on 'the stupendious, & inscrutable Judgements of God' manifest this day, Evelyn, citing 1 Peter 2.17 and Proverbs 24.21 (the text which ten months before had landed Griffiths in prison), once again drew the appropriate ideological inference: 'fear God, & honor the King, but meddle not with them who are given to change'.[91]

# 3

# *Great Zerubbabel: Charles and the Convention (1660)*

## 1 Images of the King

Seeking to present himself to Charles at Whitehall early in June 1660, Evelyn found it almost impossible to gain access to the King 'by reason of the infinite concourse of people':

> It was indeed intollerable, as well as unexpressable, the greedinesse of all sorts, men, women & children to see his Majesty & kisse his hands, inso much as he had scarce leasure to Eate for some dayes, coming as they did from all parts of the Nation: And the King on the other side as willing to give them satisfaction, would have none kept out, but gave free accesse to all sorts of people.[1]

Many of these well-wishers were, of course, suppliants and petitioners, but even for those without such self-interest Charles was an object of curiosity, for there had been no ruling king in England for over ten years and, save for the brief Scottish venture which led to the battle of Worcester in 1651, Charles himself had not been in England since he was a teenage boy in 1646. What manner of man was he?

This question had been much canvassed during the winter and spring of 1659–60. Marchamont Nedham's *News from Brussels. In a Letter from a Neer Attendant on His Majesty's Person . . . which casually became thus publique* (March 1660) played on rumours about, and fears concerning, the character, behaviour and intentions of Charles. In the form of a familiar letter from an old Cavalier, a member of the exiled court, to his friend 'Honest Jack' in London, it represents that court as frustrated and impatient for an opportunity to avenge itself for its years of exile and deprivation. Its polemical intention was to alienate support from the royalist cause, and it therefore targets particularly the Presbyterians, the prime movers of the Restoration, by revealing just what they can expect from the King's return:

> This rebellion first bubbled up in presbyterian pulpits; yet it's impolitick to say so much: We also know, 'tis more for fear of the fanaticks, than for love of us, they now are loyal; so also it is our necessity, not choice, that makes us court them: Hug them you cannot hang, at least until you can.

The possibility of a conditional Restoration, such as, in the early months of 1660, the Presbyterians hoped for, is dismissed out of hand. Charles might agree to it, but that is of no consequence: 'But he comes in on terms? and is bound up? Tush! remember that blessed line I marked in Machiavel; he's an oafe that thinks an oath, or any tender, can tame a prince beyond his pleasure.' To untrustworthiness and a despotic sense of his own prerogative the pamphlet adds bloodthirsty vindictiveness to Charles's character: 'there's fire enough in his father's ashes . . . to burn up every adversary'. The appearance of godliness in him and his court is no more than that, political expediency.[2]

Though polemical, this character of Charles as a Machiavellian voluptuary was disturbing precisely because it articulated real fears about Charles, and certainly expressed the sentiments of many of his more extreme Cavalier supporters. 'His party', alleged Nedham in an earlier pamphlet, 'are hungry, and will not be satisfied: And he having occasion to use them, must not denie them their pleasure', whatever his own inclination might be.[3] Nedham's charges prompted outraged replies which, stressing Charles's moderation, integrity and generosity of spirit, sought to inspire trust in him and confidence in the prospect of royal government. In his anonymous reply, *The Late Message or News from Bruxels Unmasked, and His Majesty Vindicated*, Evelyn solicits sympathy for the 'Innocent Prince, [who] ever since his Tender years hath been hunted like a Partridge upon the mountain from place to place'. Denying that 'that meek and gentle PRINCE' has any vengeful inclination, he presents him as one whose

> Person is so lovely, amiable, and gracefull, that it even captivates the eyes of all Beholders, and every where generates a noble and generous affection . . . so firm, constant, and obliging in his Friendships, so milde, modest and patient in his Afflictions and Sufferings; yet upon occasion so full of Princely courage and magnanimity, so knowing and discerning in his Reasons and Judgement, and by his retirement, so fitted and adapted for moderate government

that it were not possible to find a fitter ruler.[4] Though Evelyn had several times met Charles abroad during the Interregnum, his eulogy does not depend upon personal observation or first-hand experience. His description of the King's person and character is repeated verbatim from an earlier anonymous pamphlet by another royalist, Sir Edmond Peirce; it is very similar to passages in Evelyn's own *Apology for the Royal Party*, and the claims that 'A *Better Friend*, there lives not; nor a *Better Nature*' than Charles, who stands '*Firm*, to his *Temper*, and to his *Conscience*' despite of 'all *Distresses* and *Temptations*' were to be tirelessly recycled by pamphleteers such as L'Estrange.[5] Rhetorical Convention and political need dictated such sentiments.

They were given perhaps their most influential formulation in Sir Samuel Tuke's anonymous *A Character of Charles the Second, written . . . for information of the people* (April 1660). 'Finding a dawning of Liberty to assert the Truth' he, like Evelyn, seeks to disabuse the public of misrepresentations such as Nedham's. He does so by constructing an exemplary man, monarch and Christian. Charles is tall and striking (though, Tuke admits, 'the Majesty of his Countenance supplies the Lines of Beauty'), noble and graceful, his 'easinese of accesse, his Patience in Attention, and . . . Gentlenesse' evident 'both in the tone and style of his speech'. He is of solid judgement, 'a true friend to *Literature*, and to *Learned Men*', especially skilled in navigation. He is just, magnanimous, brave, merciful ('*Clemency* is as naturall to his *Majesty*, as *Courage*'), constant and trustworthy, industrious (his reputation for laziness is the consequence only of want of opportunity to act), temperate, and, up to a point, chaste. The reproach of 'habitual *Incontinence*' is the slander of enemies based merely upon some youthful indiscretions: is the King 'unfit for Government, because in his Youth he may not have been stronger than *Samson*, wiser than *Solomon*, or more holy than *David*'? It was with an eye to just such an image of Charles that, in his coronation sermon, Morley listed as the attributes of the ideal king '*Comeliness* and Gracefulness of Shape, Courtesie, and Affability of Speech, and Benigness [*sic*] of Aspect . . . Vigorous Manliness in his Mind, and a promise of Long Life in the Healthfulness of his Constitution . . . a *man of understanding and knowledge*', by which, Morley explained, he means not Machiavellian deviousness but the judgement of Solomon. Contemplating this monarch in a 1660 sermon delivered at Waltham Abbey, where he was the incumbent, Thomas Reeve exclaimed 'That this should be the Land where such a Darling of Heaven should reign!' and appealed for 'some *Apelles*' to depict the King, 'so many mercies and miracles' combine in him.[6]

For Charles, however, another kind of literary account and characterization is available. He has been called 'the luckiest monarch in English history'.[7] Certainly, he was lucky in his moment in literary history: he is the first English monarch for whom we have sustained contemporary characterizations which are, to a degree, political and psychological, rather than iconographical and panegyrical, for he is the first monarch to whom were devoted the new resources of the nascent genres of charactery, diary, autobiography, biography and historiography. Furthermore, he attracted the attention of exceptionally able writers: Dryden, Clarendon, Burnet and Halifax. Though written at different times, and for different purposes, and (in Burnet's case), existing in different states, they all draw on their first-hand knowledge of Charles in the 1660s, if coloured by subsequent experience, especially that of James II in the case of Halifax (which was rather in Charles's favour). Certain emphases, however, are common to them all, and Charles's affability is one of them. He had, to a much greater extent than any Tudor or other Stuart sovereign, and perhaps than any other English or British sovereign, the capacity to deal easily with people. This had first been evident in the escape from Worcester, when he had had to rely upon people whom he encountered in contexts ordinarily far from the experience of monarchs. With this went a disregard for the protocols and formalities of royalty such as would have shocked Charles I. He was 'so affable', says Ailesbury, 'that in the galleries and park he would pull off his hat to the meanest'. He could be quite unselfconscious. He was a great raconteur, storyteller and conversationalist, with 'a habit of conversing familiarly which, added to his natural genius, made him very apt to talk; perhaps more than a very nice judgement would approve'.[8] A certain impatience is perhaps evident in this remark and, within a year or two of the Restoration, Charles's affability was beginning to appear more of a liability than an asset to those concerned with the political management of the country. 'He was affable and easy, and loved to be made so by all about him', wrote Burnet, with 'a softness of temper, that charmed all who came near him', though he adds, caustically and characteristically, that this was only until 'they found how little they could depend on good looks, kind words, and fair promises, in which he was liberal to excess, because he intended nothing by them but to get rid of importunity, and to silence all further pressing upon him'. The 'free accesse to all sorts of people' remarked by Evelyn dismayed Clarendon, who was constantly trying to inhibit Charles and to restrain his largesse. Halifax, too, thought the King's affability cheapened by its being too general and undiscriminating, as he did the quality on which Charles prided himself, his wit, which, to Halifax's mind, was coarsened by Charles's willingness to amuse himself with his intellectual inferiors.[9]

There may, however, have been more policy to this affability than these comments allow. Most of Charles's life had been a long tutorship in the weakness of kings. Unlike his mentor and adviser Clarendon, he could barely recall a time when his father comfortably enjoyed his throne. Insecurity and instability he knew not 'as an interruption but as normality'. He himself had been on the run not just since Worcester in 1651 but since he parted from his father in 1646. His experiences in exile, often demeaning, had taught him both dissimulation and a kind of sceptical amusement at the protestations and commitments of others. He had learned how far interest will supervene and came to have, in Burnet's words, 'a very ill opinion of both men and women'.[10] He had no guarantee that 1660 marked a permanent return to England. Plots and rumours of plots abounded, and before long even the Cavalier Parliament was behaving in a disturbingly independent way.[11] His apparently easy-going indifference may be understood as a safeguard and a survival technique: it is dangerous to trust too far, to expect too much. As Halifax, with the benefit of James II's example, remarked, Charles's yieldingness, whatever foundations it might lay to the disadvantage of posterity, was a specific to preserve us in peace for his own time ... As a sword is sooner broken upon a feather bed than upon a table, so his pliantness broke the blow of a present mischief much better than a more immediate resistance would perhaps have done.

This wry wariness distinguishes him from the other males in his family. He had none of the pedantry of his grandfather, the tendency to pomposity of his father, nor of the stubborn obtuseness of his brother. He had a much clearer grasp than any of them of what was going on, and a much surer sense of both his own place in proceedings and of the part being played by others: 'Where men had chinks he would see through them as soon as any man about him' said Halifax. He 'knew men better than any that hath reigned over us' said Ailesbury, who judged him 'a great master of King-craft', lamenting that neither his father nor his brother were 'endowed with the same talent'. Buckingham once deftly distinguished Charles from his brother's much more highly developed sense of duty: 'The king could see things if he would, and the duke would see things if he could'.[12]

Charles was not lazy – he had exceptional physical energy and was throughout his life an early riser and avid sportsman[13] – but he had no patience with routine administration, giving rise to the view that, as Pepys lamented in the autumn of 1665, the King minds 'nothing but his ease': 'he showed great abilities in urgent affairs, but was incapable of application to any that were not so'. 'He hated business' says Burnet bluntly. He had a short attention span and was easily bored, 'often weary of time, and did not know how to get round the day'. 'The great art of keeping him long was, the being easy, and making every thing easy to him'. This 'love of ease', which Halifax held came to 'exercise an entire sovereignty in his thoughts', perhaps explains Charles's partnership with Clarendon, upon whose unremitting and conscientious dedication to business he could rely, though it was never a comfortable partnership on either side. 'Yet no ill nature all this while' Halifax adds to his cool assessment of Charles's bountifulness, and he affectingly concludes his *Character* with the unexpected summary statement that Charles was 'an unfortunate Prince in the beginning of his time, and a gentle one in the rest'. To have been gentle and tolerant in an age remarkable for the bitterness of its partisanship was no mean thing.[14]

Charles's religion appears to have been similarly easy-going and benign, and equally politic. Tuke claimed that he was a pious and resolute Protestant and Evelyn had insisted that Charles was 'firmly and inremoveably fixed, to the professions of the true Protestant Religion', as well they might, for this was a sensitive point. In May 1659, in his exemplary *Character of... King Charles the IId*, William Walwyn, afterwards Prebendary of St Paul's, had felt obliged particularly to insist that Charles's residence abroad had not, as often claimed, perverted him to Roman Catholicism.[15] The suspicion, however, was not so easily laid to rest. Recusant families had played a large part in Charles's escape after the battle of Worcester and these contacts contrasted very strongly with his humiliating experience of Scottish Presbyterianism in the months before. His inclination was certainly to prefer the former to the latter. He once averred to Clarendon that 'for my part rebell for rebell, I had rather trust a papist rebell then a presbiterian one'.[16] Since Worcester, Charles had spent years in Roman Catholic France, his mother was a staunch Roman Catholic who for nine years had promoted a Roman Catholic marriage for Charles and had strenuously endeavoured to convert his younger brother, Prince Henry,[17] and there were already rumours about the religious inclinations of his brother James, Duke of York. Although James did not become a convert until later in the 1660s, within nine months of the Restoration Pepys was already expressing apprehension lest he should succeed Charles, 'he being a professed friend to the Catholiques'. It would subsequently be maintained that Charles had indeed become a Roman Catholic during his exile. Thomas Carte, the biographer of James Butler, 12th Earl and afterwards 1st Duke of Ormonde, claimed that Ormonde discovered Charles's Roman allegiance in 1659 in Brussels when by chance he saw the King at mass. Burnet was quite convinced that Charles was a secret convert some years before the Restoration, and that Clarendon suspected as much. Halifax, noting Charles's marriage to a Roman Catholic and the sway of Roman Catholic mistresses, was in no doubt, 'that when he came into England he was as certainly a Roman Catholic as that he was a man of pleasure', though by this Halifax did not mean to imply any religious conviction on Charles's part: 'A general creed, and no very long one, may be presumed to be the utmost religion of one whose age and inclination could not well spare any thoughts that did not tend to his pleasures'. He attributed Charles's conversion to the social status and material splendour of Catholicism as Charles saw it in France, and to what Charles took to be its indulgence towards sin.[18] If so, Charles remained very quiet about it, even after the secret Treaty of Dover bound him to declare himself a Roman Catholic. Halifax put this down to policy ('It was not the least skilful part of his concealing himself, to make the world think he leaned towards an indifference in religion'), but it is hardly likely, in the event of his acceptance into that church, that Rome itself would have continued so discreet, even after his death. Besides, Charles was a public communicant of the Church of England throughout his life and, as James said to Evelyn, though some 'believe the Ch: of R: gives Dispensations, for going to church, & many like things . . . it was not so; for if that might have been had, he himselfe had most reason to make use of it'.[19]

To reassure people on this point, in early 1660 Hyde despatched George Morley to London to deny that Charles was a Romanist and letters and testimonials were procured from foreign Protestant divines. On 4 April, for example, Raymond Gaches, minister at Charenton, Paris, wrote to Richard Baxter at the instigation of the Earl of Lauderdale. Gaches's letter, with others also written in early April, was translated and published by Anne de La Tour d'Auvergne as *Certain Letters Evidencing the King's Stedfastness in the Protestant Religion* (1660).[20] Steadfast devotional commitment was not, however, a quality with which contemporaries credited the King:

> He often professed his belief of a Deity and of a Messiah . . . of a future state and other doctrines; but had very large notions of God's mercy, that he would not make his creatures forever miserable on account of their personal failing. Upon this notion he indulged himself in his pleasures, but had frequently his hours of retirement for the exercise of his private devotions. He laid very little stress on the different systems of religion; and would frequently take delight to tease his brother, who was very serious and zealous in his way, with reflecting on the scandalous lives of some popes, and laughing at some particular tenents of the Roman Catholics.

Burnet gives a very similar report. Though to Burnet Charles 'seemed to have no sense of religion' he yet 'said once to my self, he was no atheist, but he could not think God would make a man miserable only for taking a little pleasure out of the way'. Whatever else he was, Charles was neither an orthodox and committed Roman Catholic nor an Anglican Protestant.[21]

## 2 'Our good old Form'

> No longer let the vain Republican
> Fill with Chimera's his fantastick Noddle:
> Balance, and Ballot, and Agrarian,
> And all the Whimsies of th' Utopian Model
> Are out of doors: to the old Form we cling,
> Our good old Form; Commons, and Lords, and KING.[22]

In 1660 this sentiment could find widespread support, but it was a nostalgically appealing rather than a politically precise sentiment. What, exactly, was England's 'good old' constitutional form? There could be no doubt, at least, that it was monarchical. In 1656–7 the proposal that Cromwell should accept the crown had turned largely on the fact that, while 'the Title of *Protector*' was 'not known by the Law', that of king had been 'known by the Law of *England* for many ages, many hundred of yeares together received, and the Law fitted to it'. Legally minded and traditional opinion held that for this reason a constitutional settlement is impossible without a king. Such a view is embodied in the term *Interregnum* to denote the 1650s: an interruption in the right (monarchical) order of things. 'All the lawyers', reported Burnet, 'said, no new government could be settled legally but by a king, who should pass bills for such a form as should be agreed on. Till then, all they did was like building upon sand.' Cromwell, of course, was not persuaded, but the events of 1658–60 served only more firmly to convince conservative opinion that monarchy was the key to political stability.[23] A record of the 1657 discussions was published in April 1660 under the title *Monarchy Asserted, to be the Best, Most Ancient and Legall Form of Government* and its arguments were rehearsed in such pamphlets as the anonymous *Plea for a Limited Monarchy as it was established in this nation before the late warr*, addressed to Monck early in 1660. Such arguments now combined with a less legalistic and more pervasive feeling that in some ill-defined way monarchy was proper and natural to England. This drew strength from the institution's antiquity in Britain, which, in their enthusiasm, such advocates as the Aberdeen minister Alexander Scrougie might stretch to over 2,000 years in duration. Less precisely and more evocatively the *Plea for a Limited Monarchy* claimed that 'Monarchy in these Nations [is] more antient than Story or Record, more venerable than Tradition itself', and so 'our Laws were, as it were, under that Climate, habituated to that Air and Diet, grafted into that Stock'.[24] This sense that the institution was venerable easily combined with the more fundamental claim that the divinely created order of the world was regal, as it did in the sermons of Thomas Reeve. Government by the one, he asserted, is divinely ordained for all creatures and is practised by 'Heathens, Mahometans, the wild Tartarians, and the wise Persians and Chaldees', as well as 'amongst *Beasts, Birds, Fishes, Devils*'. 'The Government of the World' originated in Eden with 'one father of the family': monarchy is hence 'the Protarchy, the first and best government'. Reeve, who clearly had a taste for coinages, declared from his pulpit that 'I do dislike Polyarchy in Government as ill as I doe Polygamy in Marriage: let us not multiply sovereignty where God hath limited it'. If then, as the pamphlet literature now insisted, 'The People never had in them any authority or jurisdiction at all which they could give or resume upon occasion' since a king 'has his Authority immediately from God' (Romans 13.1), the return of the king would, argued Sir Edmond Peirce, bring the country back into line with the divine will: monarchy is 'the sole Government appointed by God, and Kings, and Kingdomes, his alone institution and planting, as is clear by the whole current of Scripture, from *Adam* . . . This Nation ever since its first being, even for thousands of years, owning Monarchy for its Government in all Ages and Vicissitudes.' Sir Robert Filmer's *Patriarcha*, not yet published though extant in manuscript for at least twenty years, similarly derived 'the *Naturall* Power of Kings' and 'patriarchal government' from the 'lordship' of Adam. To this way of thinking, the Interregnum had failed because it was an aberration, foreign to the genius and the history of the English and a monstrosity in the order of things: drawing his evidence from the animal kingdom and from the practice of primitive peoples, Morley argued in his coronation sermon that universal '*nature* it self doth seem to recommend' monarchy.[25]

Such confidence that monarchy was instituted by God and peculiarly English did not, however, define the monarch's constitutional role. This was the very matter over which the Civil War had been fought and what distinguished it from medieval conflicts as the first ideological war in our history: the dispute had been over not who should be king but how he should be king. The Interregnum's attempts to deal with the matter by abolishing monarchy having failed, England in 1660 found itself much relieved but not much the wiser. There was consequently no less speculation about the nature of kingship than about the character of the king. This was much debated in the pamphlet literature of 1659–61 – 'the *Presse* growns under the Subject' said L'Estrange – and the nature, as well as the merits and demerits, of monarchy remained a subject of discussion throughout the decade. One view was implicit in the words of the vote on 1 May, that 'according to the antient and fundamental Laws of this Kingdom, the Government is, and ought to be, by King, Lords and Commons'. This vote did not merely restore monarchy: it restored also the House of Lords and deprived the Commons of the supreme constitutional authority which, as the Rump, it had wielded. It proposed a mixed, or constitutional, monarchy. This view was much given to talking in terms of balance and harmony, as did the author of *The Dignity of Kingship Asserted* when seeking to reassure his readers that they need have no such apprehension of monarchical power as Milton entertained:

> *Kingship* I affirm, to be the only *desirable* government in the world, and of all sorts of *Kingly Government* or *Monarchies*, ours of *England* was most *exquisitely composed, equally tempered*, and *suited* to a *Nation* really free, and yet truly *Subject*, where *Majesty* and *subjection* made a true harmony, and the most inferior members were as equally necessary to the good of the whole, as the chief. In it the *King* was *Supreme*, the head of Law and Justice, and yet himself never had power to make, or to execute any Law... the Commons *propounding*, and *framing* the nobles *approving* and *Consenting*, the King *signing* and *confirming*, Lawes were made.

The king of England, asserted G. S., was 'a *supreme*, a *true*, but not an *absolute Monarch*', who depended upon the advice of his Privy Council and Commons and whose rule was 'purely *Paternall*... as a loving and carefull *Father*'.[26]

Proponents of this view of monarchy frequently made reference to the constraints of 'ancient laws' within which monarchy operated, arguing, like the *Plea for a Limited Monarchy*, that the *via media* of a limited or mixed monarchy suited the English genius since 'our *English* Nature is not, like the *French*, supple to Oppression, and apt to delight in that Pomp and Magnificence of their Lords', nor yet, like the Dutch, 'addicted only to Traffic, Navigation, Handycrafts, and sordid thrift'. The English way was neither to elevate the monarch above the life of the nation, nor to pursue affairs regardless of the monarch, but to integrate crown and country: the Restoration returned not merely 'a gracious PRINCE' but, asserted Sheldon in a sermon of thanksgiving in June

1660, 'together with him our *Laws, Liberties, Properties*; the *free exercise of Religious Duties*, indeed all that is or ought to be dear to a Christian Common-wealth'. Consequently, in this constitution, the king wields no autocratic power in or of himself; his role is neither dictatorial nor legislative, but executive. It is by insisting on this that the *Plea for a Limited Monarchy* recommends monarchy. While the king has the prerogative to choose his ministers, he is answerable to parliament for their conduct, and, if any object that he has 'the Power of *making War*', the safeguard is that he has 'not the Means; and then, it signified no more than giving him Leave to fly, if he could get Wings'. Whether what this tract describes was indeed the antebellum English constitution is a moot point, but, by resting its argument on the precedent of Charles I, it is able to win a hearing for the contention that English monarchy includes 'all the Perfections of a free State, and was the Kernel, as it were, of a Common-wealth, in the Shell of Monarchy, *viz.* The Senate Proposing, the People Resolving, the Magistrate Executing'. Although the royal prerogative theoretically entitles monarchs to veto bills, because of their dependence upon parliament for supply there is 'a wise and sweet necessity for the King . . . to confirm all such Bills as were convenient for the People'. The *Plea* allows that the King is privileged, and is said to be sacred, but this is merely to accord him appropriate status: alone he can accomplish nothing: 'our King, in his personal Capacity, made no Laws, so neither did he, by himself, execute or interpret any'.[27]

This reassuringly moderate line was followed by Morley in his coronation sermon when he allowed that among '*Hereditary* Monarchies one may be more desirable then another, as a *Political* rather then a *Despotical*', acting 'by Equal and Just Lawes' passed with the people's '*consent*'. Such constitutionalism, however, is frequently found in disconcerting proximity to far more absolutist sentiments. Morley's sermon in fact talks up the majesty and divinity of kingship and even G. S. can assert that there is 'none above, or singly co-ordinate with' the king and he recommends hereditary monarchy on the grounds that '*Elective* Kings are but *Conditional* Kings; and *Conditional* Kings are *no* Kings'.[28] The particular emphasis is often determined by time and circumstance. Replying to Milton before the Convention met, L'Estrange was studiously moderate and did 'not deny, but a Parliament is above a King', though even then his gloss was rather less emphatic: 'That is: the King is greater in Conjunction with his two *Houses*, than by *Himself*'. By the summer of 1660 he was more boldy stating that '*Mixt*' monarchy '*implies a contradiction*'. A year later, objecting to the misrepresentation of loyal cavaliers as 'a *Loose, Begggarly, Prophane, Tipling* sort of people', he could assert that the proclamation had been better directed against '*Those that deny the Kings Authority to be above that of the Two Houses*'.[29]

This is to argue for the unfettered prerogative of absolutism: 'Why', asked Reeve, 'is a King called a [*sic*] supreme if he hath any supreme above him? or named Lawgiver, if he himself be liable to law?' And since his is 'the power of making the universall Laws of the Kingdom', his also is 'the power of dispensing with penall Laws by Pardons, and with positive statutes about duty by Licences; Yea, in some cases, to alter and abrogat some Laws'. The king's will derived this autonomy from his divine appointment: the king is appointed and authorized directly by God, to whom alone he is answerable (Proverbs 8.15, 16; Romans 13.1). In the sermon which caused such embarrassment, Matthew Griffith overplayed this line to claim of God and the King that 'they are both *Gods*, and both *Kings*'.[30] It was this conception which was embodied in the splendour of the pageantry of the Restoration which so impressed Pepys: 'The Beauty of a King [is] the brightest thing that a nations eyes can be fixed upon . . . solacing, satisfying, triumphant . . . amiable, delectable, splendid, illustrious, supereminent, matchlesse [and] majestical'. The store of royal and divine images clustered around the symbol of the sun was raided by many a panegyric to burnish the King's image. Elias Ashmole, for example, developed the conceit of Charles's return as the rising of the sun, harnessing his horses 'Deckt in refulgent lustre', mounting his chariot, 'Throwing his usual glories round his Face', and riding across the sky as 'All sacred Lustre from about him sheds'.[31] To minds thus possessed by the divine right of kings, the obligation of the subject is absolute obedience: to oppose or resist a king is to resist the authority of God. This happy corollary was seized upon by the restored regime. An insistence on passive submission was to become an insistent theme of the Restoration authorities and the imposition of oaths repudiating a subject's right to oppose the chief magistrate, or even to endeavour to change the form of government, would become a feature of Restoration legislation.[32]

## 3 The *Declaration of Breda*

The extravagant regalia and iconography never, however, captivated Charles himself. He projected a studiously moderate and reassuring sense of his kingly authority. His informality of manner confirmed the impression created by what, for the great majority of the nation, was the first royal utterance since 1649. In the *Declaration of Breda* he, and his equally judicious first minister, Hyde, compiled one of the most delicately phrased of political documents. It intervened with extraordinary sensitivity, but decisively, in the debate on the nature of monarchy. It contrived to reassure those who had cause to fear a Restoration, to encourage those who would promote it, to indicate the lines of a settlement, but to bind neither Charles nor a restored regime to anything at all. Its notable absence of vindictiveness augured well. To its reassuring tone may in large part be attributed the subsequent willingness of the Convention to admit Charles's return without any preconditions.

The *Declaration*[33] was dated 4 April, that is, during that crucial interval between the dissolution of the Long Parliament and the sitting of the Convention, when a Restoration appeared very likely but not yet quite assured. Its business was to turn this probability into a certainty. To this end, its five brief paragraphs entertain not the least doubt of Charles's right to the throne, and say nothing of qualification to the authority of his kingship. The document thus speaks with confidence, but it avoids authoritarianism or any suggestion that it speaks for either a dangerously unbridled or a vengefully partisan power. Charles's great asset is that he is not in the least implicated in recent history. He speaks therefore with what sounds like an impartial and distanced concern. The *Declaration* first situates him with the peacemakers, with those who have 'a desire and longing that those wounds which have so many years together been kept bleeding may be bound up'. This is the monarch as healer, professing a desire to help to end the 'long misery and sufferings' of recent history. In its first paragraph the *Declaration* appeals to the most compelling argument for Restoration, the harrowing common experience of recent events and the 'general distraction and confusion which is spread over the whole kingdom'. There is no hint here of what Charles himself will gain through restoration; rather, the return of the King is presented as the condition of the return of normality and good governance, of the rule of law: 'Nor do we desire more to enjoy what is ours than that all our subjects may enjoy what by law is theirs, by a full and entire administration of justice throughout the land, and by extending our mercy where it is wanted and deserved'. The *Declaration* offers law and the subject's rights in the place of arbitrary government, justice and mercy in the place of militarism and conflict. Throughout this opening the emphasis is upon what the monarch shares with his people, with what he can offer them. The restoration contemplated is not primarily of him to his heritage (and that it would be to his power is nowhere mentioned) but, through this, of right order, and so of 'the quiet and happiness of [the] country in the restoration both of king, peers and people to their just, ancient and fundamental rights'. This is an all-inclusive restoration, not a restoration of a king's despotic power over his subjects but of 'our just rights and theirs in a free Parliament'.

The *Declaration*, then, presents a benevolent king. The second paragraph develops this with some of the most direct statements in the *Declaration*: 'to the end that the fear of punishment may not engage any' to oppose a restoration 'we do by these presents declare that we do grant a free and general pardon, which we are ready upon demand to pass under our Great Seal of England, to all our subjects, of what degree or quality soever, who within forty days after the publishing here shall lay hold upon this our grace and favour'. The comprehensiveness and exhaustiveness of that is reiterated in the following sentence:

> let all our loving subjects, how faulty soever, rely upon the word of a king, solemnly given by this present declaration, that no crime whatsoever committed

> against us or our royal father before the publication of this shall ever rise in judgement or be brought in question against any of them, to the least endamagement of them, either in their lives, liberties or estates, or (as far forth as lies in our power) so much as to the prejudice of their reputations by any reproach or term of distinction from the rest of our best subjects.

The tenor of this general clemency is pointedly applied to three specific cases: first, 'we do declare a liberty to tender consciences, and that no man shall be disquieted or called in question for differences of opinion in matter of religion which do not disturb the peace of the kingdom'; secondly, that all questions relating to 'grants, sales and purchases of land' during the Interregnum 'to and by many officers, soldiers and others' shall be 'determined in Parliament'; and thirdly that Charles is ready to consent to any act of parliament 'for the full satisfaction of all arrears due to the officers and soldiers of the Army under the command of General Monck, and that they shall be received into our service upon as good pay and conditions as they now enjoy'.

The reference there to parliament picks up a theme which runs through the *Declaration.* This is a reassuringly constitutional monarch, cognizant of the several estates and of their role in government. The 'free and general pardon' extended by Charles will not extend to 'such persons as shall hereafter be excepted by Parliament'; he does not offer a 'liberty to tender consciences' on the authority of his prerogative but through his willingness to 'consent to such an Act of Parliament as upon mature deliberation shall be offered to us for the full granting that indulgence'. These formulations contrive both to make the monarch's inclinations reassuringly clear but also to imbue him with a becoming reticence, a disinclination to impose his will; above all, they distance him from the model of his father and his personal rule in the 1630s. This is no absolutist. These formulations also, of course, and perhaps not incidentally, absolve Charles from responsibility for the ensuing shape of any constitutional settlement. That will lie with parliament.

And, in the course of 1660, the Convention did enact just such a judicious, moderate and 'constitutional' settlement as *Breda* promised.[34]

## 4 The Act of Oblivion

The *Declaration of Breda* was the keystone of the Restoration policy initially followed by Charles and Hyde. The day after Charles was publicly declared King a bill of Indemnity and Oblivion was introduced into the Convention to make good the promises of *Breda.* For Charles, this was the fundamental legislative act of the Restoration settlement upon which depended his continuing enjoyment of the crown. When, in his speech on 29 December 1660 dissolving the Convention, he hoped that it would 'be for ever called, "The Healing and the Blessed Parliament"', it was because, next to the 'Miraculous Blessing' of God's Providence, he imputed 'the good Disposition and Security we are all in' to the Act of Oblivion which the Convention had passed: 'That is the principal Corner-stone which supports this excellent Building, that creates Kindness in us to each other; and Confidence is our joint and common Security'. Early in the debates on the bill, the Speaker of the Commons asserted that 'the Disposition of his Majesty is to Mercy; he hath invited his People to accept it; and it is the Disposition of the Body of this House, to be Healers of Breaches, and to hold forth Mercy to Men in all Conditions, so far as may stand with Justice'.[35] Quite how far that was, however, proved to be an extremely teasing question. When, six weeks later, the bill was still under discussion, Charles sent a message to the Commons to speed its passage. 'The Security of King and People' both depend upon it, he insisted, since 'The great Violation, which the Laws of the Land had for so many Years sustained, had filled the Hearts of the People with a terrible Apprehension of Insecurity to themselves, if all they had said and done should be liable to be examined and punished by those Laws, which had been so violated'. Unless they could be relieved of guilt and anxiety about their past, his subjects would never commit their future wholly to him. On 11 July the Commons finally passed the bill to the Lords, with a message for its swift despatch following on 19 July. Eight days later Charles once more intervened, delivering what was published as *His Majesty's Gracious Speech to the House of Peers, concerning the Speedy Passing of the Bill of Indemnity and Oblivion.* His argument again appealed implicitly to the fragility of the Restoration. Recalling his message to the Commons and that he thought them 'too long upon that Work', he expressed his fear lest people should begin to suppose he would not keep the promise of Breda, and had he not made that promise of general pardon, 'I am persuaded neither I nor you had been now here'. If it was now suspected that he would renege on it, the Restoration itself might be in jeopardy.[36] Despite this urging, it was not until 29 August 1660 that Charles II was finally able to give his royal assent to *An Act of Free and General Pardon, Indempnity and Oblivion* (12 Car.II c.11). Its purpose was 'to bury all Seeds of future Discords' by ensuring that, in the very words of *Breda*, 'noe Crime whatsoever committed against His Majesty or His Royall Father shall hereafter rise in Judgement or be brought in Question'. It enacted that any treasonable or criminal act performed 'by vertue or colour' of the authority of king or parliament since 1 January 1638 and before 24 June 1660 should 'be Pardoned... and put in utter Oblivion' unless performed by one of the persons expressly excepted from the Act's provisions.[37]

It was these exceptions from the general pardon which had caused the four-month delay before the bill's enactment, during which Lords and Commons engaged in prolonged and heated debates over whose guilt was so heinous they could not be pardoned. Charles, in accord with the advice of Hyde, was very clear that their number should be as small as possible. In his Lords speech he professed that he never thought of excepting more than 'the immediate Murderers of my Father' and he urged the peers 'to depart from all particular Animosities and Revenge, or Memory of past Provocations' in order to pass a bill with no more exceptions than this. At the bill's introduction Monck proposed that the number of the persons excepted should be five; on 14 May the Convention decided there should be seven, and on 5 and 6 June these were named; nevertheless, on 7 June, five more were added, and their number gradually grew in subsequent debates.[38] Eventually, there were four categories of exceptions. Thirty-three persons were wholly excepted from the provisions of the Act, out of over sixty who were considered at various stages. These were men who had sentenced Charles I to death, or signed the death warrant, or been instrumental in the proceedings of the trial. They could all expect to be executed since there was no doubt that, when brought before a court of law, they would be found guilty of treason. Their only escape was to avoid capture and trial.[39] A further nineteen regicides were imprisoned under threat of execution.[40] Seven men were 'excepted out of the Act... for and in respect only of such Pains, Penalties, and Forfeitures, (not extending to Life), as shall be thought fit to be inflicted on [them] by another Act'. By this formula they escaped execution but were liable to whatever punishment should subsequently be imposed upon them. Of these seven, five were men who had been nominated to the court to try Charles I but who had taken very little part in the proceedings and had not signed the death warrant. The other two were John Phelps, one of the two clerks to the court (his journal of the trial was published by John Nalson in 1682) and Sir Arthur Haslerig. In due course, the estates of the five survivors of these seven were confiscated, they themselves were degraded and imprisoned for life, and annually they were drawn on hurdles through London to Tyburn with ropes about their necks in 'the manner of persons executed for High Treason'.[41] Finally, twenty persons were disqualified from holding public office. These were men of some prominence in the Army and in the Protectorate or republican regimes but who had not been involved in the trial of Charles, with two exceptions: the regicide John Hutchinson and Francis Lascelles who though nominated a judge, 'had never been at the High Court of Justice, and but once at any meeting with them, and at that time he declared his dissent to their proceedings'.[42] The Act also took the occasion wholly to except, 'though dead', Oliver Cromwell, Henry Ireton, John Bradshaw, Thomas Pride and twenty others deceased.

Throughout these debates the Lords and Commons tended to work against each other, the one House safeguarding those the other would penalize. The Lords' amendments to the bill omitted many of those excepted by the Commons and included those, such as Haslerig, Lambert and Vane, whom the Commons had excepted only in respect of pains and penalties not extending to life. In the event, it was agreed that Haslerig should not be wholly excepted and that the cases of Vane and Lambert, wholly excepted from the Act in addition to the thirty-three regicides, should be the subject of a parliamentary appeal to the King's mercy for their lives to be spared. This petition was successful. The Lords sought also to restrict the royal mercy so that those involved in March 1649 in the trial and execution for treason of Arthur, Lord Capel, and other lords should be excepted. This was rejected by the Commons on the very reasonable grounds that 'they do not insist upon the shedding of Blood upon the Account of the Death of Commoners'.[43] Some members, like the vitriolic Prynne, 'desirous to ruyne as many as possible of those' who had served the republic, were vindictive, but it is not the case that, as the hostile witness of Lucy Hutchinson would have it, the Presbyterians 'according to their nature fell a thirsting, then hunting after blood, and urging that God's blessing could not be upon the land till justice had cleansed it from the late King's blood'. Many members were conciliatory, and some capable of great dignity: 'the Lord Fairfax upon that subject [of the execution of Charles I] did say that if they would except any, he knew of one that was fit so to be, and that was himselfe, for that being then Generall he hindred it not when he might have done it'.[44] Many – perhaps the majority – were swayed less by straightforward political considerations or the desire either for reconciliation or revenge than by what would secure their own place in the future, by financial considerations, and by personal animosities and relationships, and by family allegiances. Many of the family ties tested by Civil War proved sufficiently resilient to safeguard individuals despite political differences: John Hutchinson, for example, was saved largely as a result of the intervention of his royalist brother-in-law Sir Allen Apsley and of Sir George Booth, on whose behalf John Hutchinson had intervened in 1659; his wife also played a decisive role, forging his signature to a letter of regret addressed to the Speaker. Bulstrode Whitelocke depended both upon such connections and upon a bribe; Ormonde was prepared to testify to Ludlow's good character; Monck's intervention secured Haslerig and his estate for his children.[45]

Since the events under discussion had occurred over ten years previously a good deal of parliament's time was spent debating matters of fact. Often, exception or pardon turned on deciding exactly what had occurred and who was responsible for it, to what extent those involved were free agents and therefore personally culpable, and how far words and deeds had been accurately recorded. Efforts were made to get at the facts. Steps were taken to bring into parliament's keeping, and to preserve, such relevant documents as Phelps's papers. William Prynne was appointed chairman of a committee to secure and examine these records. A record of the trial was read in the House, enquiry was made concerning the identity of the executioner and the Convention was extremely anxious to procure the original warrant for the execution of Charles I. This was in the possession of Francis Hacker, now imprisoned in the Tower, who had had charge of Charles I prior to his execution. His wife, Isabella, 'thinking to save her husband', procured the document, 'with all their hands and seals' and presented it to the Lords on 31 July, but without having first negotiated for her husband's liberty, or even life; he was still excepted from the act.[46] Appeal to the facts could persuade parliament to change its mind. Matthew Thomlinson, for example, who had guarded Charles I during his trial, successfully pointed out that the inclusion of his name in the list of judges excepted by the Lords was an error. Thomas Lister, also excepted as one of the judges at Charles I's trial, was deleted upon his petition that he had sat on only one day; Sir Gilbert Pickering, who attended only two sittings, was excepted by the Commons for penalties not reaching to life, but, upon his petition to the Lords, was by the Peers, as a result of Sandwich's intervention, deleted from the list of exceptions. The most signal such appeal was Richard Ingoldsby's claim that Cromwell had held his hand and forced him to subscribe the death warrant against Charles I. Reward for his recent service in the case of Lambert's revolt required that some way be found to exculpate his regicide past, and, despite its implausibility, this tale served and he was pardoned.[47] As well as mistakes and revisions of this kind, MPs were liable simply to change their minds. Richard Keeble, serjeant at law, one of the three commissioners who had charge of the Great Seal after the execution of Charles I, escaped exception in the Commons on 12 June, but not on the 16th, when he was excepted for pains and penalties not extending to life; on 13 August, he was again omitted from the exceptions; in the final act, he was among those debarred from holding public office. The regicide Adrian Scroope, like John Hutchinson 'cleared by vote' on 9 June, then surrendered to the authorities, but was nevertheless excepted from the act on 28 August, the day before it received royal assent, and, in Lucy Hutchinson's words, 'had the honour to die a noble martyr'.[48]

While these debates continued during the summer of 1660 there was consequently very considerable uncertainty about how far the act's provisions would eventually extend. A royal proclamation was issued on 6 June requiring the regicides in hiding to surrender themselves within fourteen days 'under Pain of being excepted from any Pardon or Indemnity both for their respective Lives and Estates'. This was succeeded by a succession of orders, warrants, searches, seizures and arrests during the ensuing weeks. Those at risk were much exercised by this proclamation, for the continuing debates in the two Houses, and the unpredictability of their tempers, offered no assurance that surrender would be to their advantage. The Commons held that those who gave themselves up should be shown mercy; the Lords disagreed. Ludlow was prompted to write a tract arguing 'the case of those who had rendred themselves upon the proclamation' but found it too hazardous either to have it printed or presented as a petition.[49] He himself did surrender, but he did so very apprehensively and then, after growing misgivings about the government's intentions, fled abroad, making eventually for Geneva, for 'I had a great love and inclynation to the ayre of a Commonwealth'. Even though pardoned by the Commons, at his wife's insistence John Hutchinson remained in hiding in London until his safety was guaranteed with the passing of the Act of Oblivion, a wise precaution in view of the fate of Adrian Scroope.[50] Twenty-one regicides did yield themselves. Since they 'doe pretend thereby to some favour, upon some conceived doubtfull words' in the proclamation, the Lords finally agreed that, if they 'should be legally attainted for the horrid Treason and Murther' of Charles I, their execution should be suspended until another act had been passed for that purpose. Meanwhile, they remained incarcerated. Of those who surrendered, only Adrian Scroope was denied this leniency.[51]

Nine of those who did not surrender were detected and arrested.[52] Nineteen others sought refuge overseas: some, such as Edward Whalley and William Goffe, in New England, some, such as Ludlow, Cornelius Holland, Valentine Walton and John Hewson, in Holland, Germany and Switzerland. When the Convention reconvened in November 1660 it passed an Act of Attainder (12 Car.II c.30) condemning to death those regicides who had sought to avoid capture and confiscating both their property and the estates of regicides and republicans who had died before the Restoration (notably, Cromwell, Ireton and Bradshaw).[53] However, though they might have escaped immediate penalty they continued to be at risk. Thomas Scott was either captured, or persuaded to surrender, in Brussels in the summer of 1660. John Barkstead, John Okey and Miles Corbet were given up by the Dutch authorities at Delft in 1661, and returned to England. They were executed on 19 April 1662. Two years later, in 1664, John Lisle was assassinated in Lausanne.[54] Those imprisoned in England continued to be at risk from a volatile Commons. In the summer of 1661 the Cavalier House of Commons took in hand 'the business touching those Persons that are reserved to Pains and Penalties by the Act of Indemnity, and those that are excepted out of the said Act, and those that are convicted and condemned, in the *Tower*'. On 30 July an act dealt with those reserved for future punishment (13 Car.II c.15), but the bill for the execution of 'those Nineteen Traitors in the *Tower*' (that is, the surviving regicides who had surrendered) was lost in the Lords. The irony did not escape Henry Marten, the regicide and prominent republican said to be the author of the inscription *Exit Tyrannus Regum ultimus* which had replaced the arms and statues of Charles I in public places. When, having surrendered and been tried, he was summoned to say at the Bar of the House of Lords why the Commons' proposal for execution should not be adopted, he observed that 'That Honourable House of Commons, that he did heretofore idolize, had given him up to Death; and now this Honourable House of Peers, which he had so much opposed . . . is now made the Sanctuary for to fly for his Life'.[55] At the same time as these debates, the House of Commons resolved on proceedings against Vane and Lambert. Vane was tried for treason in April 1662 and, despite his reprieve, executed, less for his past than for his present refusal to recant his belief in the Good Old Cause and for his resolute defence of his actions. Lambert, who bore himself more submissively at his trial three days later, was imprisoned for life.[56] John Hutchinson, though he had his liberty, continued under the wary eye of the authorities: in 1663 he was arrested on suspicion of complicity in the Northern Plot (though never charged or tried) and was brought to his death by the circumstances of his imprisonment. His death left of the regicides only Richard Ingoldsby alive and free from threat. Lambert, whose capture had bought Ingoldsby's good fortune, was 22 years a prisoner, first in Guernsey and then on an islet in Plymouth Sound, where he died in 1684. As late as 1689 Ludlow found he was still unwelcome in England. Richard Cromwell, whom the Act of Oblivion had passed over in silence, went abroad, harassed by creditors rather than persecution, returning to England about 1680, where he lived quietly and unmolested into the Hanoverian age. He died in 1712, having outlived all other notable public figures from the Republic and Protectorate.[57]

## 5 The Convention Settlement

Though more untidily managed than Charles had wanted, and less generous, the Act of Oblivion was the essential legislative achievement of the whole decade. Upon it the Restoration depended for, by inhibiting royalist vengeance, it prevented the restored regime's hold on power from being jeopardized by a Puritan and republican reaction. In the Lords on 29 August giving his assent to the Act, Charles professed that no one had longed for it 'more impatiently' than he and he expressed the hope that it would 'be the foundation of much Security and Happiness to us all'.[58] The decade, however, would never feel entirely secure, and many of the King's subjects would be far from happy with their plight under subsequent legislation. The Act of Oblivion did fulfil a key promise of *Breda* but that declaration promised more than a general pardon, and more was expected. Charles may have been restored without conditions, but his restoration was not unconditional. He and the Cavaliers had been wholly passive in effecting his return, but upon their own efforts would now depend whether they were to remain. In conversation with Pepys in early March 1660 Mountagu opined not only that Richard Cromwell would not long survive were he to be restored, 'no, nor the King neither... unless he carry himself soberly and well'. 'The king was not yet master of the kingdom', recalled Clarendon, 'nor his authority and security such as the general noise and acclamation, the bells and bonfires, proclaimed it to be.'[59]

From the first, Charles and his government were hence wary and insecure. Recent history had taught all too clearly that 'The angry buzz of a multitude is one of the bloodiest noises in the world'.[60] If Charles had judiciously to respect the will of parliament, so too it had to respect public opinion. Central government depended for the implementation of its policies at local level upon the gentry, especially in their capacity as JPs and as members of corporations, but local government functioned through the willingness of minor gentry and of those below the rank of gentleman – of husbandmen, yeomen, merchants – to act as government agents in unpaid offices such as those of constable and bailiff. The composition of these local government agencies was changed to reflect the change in political circumstances. New commissions of peace excluded republicans, Cromwellians and sectaries, and restored many of the royalist and episcopalian gentry to the place on the magistrate's bench which they regarded as rightfully theirs. However, though purged, their commitment to the policies of the restored regime could not be taken for granted, partly because many officers did survive from the Interregnum and partly because public protestations were not always a reliable guide to personal convictions. Without their support, government would come to a standstill, as Charles I had discovered in 1640–2 and the Rump and Army in 1659–60, and as James II would discover in 1687–8.[61]

The immediate business of the new regime – and of the Convention which had called it into being – was threefold. First, it had to provide this body of opinion with the security and stability it looked for in church and state. It had been the experience of collapsing central authority, of something approaching anarchy, and of increasing horror at the extravagance of the sects, and particularly the Quakers, which had allowed the Restoration. Clearly, the expectation was that a return to traditional forms would mean a return to reliable, just and predictable courses. Secondly, it had to negate any threat to restored monarchical government, military or civil. This was posed most obviously by the remaining regiments of the New Model Army which, even after Monck's dominance, were still made up of men who had wielded great political power and who had espoused radical politics and religion. There was an associated need to reassert more generally the authority of social superiors over those classes who, so such superiors held, had enjoyed far too much liberty of person and of mind, as well as of conscience, during the Interregnum. And thirdly, there were the government's friends, those who had suffered in the royalist cause, to reward.

The Convention addressed first the immediate and practical necessity to confirm the authority of the institutions and officers of the state. The legitimacy of the political process at national and local level and of legal jurisdiction were all vulnerable to challenge. This parliament had not been summoned by a monarch and the law courts were presided over by officers appointed by what were now regarded as illegal and usurping regimes. The Convention dealt first with its own status as a parliament. A bill introduced on 4 May put this beyond dispute and confirmed that the Long Parliament was dissolved (12 Car.II c.1).[62] Even more promptly, the vote in the Commons on 1 May to return to monarchical government was immediately followed by a resolution to set up a committee 'to offer such Expedients as may carry on the Courts of Justice of the Kingdom; and how Fines, Recoveries, Assurances, Judgments, and Decrees passed, may be confirmed and made good'. A fortnight later the *Act for the Continuance of Processe and Judiciall Proceedings* (12 Car. II c.3) was introduced. It dealt with the immediate situation by confirming the legitimacy of all court actions and legal proceedings in hand, permitting such actions to continue and ruling that decisions reached were binding. Both these acts received the royal assent within the month, on 1 June.[63] The past posed graver problems, and was the subject of another bill. By the *Act for Confirmation of Judiciall Proceedings* (12 Car. II c.12), which received the royal assent with the Act of Oblivion on 29 August, no legal proceeding or decision since 1 May 1642 could be avoided or queried on the grounds of 'want or defect of any Legall Power' in the courts. With the exception of the trial and sentencing of Charles I, they were to be treated as though the regimes which authorized them were legitimate and their ordinances 'Good True and Effectual Acts of Parliament'. The Convention, of course, believed no such thing and was embarrassed to have to acknowledge these illegitimate regimes, and even to name Oliver and Richard Cromwell, with their titles, in the Act. Lest there be any misunderstanding, the Act went on to state in unequivocal terms that nevertheless these were 'most Rebellious, Wicked, Trayterous and Abominable Usurpations Detested by this present Parliament as opposite in the Highest Degree to His Sacred Majestyes most Just and undoubted Right'.[64] The implication of this was that the public acts of the past 18 years – parliament's own proceedings – were wicked and detestable abominations, that is, not binding. The Convention was thus caught in a cleft stick. Necessity required it to recognize the legality of proceedings conducted under regimes which it could only regard as illegal. Thus, the Marriage Act confirmed the legality of all marriages conducted since 1 May 1642.[65] At one and the same time the Convention behaved as though its predecessors had enacted 'good, true and effectual acts of parliament' while on the other it denied that they could possibly have done so. This constitutional knot it did not endeavour to unravel.

While, taking its cue from the unconditional return of Charles, the Convention never debated the nature of monarchy or addressed large constitutional questions, it did in two (related) ways tackle the status and role of the crown. First of all, as early as 3 May, a bill was ordered for abolishing 'Tenures *in Capite*, and by Knights Service and Socage *in Capite*, and also of the Court of Wards'. These arcane terms referred to a number of antiquated feudal sources of income for the crown. Their abolition cut the crown off from any vestiges of feudal status and from an important source of income. The bill consequently proposed to settle £100,000 per annum on the King in lieu of wardships and liveries. This bill intermittently occupied parliament for over six months before it received the royal assent on 24 December.[66] During this time, it had become entangled with the larger question of the financial position of the monarch. On 1 May the Commons voted an assessment of £70,000 per month for three months for the royal revenue, beginning on 24 June, and a bill to put this into effect was passed on the 28th. With the Act Confirming the Convention and the Act for the Continuance of Judicial Proceedings, it completed the group of fundamental bills settling the new regime which received the royal assent on 1 June.[67] There financial matters were left until, on 31 July, a committee was set up 'to consider of settling such a Revenue on his Majesty, as may maintain the Splendour and Grandeur of his Kingly Office, and preserve the Crown from Want, and from being undervalued by his Neighbours'. On 4 September this committee reported, first, that it computed the crown's current annual income at £819,398 (from customs, feudal revenues, rents and licences and postage) and, secondly, that it recommended an income of £1,200,000 to cover the monarch's annual expenditure. How to make up the missing third much exercised the Commons. However, by now the period of provision covered by the first supply bill was about to expire and so, while the House debated where to find the missing third of the royal revenue, on 7 September it had perforce to order a bill for a further month's supply of £70,000, and yet another was passed on 28 December.[68] The need to make up the difference was made more pressing by the loss in income of (on the committee's calculation) £100,000 were the Court of Wards to be abolished. In November, the Commons finally agreed on an excise on alcoholic drinks as a preferable expedient to the assessment which had been proposed, to be levied by revising an excise bill already passing through the House. The *Act for Taking away the Court of Wards and Liveries* settled on the King, 'in full Recompence and Satisfaction', 'the Moiety of the Excise of Beer, Ale, Cyder, Perry, and strong Waters' to make up the £100,000, while its companion *Act for a Grant of Certain Impositions upon Beer, Ale and other Liquors, for the Increase of His Majesty's Revenue, during his Life*, which also received the royal assent on 24 December, settled on the King 'the other Moiety' of the excise revenue to make up the balance of the £1,200,000.[69] The Commons had devoted a good deal of time and energy to these measures. Far from seeking to keep the King on a tight rein it had rather, as it thought, provided handsomely for him. In fact, its estimate of the cost of Charles's government was lamentably short and it had, albeit unwittingly, sown the seed of a tension between crown and parliament which would grow as the decade progressed.[70]

That, however, lay ahead. The immediate potential threat to civil society and order was neither financial nor legal but military. For 15 years the Army's role in public affairs had far exceeded that of military operations. Its regiments might be scattered and broken up, its junior officers purged, its senior officers discredited, its radical fervour passed, but while it continued in existence there could be no confidence that its revolutionary might would not stir. There was, of course, no possibility of disbandment without meeting its huge arrears of pay. No one doubted that it was therefore imperative that the promise of the *Declaration of Breda* to pay its arrears should be promptly honoured, but the Convention was much exercised by how to raise sufficient funds to do so. To identify and implement 'Ways for the speedy raising of a considerable Sum of Money, for Satisfaction of the Arrears due to the Army and Navy' and 'for getting in of Money, towards the disbanding of the Army' involved prolonged parliamentary debates, the setting up of a committee 'to examine the Debts of the Navy and Army', repeated conferences between Commons and Lords, several temporary arrangements to secure the Army's monthly pay and short-term borrowings from the City. Finally, a 'greate *Tax* of Pole-mony' was 'levied for the disbanding of the Army' by an act which received the royal assent on 29 August. When this *Act for the Speedy Provision of Money, for Disbanding and Paying off the Forces of this Kingdom* was found to have raised insufficient funds, a second act was pushed through the House in three days in September, to be followed by yet a third act for supplying defects in the poll bill in December.[71] Meanwhile, the Act for Disbanding the Armed Forces had received the royal assent on 13 September. Reports on the progress of its implementation were received in November and December. By January 1661 the process, involving over thirty regiments, as many garrisons and 25 warships in England and Scotland, was all but completed.[72]

Breda had promised a liberty to tender consciences, or, at least, royal assent to an act of indulgence which parliament should present for this purpose, but the Convention did not take this up. Discussions and negotiations did take place outside the Houses, but there was no attempt within parliament to reach an ecclesiastical settlement. Like the final shape of the constitutional settlement, the nature and extent of the Church of England was left to the Cavalier Parliament to determine.[73] The one piece of ecclesiastical legislation which the Convention did pass, however, showed it far more sympathetic to the religious bias of the Interregnum than the Cavalier Parliament would be, and continued its concern to maintain order by safeguarding the authority of existing institutions, officers and proceedings. The standing of parish ministers was jeopardized by the fact that a great many of them had been appointed when central ecclesiastical authority (and certainly episcopal authority) had all but vanished. By the *Act for the Confirming and Restoreing of Ministers*, introduced on 9 May and strenuously promoted by Prynne, any man 'Ordained by any Ecclesiasticall persons' who had been placed in a benefice since 1 January 1642 was declared the 'reall and lawfull Incumbent', save when his predecessor was living and had been sequestered or ejected or there was a rival claimant who had been presented by the patron of the living but refused admission by the Triers. The effect of this was to confirm the title of the great majority of ministers appointed during the Interregnum, men usually without episcopal orders. The act thus differed from later religious legislation by making no judgement at all about the orthodoxy or churchmanship of these men, whose pastoral commitment it accepted without query. Although support for the execution of Charles I and opposition to the Restoration disqualified incumbents from keeping their livings, there was no liturgical, ecclesiastical or doctrinal test imposed, save that incumbents could not be anti-paedobaptist.[74]

There was one more matter outstanding, and perhaps the one which touched people most nearly: property. During the Commonwealth and Protectorate thousands of acres had changed hands, either through confiscation, or in order to compound, or through sales compelled by penury or local pressure. The *Declaration of Breda* had referred to parliament 'all things relating to . . . grants, sales and purchases'. The matter was beyond parliament's power to resolve. Following the Confirmation of Judicial Proceedings Act it appeared that all transfers of title by due legal process, however occasioned, were binding, while confiscations and sales on behalf of the Republic and Protectorate might not be. This suggested that anyone who had sold land would have no claim for its recovery, while anyone whose land had been confiscated might have a claim. This distinction, however, hardly accorded with experience. Many sales of land had been, in effect, compelled, by poverty brought on through the losses incurred in supporting the royalist cause, by fines or taxes, or by the cost of compounding. Confiscations were of different types: crown lands sold by the Commonwealth and Protectorate; church lands seized and sold; the private estates of Cavaliers sold because they could not, or would not, compound by paying fines. In each case the estates might have been subsequently sold, perhaps more than once. No legislation could cope with this confusion. Various kinds of expedient were adopted, and different solutions arrived at, in different cases. Private agreements might be reached, or there might be recourse to law, to petitioning of the King or other patron, or to a private bill of parliament. The Commons was itself petitioned by purchasers seeking confirmation of their titles and during the summer and autumn the House several times considered the matter. A Grand Committee for Sales was set up to make proposals, and bills guaranteeing long leases to purchasers, or guaranteeing their estates, or offering compensation were introduced (the first as early as 4 May), but none was carried through. However, the Lords did agree on the restitution of crown lands to the royal family and the Commons, tacitly accepting this, on the return of church lands.[75]

Whether or not the result was a redistribution of land ownership is debated. While many old landowning families did manage to recover their estates, sometimes even before the Restoration, new landholders often retained the estates which they had first acquired in the 1640s and 1650s. It has hence been argued both that a legacy of the Interregnum was a rejuvenated and politically radicalized landowning class, and that it did not see any substantial alteration in the profile of the propertied gentry or any lasting injection of new blood.

The point is significant because it may well bear on the development of political opposition, and of political parties. If indeed a good many families originally Puritan, parliamentarian or republican, joined the landowning gentry, then the development of a country opposition – ultimately, of the Whigs – has an explanation. Among royalist gentry, impoverishment and privation would prove a fertile seedbed of disillusionment. Permanent loss of estates, the exchange of ownership for tenancy, or the recovery of lands only after long and expensive legal proceedings and at punitive expense or mortgage cost, might easily breed disenchantment and the belief that Presbyterians were far more favoured by the new regime than its constant adherents. It was a sentiment which might well turn from disillusionment to outright opposition. Thomas Bruce, 2nd Earl of Ailesbury, held that '"Whiggism"... sprang by degrees from the discontent of noble families and of many good families of the first gentry in the Counties whose ancestors were sequestered, decimated and what not on account of their steadfast loyalties'.[76]

Certainly, whether justified or not, royalists were much given to expressions of discontent in the months following the Restoration, and their grievances were not confined to questions of land ownership. The suspicion that Charles and his ministers were more anxious to appease old enemies than to reward old friends spread easily and swiftly. To the royalist Roger L'Estrange it was the Presbyterians who in 1661 appeared to be the 'white boys' in favour, just as they had formerly done to the republican Lucy Hutchinson. 'We find', he complained in his *A Caveat to the Cavaliers* (1661), 'the *Court* dangerously throng'd with *Parasites*: *Knaves* represented to the *King*, for *Honest* men, and *Honest* men for *Villeins*: a watch upon his Majesties Eare, to keep out better Enformation; *seditious Ministers* protected', and he warned the King to beware '*Temporizing Friends*' as much as '*unconverted Enemies*'.[77] After all, the grandest and most ostentatious rewards went to parliamentarians and Cromwellians, to Monck and Mountague, who, as Duke of Albemarle and Earl of Sandwich respectively, received vast estates, while others who had held high office in Interregnum regimes were prominent in the Restoration government. It was an embarrassing fact that to such men, rather than to royalists, was due the Restoration. Political prudence and the spirit of Breda both dictated that the government should not exclude those who had brought it into being and who might yet dissolve it. Charles's Privy Council was consequently judiciously mixed. Its thirty members included the dukes of York and Gloucester (members by right as royal dukes), sixteen royalists,[78] four erstwhile Cromwellians[79] and eight Presbyterian parliamentarians who had opposed the Protectorate.[80] Ministries and household offices were distributed with a similar conciliatory sensitivity. Hyde remained Lord Chancellor, Monck became Captain-General for the Army; Morice joined Nicholas as a Secretary of State; the Duke of York was Lord High Admiral, Mountague Vice-Admiral; Ormonde was made Lord Steward, Northumberland Lord High Constable;

Southampton became Lord Treasurer and Ashley Chancellor of the Exchequer. Similarly, throughout the nation, examples can be found of erstwhile royalists, parliamentarians and Cromwellians all being appointed as judges, lords-lieutenant and deputy-lieutenants of counties and justices of the peace.[81]

Charles himself appears to have been personally generous, liberally handing out to royalists peerages, baronetcies, knighthoods, offices, estates and pensions, to the dismay of his Lord Treasurer, Southampton, and his Chancellor, Hyde. Almost inevitably, in the heady days following the Restoration, expectations ran unchecked and claimants far exceeded resources. Disappointment was inevitable. In his *Memoirs* Bulstrode came as close as his royalism would allow to criticism of Charles's 'trimming Indifferency' in 1660, 'to disoblige his old Friends, in hopes of getting new ones': 'they who suffered for his late royal Father, were not the better for all his immoderate Bounties'. This dissatisfaction was displaced on to Charles's first minister, Hyde. The Chancellor, noting a tendency among supplicants to exaggerate past service and sacrifices, was not much impressed by complaints of neglect but, as the man who was 'thought to have most credit with his master, and most power in his counsels' and the one to whom were referred supplications and petitions, he attracted the animosity – 'implacable hatred' Burnet calls it – of those who felt themselves aggrieved when their suits were refused. That at the same time former enemies were so conspicuously rewarded with office further fuelled resentment with the man responsible for royal policy: Presbyterians and Cromwellians 'were put in great posts by the earl of Clarendon's means, by which he lost most of the cavaliers, who could not bear the seeing such men so highly advanced and so much trusted'. Clarendon certainly resisted attempts by the Cavalier Parliament in 1661 to rewrite the Act of Oblivion on the grounds that 'it was the making those promises had brought the king home'.[82]

What mattered less than whether the fault lay in the exaggerated claims of the suitor or in the niggardliness of the patron was the perception of neglect. *An Humble Representation of the Sad Condition of Many of the King's Party* (1661), though willing to comply with the Act of Oblivion for the sake of the public good, feared that in drafting it MPs 'did but too well remember our enemies, and only forget us'. 'The angry men, that were thus disappointed of all their hopes', records Burnet, 'made a jest of the title of it, *An act of oblivion and indemnity*, and said, the king had passed an act of oblivion for his friends and of indemnity for his enemies.' And for such as L'Estrange, they continued to be enemies, act or no act: it 'saves them from the *law*, but *in Foro Conscientiae* 'tis no acquital; It discharges the *Penalty*, but not the *Crime*'.[83] Pepys records hearing, in March 1662, Robert Creighton, a chaplain to the King and afterwards Bishop of Bath and Wells, remonstrating in a sermon before Charles that

> it had been better for the poor Cavalier never to have come in with the King into England again; for he that hath the impudence to deny obedience to the

> lawful magistrate and to swear to the oath of allegeance &c, were better treated nowadays in newgate then a poor Royalist that hath suffered all his life for the King is at Whitehall among his friends.

Pepys himself had first-hand experience of 'discontented Cavaliers that thinks their Loyalty is not considered', to whom he refers as a recognized type in Restoration London. In December 1665 he was disturbed when the royalist Sir James Bunce, 'I know [not] whether in earnest or jest', averred 'this is the time for you . . . that were for Oliver heretofore; you are full of imployment, and we poor Cavaliers sit still and can get nothing'.[84]

# 4

# *Royal Servants: Clarendon and the Cavalier Parliament (1661–1667)*

## 1 Court and Country

The moderate and constitutional settlement worked out by the Convention in 1660 would not long endure.[1] Reactionary partisanship swiftly became far more characteristic of the political and religious life of the nation than compromise and conciliation. This first expressed itself in the elections to the Cavalier Parliament which reduced the Presbyterian representation to all but negligible proportions. Just under half those returned were Cavaliers who had either been in arms for the King themselves, who had fathers who had fought for him or who had been engaged in royalist conspiracies during the Protectorate. The remainder were overwhelmingly of episcopalian and royalist temper. Presbyterian members numbered between 37 and 50. 'We have great hopes', wrote the Secretary of State Sir Edward Nicholas, 'that this will prove a very happy Parliament, there being few Presbyterians in it.'[2] This House of Commons proved to be far more determined upon drastic courses with their erstwhile foes both than the Convention had been, and than either Clarendon or Charles could have wished: they were 'so high and so hot, that, unless the court had restrained them, they would have carried things much farther than they did, against all that had been concerned in the late war'.[3]

Cavalier the House might have been, but not compliant. It soon proved that it could have a mind of its own, for, while it was zealously for the King, and in some respects a less inhibited advocate of his cause than either he himself or his Chancellor, the Commons very soon proved to be equally zealous in defending its own prerogative and very unwilling to allow the King unfettered scope to pursue his own way. In order to secure monarchical government the restored regime and the Convention had tiptoed very carefully around constitutional matters. The Convention's settlement had not tackled the very issue which had broken the kingdom's mould, namely the relationship between king and parliament, between executive and legislature.

The failure to secure terms for Charles's return, still less anything approaching an agreed constitution, left the work still to do. Burnet held that 'To the king's coming in without conditions may be well imputed all the errors of his reign';[4] to it also may be imputed the series of crises through which Charles's reign lurched as rival hypotheses sought to define the chimera which was the Restoration's constitution. The first of them, ominously detectable within two or three years of the King's return, came to a head in 1667, and the next shortly after the close of the decade, in 1672. By the late 1670s the throne itself was hardly less at risk than it had been in the 1640s.

These tensions were evident within the Cavalier Parliament itself. Conspicuous in the Lords and among the King's ministers and advisers were such high prerogative men as George Villiers, 2nd Duke of Buckingham, Sir Charles Berkeley, created Viscount Fitzharding in 1663 and Earl of Falmouth in 1664, and Henry Bennet, in 1663 created Earl of Arlington. During a conversation in February 1664 'bewailing the posture of things at present' and that the King is 'led away by half a dozen men, that none of his serious servants and friends can come at him', Pepys reports hearing that 'these people about our King . . . tell him how neither privileges of Parliament nor City is anything; but his will is all and ought to be so'.[5] Such men did not at all care to have it suggested that the monarch in any sense shared sovereignty with parliament. At the trials of regicides in October 1660 Sir Robert Hyde, Lord Chief Justice of King's Bench, stated that 'the king is above the two houses. They must propose their laws to him. The laws are made by him, and not by them, by their consenting, but they are his laws.'[6] This view had its supporters in the lower House too. Burnet reports that in 1667, as part of their campaign to discredit Clarendon, 'many members of the house of commons, such as [Sir Thomas] Clifford, [Sir Thomas] Osborne, [afterwards Earl of Danby, Sir Robert] Carr, [Sir Thomas] Lyttleton, and [Sir Edward] Seymour, were brought to the king, who all assured him that upon his restoration they intended both to have raised his authority and to have increased his revenue, but that the earl of Clarendon had discouraged it'. In the Chancellor's more restricted notion of the royal prerogative, king, parliament and law formed an indissoluble trinity: Clarendon 'all along declared himself for the ancient liberties of England, as well as for the rights of the crown' and, following the Restoration, would neither 'stretch the prerogative beyond what it was before the wars' nor maintain those measures extorted from Charles by the Long Parliament.[7] Still more muted in their estimate of the royal prerogative were peers sympathetic to Presbyterians and Independents, such as William Russell, 5th Earl of Bedford, Denzil, Baron Holles, and Philip, 4th Baron Wharton. In the Commons, nonconformist sympathies combined with scepticism about the pretensions of the court in such members as the former New Model Army officer Colonel John Birch, Richard, the eldest son of John Hampden, and another son of a famous Puritan family, Sir Edward Harley. Andrew Marvell, the member for Hull, though retiring in debates within the House, was the most scathing satirical spokesman outside of MPs unimpressed by Clarendon's constitutionalism and dismayed by what they took to be the court's absolutist inclinations.[8]

Consequently, the government could by no means rely upon the unquestioning support of the Commons. Management of its members was called for in order to secure a majority for court policies.[9] Clarendon, as Chancellor Charles's first minister, never found this to his taste. In his view, ministers should not seek to manipulate parliament, just as parliament should not seek unduly to fetter the King. His was a traditionalist's faith in the harmonious working of the constitution which relied upon the memory of the disastrous experience of the 1640s to persuade parliamentarians and ministers to work together. At the end of the decade Coventry told Pepys that Clarendon had misapprehended the strength of loyalists' relief at the Restoration and 'thought he could have the command of Parliaments for ever, because for the King's sake they were awhile willing to grant all the King desire[d]'.[10] As the years passed, this want of constraining relief and gratitude grew more pronounced. Cavalier bitterness at what was perceived as court ingratitude[11] and discontent with the administration's performance combined with the effect of by-elections to foster oppositional tendencies. Through this parliament's long 17-year history there would be some 350 by-elections; by 1667 112 seats had changed hands. Very few of the new members returned on these occasions had any previous parliamentary experience.[12] In a general way, these newer members represented an inclination to oppose the court rather than to side with it. They were on the whole younger than those for whom the 1640s were still a powerful persuasive to quiescent loyalism and so more struck by the costs and inadequacies of monarchical administration than by the glories of the ideal of monarchy. They strengthened the critical temper represented by such original members as Monck's brother-in-law Sir Thomas Clarges. Nevertheless, though in the early 1660s Charles could indicate to Clarendon that 'our frindes' in the Commons should have directions, the Chancellor continued to view the manipulation necessary to secure a working majority in the House as ignominious and unseemly. There is something in Dryden's distinction between 'emp'ric politicians' who 'use deceit' and Clarendon who works 'by means as noble as your end'.[13]

With the exile of Clarendon in 1667 the tone of politics changed radically. The Cabal did appreciate the need to secure results, and it was none too scrupulous about the means.[14] Bribery now became a standard feature of parliamentary management and corruption a normal part of political life. To them especially is due the building of the court party to promote the King's business. By February 1670 an MP could observe that 'the face of affairs are much altered; the Courtiers now carry all before them in the House of Commons'.[15] The work of Thomas Clifford, the 'Bribe Master General', was especially important. According to Burnet, when first elected to the House in 1660, as MP for Totnes, Devon, Clifford sought the patronage of Clarendon, but, failing of this, he 'struck in with his enemies and tied himself particularly to Bennet', 'whose creature he is and never from him', wrote Pepys in 1667. Since he first joined the government as Secretary of State in October 1662 Bennet, who 'had the art of observing the king's temper, and managing it beyond all the men of that time', had been at odds with Clarendon and, wrote Burnet, 'began to raise a party in opposition to the earl of Clarendon'.[16] Through patronage, the offer of offices (often ancient and obscure sinecures in the crown's gift carrying no duties), or straightforward gifts of money, Clifford and Bennet, concentrating, it seems, on needy Cavaliers, developed a core of reliable Commons support. By 1670 they could count on over 100 MPs. Clifford's work has been said to have created the essential characteristics of Commons politics for the next 150 years.[17]

In its earliest form this management of parliamentary business was an expedient to ensure government success with particular measures. It implied little, if anything, about the views of members. However, as the decade progressed, it began to develop from an administrative expedient into an expression of ideological commitment. At the Restoration, *Cavaliers* 'was the distinguishing name of all that had been of the king's party', while his opponents were designated *Presbyterians* or *fanatics*, though Presbyterian support for the Restoration was grudgingly and sceptically recognized in the term *new Cavaliers*. *Presbyterian* continued in pejorative use throughout the decade, but, though Marvell could in 1675 still write in a letter of the 'Episcopal Cavalier Party', *Cavalier* gradually became confined to a particular brand of hedonistic royalism.[18] From the mid-1660s contemporaries began to speak rather of rival Court and Country groupings in parliament, the terms gaining currency through the crisis of the Dutch war and the ousting of Clarendon. In this usage, *Court* and *Country* refer respectively to supporters of the royal executive (as the choice of ministers of state lay with the King they tended to be his close confidants, that is, members of the court) and of the parliamentary legislature (*Country* presumably because of the alliterative neatness of the semantic distinction). In 1666 Pepys wrote of 'all the country gentlemen' being 'publicly jealous of the Courtiers in the Parliament' and the following year of the opposition to the court of 'the gentlemen of the country' in the Commons. In his satirical attack on the government in his *Last Instructions to a Painter*, written probably between Clarendon's resignation on 30 August 1667 and his flight on 29 November, Marvell directed the painter in depicting the Commons to 'Describe the *Court* and *Country*, both set right, / On opposite points, the black against the white'. Marvell, a former Cromwellian and now a Country party man, develops a contrast between the integrity and straightforwardness of 'the *Country Justice* on his Pad' and 'Plain *Gentlemen*' in stagecoaches coming up to London to take their seats and 'the *Courtiers* fine', 'fresh as from the Mint', who 'Salute them'. When, in a mock heroic account of parliamentary debates, he characterizes the Country party as 'A *Gross of English Gentry*, nobly born, / Of clear *Estates*, and to no Faction sworn; / Dear Lovers of their King, and Death to meet, / For Country's Cause, that Glorious think and sweet', *Country* no longer denotes a rural and provincial alternative to the town, but the interest of the nation rather than of the crown. Writing of political rivalry in 1671 Burnet could speak of 'the names of the Court and Country party'.[19] By the early 1670s an MP could distinguish between 'this side of the house, and that side'. Under the pressures of anti-court feeling aroused by the second *Declaration of Indulgence* in 1672, this sense of identity among opposition MPs further developed through their habit of meeting in London taverns to plan tactics, leading to the founding in 1674 of the Green Ribbon Club which met at the King's Head Tavern in Chancery Lane.[20] During the Exclusion Crisis these groupings began to coalesce into more coherent parties, now known almost exclusively by the terms *Whig* and *Tory*, though both terms antedate the Restoration and both are religious in origin.[21]

Within fifteen years of the Restoration contemporaries were interpreting their own history in terms of this opposition. In 1675 Shaftesbury, a former Presbyterian, at this date a man of the Country party, and soon to be the preeminent Whig leader, if not their creator, wrote of 'a Project of several Years standing... *To make a distinct Party* from the rest of the Nation of the High Episcopal Man, and the Old Cavalier', for whom 'Monarchy as well as Episcopacy [is] *Jure Divino*, and not to be bounded, or limited by humane Laws'. He derived this from the Corporation Act of 1661. In his *Account of the Growth of Popery and Arbitrary Government* (1677), Marvell traced back to the mid-1660s a pro-Catholic Court party design to rule through a standing Army rather than parliament. On the other side of the political spectrum, Edmund Bohun wrote seven years later of a Whig plot to destabilize the state 'from the Time his Majesty set his Foot upon the English shores at his Return'.[22] Most emphatically, Daniel Defoe, in the first decade of the next century, discerned 'two contending Parties' throughout seventeenth-century history, 'distinguish'd, *as in like Cases*, by Names of Contempt; and tho they have often changed them on either side, as Cavalier and Roundhead, Royalists and Rebels, Malignants and Phanaticks, Tories and Whigs, yet the Division has always been barely *the Church and the Dissenter*, and there it continues to this Day'.[23]

## 2 The Cavalier Settlement

When, at the opening of the Cavalier Parliament on 8 May 1661, Charles addressed the assembled members he made it clear that he anticipated no change in government policy. Recalling that in his speech at the close of the Convention he had hailed the Act of Oblivion as the cornerstone of the nation's peace and security, he stated bluntly: 'I am still of the same Opinion . . . I shall never think him a wise Man, who would endeavour to undermine or shake that Foundation of our Public Peace, by infringing that Act in the least Degree'.[24] He accordingly recommended to the new parliament two bills ready-prepared to confirm the private and public acts of the Convention. When, that summer, the Speaker of the Commons, Sir Edward Turner, presented these bills for the royal assent, it was with a tactful acknowledgement of the King's commitment:

> that we might with some Chearfulness see Your Majesty's Face, we have brought our Brother *Benjamin* with us; I mean, Your Act of Oblivion: I take the Boldness to call it Yours, for it is by many Titles; Your Majesty first conceived it at *Breda*; You helped to contrive and form it here in *England*; and, we must all bear You Witness, You laboured and travailed till it was brought forth.[25]

This compliment disguised how far in fact the temper of the House of Commons now was from the King's, and how unwilling it had been to confirm the Act of Oblivion as he wished, without modification. On 14 June, records the House's journal, the question whether the Act should be confirmed 'took up long Debate', a debate which was continued on the 15th and 19th. On the 22nd the House received a curt letter from Charles in which, after reminding members of 'the Value We set upon the Act of Indemnity, as We have great Reason to do' and that he had urged its swift despatch in the Convention, he declared that he would assent to no bills presented at the summer recess unless they included confirmation of that Act 'in the same Terms We have already passed it'. The Commons then complied, and on 8 July Charles came specially to the Lords to assent to *An Act for Confirming Publique Acts* of the Convention.[26] Only a royal threat, however, had wrung this from parliament. It was already clear that this House of Commons was of a less forgiving nature than its monarch. The House went on to move against those reserved by the Act of Oblivion for pains and penalties not extending to life and to seek the execution of those regicides who had surrendered. In this they failed, for there was no government support for the motion. When, in a note passed to Charles at a Privy Council meeting, Clarendon asked whether it were not better the execution bill 'should sleep in the houses [of parliament], and not be brought to you', Charles wrote in reply, 'I must confesse that I am weary of hanging except vpon new offences' and agreed that Clarendon should prevent its presentation for assent, 'for you know that I cannot pardon them'. Accordingly, the bill was not discussed in the Lords.[27] Charles's reply not only shows him less sanguinary than the Commons; it also recognizes how circumspect he had need to be in circumventing their bent.

If the House was less generously disposed than the King, it was also without the lingering sensitivities of the Convention. It forthwith set about the formal and public humiliation of the legislative, legal, religious and intellectual bases of the previous regimes, a vindictiveness which its predecessor had eschewed. On 17 May the Commons voted that the Solemn League and Covenant should be burned by the public hangman, and ten days later the legislation establishing the Commonwealth was similarly consigned to the flames. Evelyn watched 'the *Scotch-Covenant* burnt' with precisely the reflection desired by the authorities: 'o prodigious change'.[28] In the summer, works by Milton, whose arrest had been ordered by the Commons on 16 June, and by John Goodwin were ordered to be publicly burned.[29] The attainder of Strafford was annulled on the grounds it had been secured through mob violence[30] and on 30 July the royal assent was given to a bill repealing the Long Parliament statute which had excluded bishops from the House of Lords. Presenting this bill the Speaker of the Commons described the 1640 statute as the first step on the road to constitutional disintegration. 'We found', he claimed, that James's adage 'No Bishop, No King', was 'true; for, after they were put out, the Fever still increasing, in another Fit the Temporal Lords followed, and then the King Himself. Nor did the Humour rest there; but, in the Round, the House of commons was first garbled, and then turned out of Doors'.[31] This readiness to suppose that political disposition could be inferred from religious affiliation had declared itself at the opening of the Cavalier Parliament. On 13 May the Commons ordered that on Sunday 26 May all members should receive the sacrament in St Margaret's, Westminster, 'according to the Form prescribed in the Liturgy of the Church of *England*', that a record should be kept of their attendance, and any absentees prevented from taking their seats in the House until they could present a certificate of compliance.[32]

This reducing of the sacramental office to a political fitness test was a coarsening of devotion and a cheapening of conscience which, in its subsequent legislation, the Cavalier Parliament was to find very serviceable. The Convention had never supposed that a man's loyalty to the crown could be inferred from his posture and words at prayer, and it had consequently seen no need to circumscribe either doctrine or forms of worship to ensure political conformity, anymore than it had felt obliged to imposed doctrinal or liturgical tests upon the clergy to guarantee religious orthodoxy. The Cavalier Parliament, however, believed that something far more interventionist was required to ensure the continuing political and religious health of the nation. To its reactionary temper the Convention's settlement of the nation's affairs appeared only half-heartedly to have turned its back on the past. Far too many doubtful, if not downright dangerous, notions and practices were still tolerated. The Cavalier Parliament demanded far sterner dealing with the clergy than was provided for by the Act for Confirming Ministers[33] and a rigorous policing of religious and political sentiment. In the pursuit of these aims it embarked upon a rigorous legislative programme as soon as it opened. Within eighteen months it had established a much more repressive and partisan regime than anything proposed in the Convention, one which sought to confine governmental and ecclesiastical office to those of impeccably royalist and episcopalian sentiment, to restrict the free association of people, and to limit the exchange of ideas and of information.

With the Army no longer a focus for radical political opinion or an alternative centre of power, steps were taken to ensure that the general public could not again assemble to become a challenge to the will of parliament and to prevent the circulation of dissident ideas. Parliament sought first to prevent any possibility of a recurrence of the insurgency of the 1640s. Building on an earlier Elizabethan treason act (13 Eliz. c.1) the *Act for the Safety and Preservation of His Majesties Person and Government against Treasonable and Seditious Practices* extended the range of treasonable practices to include the spoken and written word. 'Because the growth and increase of the late troubles & disorders did in a very great measure proceed from a multitude of seditious Sermons Pamphlets and Speeches dayly printed and preached with a transcendent boldnes defaming the Person and Government' of Charles I and II, it enacted that to 'imagine invent devise or intend' death or harm to the king is treason, whether by 'Printing Writing Preaching or Malicious and advised speaking'.[34] This curtailment of the liberty of the press and of speech received the royal assent on 30 July, at the same time as *An Act against Tumults and Disorders upon Pretence of Preparing or Presenting Publick Petitions*. This again took its cue from the past and again sought to suppress expressions of hostile popular opinion. It sought to prevent any mobilization of hostile public opinion or pressurizing of parliament by making it illegal for more than twenty persons to sign, and more than ten to present, any petition to parliament 'for alteration of matters established by Law in Church and State', unless the petition had been approved by three or more JPs or by a majority of the Grand Jury of the county, that is, local gentry, magistrates and leaders, who would not look kindly on any challenge to the traditional hierarchy.[35] Ten months later, the Licensing Act re-introduced the pre-publication censorship of all printed material.[36] A similar impatience with popular dissent was expressed by the Quaker Act of 1662. This dealt with the most disturbing of the radicals and their apparent challenge to due legal process by imposing for a first offence a fine of up to £5 and three months' imprisonment, up to a £10 fine and six months in prison with hard labour for a second offence, and either voluntary exile or transportation for a third offence, upon anyone who refused to take an oath or who was part of a gathering of more than five adults assembled 'under pretence of joyning in a Religious Worship not authorized by the Lawes of this Realm'.[37] The desire to reduce the mobility of the 'lower sort' was at least in part responsible for the 1662 Poor Relief Act. On the grounds that persons who moved from parish to parish in search of woodland and common grazing land deplenished parish resources and themselves 'att last become Rogues and Vagabonds', it empowered JPs to return to their previous place of settlement anyone coming to settle in a parish in a property worth less than £10 per annum. JPs could, however, license labourers and cottagers when their labour was beneficial.[38]

While these measures controlled public displays and expression, the Corporation Act ensured that local government would be conducted by persons sympathetic to the new regime. It represented a more drastic toughening of the regime's stance and a more deliberate move away from the spirit of Breda. On many town councils there still remained men who had been elected during the Interregnum and who had been sympathetic to, or active supporters of, one or more of its regimes. The validity of their election was thus open to some challenge, but, more to the purpose, their loyalty to the new regime might be less than complete. To ensure that city and borough councils were run by 'persons well affected to His Majesty and the established government', the Corporation Act, read in the Commons for the first time on 19 June 1661, authorized the appointment of royal commissioners, operating between February 1662 and March 1663, to purge councils of undesirable members by requiring all mayors, aldermen, council members, magistrates and local officials to take the oaths of allegiance and supremacy, to renounce the Covenant and to subscribe a declaration denying it to be lawful to take up arms against the King 'upon any pretence whatsoever' and abhorring 'that Trayterous Position of taking Arms by His Authority against His Person'. Furthermore, no person was henceforth to be elected to public office who had not received the sacrament of the Lord's Supper 'according to the Rites of the Church of England' within the year preceding their election. This was a politically partisan and unprecedentedly systematic and deliberate attempt to purge the political nation of anyone not wholly committed to the new regime. It also extended the process of turning a sacrament into a political test begun by requiring MPs to observe the Prayer Book Holy Communion rite. And since there had as yet been no final settlement of ecclesiastical affairs and the episcopal Church of England enjoyed no legally superior status to other churches and congregations, the Act also shamelessly pre-empted discussions and anticipated settlement favourable to the Cavalier and episcopalian interest.[39] This was of a piece with the Commons' attempt to replace the Convention's Act for Confirming Ministers with an act which would have ejected more Interregnum clergy from their livings. This bill was killed by Clarendon's efforts in the Lords in February 1662,[40] but he was unable to prevent the equally stringent Act of Uniformity from reaching the statute book. The open-mindedness of the *Declaration of Breda* and its toleration of 'liberty of conscience' were now but memories. The most signal mark of the temper of the Cavalier Parliament in the 1660s was its determination through penal legislation to prevent the comprehension of Puritanism within, and to refuse toleration of it without, the established church.[41]

It was chiefly through the Treason Act that the Cavalier Parliament settled the constitutional question left over from the Convention. It did so by very firmly shutting the door on the past. The Convention's Confirmation of Judicial Proceedings Act had recognized as binding the proceedings of courts of law but not the provisions of public enactments. The Treason Act affirmed that there was no obligation from any oath or engagement imposed by the Long Parliament or Rump, that the Solemn League and Covenant was illegal, that there is no legislative authority in a parliament without a king, that the Long Parliament is certainly dissolved and that all 'pretended Orders and Ordinances of both or either Houses of Parliament . . . to which the Royall Assent . . . was not expresly had or given . . . are and soe shall be taken to be null and void'. At a stroke, this put the clock back to 1641: all subsequent legislation passed without the agreement of Charles I or Charles II was annulled. There was hence no need to scrutinize and individually to annul subsequent ordinances since nothing subsequently enacted was legal or binding. The constitutional experiments of the Interregnum, every one and every form of every one, were thereby scrapped without more ado, and certainly without discussion.[42]

While this obliterated the public acts of the Interregnum it also ensured that the reforming legislation of the early months of the Long Parliament was retained. This was a more moderate settlement than some desired, for there were those who wished to reverse the 1641 concessions and to return to the high days of Charles I's personal rule. The prerogative courts and non-parliamentary taxation – the financial and executive agencies of absolutist rule – found no champions. There was no move to restore to the monarch the right to levy ship money, or to reconstitute the courts of Star Chamber and High Commission, and, as we have seen, the crown's feudal rights were abolished. These reforms had enjoyed Hyde's support, and his constitutionalism had no desire to see them undone. However, the more radical measures introduced by John Pym late in 1641 and 1642 did not survive and the 1640 Triennial Act, which had provided for the summoning of a new parliament after a break of three years, if need be 'without any further Warrant or direction from His Majestie', was repealed expressly as a 'Derogation of His Majestyes just Rights and Prerogative inherent to the Imperiall Crowne of this Realme'. The new Act did require that sittings of parliament should be held at least every three years but by dropping the provision for an automatic calling of parliament if the monarch failed to comply with the law it did not derogate from the right of the crown to summon parliament. This bill was passed by the Lords *nem. con.* on 31 March 1664, only two days after the House had received it from the Commons, and the Lords, 'conceiving the said Bill to be a Matter of great Importance', immediately informed the King of its unanimous decision and invited him to come to assent to it as soon as possible. Charles was there five days later not only to assent but to give his hearty thanks for the act, 'For the Act you have repealed could only serve to discredit Parliaments, to make the Crown jealous of Parliaments, and Parliaments of the Crown, and persuade Neighbour Princes that *England* was not governed under a Monarch'.[43] In a similar vein the Militia Act vested sole control of military forces in the monarch by declaring that neither House of Parliament could pretend to the authority to command any military forces.[44] The scare caused by Venner's rising in January 1661 permitted the establishment of a small (*c*.3,000 infantry) standing Army ('his Majesty's Life Guards') under Charles's control. In 1661, as a result of his marriage treaty with Portugal, Charles raised further troops for overseas service in Tangier and the Peninsula. These steps did not recreate the New Model (though many Cromwellian veterans enlisted) but Charles II did have at his disposal a force not available to his father.[45]

This was an impressive body of legislation, much the heaviest of the decade,[46] from which the royal prerogative emerged in robust shape. The crown regained sole control of the armed forces and the discretion to call, prorogue and dissolve parliament. The monarch continued to have sole right to choose ministers, he remained free to determine foreign policy, to appoint all officers of state, to veto legislation and, though this was a disputed area, the prerogative right to suspend statute law or exclude individuals from its provisions. The mere expression of discontent with the monarchy now ran the risk of a charge of treason. Together, these measures clearly signalled the reduction of Presbyterian representation and influence: 103 MPs did vote against the burning of the Covenant, but 228 voted for. That the Presbyterians were certainly no longer Lucy Hutchinson's 'white boys' is indicated by Pepys's opinion that the bill for restoring the bishops to their place in the Lords had not been introduced 'so soon but to spite Mr Prynne, who is every day so bitter against them in his discourse in the House'.[47]

## 3 'The fat *Scriv'ner*'

Rarely can a politician have had such cause for satisfaction as had Clarendon in 1660. Charles had returned without bloodshed at home or indebtedness abroad. Clarendon's waiting game, which had so frustrated more hectic royalists' spirits in the 1650s, was splendidly vindicated. Vindicated, too, was his refusal to countenance binding and submissive leagues with any continental power and his resistance of Henrietta Maria's attempts to bring the Stuarts within the Roman and Bourbon orbit. Nor could the signal failures of the 1650s – the ignominious Scottish venture, the invasion of England – be laid at his door since they had been undertaken against his advice. As the man who, ever since the setting up of the 14-year-old Prince's own court in the west in 1645, had been Charles's chief adviser, strategist and political mentor, Clarendon was the dominant political figure at the Restoration. As Lord Chancellor he was Speaker of the House of Lords, and, elevated to the peerage at the Coronation, he was the councillor closest to the King and the most likely source of patronage: as Dryden, in panegyrical vein, put it, 'The nation's soul (our monarch) does dispense / Through you to us his vital influence; / You are the channel where those spirits flow, / And work them higher as to us they go'.[48]

However, as a commoner and a lawyer Clarendon conspicuously lacked the aristocratic mien of an Ormonde or the *élan* of a Buckingham. His attentiveness to business, his administrative efficiency and his legalistic pedantry attracted a disdain which found these qualities small recommendation at court. This resentment was exacerbated by his manner. His moralizing and contempt for impropriety of any sort, and his tendency to pomposity and to smugness, irritated cavalier spirits: 'He was haughty, and was apt to reject those who addressed themselves to him, with too much contempt'; he had 'too magisterial a way'. That he was overweight, and afflicted by gout, made him a ready target for opponents, who caricatured him as an over-promoted, portly secretary. Charles did recognize his merits, but even with the King his relations were not easy. Clarendon, dismayed by Charles's informality and (often generous) impetuosity, unimpressed by his wit, and appalled by his licentiousness, could adopt towards his monarch the air 'of a governor, or of a lawyer'.[49] His temperament was better suited to the court of Charles I, which is perhaps why that king had selected him as a suitable guide for the heir. He was, however, the very last person Charles II would himself have chosen as friend or adviser. Others pressed in as far more congenial, and herein lay the seeds of disaster.[50] He enjoyed too little factional support at court to counter the widespread animosity which was ready to put the worst construction upon his motives and actions. Eventually, Charles succumbed to it: the restored regime's most laborious servant would be the only one to have to go on his travels again.

It was Clarendon's daughter who first revealed his vulnerability. When, in early October 1660, it became known that Anne Hyde was pregnant she named James, Duke of York, as the father and claimed that they had been secretly married in the Chancellor's own house. Though York denied this, 'she was a woman of a high spirit. She said she was his wife, and would have it known that she was so'. It was soon evident that Anne had spoken no more than the truth and by January 1661 she was publicly recognized as Duchess of York. This clandestine marriage outraged the royal family – Henrietta Maria could hardly be persuaded to meet her daughter-in-law. Clarendon was equally dismayed by this turn of events, but it nevertheless made him the object of resentment and envy since he all too clearly stood to gain by this connection with the royal family. With the King unmarried, Anne was in the way to become Queen of England, and the mother of kings. This was easily construed as ambition in Clarendon to see 'His dear *Clarinda* circled in a Crown' and to found a Hyde dynasty; 'the fat *Scriv'ner* durst begin to think / 'Twas time to mix the royall Blood with ink'.[51] This was more than sufficient ammunition for jealous courtiers and for Henrietta Maria, who maligned both Clarendon himself with charges of conspiracy and his daughter with charges of promiscuity. Even when allowance is made for Clarendon's rhetorical representation of a monarch such as Charles did not always make in life, his account of the interview between the two is all to Charles's credit. 'All the earl of Clarendon's enemies rejoiced' at this episode, as certain 'to raise envy high against him, and make the king so jealous of him' but Charles stood by his Chancellor, while Clarendon himself 'looked on it as that which must be all their ruin sooner or later'.[52]

This affair became embrangled with the King's own marriage. Within a year of the Restoration a marriage treaty was agreed with the Portuguese who offered the Infanta Catherine with the fabulous dowry of Tangier, Bombay, trading rights in the Portuguese empire and £1,500,000. This was undoubtedly a strong incentive to the impecunious court, who were unpersuaded that rival Spanish approaches could equal it.[53] Catherine of Braganza had been brought up in a convent, knew no English and had very little knowledge of English affairs. Nor had she any of those physical features or arts which attracted Charles.[54] Nevertheless, he wrote elatedly of the wedding night in a letter to Clarendon 'the day after their marriage, by which it appeared very plainly, if not too plainly, that the marriage was consummated, and that the king was well pleased with her', and in the month following their marriage on 24 May 1662 he gave every impression of pleasure in his wife.[55] The promised dowry, however, remained largely unpaid and by the summer it had become apparent that, despite Charles's raptures, the marriage was far from happy. These circumstances did not reflect well on those involved in having secured the marriage, but, more disturbingly, its failure to produce an heir strengthened the probability that Clarendon's grandchild would sit on the throne. Though he protested that he had not initiated the match and 'had no other hand in that matter than as a counsellor', this prospect provoked the allegation that, as Burnet reported and Ailesbury believed, Clarendon had contrived the match in the knowledge that Catherine was barren 'on design to raise his own grandchildren'.[56]

Charles would hardly have taken this charge seriously (as Burnet points out, neither Clarendon nor Catherine could have known she would not conceive), but Clarendon's forceful taking of Catherine's side in her argument with Charles over the Countess of Castlemaine certainly strained the relationship between King and Chancellor. Barbara Villiers was the daughter of William Villiers, 2nd Viscount Grandison and a second cousin, once removed, of Buckingham. By the age of 15 she was a famed London beauty and mistress of Philip Stanhope, 2nd Earl of Chesterfield; in April 1659, at the age of 19, she married Roger Palmer, whom she accompanied when in May 1660 he waited on Charles at Breda. The rumours that she was Charles's mistress which began to circulate soon after the Restoration were confirmed by the autumn of 1661. In December Palmer was created Earl of Castlemaine, but the patent's confining the title 'to the males got on the body of this wife, the Lady Barbary' by her husband ensured the extinction of his ennobled line, 'the reason whereof', Pepys drily remarked, 'everybody knows': it was the elevation of the wife which was intended, and her services which had earned it. Humiliated by the King's 'great deal of Familiarity' and 'dalliance' in public with his wife, the Earl left the country in July 1662.[57] 'The night that the bonefires were made for joy of the Queens arrivall', Charles was, reports Pepys, with the Countess at her house in King Street in Westminster, as he had been every night that week, where 'there was no fire at her door, though at all the rest of the doors almost in the street; which was much observed'. There was certainly an expectation in London society that, after his marriage, 'my Lady Castlemayne will keep in still with the King', and so no one supposed that it was her nobility which was at stake when Charles insisted on having the Countess's status recognized by her becoming a part of the royal household as a Lady of the Queen's Bedchamber. When 'the Queene did prick her [the Countess] out of the list presented her by the King, desiring that she might have that favour done her or that he would send her from whence she came', Clarendon took Catherine's side against Charles, arguing the cruelty of thus humiliating the Queen. Opposition, however, proved futile. Charles dismissed Catherine's Portuguese ladies-in-waiting and the friendless Queen received the King's mistress in August. With Charles spending four or five nights a week with her, the Countess now held sway.[58] Pepys thought Charles's stealing from the Countess and returning each morning 'all alone privately' through Whitehall Garden, 'so as the very Centry's take notice of it and speak of it', 'a poor thing for a Prince to do', but there was no need for such indignity after April 1663, when, the King 'having not supped once with [the Queen] this Quarter of a year, and almost every night with my Lady Castlmayne', the Countess finally 'removed, as to her bed, from her house to a chamber in White-hall next to the King's owne'.[59]

Her sway was political as well as sexual. 'At mistress Palmer's lodgings' Charles 'held as it were a court' which his ministers attended, all save Clarendon and Southampton, who refused to do so. Indeed, the Countess received an Irish title because Clarendon, as Keeper of the Great Seal, refused to pass an English patent and the ennoblement had consequently to pass under the Irish seal.[60] In the *Continuation* to his *History of the Rebellion* he registers this disapproval by refusing to recognize her title: she is referred to only as 'the lady', and never named. (Burnet, too, reduces her to 'the mistress' in his *History of His Own Time*.) There was, however, a price to pay for this disdain. Through the Countess's hold over Charles, by whom he was 'bewitched' and whom she 'commands', 'none in the Court hath more the King's eare now then Sir Ch. Barkely and Sir H. Bennet and my Lady Castlemayne, whose interest is now as great as ever'.[61] At this alternative court gathered the opposition to

Clarendon. In May 1663 Pepys was told by Sir Thomas Crew, a Puritan and former member of Oliver and Richard Cromwell's parliaments, that

> the King doth mind nothing but pleasures and hates the very sight or thoughts of business. That my Lady Castlemayne rules him; who he says hath all the tricks of Aretin that are to be practised to give pleasure – in which he is too able, hav[ing] a large ———; but that which is the unhappiness is that, as the Italian proverb says, *Cazzo dritto non vuolt consiglio.* If any of the Sober counsellors give him good advice, and move him in anything that is to his good and honour, the other part, which are his counsellors of pleasure, take him when he [is] with my Lady Castlemayne and in a humour of delight and then persuade him that he ought not to hear or listen to the advice of those old dotards or counsellors that were heretofore his enemies, when God knows it is they that nowadays do most study his honour. It seems the present favourites now are my Lord Bristoll, Duke of Buckingham, Sir H. Bennet, my Lord Ashley, and Sir Ch. Berkely; who among them have cast my Lord Chancellor upon his back, past ever getting up again; there being now little for him to do, and waits at court attending to speak to the King as others do – which I pray God may prove of good effects, for it is feared it will be the same with my Lord Treasurer [Southampton] shortly.[62]

Of these, George Digby, 2nd Earl of Bristol, had opposed Hyde's cautious pursuit of a negotiated settlement between Charles I and parliament and had energetically advocated outright victory in the Civil War to secure an unlimited monarchy. During the Interregnum he became a convert to Roman Catholicism and urged this course on Charles II as a means to secure foreign support. He was flamboyant, lively, a gambler, and scornful of Clarendon. He became a close associate of Henrietta Maria after she returned to England in 1662, and she had no more love than Bristol for the man who throughout the 1650s had opposed her attempts to nail Charles's colours to the Bourbon mast. She 'hated him mortally' was Clarendon's succinctly stated view. Buckingham, the most brilliant of the courtiers, 'studied with all his wit and humour to make lord Clarendon and all his counsels appear ridiculous, and lively jests were at all times apt to take with the king'.[63] Sir Charles Berkeley, afterwards made Earl of Falmouth without, opined Burnet, 'any visible merit, unless it was the managing the king's amours', was 'the most absolute of all the king's favourites'; 'of no good nature' says Pepys.[64] In contrast, the former Cromwellian Antony Ashley Cooper, afterwards Earl of Shaftesbury, did not share the dissolute ways of this bedroom Cabal, but he did recognize the political advantage of what Clarendon called 'a league defensive and offensive' and of having the 'entire trust' of Castlemaine.[65] Sir Henry Bennet, in 1663 created Earl of Arlington, also stands apart as a highly educated, dedicated and skilful politician and administrator. Perhaps for this reason, Clarendon showed himself very wary and suspicious of the man who in October 1662 replaced Clarendon's old friend and colleague

Sir Edward Nicholas as Secretary of State, 'to the satisfaction of his own ambition', while Bennet's post as Keeper of the Privy Purse went to Berkeley, whom the King 'every day loved with more passion, for what reason no man knew or could imagine' commented the perplexed Clarendon.[66] Bennet soon became a close adviser of Charles, taking over from Clarendon the role of intermediary between the King and his wife, and giving rise to rumours that, as Pepys put it in October, 'the young men get the uppermost, and the old serious lords are out of favour'. Clarendon was still Chancellor, but there were now two 'great factions at Court', one clearly in the ascendant: 'none in Court hath more the King's eare now then Sir Ch. Barkely and Sir H. Bennet and my Lady Castlemayne'. 'All the world did judge', observed Pepys in 1663, 'the Chancellor to be falling from the time that Sir H. Bennet was brought in.' Clarendon himself wrote (of 1665) that 'though the king seemed to continue the same gracious countenance towards the Chancellor which he had used ... yet he himself found, and many others observed, that he had not the same credit and power with him'.[67]

There had been a first attempt to dislodge Clarendon in the summer of 1663. In April Pepys heard from Sandwich that 'Sir H. Bennet and my Lord Bristoll and their faction are likely to carry all things before them ... and perticularly against the Chancellor, who he tells me is irrecoverably lost'.[68] Bristol, the prime mover of this attempt to impeach the Chancellor for high treason, presented to the Lords articles of impeachment which had chiefly to do with the furtherance of popery and the accusation that the Chancellor had received a huge bribe for the sale of Dunkirk which, after negotiations through the summer of 1662, had been sold to the French for 5 million *livres* in October, to public outcry at the humiliation of losing an overseas possession, and at losing it to France. As chief minister and agent of the sale Clarendon attracted this criticism.[69] Clarendon, however, was not deserted by the King, who informed the Lords that he knew the charges against his Chancellor to be false. The impeachment failed and Bristol, under threat of arrest himself as a Catholic recusant, had to go into hiding.[70]

Popular animosity soon found another target. Clarendon had been granted a piece of land near St James's Fields where, in Piccadilly, he began in 1664 to build a huge mansion. By Burnet's sympathetic account, 'he intended a good ordinary house, but, not understanding those matters himself, he put the managing of that into the hands of others, who run him into a vast charge of about 50,000*l*. ... it raised a great outcry against him'. To spend three years constructing this residence as London endured the effects of plague, fire and the Dutch war appeared an insensitive, extravagant and triumphalist gesture: 'It was visible that in a time of public calamity he was building a very noble palace'. Soon after construction began it was called by 'common people ... Dunkirke-house, from their opinion of his having a good bribe for the selling of that town'; 'Others called it Holland house, because he was believed to be no friend to the war: so it was given out that he had money from the Dutch'. It focused hostility to the Chancellor, both in such popular displays of discontent as when, in June 1667, 'some rude people . . . cut down the trees . . . and broke [the] windows; and a Gibbet either set up before or painted upon [the] gate, and these words writ – "Three sights to be seen: Dunkirke, Tanger, and a barren Queen" ', and in such coterie attacks as the verse satire (probably Marvell's) 'Clarindon's House-Warming', which repeats the charges of bribery and of disregard for the nation's sufferings.[71]

Charles's libido then again complicated life for his Chancellor. Frances Stuart, 'La belle Stuart', born in 1647, was the daughter of Walter Stuart, a physician in the household of Henrietta Maria, where her beauty attracted the attention of Louis XIV. She was appointed Maid of Honour to Catherine early in 1663 and when, that summer, Pepys saw her, he was moved to write that 'with her sweet eye, little Roman nose, and excellent *Taille*, is now the greatest beauty I ever saw I think in my life; and if ever woman can, doth exceed my Lady Castlemayne.[72] What Pepys noticed, so did Charles, but his advances were refused.[73] Clarendon himself enters the story in early 1667 when Charles investigated the possibility of divorce with, it seems, a view to marrying Frances.[74] When Charles Stuart, 3rd Duke of Richmond (Charles's cousin) himself proposed to her, the King, in seeming condescension but, by Burnet's account as a ruse to gain time, ordered Clarendon to look into the appropriate marriage settlement. If so, it was a ruse which failed, for Frances eloped with the Duke and, without royal permission, they were secretly married on 30 March. Evelyn told Pepys that on her side the marriage was contracted in desperation, 'for it was come to that pass, that she could not longer continue at Court without prostituting herself to the King, whom she had so long kept off'. That summer Pepys heard another story, that 'the Duke of York and Chancellor were jealous of' the King's intention to marry her and, lest Charles should 'wipe their noses of the Crown . . . did do all they could to forward the match with my Lord Duke of Richmond, that she might be married out of the way'. This was the version of events which gained currency and which Burnet recorded: that, to preserve his own grandchildren and prevent any possibility of Charles's marriage to a fertile bride, Clarendon advised Frances Stuart to close with the Duke before such an advantageous opportunity was lost. It was a version which Charles's frustration and anger disposed him half to believe, but when, on 30 August, he satisfied members of 'my Lady Castlemayn's faction' by finally dismissing his Chancellor, Charles had greater cause than personal resentment. Whether or no the King believed either that Clarendon had intervened in his personal life or that he had dynastic ambitions, the humiliation of England's defeat in the Dutch war demanded a scapegoat, and younger, ambitious politicians knew whose time had come.[75]

## 4 The Costs of War

The immediate occasion of the second of the three seventeenth-century wars between the United Provinces and England was England's claim to exclusive trading rights on the coast of Guinea. In 1660 the Royal Company of Adventurers Trading into Africa had been incorporated, with Prince Rupert as its first governor, the Duke of York as his successor in 1664, and such courtiers, Privy Councillors and military leaders as Albemarle, Arlington, Berkeley, Buckingham and Sandwich among its members or 'assistants'. As a royal company, it also, of course, enjoyed Charles's support. This was a formidable array of interest and influence. In 1661 it despatched Sir Robert Holmes to dispossess the Dutch of their holdings in West Africa, action of which the Privy Council approved in January 1662. The Dutch response was to seize Royal Company ships off West Africa and to blockade the Gold Coast. Holmes was then secretly authorized to engage in hostilities against Dutch ships, forts and settlements, resulting in the seizure of African settlements and of New Amsterdam in August 1664. That winter, however, the Dutch Admiral Michael de Ruyter took a fleet south and by February 1665 had recovered nearly all the Dutch African possessions: at the Exchange on the 22nd of that month Pepys, 'among the merchants', heard 'fully the news of our being beaten to dirt at Guiny by De Ruyter with his fleet'. The Royal Company appealed to Charles for aid and, with a bellicose parliament and anti-Dutch feeling running high, on that same 22 February war was declared on the United Provinces.[76]

Led by Admiral Robert Blake the English had gained an emphatic victory in the First Dutch war (1652–4), a victory which added large numbers of Dutch merchant ships to the English fleet and secured enforcement of the provisions of the Navigation Act of 1651. This restricted the English export–import trade to either ships of the goods' country of origin or English ships (thus cutting out the Dutch as handlers).[77] In 1665 there was consequently an expectation both of victory and of profit. In June that year such optimism was encouraged by the English naval victory at the battle of Lowestoft under the Duke of York as Lord High Admiral. However, that victory was less decisive than it might have been because Henry Brouncker, a member of the Duke of York's household, in the Duke's name but without his authority, called off the pursuit of the enemy's ships, which consequently were not taken. In July, Sandwich despatched ships to blockade the Dutch fleet in Bergen, only to have his ships beaten off and for the Dutch fleet to mount an effective blockade of the Thames for three weeks in October. This, rather than the victory off Lowestoft, was the sounder omen. The next year Monck was beaten by de Ruyter in the Four Days' Battle (1–4 June 1666) as a result of the fleet's having been divided between him and Prince Rupert. A year on again, and on 10 June 1667 de Ruyter sailed up the Medway, burnt the English fleet at Chatham, towed away *The Royal Charles* on which Charles had sailed for Dover in 1660, and blockaded the Thames.[78] An enemy incursion of this boldness and the loss of the fleet without its even having fought a battle were an unprecedented ignominy, and one which, following so hard upon the Plague and the Fire of London, offered all too compelling evidence of England's sorry decline since the days of Cromwellian prestige and, as it might seem to some, divine favour.[79] As a guardian of the national interest, the Restoration regime was thoroughly discredited.

This humiliation fuelled the suspicion that from the first the war had been a court expedient to raise funds, and that its dismal failure was due to those funds having been misdirected to improper ends. Supply for the war had been a bone of contention from its commencement. In his speech to the Commons on 24 November 1664 Charles had had explicitly to scotch the idea that were funds granted by parliament he would negotiate a quick peace in order to retain the monies. Parliament made a first, unprecedented grant of £2,500,000, which was succeeded by a further £1,250,000 voted by the Oxford Parliament in 1665, granted specifically for war purposes only. The Commons' response to the subsequent sorry tale of incompetence was in December 1666 to vote for the setting up of a Commission of Public Accounts to examine and inspect the expenditure of former grants.[80] By assuming a right in the Commons to scrutinize royal expenditure, this unprecedented financial audit had clear constitutional implications. Traditionally the crown had been free to manage its own revenue as it saw fit. To investigate how effectively the King's ministers had managed public finances, and to pursue suspicions of embezzlement, was to come perilously close to raising questions about the King's prerogative right to choose his own ministers. It was, Clarendon agreed with Charles, 'such a new encroachment as had no bottom'. 'The court', wrote Burnet, 'was much troubled to see an inquiry of this kind set on foot. It was said the king was basely treated, when all his expense was to be looked into.' Pepys was similarly alive to its political implications when he observed that the 1666 vote for the Commission 'makes the King and Court mad – the King having given order to my Lord Chamberlain to send to the playhouses (and bawdy houses) to bid all the Parliament-men that were there to go to the Parliament presently – this is true, it seems – but it was carried against the Court by 30 or 40 voices'. The challenge felt by the Court party and by Charles is caught in the King's remark, reported by Burnet, that 'he did not wish to be like a Grand Signior, with some mutes about him, and bags of bow-strings to strangle men as he had a mind to it: but he did not think he was a king, as long as a company of fellows were looking into all his actions, and examining his ministers as well as his accounts'.[81]

This irritation had been growing in Charles ever since his return. The poverty of the crown and Charles I's recourse to doubtfully legal means of raising revenue had contributed greatly to the circumstances which produced civil war in 1642. Any secure constitutional settlement needed to make such provision for the King and for his executive duties as would not tempt him again into extreme measures to raise money. In this, the Convention signally failed. Parliament refused to accept any responsibility for the debts which Charles II had inherited from his father, or for those personal debts he had incurred during his exile. Hence, Charles was £800,000 short within a few months of recovering his throne. Parliament continued the traditional distinction between 'ordinary' and 'extraordinary' revenue, thus compelling the crown to seek any additional funding through parliament, a tolerable situation had there been a dependable and sufficient ordinary income, but parliament's provision for the ordinary revenue was inadequate. In September 1660, on the advice of a parliamentary committee of inquiry into the royal finances, the Convention had agreed that the government's ordinary annual revenue should be £1,200,000 and that provision needed to be made to supply about a third of this.[82] The Cavalier Parliament went some way towards recognizing the difficulty when, in the spring of 1661, it passed bills for voluntary donations to the King and for the speedy collection of all tax arrears, and, in the autumn, it agreed a grant of £1,260,000 in respect of royal debts and costs. More durable measures were taken early in 1662 when, in addition to the traditional grant of revenue from customs and excise, it voted Charles II an income from the excise tax on alcoholic liquors established in 1643 and from a new hearth tax.[83] The crudity of the Hearthmoney Act (14 Chas. II c.10) and its indiscriminate imposition of a tax of 2s. per hearth or stove upon all occupiers (falling, if the property were vacant, upon the owner), regardless of their status or wealth, made it deeply unpopular. In June 1662 Pepys reported a general 'Clamour against the Chimny-money' with the threat that 'they will not pay it without force'. Its reliance upon householders' self-assessment of the number of their hearths also made it very inefficient.[84] Neither it, nor the other sources of royal income, yielded the sums anticipated, so that an annual income of £1,200,000 was never achieved. Between 1660 and 1664 crown revenues fell short annually by between £300,000 and £400,000. By 1664 the debt was some £1,250,000. The effects of the Dutch war, the Plague and Fire, then saw the ordinary revenue slump to only £700,000 in total in 1665 and 1666.[85] It was inability to meet the costs of war which compelled the English to conclude negotiations on a peace treaty at Breda on 21 July 1667, conceding the territorial claims of the Dutch in West Africa and Nova Scotia (though New Amsterdam, now New York, was retained) and their demands for compensation and reparation.[86]

A convincing step to regain financial control was taken when, upon the death of the Lord Treasurer Southampton in May 1667, the Treasury was put into commission. This was against the advice of Clarendon, a great admirer of the integrity and loyalty of his old friend Southampton. He would have preferred a peer of similar conservative and traditional character to take over, arguing that commissioners 'were more suitable to the modelling a commonwealth, than for the support of monarchy'. Charles, however, proved in this to be shrewder than his Chancellor. The six commissioners – Albemarle, Ashley, Clifford, Sir William Coventry, Sir John Duncombe and, as Treasury Secretary, Sir George Downing – were able, as a group, to take a much more hardheaded and disinterested view of financial administration than any individual. Their initiative and determination in investigating and reforming the antiquated procedures of the Treasury have been described as 'electrifying', 'galvanizing' and 'dramatic' in their effect, and as having laid the foundations of the modern Treasury.[87] However, the continuing work of the Commission of Public Accounts during the last years of the decade remained a constant reminder to Charles of his financial insecurity, encouraging his inclination to cast envious glances at his cousin in France. That the recovery of his throne had not brought relief from impoverishment, and that he was now as ignominiously dependent upon parliament for supply as he had been upon the largesse of others during the Interregnum, go far to explain the negotiations over the Treaty of Dover with which the decade ended.[88]

## 5 'The old man's going away'

For the humiliation of the war and for what, materially and financially, it had cost the nation, someone had to pay. Clarendon's unpopularity marked him down as the obvious scapegoat for military, administrative and financial incompetence, but it was Charles's final abandonment of the Chancellor whose uncongenial manner had so often tried his patience which sealed Clarendon's fate. Charles had never quite believed in his Chancellor's commitment to the material well-being of the monarchy. In 1660–1 it had been supposed that the figure of £1,200,000 might easily have been £2,000,000 had not Clarendon 'had no mind to put the king out of the necessity of having recourse to his parliament', and Charles was said to believe that Clarendon 'could have raised both his authority and his revenue much higher'. He now blamed his Chancellor for not having prevented the apparent invasion of his prerogative represented by the Commission of Public Accounts. 'The truth is', he wrote to his sister, Henriette-Anne, Duchess of Orleans ('Minette'), 'the ill conduct of my Lord Clarendon in my affairs has forced me to permit many inquiries to be made, which otherwise I would not have suffered the Parliament to have done.'[89] With 'The mistress, and the whole bedchamber... perpetually railing' at Clarendon and with Charles's patience stretched over Frances Stuart, what had for him always been Clarendon's unappealing manner became insupportable when the political advantages of retaining his services no longer outweighed the odium he attracted. When the 'ill conduct' of the war, 'those terrible calamities of the plague and fire of London, with that loss and reproach he suffered by the insult at Chatham, made all people conclude there was a curse upon his government', Charles had need of a decoy. Arlington and Coventry could give Charles good evidence of Clarendon's stultifying effect on, and patronizing attitude to, those seeking to manage public affairs, and the King knew well, as he wrote to Ormonde, that he 'could not retain the Chancellor and do those things in parliament that I desired'. In the summer of 1667 Pepys heard that 'the King doth say that he will have the Parliament meet, and that it will prevent much trouble by having of him out of their envy, by his place being taken away – for that all their envy will be at him'. To Minette Charles wrote: 'his behaviour and humour was grown so unsupportable to myself, and to all the world else, that I could no longer endure it, and it was impossible for me to live with it, and do those things with the Parliament that must be done or the government will be lost'. When, at an interview on 26 August, Charles warned Clarendon that he faced impeachment by parliament, the Chancellor refused to resign. By his own account, as Clarendon crossed the garden at Whitehall after this meeting, 'the lady, the lord Arlington, and Mr May, looked together out of her open window with great gaiety and triumph'. The next day, Pepys heard a version of the same story, 'how this business of my Lord Chancellors was certainly designed in my Lady Castlemaine's chamber, and that when he went from the King on Monday morning, she was in bed (though about 12 a-clock) and ran out in her smock into her Aviary looking into White-hall-garden, and thither her woman brought her nightgown, and stood joying herself at the old man's going away'. On 30 August Charles sent Secretary Morice with a warrant to require of Clarendon the Great Seal.[90]

'The Chancellor believed that the storm had been now over', but this was far from the case. Rather, his weakened position encouraged further hostility. When parliament, having been summoned for 25 July, was four days later prorogued until 10 October, it was upon Clarendon that disgruntled MPs, put to the expense and trouble of a needless summer journey to London, vented their discontent. On 15 October Lords and Commons presented the King with an address of thanks for his removal of his Chancellor, and Charles in reply undertook never again to employ him 'in any publick Affairs whatsoever'.[91] The first parliamentary attack on Clarendon came on 26 October, and on 11 November it was agreed in the Commons by 161 votes to 89 that there was cause for impeachment.[92] Despite this convincing vote, evidence of wrongdoing was not to be had, as Clarendon, with his customary rectitude, knew it would not be. The Commons could offer to the Lords only 'a general impeachment . . . without any special matter' and Clarendon was more than ready to be brought to trial to demonstrate its speciousness. He refused enticements to flee the country and adjured his friends to disown him were he to be found guilty of any corrupt practice. What was driving the impeachment process was the ambition of younger politicians frustrated by Clarendon's monopoly of power and encouraged by Buckingham (who spent a month in the Tower in the summer of 1667 for fomenting opposition). Coventry, who did not believe Clarendon to be corrupt, nevertheless considered him unfit for office on the grounds that, as he explained to Pepys in September, while Clarendon 'was so great at the Council-board and in the administration of matters, there was no room for anybody to propose any remedy to what was amiss or to compass anything, though never so good for the Kingdom, unless approved of by the Chancellor'.[93]

The determination of the Commons to proceed was not, however, matched by the Lords, who on 20 November confirmed their resolution of 14 November to reject the Commons motion for impeachment, though the minority of 28 (which included Buckingham) entered their dissent in the journal. The majority acted less out of sympathy for Clarendon than from self-interest. Pepys heard that 'this stiffness of the Lords is in no manner of kindness to my Lord Chancellor... but that they do fear what the consequence may be to themselfs should they yield in this case'. Their lordships, reports Burnet, 'thought that a general accusation was only a clamour, and that their dignities signified little if a clamour was enough to send them to prison'. The Derbyshire MP John Milward recorded in his diary that the Lords feared that 'if a Peer may be committed upon a general impeachment the Commons may impeach all the Lords one by one, and so take them all away or leave the House very thin'.[94] The case became the subject of heated debates within the Lords, where peers were 'very high one against another', and between the two Houses. On 29 November the Lords again affirmed that the evidence from the Commons did not justify Clarendon's arrest, which the Commons declared an obstruction of justice on the part of the other House. In this dissension, Clarendon was persuaded that it was in the best interest of both the King and of parliament, as well of himself and his family, for him to withdraw himself. On the night of 29–30 November he took ship secretly for France.[95] When this was reported to the Commons on 3 December his opponents of course interpreted it as a confession of guilt and the House ordered to be burnt by the public hangman as scandalous and seditious his letter from Calais to the Lords protesting his innocence and that he had not left the kingdom 'for fear, or out of any consciousness of guilt, but only that he might not be the unhappy occasion of any difference between the two houses, or of obstructing public business'.[96] On 18 December the Commons passed a bill banishing him from all English dominions and making it a treasonable offence to correspond with him. It passed in the Lords the next day.[97]

Clarendon was, after Charles himself, the dominant political figure of the 1660s. He stood out against the corrupt, the disorderly and the unconstitutional, but his was a lonely voice and, as the administration's first minister, it was precisely with court indulgence, executive mismanagement and arbitrary government that he came to be identified. It was his opposition to despotic and baroque tendencies which strained his relationship with Charles and isolated him from the court and the Castlemaine coterie, who found him tedious and pompously moralistic, pedantic in his appeal to legalities ('the Chancellor had been bred of the gown' he says of himself), and risible in his regard for tradition. Evelyn, who declared Clarendon 'my particular friend on all occasions', remarked that he 'kept up the forme & substance of things in the nation with more solemnity than some would have'.[98] This is writ large in his *History of the Rebellion.* Its shapely Ciceronian periods would have been old fashioned even before the Civil War: in the age of Locke they recall Richard Hooker. Their assured rhetorical patterning is at odds with the disharmony of the decade, and with the experience of the Chancellor himself; they articulate an ideal of harmony and order which, for all the Chancellor's efforts, the decade would not restore to England.

# 5

# *Fathers in God: The Church of England*

## 1 The Worcester House *Declaration*

Public England in 1660 was joyous, and episcopalian England was most joyous of all. Not for a moment did anyone doubt that the restoration of kingly government in the state would be accompanied by the restoration of the government of bishops in the church. There was, however, something of a question over the exact nature of the restored episcopal church, just as there was over the nature of the restored monarchy. A delegation of Presbyterian ministers was despatched to Breda to welcome Charles, but the Presbyterians who had chiefly effected the Restoration took no prior steps to safeguard their own religious future. Charles's return was as unconditional in ecclesiastical matters as it was in constitutional: the Convention no more prescribed a church settlement than it did a political one. This was no cause of dismay to Baptists, Quakers and many Independents, who suspected any Presbyterian inclination towards a treaty with the King as likely to impose upon them a uniformity as intolerant as the episcopalian. While the Presbyterians hoped for a church settlement sufficiently broad to include (or *comprehend* in contemporary terminology) them within the national church, these congregational and radical groupings looked for toleration (or *indulgence*) to worship independently.

For six months or so the signs were promising for supporters of comprehension at least. The *Declaration of Breda* had sounded as conciliatory a note in religious matters as in political, and there was every indication that, in recognition of what the Restoration owed to Presbyterian opinion and of the continuing Puritan inclinations of a large part of the population, the national church would be established on sufficiently broad terms to allow it to accommodate both episcopalian and Puritan opinion: 'Some plain and moderate Episcopal Men thought of Reconciliation and Union with the . . . Presbyterians; yea, and a Reward to the Presbyterians for bringing in the King'.[1] Preliminary discussions between these moderate episcopalians and Presbyterian divines appear to have begun as early as March 1660. On 25 April, on the eve of the Restoration, John Gauden, afterwards Bishop of Exeter, met the Presbyterians (or, as they would have preferred to be known, 'Reconcilers')[2] Richard Baxter and Thomas Manton at the house of Nicholas Bernard, formerly chaplain to James Ussher, Archbishop of Armagh. Their discussions were sympathetic to a form of moderate, or 'primitive', episcopacy, such as that proposed by Ussher as a basis for church union in the 1640s.[3] This greatly reduced the size of episcopal sees and limited the authority of bishops by associating it with presbyters and restricting it to a single church, with a merely presidential role over other churches. In the spring of 1660 there seemed every likelihood that this conception of *episcopus praeses*, rather than '*Episcopus Princeps*; indued with *sole* Power both of *Ordination* and *Jurisdiction*', would prevail. Baxter, with the Smectymnuan Edmund Calamy and Gauden chosen to preach at the opening of the Convention, 'told them it was easy for moderate Men to come to a fair Agreement, and that the late Reverend Primate of *Ireland* and my self had agreed in half an Hour'. These words prompted 'many moderate Episcopal Divines' to seek him out to ask 'what those Terms of our Agreement were', 'and we agreed as easily among our selves in private, as if almost all our Differences were at an end'.[4] Gauden was the dedicatee of John Lloyd's *Treatise of Episcopacy* (1661), which preferred 'Ignatius' episcopacy' to 'the English diocesan frame' and he was himself the author of the moderate *Slight Healings of Publique Hurts* (1660). And Baxter was fond of repeating that Morley then opined that no one had written better of episcopacy than Baxter in his *Five Disputations of Church Government* (1659), which had argued for 'reduced episcopacy'.[5]

The restored regime fully supported this tendency towards reconciliation. Morley was despatched to England by Hyde in March 1660 and engaged in discussions with William Bates and other Presbyterian divines, including Baxter, whom he sought out as 'a Moderate Orthodox Man'. In April, Charles himself expressly encouraged Morley to have 'frequent conferences' with the Presbyterians, 'that if it be possible, you may reduce them to such a temper, as is consistent with the good of the Church'.[6] Following the King's return, 'for the Gratifying and Engaging some Chief Presbyterians, that had brought in the King; by the Earl of *Manchester*'s means' a number, including those involved in continuing meetings to discuss the governance of the restored Church of England, were appointed chaplains to Charles.[7] When Charles learned of these contacts from Lord Broghill (afterwards Earl of Orrery), he 'took it very well, and was resolved to further it'. At a personal audience with Baxter, Reynolds, Calamy, Simeon Ashe, John Wallis, Thomas Manton and William Spurstowe at the lodgings of Edward Montagu, 2nd Earl of Manchester (now Lord Chamberlain), attended also by Hyde and Henry Jermyn, Earl of St Albans, Charles heard from the Presbyterian ministers (and in particular from Baxter) a protestation of their loyalty and of their detestation of Cromwell's usurpation, a plea that he should not be misled by misrepresentations of them as factious and fanatical, and a reassurance of their desire for a comprehensive church settlement. He

> gave us not only a free Audience, but as gracious an Answer as we could expect: professing his gladness to hear our Inclinations to Agreement, and his Resolution to do his part to bring us together; and it must not be by bringing one Party over to the other, but by abating somewhat on both sides, and meeting in the Midway; and that if it were not accomplished, it should be long of our selves, and not of him: Nay, that he was resolved to see it brought to pass, and that he would draw us together himself.[8]

As a result of this meeting, proposals for a settlement were invited from the Presbyterian side. Drawn up during the early summer, these focused on church government, 'for that was the main Difference: if that were agreed there would be little danger of differing in the rest', with some recommendations touching liturgy and worship. Doctrinal differences were never raised as a threat to church unity. The Presbyterians proposed, in church government: the model of reduced episcopacy drawn up by Ussher, 'without a Word of alteration . . . that the World might see . . . that we pleaded not at all with them for *Presbytery*, unless a *Moderate Episcopacy* be *Presbytery*'; in liturgy: that the Prayer Book should be subject to revision by a group of 'Learned, godly, and Moderate Divines of both Perswasions', before being re-imposed; and, in ceremonies: that disputed incidentals, such as the use of the cross in baptism and kneeling to receive the sacrament, should not be imposed but left to the individual conscience.[9]

These were remarkably moderate and restrained propositions but they conflicted with two convictions of growing influence among episcopalians: first, that diocesan episcopacy (or prelacy) was essential not merely to the well-being but to the being of the church, no less than monarchical rule by a single person was essential to right order in the state; secondly, that submission to that authority, leading to uniformity in religious observance, was the mark of a Christian state.[10] The episcopalians did agree to the revision of the liturgy 'by such discreet Persons as his Majesty shall think fit', but it was with some justification that Baxter nevertheless characterized their reply to the Presbyterian proposals as a 'Paper of bitter Oppositions', for it contrived to associate the case for moderate episcopacy with the sedition of the Interregnum, with democratic anarchy and with discontent at the restoration of monarchy. It expressed surprise that anyone should claim that 'Administration of government by one single Person' was to be avoided in the church for fear of partiality and corrupt practices when such an idea, 'if applyed to the Civil State, is a most dangerous Insinuation'. Lest the point be missed, the reply went on:

> we verily believe what Experience and the Constitutions of Kingdom, Armies and even private Families sufficiently confirmeth (in all which the Government is

> administered by the Authority of one single Person . . . ) that the Government of many is not only most subject to . . . Evils and Inconveniencies, but more likely also to breed and foment perpetual Factions both in Church and State, than the Government by one is or can be.

In short, 'No bishop, no King'. Any suggestion that individuals might vary ceremonial practice was similarly rejected as a licence to question and challenge the competence of properly constituted authority. That some ceremonies were queried is occasioned less by the practices themselves than by 'the unsubduedness of some Mens spirits' which are 'more apt to contend, than willing to submit their private Opinions to the Publick Judgment of the Church'. It is not the business of conscience to pretend to arbitrate between an individual and ecclesiastical law but to submit to 'lawful Authority' in church as in state.[11]

Nevertheless, political opinion continued more sympathetic. Debates in the Commons in July and August showed a willingness to consider moderate or 'primitive' episcopacy, and on 4 September the House felt able to pass the Act for Confirming Ministers which recognized the legitimacy of non-episcopal orders and imposed no liturgical or ceremonial test upon ministers. There were some ejections as a result of this act, but by far the majority of Interregnum clergy were confirmed in the livings they had held in the Cromwellian church.[12] The Convention was not, however, confident of its competence in ecclesiastical matters and, following debates on 9 and 16 July, on 20 July it had referred the matter to the King and such divines as he should appoint. The government undertook to forward this motion: in his speech at the adjournment of the Convention on 13 September, Hyde spoke for reconciliation and compromise and promised a royal declaration on religion.[13] A first draft of this declaration had been received by the Presbyterians on 4 September. A meeting to discuss and revise this draft, at which the King was present, was held on 22 October at Hyde's residence, Worcester House.[14] Baxter left this meeting 'dejected, as being fully satisfied that the Form of Government in that Declaration would not be Satisfactory', but three days later he 'met the King's Declaration cried about the Streets, and I presently stept into a House to read it', whereupon he found, to his surprise, that 'the Terms were (though not such as we desired, yet) such as any sober honest Ministers might submit to'. It provided for 'the advice and assistance of presbyters' in ordination and the exercise of episcopal jurisdiction; the appointment of suffragan bishops in large dioceses; the prohibition of 'arbitrary' episcopal power; the calling of a synod to revise the Prayer Book; and the toleration of 'the private consciences of those who are grieved with the use of some ceremonies'. Baxter was 'so much pleased with it' that he gave the Chancellor 'hearty thanks' for the revised Declaration.[15]

This moderation was matched by the episcopal consecrations of the autumn. The government had delayed filling the bench of bishops during the summer and now that it moved to do so it included men of known moderation. By 1660, 17 of the 26 English and Welsh sees were vacant.[16] Earlier in the summer offers of preferment to a number of Presbyterians seemed to confirm the goodwill of the restored regime: the bishoprics of Hereford, Norwich, and Coventry and Lichfield were offered to Baxter, Edward Reynolds and Edmund Calamy respectively and the deaneries of Rochester, Coventry and Lichfield, and York to Thomas Manton, William Bates and Edward Bowles.[17] Only Reynolds accepted, but the episcopalians consecrated in October and December 1660 and in January 1661 included such men as Gauden, John Hacket, Humfrey Henchman, Robert Sanderson and Nicholas Monck.[18] These were not men identified with 'the prelatical party', the 'high episcopal men', the 'Laudians', as they were variously styled. Gauden had demonstrated his commitment to a comprehensive church settlement and Sanderson excelled in precisely that practical and casuistical divinity which the Puritans especially valued.[19]

If, during the summer, the Presbyterians thus seemed to have good cause to anticipate a church settlement sufficiently broad to accommodate them, developments in the autumn augured less well. Parliament was adjourned the day Charles signed Prynne's bill (13 September), so there could be no further legislative progress for some weeks. There were divisions in the Presbyterian ranks, between the Baxterians and those committed to a strict Presbyterian church polity, who declined to sign *The Humble and Grateful Acknowledgment of Many Ministers . . . to his Royal Majesty for his . . . Late Declaration concerning Ecclesiastical Affairs* 'because their thanks would signifie an approbation of Bishops, and Archbishops which they had covenanted against' in the Solemn League and Covenant.[20] The Independents were put out that they had not been represented at the negotiations and dismayed that there was no word of toleration for those of congregational views (including the Baptists) who had no interest in a national church and could not accept the terms of the *Declaration*. In response to their petitions, Hyde had raised the question of toleration for those outside the established church during the Worcester House meeting and Baxter had felt obliged to speak against any toleration which might 'secure the Liberty of the Papists'. This would long rankle with the Independents.[21]

More significantly, while the legislative process was stalled and ominous divisions were appearing in the Puritan ranks, restoration of the episcopal Church of England was taking place at grassroots level without any direction or sanction from central government and regardless of the discussions in London. Not until 30 July 1661, when by the Treason Act all acts and ordinances of parliament which had not received the royal assent were officially declared void, was it clear that laws forbidding the use of the Prayer Book were no longer in force.[22] That, however, was the popular (and clerical) assumption long before this. Some ministers, like Clement Barksdale in

Gloucestershire, resolved as early as May 1660 on use of the Book of Common Prayer. By the summer this was possible for many of those who, like Evelyn, had attended illicit Church of England services in London during the Interregnum, when, in the Old Testament imagery which nonconformists after 1662 would apply to their plight, the church was 'in Dens & Caves of the Earth'. Under 8 July 1660 Evelyn wrote that 'From hence forth was the *Liturgie* publiquely used in our Churches, whence it <had> ben for so many Yea<r>es banish'd'. On 1 July Pepys heard 'a good sermon' in Westminster Abbey 'but no Common Prayer yet', which implies the expectation that he soon would hear it. On 5 August he went to St Margaret's, Westminster, 'where the first time I ever heard Common Prayer in that church'. Not until 4 November did Daniel Milles, minister of Pepys's parish church of St Olave's, Hart Street, 'begin to nibble at the Common Prayer by saying "Glory be to the Father", &c after he had read to two psalms. But the people have beene so little used to it that they could not tell what to answer.' A week later, however, he 'did... begin to read all the Common Prayer, which I was glad of'.[23]

This tendency received at least implicit encouragement from the King. Charles had told the Presbyterian delegation at Breda 'with some warmth, that, whilst he gave them liberty, he would not have his own taken from him', that he 'would never in the least degree discountenance the good order of the Church in which he had been bred by his own practice' and that, believing the Prayer Book liturgy to be 'the best in the world', he would have 'no other used in his own chapel'. In the royal chapel at Whitehall the organ had been restored and was being played by mid-June; by the beginning of July, the choristers were wearing surplices. This reflected the Laudian inclinations of Brian Duppa, Lord Almoner, and Bishop of Salisbury, and of Gilbert Sheldon, then Dean of the Chapel Royal, but these practices were swiftly adopted throughout the capital. On that same 4 November when Milles began to venture on the Prayer Book liturgy, Pepys heard the organ play for the first time in Westminster Abbey. By the end of 1660 this had become such an attraction that the crowds wishing to hear it caused 'great confusion'. Organs were similarly restored, as were cathedral interiors, throughout the provinces; Pepys found that at Rochester 'now a-tuning' in April 1661. When, in July 1661, he visited the chapel of King's College, Cambridge, he was struck by 'the schollers in their surplices at the service with the organs – which is a strange sight to what it used to be in my time'. Without waiting for the outcome of discussions in London, the sounds and sights of the national church abolished in 1645 were gradually returning through the summer and autumn of 1660. As they did so, the negotiations in London became increasingly isolated from the ecclesiastical state of the nation. 'The poore *Church* of *England*' which only a year before had appeared to be 'breathing as it were her last, so sad a face of things had over-spread us', was now revived in fact, if not yet in law.[24]

Similarly, the Church of England's government and clergy were re-establishing themselves without waiting on central authority or the formulation of a national policy. Cathedral chapters were reconstituted in response to pressure from clergy seeking positions, the surviving bishops reclaimed their sees as of right, and the consecrations of new bishops were untroubled by questions about the nature and extent of episcopal authority. Though they were at first hardly received with popular acclaim – seeing five bishops 'all in their habitts' at the consecrations on 4 October 1660 in Westminster Abbey, Pepys remarked that 'at their going out, how people did most of them look upon them as strange Creatures, and few with any kind of love or Respect' – there were already signs of confident assertiveness in the extolling of the highest prelatical notions. John Sudbury's *Sermon* on the occasion, a celebration of 'the Dignity and pre-eminence, the Power and Authority' of the bishop's office as no less crucial to the stability and well-being of the church than monarchy to that of a kingdom, left no doubt that the restrictions of episcopal power proposed in the *Declaration* were far from the thoughts of those present.[25]

These developments were outrunning Charles's conciliatory policy and the aspirations of Worcester House. When parliament reconvened on 6 November the combination of disunity among the Presbyterians, a grassroots revival of the Church of England at parish level, revitalized episcopalian MPs returning from their constituencies and the increasing confidence of the replenished bench of bishops had quite changed the ecclesiastical temper. When the motion to pass the *Declaration* into law was put on 28 November it was lost 183–157. It was the crucial moment: after this vote, the exclusion of Puritan opinion from the established church was only a matter of time. 'So there', wrote Marvell in a letter, was 'an end of that bill and for those excellent things therein.' As a later satirist – perhaps Marvell again – put it: 'Then Bishops must revive, and all unfix, / With discontent to content twenty six'.[26] Baxter had feared that the *Declaration* 'was but for present use, and that shortly it would be revok'd or nullified' and that apprehension now seemed justified. Burnet was convinced that Sheldon was from the first determined wholly to exclude Puritan opinion from the established church, but Baxter's final judgement rejected the notion that 'nothing but Deceit and Jugling was from the beginning intended', holding rather that 'when they came in, it was necessary that they should proceed safely, and feel whether the Ground were solid under them, before they proceeded to their Structure'.[27]

## 2 The Act of Uniformity

The vote of 28 November 1660 was the turning-point. Not only was Presbyterian representation in the Cavalier Parliament which met on 8 May 1661 reduced to about fifty members,[28] but during the winter any lingering concessionary inclinations towards the Puritans had been rudely discredited by 'some discontented schismaticks' who, on 6 January 1661, had 'raised a small rebellion in London'. Thomas Venner's Fifth Monarchist uprising was indeed a 'small rebellion', involving perhaps fifty people who were quickly overcome, but its suddenness and bloodiness did much to convince apprehensive royalists and episcopalians that this was what could be expected from Puritans of any stamp.[29] In vain did Quakers and Baptists dissociate themselves from the uprising.[30] Throughout 1660 Secretary of State Sir Edward Nicholas had been receiving reports of 'wicked and disaffected persons . . . termed Quakers', 'great store of anabaptists and quakers . . . in every corner of the country' and of regular meetings of over 1,000 at Bristol 'to the great affrighting of this City'. Venner's rising merely confirmed what he and the government already supposed they had good reason to believe: that 'under the spetious pretence of Religion & piety' enthusiasts hid 'their horrid designes'. A royal proclamation of 10 January forbade meetings of 'Anabaptists, Quakers and Fifth Monarchy men, or some such like appellation' held 'under pretence of serving god', and upwards of 4,000 Quakers and Baptists were swiftly gaoled.[31] That any form of religious dissent was but a hypocritical cloak for rebellious sedition and political subversion was the firm conviction of the great majority of members returned to the Cavalier Parliament, men whose royalism had been further stirred by the coronation of Charles II, with full episcopal splendour, on St George's Day, 23 April.[32]

Convinced that any toleration of Puritanism was likely to lead to disorder, the majority of the members of the Cavalier Parliament refused to tolerate any dissent from, or diminution of, the episcopal ideal. It was, after all, fidelity to the Church of England which had inspired Charles I's martyrdom. Both his memory and the security of the realm required a return, without qualification and without exception, to full-blown prelacy. MPs promptly voted to have their members receive the sacrament according to the Prayer Book rite, to have the Solemn League and Covenant burned, and to restore the bishops to the Lords.[33] The bishops took their seats at the start of the second session in November; earlier, in May, Convocations of the clergy had been summoned to meet in York and London and there were soon increasing signs that the church hierarchy, now firmly re-established, shared the proclivities of MPs.[34] Consequently, although the Savoy Conference was convened on 15 April 1661 to discuss Prayer Book revision, as promised in the *Declaration*, it was not in the conciliatory and constructive spirit envisaged; still less was it a meeting of equal parties. What had, in 1660, been proposed as a conference between equals was, six months later, something very different: the twelve Presbyterians were from the first on the defensive, pressed into the role of suppliants requesting changes in what was assumed to be the established order.[35] 'We spoke to the Deaf' was Baxter's summary conclusion, and 'could prevail with these Prelates and Prelatical Men, (after so many Calamities by Divisions, and when they pretended desires of Unity), to make no considerable Alterations at all' to the Prayer Book. Baxter's own inexpert negotiating skills seem, however, to have helped to close the episcopal ears. He took upon himself the main management of the Presbyterian case, but by the comprehensiveness and minuteness with which he presented it, caused only irritation and impatience. Morley wrote that the delegates were 'tending to an amicable and fair compliance, which was wholly frustrated by Mr Baxter's furious eagerness to engage in disputation'. Izaak Walton recorded that even the 'patient' Robert Sanderson, Bishop of Lincoln, was moved to expostulate 'with an unusual earnestness' at Baxter's '*pertinacious confidence and less abilities*'. Clarendon similarly blamed Baxter for the breakdown of the conference.[36] With the collapse of the Savoy Conference the revision of the Prayer Book was taken over by the Canterbury Convocation. Although Baxter bitterly stated that the result was a book 'more grievous than before' the revisions in fact showed some responsiveness to the Presbyterian exceptions raised at the Savoy. There were grounds for the claim in its preface (written by Sanderson) that it was a moderate document tending 'to the preservation of Peace and Unity in the Church'.[37] This could not, however, be said of the Act of Parliament to which it was attached.

On 25 June, even as the Savoy Conference was in session, the House of Commons appointed a committee to look into the legislation which had abolished church courts in 1641 and the laws relating to the liturgy. It was charged with drafting a bill to ensure future uniformity of practice in worship and conformity to the liturgy of the Church of England.[38] Bills repealing the 1641 legislation and for uniformity of worship were passed by the Commons in July, but the latter was not taken forward by the Lords.[39] This uniformity bill was comparatively lenient, requiring only the use of the Prayer Book, but by the spring of 1662 it had become an altogether more stringent measure. It was a severely revised uniformity bill which finally passed from the Commons to the Lords on 13 March 1662 and received the royal assent on 19 May, one which, far from holding out the hope of comprehending the Presbyterians within the national church, was generally expected, wrote Pepys, to 'make mad work among the presbyterian ministers'.[40]

The preamble to the *Act for the Uniformity of Publique Prayers and Administration of Sacraments* (14 Car.II c.4) made clear both the political incentive behind the statute and the shaping effect upon it of the events of the Interregnum.[41] It began by looking back approvingly to the 1559 Elizabethan Act of Uniformity (1 Eliz. c.2) and asserted that it was 'the great and scandalous neglect of ministers' of its prescribed liturgy and the determination of many 'wilfully and schismatically' to refuse to attend their parish churches which had created the 'Factions and Schisms' which caused such 'great mischiefs and inconveniences during the time of the late unhappy troubles'. It affirmed that 'nothing conduceth more to the setling of the Peace of this Nation . . . nor to the honour of our Religion and the propagation thereof then an universall agreement in the Publique Worshipp of Almighty God'. Uniformity of worship, that is to say, safeguarded the political nation as much as it inspired religious devotion. As Richard Allestree put it in a 1662 *Sermon . . . on . . . the Anniversary of His Sacred Majesty's Most Happy Return*,

> when men once depart from Uniformity . . . why may not divisions be as infinite as mens phansies? . . . It is *one God, one Faith, one Worship* makes *hearts one.* Hands lifted up together in the Temple they will joyn and clasp: and so *Religion* does fulfill its name *a religando*, binds Prince and subjects all together; and they who thus do *seek the Lord their God*, will also *seek David their King.*[42]

On these grounds and to this end the Act required every minister henceforth to use the Book of Common Prayer in places of worship, and only the Book of Common Prayer, and never to pray or preach without it. All other forms of worship were outlawed. Every beneficed clergyman was required on a Sunday before St Bartholomew's Day in his church 'openly and publiquely before the Congregation there assembled [to] declare his unfeigned assent & consent to the use of all things' prescribed and contained in the Book of Common Prayer. Any man who neglected to do so was *ipso facto* 'deprived of all his spiritual promotions'. Such a declaration had in future to be made before any minister could be admitted to a living. Incumbents had further to subscribe a declaration of the illegality and invalidity of the Solemn League and Covenant and to renounce the taking up of arms against the king. And finally the Act broke decisively with England's history since the Reformation by recognizing the validity only of episcopal orders. Any incumbent not episcopally ordained by Bartholomew's Day was deprived.[43]

Taken together, these provisions were far more rigorous than the old Elizabethan Act, which had not mentioned orders and had required only a general undertaking to use the Prayer Book, not a public approval of every jot and tittle in it. The stringency of the Act was unprecedented, and there was very considerable apprehension at what its effects might be. In June 1662 it was reported to Sir William Compton, erstwhile member of the Sealed Knot group of royalist conspirators and now master of the Ordnance, that Fifth Monarchists and republicans did but stay their hand until the more numerous Presbyterians, having 'tasted the scourge of the Act of Uniformity', joined them in a general uprising. In July, Secretary Nicholas received similar information that Commonwealthsmen were waiting only for Presbyterians to take the lead. Throughout the summer Pepys made anxious entries in his diary. On 22 June he was afraid that 'the Bishops will never be able to carry it as high as they do', and at the end of that month he recorded, 'All people discontented', the fanatics that 'the King do take away their liberty of conscience', and he feared 'the heighth of the Bishops, who . . . will ruin all again'. On 17 August (the last Sunday before 24 August), having heard William Bates's farewell sermon, he wrote: 'I hear most of the Presbyters took their leaves today. And the City is much dissatisfied with it. I pray God keep peace among us and make the Bishops careful of bringing in good men in their room, or else all will fly a-pieces.' On Bartholomew Day itself reports of disrupted services and the ripping apart of prayer books sounded 'very ominous'. On 31 August he prayed 'God preserve us!' since 'discontents ... by reason of the presbyters', rumours of plots and the imprisonments of nonconformists 'bode very ill'. On 3 September, the anniversary of Cromwell's victories at Dunbar and Worcester, and of his death, a rising of 'Fanatiques and the Presbyters' was anticipated. It was with considerable relief that on 30 September Pepys recorded that the Bartholomeans had 'gone out very peaceably and the people not so much concerned therein as was expected'. That same month Secretary Nicholas was relieved to find that all was quiet: many Presbyterians had conformed and London was generally appreciative of the quality of the preaching of the conformist ministers.[44]

Although a very substantial number felt unable to comply with the act and were forced to abandon their livings,[45] the great majority of parish ministers submitted and conformed, as the majority had done during the Interregnum. This is not to imply that to a man the clergy of the Church of England discovered a passionate commitment to the Prayer Book, or even to episcopacy. Many were so committed, but Puritan opinion was not excluded from the established church overnight. Though they might be sharply divided over church order and ceremonies, there was no doctrinal division between conformists and nonconformists, or, at least, no difference any greater than could be found within either camp. In the main, they shared an equal abhorrence both of Romanizers and of fanatics, and in many conformists a Puritan temper remained. Subscription to the Prayer Book was by no means always wholehearted, nor was it always strictly followed. Ralph Josselin, vicar at Earls Colne, Essex, since 1641, subscribed in 1662, but for 20 years maintained only a half-hearted conformity, of the sort Puritans had practised since Elizabethan times. He could bring himself to only intermittent and partial use of the Prayer Book and never wore a surplice. He was the subject of repeated complaints to his diocesan from both parishioners and neighbouring clergy, and was constantly apprehensive of archidiaconal and episcopal visitations. At last, on 16 May 1680, he put on the surplice which, he wrote in his diary, 'I see no sin to use, and shall endeavour to live as quietly as may bee to the end of my race'.[46] Josselin and others like him were able to continue to disregard the strict terms of conformity for the simple reason that the Restoration church lacked the means to enforce uniformity of practice. Ecclesiastical courts were inefficient and could not compel attendance. The church hierarchy might direct and admonish, but there were few sanctions it could apply to bring its clergy into line. On the bench of bishops itself there were men like Gauden and Reynolds who were sympathetic to the nonconformists and who, deeply dismayed by the divisiveness of the Act of Uniformity, connived at non-compliance in their dioceses. Theirs, however, was not the temper of the Primate of All England.[47]

## 3 Comprehension, Indulgence and the Clarendon Code

Although in the 1630s Gilbert Sheldon, consecrated Bishop of London in October 1660 and elevated to the archbishopric of Canterbury in August 1663, had been a member of the moderate and eirenical Great Tew circle of scholars and divines, the Act of Uniformity was his act; to it, and its principle of exclusion, he remained absolutely committed. When, before the royal assent, Clarendon endeavoured to moderate its provisions and, after, to mitigate its effects, he was prevented by Sheldon.[48] To an extraordinary degree, Sheldon came to identify with religious nonconformity all that was threatening to church and state and he bent his endeavours to its extirpation. Religious persecution, coercion of conscience and Sheldon went together:

> 'Tis only a resolute execution of the law that must cure this disease, all other remedies serve and will increase it; and it's necessary that they who will not be governed as men by reason and persuasions should be governed as beasts by power and force, all other courses will be ineffectual, ever have been so, ever will be so.[49]

From this point of view there was a stark simplicity about matters of conscience: it is a political and a religious duty to submit to the law. There could no more be a loyal nonconformist than there could be a sincerely religious one. For Sheldon, the Restoration could be secured only by a future from which nonconformity had been banished, but gentry and law officers proved rather less wedded to high church policies, and less hostile to Puritanism, than the Primate could have wished. The failure of officials to implement penal religious legislation was a constant source of frustration to Sheldon.[50] Even in the Cavalier Parliament itself there remained some regard for Puritanism and a less than total commitment to its harassment, degradation and expulsion from the Church of England.[51]

It was hence never his intention that the Act of Uniformity should purge the established church only to allow alternative religious traditions to flourish outside it. Toleration was no more to his mind than comprehension. Having ejected nonconformity from the Church of England, ensuing penal legislation sought to eject it from England. This was the business of the *Act to Prevent and Suppresse Seditious Conventicles* (16 Car.II c.4) of 1664, passed on the pretext of the incompetent and poorly supported Derwentdale Plot.[52] This reinforced 35 Eliz. c.1 by making generally applicable the provisions of the 1662 Quaker Act. As a remedy 'against the growing and dangerous Practice of Seditious

Sectaryes and other disloyall persons who under pretence of Tender Consciences doe at their Meetings contrive Insurrections' it prohibited any assembly for religious worship or exercise conducted 'in other manner then is allowed by the Liturgy or practise of the Church of England' which was attended by more than five persons not of the same household. In short, it prohibited all but the most private of prayers unless the Prayer Book was used (and regardless of whether the meeting was in fact seditious). Contravention of the Act incurred a fine of up to £5 for a first offence, up to £10 for a second and for a third conviction either a £100 fine or transportation for seven years (but not to either Virginia or New England), whence it was commonly known as 'The Act of Banishment'. The Quaker Edward Billing pointedly recorded an occasion when this sentence was passed on some Quakers and the judge, uncertain where to send them, 'mentioned *Hispaniola* (a place that never yet belonged to *England*) and one that stood by and heard him, said *Oliver did not get that for you*'. Even without such grim farce the ultimate penalty was not easily enforceable, ships' captains and crews on occasion refusing to carry those banished, 'it being contrary to the Lawes of England to transport men without their consent'.[53]

Having, as it hoped, dispersed their adherents, parliament turned to the Bartholomeans themselves, denying them not only ministry but, in effect, any livelihood. The *Act for Restraining Non-Conformists from inhabiting in Corporations* (17 Car.II c.2), or Five Mile Act, of 1665, prohibited ordained men who had not assented to the Prayer Book from coming within five miles of any corporation, parliamentary borough or place where, since the Act of Oblivion, they had ministered, taught or preached, unless they had taken the 'Oxford Oath', so called since the Act was passed by parliament meeting at Oxford while many nonconformist ministers laboured in plague-ridden London. This comprised a declaration of non-resistance repudiating the taking up of arms against the king and an undertaking 'not at any time [to] endeavour any Alteration of Government either in Church or State', upon pain of a £40 fine. There was some demur at such a comprehensive disclaimer, but Sheldon drove the bill forward inveighing against 'tenderness for ill men'. The method of enforcement was as distasteful as the Act's prohibition of any attempt (rather than any *unlawful* attempt) at political or ecclesiastical reform was tyrannical: of the fine, one third went to the crown, one third to the poor of the parish where the offence was committed, and the final third was available to be claimed by any informer whose disclosure had led to the conviction. It was the beginning of a nasty trade.[54]

The First Conventicle Act lapsed on 1 March 1669; its 1670 successor was more stringent in its penalties, more determined to ensure its enforcement and prepared to allocate a still more prominent role to informers (22 Car.II c.1). The Second Conventicle Act empowered any one justice of the peace (the previous act had required two justices to convict) on the evidence of a confession, two witnesses, or merely 'by notorious evidence and circumstance of fact', to convict an accused of attending a conventicle. The simple satisfaction of the justice was to be taken as 'a full and perfect conviction', to secure which he had power to 'break open and enter into any house or other place' where a conventicle was suspected. In any case of dispute, it required its provisions to be interpreted 'most largely and beneficially for the suppressing of conventicles'. While it reduced the penalty imposed upon anyone attending a conventicle, this Act now imposed a £20 fine upon any person permitting their property to be used for a conventicle and a £40 fine upon anyone preaching at one, a £5 fine upon constables and other officers who did not actively pursue offenders and upon those who refused to inform, and a £100 fine upon JPs who did not enforce it. Furthermore, unlike the First Conventicle Act, this Act had no term placed upon it.[55] To those dismayed at the compulsion to inform (it was commonly known as the Informing Act) and the power given to individual justices, the Act appeared to be an erosion of fundamental liberties, 'the Quintessence of arbitrary Malice' as Marvell called it. This case was argued in such anonymous pamphlets as *The Englishman, or a Letter from a Universal Friend* (1670) and *Some Seasonable and Serious Queries upon the Late Act against Conventicles* (1670), which was reported to Secretary Williamson as 'A most seditious Pamphlett', tending 'as much as is possible . . . to the stiring vp of Sedition and Rebellion'.[56]

Despite this body of legislation and the politicking of Sheldon there were yet intermittent attempts to keep the spirit of Breda alive. The declarations of Breda and of Worcester House had already suggested that, whether out of policy, inclination or jealousy of his prerogative, Charles was a good deal less vindictive and a good deal more catholic in religious matters than the hierarchy of the Church of England. On 11 May 1661 he issued a proclamation freeing Quakers imprisoned following Venner's uprising, and on 22 August 1662 another proclamation released Quakers imprisoned for holding conventicles unlawful under Elizabethan statute, and as a direct result of his intervention Quakers sentenced to death were pardoned. George Fox was sufficiently persuaded of Charles's clemency to appeal directly to him as the most efficacious means of securing relief.[57] Following the royal assent to the Act of Uniformity on 19 May 1662, Charles began to explore the possibility of alleviating its effects through the exercise of what he took to be his prerogative right in ecclesiastical matters. However, when Clarendon sounded out the likely response he received only a guarded reply from the Presbyterians who were very wary of ranging themselves against parliament by accepting what might prove unconstitutional means of relief. These misgivings at the monarch's overriding parliament's legislative authority were addressed when, on 26 December 1662, Charles issued what has inaccurately become known as his first *Declaration of Indulgence*. Recalling his promise at Breda of 'a liberty to tender consciences' with the observation that parliament has 'never thought fit' to offer an act for that purpose, and pointing out that the Church of England was now secured through the Act of Uniformity, he proposed 'without invading the freedom of Parliament, to incline their wisdom at this next approaching sessions to concur with us in the making some such Act for that purpose as may enable us to exercise with a more universal satisfaction that power of dispensing which we conceive to be inherent in us'.[58]

This, however, encountered another difficulty: while Independents and Baptists would have welcomed such a toleration, to Reconcilers such as Baxter it conjured up the abhorrent prospect of a permanent schism in the religious life of the nation. Furthermore, there was a deep suspicion that the intended beneficiaries were the Roman Catholics, the 'greatest part of whom', so Charles averred in the *Declaration*, have 'deserved well from our royal father of blessed memory, and from us' and who were not excluded from it. Baxter and the Presbyterians consequently found themselves arguing the same case as Sheldon, and they refused to offer an address of thanks. On these twin grounds – of the exercise of the royal prerogative to overrule parliament and the toleration of popery – the Commons, when they reconvened on 18 February 1663, refused to ratify the *Declaration*. On 27 February the Commons presented the King with an address which foresaw that such a policy would jeopardize the standing of the Church of England and, ultimately, encourage popery.[59] This episode was one of the first indications both that the Cavalier Parliament was prepared to disoblige its King if he threatened to encroach on its rights and that the nonconformists were unwilling to become royal lackeys in order to secure their own relief. When, in 1672, Charles II issued his second *Declaration of Indulgence*, the same parts would be played out, and in 1688 this alliance of nonconformists and their persecutors would be re-established against James II, to far greater consequence.

While the issue of toleration languished, that of comprehension came to life again following the fall of Clarendon in 1667. In one of his finer moments, Buckingham in the autumn of 1667 promoted a scheme for 'a comprehension of such of the dissenters as could be brought into the communion of the church, and a toleration of the rest', which was supported by Arlington, chiefly on the grounds that it would extend to papists. On 21 December 1667 Pepys heard that 'the Nonconformists are mighty high and their meetings frequented and connived at; and they do expect to have their day now soon, for my Lord of Buckingham is a declared friend to them, and even to the Quakers', while 'the Archbishop of Canterbury is called no more to the Caball'.[60] Sheldon's loss of influence was evident in his inability to secure the passage through parliament of an immediate successor to the 1664 Conventicle Act, which lapsed on 1 March 1669, and in his acquiescence in 1668 to the consecration as Bishop of Chester of John Wilkins, Cromwell's brother-in-law and a known supporter of comprehension who enjoyed the favour of Buckingham.[61] The credit which the nonconformist ministers had accrued for serving in the plague-ridden capital stood them in good stead, and throughout 1668 and 1669 their stock was high. For the first time, they dared to build meeting houses.[62] In January 1668 Baxter heard from Thomas Manton that Sir John Baber, physician to Charles II and a nonconformist sympathizer, had indicated that 'it was the Lord Keeper's desire to speak with him and me, about a Comprehension and Toleration'. Orlando Bridgeman had replaced Clarendon as Lord Keeper, and he was a recognized Presbyterian sympathizer. Following negotiations,[63] agreed terms were framed into a parliamentary bill by Sir Matthew Hale, Lord Chief Baron and Baxter's admired friend, but parliament proved unsympathetic. On 10 February 1668 it voted to desire the King to put out a proclamation for the enforcement of the laws against nonconformists and, there being 'a rumour abroad of some Motions or Act to be offered for Comprehension or Indulgence . . . That no Man should bring in such an Act into the House', though in Pepys's view, a comprehension bill was 'much desired by the greater part of the nation'.[64] If so, Charles, rather than the Commons, was in tune with the nation. In the autumn of that year Manton again heard from Baber, this time to the effect that 'the King was much inclined to favour the *Non-conformists*'. About September, Manton and other nonconformists were received at Arlington's lodgings by Charles, who promised that he would 'doe his utmost to get us comprehended within the Publicke Establishment'. Nothing, however, came of this undertaking.[65]

Or, at least, nothing to the nonconformists' purpose. These moves towards the relaxation of religious policy sufficiently alarmed supporters of the established Church of England to rally them to its defence with the cry, reports Burnet, 'that the church was undermined and betrayed'. 'The talk of Liberty', wrote Baxter, 'did but occasion the writing many bitter Pamphlets against Toleration.'[66] The decade ended with a concerted press campaign to kill any initiative towards alleviating the proscription of dissent: Simon Patrick's *A Friendly Debate between a Conformist and a Nonconformist* (1669), the *Discourse of Ecclesiastical Politie* (1669) by Sheldon's chaplain, Samuel Parker, and William Assheton's *Toleration Disapprov'd and Condemn'd* (Oxford, 1670) appeared in quick succession. The ever-ready L'Estrange issued an enlarged edition of his *Toleration Discussed* to fend-off this resurgence of the threat he had dealt with in 1663.[67]

## 4 Laudians and Latitude-men

This hostility towards dissent was particularly marked in one group within the established church. During the Interregnum the aging bishops (by 1658 their average age was 73) had not provided either spiritual or intellectual leadership of the episcopal church in its eclipse, nor had they much stirred themselves about the very survival of the church's orders. There were some ordinations, but no consecrations to bishoprics, much to Hyde's frustration. From his exile he sought to rouse the bishops, but to no avail.[68] In this extremity the survival of the episcopal Church of England came to depend upon the theological, casuistical, homiletic and devotional writing of such younger men as Henry Hammond, Jeremy Taylor and Robert Sanderson. They provided an apologia for the Church of England which, against Presbyterians and Independents, defended the Prayer Book and insisted upon episcopacy as essential to its identity.[69] To a Puritan such as Baxter, this represented a fundamental break with the established church's Reformation heritage. Whereas those he called 'the old common moderate sort' of bishops 'differed not in any considerable points from those whom they called Puritans', taking 'Episcopacy to be necessary *ad bene esse Ministerii & Ecclesiae*, but not *ad esse*; and took all those of the *Reformed* that had not Bishops, for true Churches', the 'other sort', of what he styled the 'New Prelatical way', who began 'in *[William] Laud, [Richard] Neale, [John] Howson, [Richard] Corbet* and *[John] Buckeridge* with *[Richard] Montagu*' and 'followed Dr. *H[enry] Hammond*... held that Ordination without Bishops was invalid, and a Ministry so ordained was null, and the *Reformed Churches* that had no Bishops, nor Presbyters ordained by Bishops, were no true Churches, though the Church of *Rome* be a true Church, as having Bishops'. In his view, though the former 'were more numerous and elder', 'yet Dr. *H. Hammond* and the few that at first followed him, by their Parts and Interest in the Nobility and Gentry, did carry it at last against the other Party'.[70] Certainly, theirs was the view which, in 1662, was legislatively inscribed in the Act of Uniformity.[71] Such insistence upon the necessity, rather than the desirability, of episcopacy, was accompanied by the conviction that schism is the supreme sin, because it was a refusal of authority, a kind of rebellion. Although the Church of England's own separation from Rome was an awkwardness seized upon by nonconformist apologetics, the reply was straightforward: as a national church the Church of England was empowered both to take its own decisions and to require compliance with them. The separation of individuals, or groups of individuals, on grounds merely of private conscience was quite a different matter.[72] Toleration was a licence for anarchy.

Although it was hardly to be realized in the 1660s, the future lay not with these new prelatists but with moderate episcopalians, or, as they were then coming to be called, Latitudinarians, who opposed partisan exclusivity and dogmatism in both theology and ecclesiology. Their ecclesiastical inclination was towards comprehension – Edward Stillingfleet had published an *Irenicum* in 1659 – and their doctrinal towards reasonableness and moderation in the interpretation of the Christian life.[73] No less than the 'new prelatists' they were the product of a reaction to the experience of the Interregnum, but a contrary reaction. The earliest account of their origins in the 1650s explains that, as they were 'in opposition to that hide-bound, strait-lac'd spirit that did then prevail, they were called *Latitude-men*; for that was the first original of the name'. They were, says Baxter, 'mostly *Cambridge*-men, *Platonists* or *Cartesians*, and many of them *Arminians*... ingenious Men and Scholars, and of Universal Principles, and free'. Burnet, writing later, gives a fuller account:

> They declared against superstition on the one hand, and enthusiasm on the other. They loved the constitution of the church, and the liturgy, and could well live under them: but they did not think it unlawful to live under another form. They wished that things might have been carried with more moderation; and they continued to keep a good correspondence with those who differed from them in opinion, and allowed a great freedom both in philosophy and in divinity: from whence they were called men of latitude. And upon this men of narrower thoughts and fiercer tempers fastened upon them the name of Latitudinarian.[74]

From the pulpit of St Lawrence Jewry, John Wilkins, John Tillotson and Benjamin Whichcote successively preached in such a strain, supported by Stillingfleet and Edward Fowler elsewhere in London. In the 1660s they maintained friendly relations with leading nonconformists and were involved in the attempts to reach an accommodation with them in 1667–8. All save Whichcote would succeed to bishoprics in the coming decades, Tillotson to the archbishopric of Canterbury under William III.[75]

While these two traditions differed greatly in their estimate of the importance of episcopacy and in their relations with nonconformists, in their homiletic and pastoral aspects they were remarkably similar. Here, a distinctive bias emerged. Detecting in the 'wilderness years' of the Interregnum divine retribution for the murder of Charles I, sermons in the early 1660s insisted that amendment of life was the only proper response to such a divine mercy as the Restoration. The dates 30 January and 29 May were instituted as perpetual anniversaries[76] with specially composed forms of Morning and Evening Prayer which expressed contrition for the nation's past misconduct and gave thanks that England was delivered from rebellion and tyranny. Sermons on these anniversaries – and especially on 30 January – dwelt on the need to expiate the guilt of the past and to resolve upon renewed religious commitment: the chaos of the Civil War and (as it was presented) Interregnum was as much moral as political; the execution of Charles I was seen both as the epitome of this national falling away and as the clearest expression of divine displeasure. Civil war and regicide were God's chastisement even as they were manifestations of that very turpitude for which punishment was due. While the schismatic and rebellious proclivities of radical Puritans were the immediate causes of the regicide, the nation's indulgence in 'swearing and drunkenness, chambering and wantonness, pride and profaneness' created the circumstances in which it became possible. 'The reformation of our manners', then, 'wil be the properest answer to such a blessing' as the Restoration.[77]

However, Thomas Pierce's adoption of the locution *reformation of manners* intimates that *reformation* is not being used here quite as it would be in Puritan discourse. Pierce is chiefly interested in how people behave, how they comport themselves; their interior lives concern him far less. Subjectivity, that key contribution of Puritanism to our culture, engages Church of England divines very little. We hear far less of *godliness* from them than we do from nonconformists, and far more of *piety, manners, course of life, conversation.* The sermons of the Church of England are concerned not with the processes of conversion, nor with the demands of introspection, nor with the ecstasies and despairs of faith, but with, in the words of Taylor's famous title, *The Rule and Exercise of Holy Living.* Their theological bias was away from the introspective tendency in Calvinism and its predestinarian stress on faith, towards a holiness which was defined largely in terms of duty, orderly devotion and regular religious habits, a spirituality which was neither heady nor enthusiastic.[78] In the place of solifidianism there is a stress on godliness as a way of life, not a mode of being. 'Practice is the nature, and custom the perfection' of the holy life, wrote Robert South.

> For it is this which translates Christianity from a bare notion into a real business; from useless speculations into substantial duties; and from an idea in the brain into an existence in the life . . . The grand deciding question at the last day will be, not, What have you said? or, What have you believed? but, What have you done more than others?[79]

This emphasis was epitomized in what became the definitive work of practical divinity for the episcopal church, *The Practice of Christian Graces, or The Whole Duty of Man* (1658), prefaced by Henry Hammond and almost certainly written by Richard Allestree.[80] Its choice of biblical text is significant: 'we should live soberly, righteously, and godly, in this present world' (Titus 2.12). *Sober* is a key term. In reaction against the experiential and enthusiastic religion of the Interregnum the emphasis here is upon the orderly, the commonsensical and the judicious. The independent or individualistic, the socially disturbing, is eshewed: this Christianity is socially respectable, if not genteel.[81] Generally, there was not much attempt to think through the soteriological implications of this homiletic strain, at least not until George Bull's assault on the doctrine of justification by faith in his *Harmonica Apostolica* (1669), but opponents were in no doubt of its Arminian – even Pelagian – bias, which, they charged, reduced divinity to moralism.[82] This, certainly, was Bunyan's charge against Edward Fowler's *The Design of Christianity* (1671).[83]

There was a clear political dimension to such holy living. The price an established church pays for its privilege is support of the state: ever since the Tudor 'Homily against Disobedience and Wilful Rebellion' the ministers of the Church of England had been expected to inculcate good citizenship, that is, obedient citizenship. The restored episcopal church, however, was still more intimately bound to the state: recent history taught just how dependent it was upon its political masters, and how alarmingly vulnerable: its preservation required the preservation of the state. Where the impulse of Interregnum Puritanism had been revolutionary and disrespectful towards traditions, the impulse of this re-established church was conservative and (at least until pushed too far by James II) deferential. Stability it prized above all else. Religious and political duty consequently now became indistinguishable (just as religious dissent became indistinguishable from sedition): good Christians are loyal subjects. On officially proclaimed fast days for natural disasters or military defeat and on days of thanksgiving for national successes, preachers developed the theme that the well-being of the nation was tied to its political loyalism. God blessed quiescent monarchical states as he visited affliction upon rebellious and republican ones. This was the specific task of preachers on 30 January, when they were required either to read parts of the Elizabethan homily against rebellion or to deliver a sermon of their own composition on this theme. In episcopal discourse, passive obedience became the public and political expression of Christian commitment.

The established church was thus a bulwark of the establishment. A main business of its ministers was to inculcate civic duty and obedience, and of its parishioners to submit themselves to authority. The anniversaries of 30 January, 29 May and 5 November were particular opportunities to promote these ideas, but in truth to go to the parish church was to visit an organ of government at any time of the year. Royal proclamations and acts of parliament, as well as the minister's own declaration of submission to the Act of Uniformity, were read from the pulpit. The building itself represented to the congregation social and political order, with reserved pews for the socially privileged, elaborate funerary monuments testifying to local dignitaries, and mayoral and royal regalia as prominent as religious icons. With the parish church so deeply embedded in the community, the notion of ministerial vocation becomes problematic. For nonconformists it was clearer: ministry involved renunciation and separation; for conformists, it might very well present itself as a means of incorporation and betterment. Incomes were not handsome, but well above average, and the parson could claim to be a gentleman.[84]

There is one other distinctive theme: the fruits of such 'reformation of manners' would be contentment in this world. '*Peace*, and *plenty*, living *securely*, and at *ease*', Pierce assured his auditors, are 'the pleasant *effects*' of such a deliverance as the Restoration.[85] To jeopardize the one is to jeopardize the other; Christian obedience is the way to security and happiness in the political, social and spiritual realms. This is not a challenging religion of renunciation; on the contrary, it was openly self-interested and worldly: 'surely', Tillotson wrote, 'nothing is more likely to prevail with wise and considerate men to become Religious, than to be thoroughly convinced, that *Religion* and *Happiness*, our *Duty* and our *Interest*, are really but one and the same thing considered under several notions'.[86] Texts such as 1 John 5.3 and Matthew 11.29–30 were adduced to argue that the Christian life, though demanding, is neither miserable nor impossibly onerous – the role of suffering, which plays so large a part in nonconformist discourse, is here hardly mentioned. It is hard not to suppose that a comfortable and genteel life beckons the true believer.

## 5 Giant Pope

The 'new prelatists' insistence upon its episcopal nature in their defence of the Church of England against Puritanism carried with it an implication which was potentially alarming. If episcopacy is the distinguishing feature of a true church, then the apostolic succession is fundamental. Since England's episcopal orders derived from Rome's, this was to tie the integrity of the Church of England to that of Rome, and that, as Baxter noted,[87] was to acknowledge the legitimacy of the Church of Rome while denying it to non-episcopal churches. It was the Restoration ecclesiastical settlement which Peter Heylyn had in his sights when in his history of the Reformation, *Ecclesia Restaurata* (1661), he stressed the episcopal continuity of the English church with Rome. Among episcopalians the older Protestant view of the pope as Antichrist might still be argued, as it was, for example, by Henry More in *A Modest Enquiry into the Mystery of Iniquity* (1664), but increasingly it was becoming outmoded. It belonged with the enthusiasts, the intemperate, and the vulgar. Neither Hammond nor Sheldon accepted the identification.[88] No more did such moderate nonconformists as Baxter, but, while Baxter willingly recognized the possibility of true Christian commitment and of salvation within the Roman communion, he was deeply alarmed by what he believed to be the tendency of some of the prelatists' warmer feelings towards Rome. Many committed episcopalians defended the distinctiveness of the Church of England as a national church, but there were those for whom the implication of their high churchmanship was that the Church of England's independence was merely accidental and temporary. Such views revived the fear which Laud's archiepiscopate had generated in the 1630s, that the episcopal hierarchy sought the reunification of Western Christendom under the pope as its patriarch. Following the Restoration, Baxter discerned just such ambitions in Peter Heylyn, whose *Cyprianus Anglicus* (1668) confirmed his worst fears:

> *Heylin* (in *Laud*'s Life) and *Thorndike* (in three late Books) do plainly tell the World, that one Business to be done is, to open the Door of the Church of *England* so wide, by reconciling means, that the Papists might be the easilier brought in to

us, and may find nothing to hinder the moderate sort from coming to our Assemblies . . . and so all notes of Distinction may so far cease.[89]

While the established church was reawakening among nonconformists such suspicions of a drift towards Rome, the political scene was no more reassuring. Charles was suspected of being a Roman Catholic even before the Restoration,[90] and his *Declaration of Indulgence* of 26 December 1662 so increased fears of his pro-Catholic leanings that in his speech at the opening of parliament on 18 February 1663 he had had to address the issue directly, explaining that he intended no general toleration of Catholicism. To mollify anti-papist feeling he issued a proclamation ordering Roman priests and Jesuits to leave the country. That endeavouring to bring in popery should be one of the charges preferred against Clarendon by Bristol was, as Pepys observed, 'my Lord Bristoll being a Catholique himself . . . very strange'; but Bristol knew well enough what parliament would expect of a traitor to England.[91] Tirades against popery, and the introduction of bills to prevent its spread, were a feature of the decade's parliamentary business. There was, furthermore, a pronounced pro-French Roman Catholic faction at court, centred on the Queen Mother and the Duke of York, and including St Albans, Arlington and Clifford, as well as Bristol. As early as February 1661 Pepys records concern that James might eventually succeed because he was 'a professed friend to the Catholiques'.[92] There were fears (hardly compatible) both that the Catholics might not be sufficiently patient to wait for James to succeed in the course of nature and that the Roman Catholic faction, with Charles, were working to agree with Louis XIV means to return England to Roman Catholic allegiance. In 1666, St Albans did indeed begin secret negotiations with France, leading to Charles's agreement for a year not to enter into any alliance contrary to French interests.[93] At the end of the decade he would take a leading part in the negotiations which led to the Treaty of Dover.[94] Nonconformist and Whiggish fears had much to feed them: in a vein very similar to Baxter's, Marvell was to argue in *An Account of the Growth of Popery, and Arbitrary Government* (1677) that there was no less than a concerted design in the state to promote the designs of France and to revert to popery.[95]

With such suspicions abroad, the Fire of London irresistibly incited popular anti-Catholicism. Although the Dutch were suspected, the papists were the favourite scapegoat for the Fire, and particularly French papists. For several weeks afterwards, Pepys feared 'a fatal day . . . of some great mischiefe', probably a papist massacre in the capital to overthrow the Protestant government.[96] Parallels between the fire and the Gunpowder Plot were not confined to 5 November sermons which, in 1666, insisted with more than usual vigour that papist principles and policies remained those of Guy Fawkes. There was even a rumour that the Duke of York himself was implicated, which, though 'with very little appearance of truth', grew says Burnet, 'to be generally believed'.[97] On their title pages, popular accounts of the proceedings of the parliamentary Committee of Enquiry set up to examine the causes of the Fire of London advertised *informations touching the insolency of the Popish Priests and Jesuites, and the increase of Popery.*[98] In November in response to parliamentary pressure following the Fire, a royal proclamation once again banished 'all Popish Priests and Jesuites'. General suspicions appeared to be confirmed when the Enquiry found French Catholics and Jesuits the likeliest culprits and a French Roman Catholic was duly executed.[99] In June 1667, at the nadir of English fortunes in the Dutch war – papists were blamed for the Medway disaster too – Pepys heard people 'talking treason in the streets openly; as, that we are bought and sold and governed by Papists and that we are betrayed by people about the King and shall be delivered up to the French and I know not what'.[100] In the history of early modern English anti-popery the 1660s were a relatively calm decade, but anxiety at what the papists might be about was a distinct thread in the pattern of its insecurity.

# 6

# 'The Patience of Heroic Fortitude': Nonconformity, Sedition and Dissent

## 1 'Fall'n on evil days': Milton and Bunyan

That the seventeenth-century's most influential and enduring works in poetry and in fictional prose were both the product of the Puritan imagination might give us pause for thought, but still more striking is the fact that each is decisively shaped by the 1660s and articulates opposition to the Restoration settlement. *Paradise Lost* and *The Pilgrim's Progress*[1] represent the experience of the Restoration from the point of view of those whose political and ecclesiastical hopes were destroyed by Charles's return. The pairing is not an obvious one, for Milton's world of educational and political privilege had nothing in common with the provincial, largely oral culture which shaped Bunyan. In poetry Milton was heir to Europe's classical and Renaissance tradition, while in prose his had been the authorized voice of the state. He may have shared some of his notions with radical Puritans, and there may be affinities between his emphases and those of Bunyan,[2] but he did not share either Bunyan's Calvinist theology or his cultural temper. 'Brought up . . . in a very mean condition, among a company of poor Countrey-men', Bunyan 'never went to School to *Aristotle* or *Plato*'. He draws on folk culture and has in mind a popular readership. Milton, though he may have allowed the general populace to escape from Samson's destruction, allows them neither political nor cultural authority. There is no place for the 'rude multitude' in the perpetual 'general councel of ablest men' which in *The Readie and Easie Way* he proposed should govern the commonwealth, nor do the vulgar form any part of that 'fit audience' for his epic in whom he anticipated an informed sensitivity to literary decorum and to historical precedent.[3]

In November 1660, however, both men found themselves in prison, Bunyan under the old Elizabethan Act against Conventicles, and Milton by order of the Commons.[4] Bunyan had begun what would prove to be a term of imprisonment lasting over eleven years. Milton was released in December 1660, but, though not in confinement, he continued to live for much of the 1660s, as his friends Andrew Marvell and the Quaker Thomas Ellwood both remarked, 'a private and retired Life', a life in this respect not dissimilar from Bunyan's, and perhaps similar in other respects too, if reports of Milton's impoverishment and miserable circumstances are to be believed.[5] Both were discredited men, marginalized and ostracized, sharing in that larger disappointment which afflicted all who had been committed to the Good Old Cause and to Puritanism.[6] This coincidence of experience leads to the construction of strikingly similar literary personae.[7] In the 1660s Bunyan's texts repeatedly advertise themselves as prison books. The title page of *Christian Behaviour* (1663) identifies its author as 'a Prisoner of *Hope*', and the first edition was subscribed '*Farewel. From my place of Confinement* in Bedford, *this* 17th *of the* 4th *Month*, 1663'. Notifying that, *inter alia*, it will relate what its author 'hath met with in Prison', the title page of *Grace Abounding* attests that the complete text 'was written by his own hand *there*'. Most famously, the 'Denn' upon which the narrator happens as he 'walks through the wilderness of this world' at the opening of *The Pilgrim's Progress* is marginally glossed 'Gaol'.[8] Similarly, despite the very different generic obligations of epic, the narrator of *Paradise Lost* is located in a situation marked by danger, isolation and, apparently, impotence. The opening paragraph of *Paradise Lost* may blazon the exalted Renaissance conviction that it is the business of epic to inculcate religious, moral and political wisdom, but this epic poet is far removed from the cultural and political centres of power which might authorize him to treat such matters: he speaks

> with mortal voice, unchanged
> To hoarse or mute, though fallen on evil days,
> On evil days though fallen, and evil tongues;
> In darkness, and with dangers compassed round,
> And solitude.[9]

These lines may derive from Milton's particularly dangerous situation immediately following the Restoration, when he was in hiding and when he was most vociferously assailed by 'evil tongues'. During 1660 he was variously saluted in print as a 'musty Pedant' whose pen was 'dipt in the blackest and basest venome', a 'base Scribe' and '*Billingsgate* Author', 'wonderfully... stricken blind for his seditious antimonarchism', a 'blind Adder' spitting poison who proves that 'Devils may indue Humane shapes'.[10] However, in fashioning a textual self oppressed by adverse circumstances Milton is not satisfying a straightforwardly autobiographical motive; his business is apologetic. For Milton to insist that in such 'evil days' he sings 'unchanged / To hoarse or mute' is to identify the epic poet with the John Milton of the 1640s and 1650s whom the reader would know 'as the defender of divorce, regicide and the republic'.[11] It is to assert a continuity between that earlier polemical voice and the imaginings of the inspired poet and affirms, despite his lamentable predicament, a continuing commitment to the Good Old Cause, a commitment which in the poem wins divine approval. When Abdiel returns to Heaven having refused to join Satan's rebellion, he is commended by the Father for having 'maintained / Against revolted multitudes the cause / Of truth', for having borne 'Universal reproach' and submitted to being 'Judged... perverse'; but these are commendation which better suit Milton's witness than Abdiel's, and not only Milton's. The nonconformist heirs of the Puritans had witnessed the revolt of multitudes in 1660, and had subsequently borne all but universal reproach. That their cause was nothing but perversity was a commonplace of polemic, preferred repeatedly by such champions of the new order as Sir Roger L'Estrange. When Abdiel later confronts Satan on the field of Heaven, the identification of his cause with that of nonconformity becomes all but explicit in Abdiel's references to his 'dissent' from Satan and to the loyal angels as 'my sect':

> there be who faith
> Prefer, and piety to God, though then
> To thee not visible, when I alone
> Seemed to thy world erroneous to dissent
> From all: my sect thou seest, now learn too late
> How few sometimes may know, when thousands err.[12]

Following the Restoration, only one group of people was known as 'dissenters' and 'sectarians', few in number, and judged by the prevailing royalist and episcopalian ideology both erroneous and perverse, enemies to the established church and to the state, and hence to God. Yet here these very terms denominate not rebelliousness and sedition, as in common usage, but opposition to Satanic rebellion. A lexical reversal has been effected: the thousands who err are no longer the dissenters but those who stand against the dissenters, that is, episcopalians and royalists against Puritans. And the epic poet places himself in their dissenting camp: Abdiel cannot 'change his constant mind'; Milton sings 'unchanged'.[13] The 'servant of God' commended by the Father is a dissenter.

Bunyan is similarly concerned to vindicate himself against the 'revolted multitudes'. Through his imprisonment he associates himself with a preeminent Christian exemplar, St Paul. From the account in Acts 23–4 of the charges preferred against Paul before Felix, the Roman procurator of Judaea, Bunyan infers that '*an hypocritical people, will persecute the power of those truths in others, which themselves in words profess*', and, tellingly, he adds (probably in 1665): 'I am this day, and for this very thing persecuted by them'.[14] In what may be the first piece he wrote following his arrest, the tract *I Will Pray with the Spirit* (1662?), he contrasts the sincerity of true spirituality with the hollow formalism of liturgies and prescribed rites. Understandably, Bunyan's name does not appear on the title page, for this argument informs an openly oppositional text. In 1661 or 1662 to denounce 'those men that are so hot for the Forms, and not the Power of prayer' was perforce to denounce supporters of the Book of Common Prayer, that is, the fiercely episcopalian members of the Cavalier Parliament and Church of England. They would be less than impressed to learn that

> Scarce one of forty among them, know what it is to be born again, to have communion with the Father through the Son; to feel the power of Grace sanctifying their hearts: but for all their prayers, they still live cursed, drunken, whorish, and abominable Lives, full of Malice, Envy, Deceit, Persecuting of the dear Children of God. Oh what a dreadful after-clap is coming upon them! which all their hypocritical assembling themselves together, with all their prayers, shall never be able to help them against, or shelter them from.

It is above all their 'Persecuting of the dear Children of God' which situates these episcopalians, and consequently the author, for it sets the former in the tradition of Edmund Bonner, 'that blood-red Persecutor', and identifies the speaker as one of 'God's People' who, 'as it hath alwayes been, *Ezra* 4.12, to 16.', are vilified, maligned and oppressed. Bunyan is to be counted among the Lord's 'poor tempted and afflicted People', for he is in gaol, and if you

> look into the Goals in *England*, and in to the Alehouses of the same . . . I believe, you will find those that plead for the Spirit of Prayer in the Goal, and them that look after the Forms of mens Inventions only, in the Alehouse.[15]

Bunyan's 'alehouse', the haunt of the unregenerate oppressors of the faithful, is the demotic equivalent of the 'barbarous dissonance / Of Bacchus and his revellers' whom, in their Cavalier riot, Milton distinguishes from his 'fit audience' in *Paradise Lost*. As in the alehouse are to be found the royalist and episcopalian 'Persecutors of the dear Children of God' who conscientiously scruple the Book of Common Prayer, so in the riotous horde of Bacchus's train are to be found those who, Michael foresees, 'Spiritual laws by carnal power shall force / On every conscience',

> Whence heavy persecution shall arise
> On all who in the worship persevere
> Of spirit and truth; the rest, far greater part
> Will deem in outward rites and specious forms
> Religion satisfied; truth shall retire
> Bestruck with slanderous darts, and works of faith
> Rarely be found.[16]

At odds with their age, both Bunyan and Milton are, then, concerned to vindicate their dissent from, and stand against, prevailing ideology. To this end they set the contemporary world not within the providential history preferred by royalist and episcopalian writing, but in a biblical context whose emblematic and typological patterns offer a very different exegetical key. Their *apologiae* rest upon a representation of the Christian life validated by suffering. In *The Pilgrim's Progress*, Evangelist warns Christian and Faithful that they 'must through many tribulations enter into the Kingdom of Heaven' and that 'in every City, bonds and afflictions abide in you; and therefore you cannot expect that you should go long on your Pilgrimage without them, in some sort or other'. In the town of Vanity, 'you will be hardly beset with enemies, who will strain hard but they will kill you'. This inescapable experience of repression and persecution is epitomized in the trial before Vanity's Lord Hategood, as cruelly bent upon the elimination of all dissent as was the future Chief Justice of the King's Bench, Sir John Kelyng, at Bunyan's own trial.[17] Bunyan's *Prison-Meditations* of 1665 were *Directed to the Heart of Suffering Saints and Reigning Sinners*. The adjectives are all but definitive. In Books XI and XII of *Paradise Lost* just such a vision of the sad predicament of suffering saints in the hands of reigning sinners recurs throughout Michael's preview of human history as 'the world go[es] on, / To good malignant, to bad men benign'.[18] Milton's Samson[19] is 'fallen on evil days', blind, confined, a 'prisoner chained', scarce able to 'draw / The air imprisoned also, close and damp, / Unwholesome draught', and in despair that he is apparently 'cast off as never known' by God and left 'helpless' in the power of his 'cruel enemies'. His plight prompts the Chorus to adduce examples of God's apparently arbitrary dealings with his elect which Bunyan's Evangelist would recognize: abandoned to the 'heathen and profane', 'captived' and brought before 'unjust tribunals, under change of times / And condemnation of the ingrateful multitude'.[20]

There can be little doubt which 'change of times' Milton had chiefly in mind. What is represented in *Samson Agonistes*, as in *The Pilgrim's Progress*, is the world of the Restoration from the point of view of nonconformist experience. The dominant ideology figured the return of Charles as a divine mercy, unique, unprecedented, inexplicable, but for Milton and Bunyan, the Restoration and its culture epitomized the hostile wilderness of this world,[21] all too easily explicable and unremarkable save for the clarity with which it represented the adverse circumstances the saints are to expect in all ages. In contrast to the homiletic emphasis developing in the established church,[22] in the nonconformist tradition Christianity is set at odds with the world: 'the people of God are a suffering people' Bunyan would succinctly state in *Seasonable Counsel: or, Advice to Sufferers* (1684). 'Who best / Can suffer, best can do' declares Milton's Son of God. Matthew 5.11 ('when men shall revile you, and persecute you, and shall say all manner of evil against you falsely for my sake; rejoice, and be exceeding glad, for great is your reward in heaven') encouraged Bunyan to embrace suffering as a validation of his testimony: 'it belongs to my Christian profession, to be vilified, slandered, reproached and reviled'. *No Cross, No Crown,* as the Quaker William Penn curtly entitled the work he wrote while a prisoner in the Tower in 1668: 'To reign, it is necessary first to suffer'.[23] Far from signalling just retribution (as episcopalians and royalists were wont to allege), loss of power at the Restoration and consequent persecution come to signify divine approbation. Through such trials, Christians grow in grace: 'afflictions, and so every service of God, doth make the heart more deep, more experimentall, more knowing, and profound'. There is, though, a greater promise: 'Blessed are they that are persecuted for righteousness' sake, for theirs is the Kingdom of Heaven' (Luke 6.22). Nonconformists discerned in their sufferings evidence of election, an assurance of salvation: 'there is a reward for the afflicted, according to the measure of affliction'.[24]

In a construction much indebted to John Foxe, nonconformist writing consequently seized upon persecution as a confirmation of witness which could invoke a tradition stretching back through 'worthy *Wickliff, Hus, Luther, Melancton, Calvin,* and the blessed Martyrs in Q. *Maries* dayes', 'the holy and goodly Martyrs and Saints... *Hus, Bilny, Ridly, Hooper, Cranmer,* with their Brethren', to the early church.[25] For its part, the persecuting Restoration regime was set in an equally venerable tradition, that of Antichrist: '*Nebuchadnezzar*', writes Bunyan, 'will have his *Fiery-Furnace,* and *Darius* his *Lyons-Den* for *Nonconformists,* Dan. 3.6 & 6.7, *&c.*'; 'the *Papists* and their *Companions*: How many have they in all Ages *hanged, burned, starved, drowned, wracked, dismembred,* and *murdered,* both openly and in secret', 'that dissented from them'?[26] Bunyan's lexical choices here are as pointed as Milton's in connection with Abdiel. To denominate *nonconformists* those whom Nebuchadnezzar and Darius persecute and *dissenters* those whom the papists and their companions torture implicitly identifies them with those of Bunyan's contemporaries who suffer at the hands of the Restoration judicial system. To the royalist and episcopalian authorities is allocated the role of Babylonish, Median and Romish oppressors. Are not Nebuchadnezzar and Darius cited approvingly by the judge at the trial of Christian of Faithful?[27]

The Restoration world is, then, Babel, it is Nebuchadnezzar's Babylon, the Fair of the Prince of Vanity, an idolatrous Philistia devoted to Dagon, the kingdom of Beelzebub, the domain of the Great Whore. These are types of tyranny, oppression, superstition and Romanism, and consequently of the Devil. We may therefore suppose in the fourth line of *Paradise Lost* – 'Till one greater man restore us' – some slippage between being restored to divine favour from the machinations of Satan and being restored to liberty from the oppression of tyrants. One man had recently been involved in a very notable restoration and one which, in the eyes of its beneficiaries, rendered superfluous any further work of restoration. It is precisely from the 'evil days' of that 'restoration' that *Paradise Lost* turns away to the promise of restoration offered by its 'greater man'.

## 2 The Experience of Persecution

The Act of Uniformity distinguished only two categories of religious practice: conformist and nonconformist. The crudity of this distinction disguised the great diversity of opinion now excluded from the established church. The largest grouping was of those popularly called Presbyterians, perhaps a majority of whom belonged with Baxter and his 'Reconcilers', 'mere Christians', 'mere Catholics', 'of no Sect or party, abhorring the very Name of Parties'.[28] Their withdrawal from the established church was prompted not by any one of the clauses of the Act of Uniformity but rather by the Act's general implication that subscription to its provisions was an essential qualification for Christian fellowship. This exclusivity they rejected on the grounds that true Christianity is compatible with a wide range of theological opinions, liturgical practices and ecclesiastical structures. This was the case which Marvell would argue against zealously partisan conformists: 'Truth for the most part lyes in the middle, but men ordinarily seek for it in the extremities', with the disastrous results which have been evident in Christian history ever since the Council of Nicea, 'For one that is a Christian in good earnest, when a creed is imposed, will sooner eat fire than take it against his judgement'. Many things stand in need of correction 'which are far more ruinous in Consequence, than the dispensing with a Surplice' and, rather than subscription to the Act, Marvell ironically recommends as his own test of fitness that applicants for the ministry be set to read the Bible: ''Tis a very good Book, and if a man read it carefully, will make him much wiser'.[29]

To men of this mind, no scruple which does not touch the basic doctrines of Christianity is sufficient justification for excluding anyone from communion. 'As long as we all agree in Fundamentals', wrote Baxter, 'we are of one Religion for all our Differences'; he who 'would unite the Church in Kings, in Councels, in any humane devices, will but divide it'. The Act of Uniformity was such a divisive device, needlessly fracturing the church. John Howe was, so Edmund Calamy (grandson of the Smectymnuan) recorded, for '*Union and Communion of all visible Christians; and for making nothing necessary to Christian Communion, but what Christ hath made necessary, or what is indeed necessary to one's being a Christian*'. When John Wilkins expressed surprise that men of Howe's '*Latitude*... continu'd Non-conformists', Howe replied: 'That that *Latitude* of his, which he was pleas'd to take notice of, was so far from inducing him to Conformity, that it was the very thing that made and kept him a Nonconformist'. The nonconformity of these men was, ironically perhaps but perfectly sensibly, a witness against the legislation which made nonconformity a possibility.[30]

For Presbyterians of less latitude, particular clauses in the act formed the chief obstacle to conformity. It was by Howe that the difficulty of re-ordination was famously put to Seth Ward, Bishop of Exeter, when the Bishop asked 'what hurt is there in being twice Ordain'd?': '*Hurt*, my Lord, says *Mr Howe* to him; the Thought is shocking; it hurts my Understanding; it is an absurdity: For nothing can have two Beginnings'.[31] A second ordination inevitably invalidated the prior ordination by presbyters, which was as intolerable to some as was repudiation of the Solemn League and Covenant to others. Although Presbyterians did not object to a set liturgy *per se* they had, as the Savoy Conference had shown, very considerable objections to the Book of Common Prayer. Furthermore, many who, though disapproving, might be prepared to use its forms, could not bring themselves to make the required affirmation of *assent and consent* to all it contained. In any case, it was quite simply impossible for many ministers who lived outside London to see the revised Prayer Book before the subscription date, since very few copies had in fact been printed by then. Burnet records that many 'well affected to the church' could not subscribe 'to a book that they had not seen' and so 'left their benefices on that very account'; how, asked Baxter pointedly, came 7,000 to consent to a book 'which they had never seen', 'unless it was by changing with the times?'[32]

So-called Presbyterians of the stamp of Baxter and Howe, who retained hopes of eventual comprehension within a more broadly based national church, adopted a number of terms to distinguish themselves as unwilling nonconformists. Baxter spoke of 'mere nonconformists' and sometimes 'episcopal nonconformists'. 'Partial conformists' and 'old Puritans' were other terms used. The anonymous authors of *A Short Surveigh of the Grand Case of the Present Ministry* (1663) described themselves on its title page as 'conformable Nonconformists', initiating an oxymoron which would survive at least until John Cheyney's *The Conforming Non-conformist and the Non-conforming Conformist* of 1680. This was no mere play on words. These locutions both capture the tension inherent in the position of these men and accurately reflect their practice. Unable to conform to a deliberately exclusive church, they would not yet separate from it completely. Their habit of occasional communion with parish churches was in origin a religious practice which endeavoured to refuse the partisan loyalty demanded by the Church of England without lapsing into another, and equally damaging, separatism. In 1702 Edmund Calamy told Burnet that it had been practised 'by some of the most eminent of our ministers since 1662, with a design to show their charity towards the church'.[33]

For other nonconformists, however, there could be no question of communion with what was only doubtfully, and for some certainly was not, a true church. Howe distinguished between those who, like himself, found the Church of England defective but not essentially flawed and those who judged the established church 'so insufficiently Reform'd, as to want as yet the very being of a true Christian Church'.[34] The majority of these were to be found among the Independents and Baptists. Their quarrel was neither with the exclusivity of the Act of Uniformity in general nor with its provisions in particular, but with its premise that an ecclesiastical organization whose membership was coterminous with the nation's population could in any sense be a church. Theirs was a congregational ideal of church order and membership which rejected the state's authority in religious matters, as did John Owen's *Discourse concerning Liturgies and their Imposition* (1662). Owen had been advocating a congregational system since his *Eshcol: a Cluster of the Fruits of Canaan* (1648). He had been a prime agent in formulating the congregational *Savoy Declaration of Faith and Order* in 1658 and he remained true to this ideal after 1662, in, for example, *A Discourse concerning Evangelical Love, Church-Peace and Unity* (1672). 1 Corinthians 5.11 was the oft-cited proof-text. More radical still were the Quakers. Although their histrionic and demonstrative behaviour of the 1650s declined in the 1660s, their writings continued to deploy the imagery of Old Testament oracles to express the detestation felt by those for whom all traditional churches were 'cages of unclean spirits', 'synagogues of Satan'.[35]

The separation of such persons from the Church of England was a good deal firmer than was the Presbyterians', of whom, by and large, they had no very high opinion. 'Being more than the rest against the Bishops, Liturgies, Ceremonies, and Parish-Communion', wrote Baxter, they characterized 'those of us that were of another mind, and refused not Parish-Communion in some Places and Cases' as 'luke-warm Temporizers, Men of too large Principles, who supt the Anti-christian Pottage, though we would not eat the Flesh'.[36] The Clarendon Code, however, made no distinction between these 'temporizers', who looked to a more liberal national church, and those committed to independent congregations. The effect of the persecution which it visited on all regardless was, as the decade wore on, to lessen the force of their ecclesiological differences among nonconformists themselves. Presbyterians were compelled perforce into a congregational church order. Their 'Congregations were, through necessity, just of Independent and Separating Shape, and outward Practice, though not upon the same Principles'.[37] The history of nonconformity during the next 20 years is thus largely the history of the frustration of the aspirations of the moderate Presbyterians and the increasing identification of nonconformity with this separatist position, a history registered by the gradual supersession of the word *nonconformity* by *dissent*.[38]

The new state of things was evident long before the Act of Uniformity came into force in August 1662. Magistrates and judges had immediately assumed that the Restoration had put back into their hands a body of common and statute law already quite sufficient to harry nonconformists. The Elizabethan Act of Uniformity (1 Eliz. cap.2) and the Jacobean Act against Popish Recusants (3 Jac.I. cap.4) both provided for the fining of absentees from sabbath worship in the parish church ('Sunday shillings'), but more serious, and more serviceable, was the Elizabethan Act against Conventicles (35 Eliz. cap.1, *An Act for Retaining the Queen's Subjects in their Due Obedience*), whose penalties included banishment and death for those who refused to conform after three months' imprisonment, the latter sentence actually being passed, though not carried out, on 12 Aylesbury Baptists in 1663.[39] It was under this Act that Bunyan was imprisoned and it continued to be invoked even after the Acts of the Clarendon Code were on the statute book, since its penalties were more severe than those of Restoration legislation. Itinerant Quakers were liable to public whipping under the Elizabethan Vagrancy Act (39 Eliz. cap.4), and their refusal of oaths rendered them liable to prosecution under both Elizabethan and Jacobean statutes (5 Eliz. cap.1; 3 Jac.I cap.4; 7 Jac.I cap.6), which provided for the tendering of the oaths of allegiance and supremacy to anyone over the age of 18. Persistent refusal incurred the penalty of *praemunire* (forfeiture of all goods and imprisonment during the king's pleasure), again an attractively harsher penalty than any provided by the Clarendon Code. Quaker outdoor meetings were further liable to be charged with the common law offences of unlawful assembly and riot. It was for perpetrating a riot and disturbing the peace (and not for holding a conventicle) that William Penn and William Mead were famously brought to trial at the Old Bailey in September 1670.[40]

To this body of law the 1660s added the 'Clarendon Code'.[41] It visited upon nonconformists the most sustained persecution in English history, and, as it was wholly unsuccessful in its aim, the last. It did not compel conformity to the Church of England, nor destroy nonconformity, but established dissent and, before the century was out, the fact of religious pluralism and toleration. A total of 1,909 ministers, lecturers, teachers and university college heads and fellows were ejected, 695 of them under the 1660 Act for Confirming Ministers, of whom 59 succeeded in securing another benefice only to be ejected gain in 1662. Very few of these ejected ministers subsequently joined the 7,000 or so conformist clergy and, though there was some talk that ministers, with their congregations, might emigrate to New England, repeating the 'Great Migration' of persecuted Puritans in the 1630s, only 15 ministers in fact crossed the Atlantic; a further 10 took up residence in Holland, and a few elsewhere. Large though the figure of 1,909 is, it includes only those who had been beneficed in the Cromwellian church. It is consequently a measure chiefly of Presbyterian opinion, for many Independents, most Baptists and all Quakers had had nothing to do with the state church and so were never put out because they had never been in. The figures include only 194 known Independents and 19 known Baptists.[42] The number who followed these men and were prepared both to absent themselves from parish worship and to run the risks involved in attending conventicles is extraordinarily difficult to compute. It appears that it was in the region of 150,000–200,000 in the

1660s, in a total population of perhaps 5 million, or an adult population of perhaps 3.4 million.[43]

The provisions of the Clarendon Code itself witness to the difficulty of ensuring its enforcement. The need both to bribe informers and to fine law officers who failed to pursue suspects indicates the degree of coercion required. The Corporation Act and the remodelling of the Commissions of Peace did not succeed in removing all sympathy for the nonconformists, or even all nonconformists, from the ranks of local government and the justiciary. Consequently, the government could never depend on its policy being rigorously enforced at all times in all places. Quite the contrary: the pattern of persecution was dependent upon local circumstances, upon the disposition of the local gentry, of the justices and of the community. Sheldon and like-minded bishops were dismayed by their inability to compel JPs to proceed against conventicles.[44] Indifference and lethargy might be as strong disincentives to action as actual sympathy, but, on the other hand, of course, there were cases of JPs who were as fanatically zealous as Sheldon could wish. In our decade there seems generally to have been, as might be expected, stringent application initially but then, as the likelihood of any serious threat from subversion receded, as the government's own inadequacies became more apparent, as national disasters occupied minds, effective persecution declined, a situation which the stringency of the Second Conventicle Act was intended to address.[45]

The nonconformist community quickly developed strategies to counter the regime's attempts at its extirpation. In September 1670 it was complained of Quakers at Bristol that 'Notwithstanding all the endeavours of the Magistracy they cannot suppresse them by reason of theyre many trickes & evasions'. One such trick was for congregations to avoid infringing the Conventicle Act by meeting in small groups of no more than five, with the minister repeating his sermon to each, or preaching from the window of one building to small groups of auditors gathered in adjoining houses with their windows open. Meetings might be held at irregular hours, or at night, with the members of the congregation arriving by different routes and the minister disguising his business by carrying the tools of a trade. Look-outs were posted, enabling the minister to leave and the congregation to assume the character of a social occasion before officers arrived. The definition of a conventicle in the First Conventicle Act as a meeting of more than five persons 'over and above the members of the household' appeared to put meetings not held in houses beyond its scope, and congregations frequently met outdoors. The Second Conventicle Act more carefully specified 'any place ... house, field or place where there is no family inhabiting', but to meet on common land still avoided the landowner's or householder's fine which that act imposed.[46] Fox generally disdained such attempts to avoid detection and the Quakers on the whole refused to employ such expedients: Edward Billing admonished them not to 'run shirking into holes, or skulk into corners by *threes* or *fours*'. A resolute witness became the

Children of Light, for, though 'the Furnace were or should be made seven times hotter than it already is', 'our mouths were not opened by, neither can they be shut in the will of man; insomuch, that what we receive in secret, that declare we openly and freely'.[47] When their meetings were disturbed and their members imprisoned, the remaining Friends, often women and children, would meet as openly as before, in the street if need be. Baxter, though in no doubt they were misguided and deluded, recognized the constancy of their profession. So, too, did Pepys. It both impressed and distressed him: 'They go like lambs, without any resistance. I would to God they would either conform, or be more wise, and not be ketched'.[48]

Once arrested, the accused could expect conviction if they were brought to trial. They received no notice of the precise charge until it was read in court, and so had no chance to prepare a defence. Sworn testimony could not be challenged and cross-examination was hardly practised. The defendant could not appear in his or her own defence. Virtually the only way to secure an acquittal was by challenging details in the indictment, with a view to invalidating it, a strategy at which Quakers became especially adept.[49] The defendant could expect to meet a hostile court, justices and judges, though a conspicuous exception was Sir Matthew Hale, in 1671 appointed Chief Justice of the King's Bench, 'the pillar of Justice, the Refuge of the subject who feared oppression and one of the greatest Honours of his Majesties Government' in Baxter's words. He was the only judge to listen sympathetically to a plea from Bunyan's wife, answering her 'very mildly'.[50] More usually, however, judges appointed during the king's pleasure could be expected to be self-interestedly and subserviently compliant to the government's wishes, if not enthusiastically vindictive, while JPs sitting on the bench were unlikely to be sympathetic (else no arrest would have been made). And finally, little hope could be vested in the jury, for its scope to exercise independent judgement was severely circumscribed in courts whose presiding judges took it to be the jury's duty to receive direction from the bench. Jurymen might be bullied and effectively imprisoned, perhaps without nourishment, until they returned a verdict to the judge's liking, or risk imprisonment themselves for contempt if they resisted such pressure. After a trial of Quakers at Nottingham in 1665, members of the jury confessed to having convicted defendants because 'they feared... the *Judge* would have laid them by the heels' had they returned a verdict of not guilty. In 1670 the acquittal of the Quakers William Penn and William Mead made legal history on this point. The jury which had maintained its 'not guilty' verdict contrary to the advice of the judge and despite being kept two days and nights without food or water was imprisoned until payment of a fine of 40 marks by each juror for contumacy. The foreman, Edward Bushel, sued for a writ of Habeas Corpus, and Sir John Vaughan, Chief Justice of the Common Pleas, upheld his plea that he had properly fulfilled his duty as juryman in returning what he had inferred from the evidence presented: 'the Jury, and not the Judge, resolve and find what the Fact is'. 'Never thing, since the King's Return', wrote Baxter', 'was received with greater Joy and Applause by the People' than this verdict.[51]

## 3 Nonconformist Culture

The nonconformist response to persecution was in the main quietist. The great and heady days of revolution and of millenarianism were over. Writing in 1664, Baxter touches a note recurrent in nonconformist thought:

> I am farther than ever I was from expecting great matters of Unity, Splendor or Prosperity to the Church on Earth, or that the Saints should dream of a Kingdom of this World, or flatter themselves with the Hopes of a Golden Age, or reigning over the Ungodly... on the contrary I am more apprehensive that Sufferings must be the Churches most ordinary Lot, and Christians must be self-denying Cross-bearers.[52]

John 18.36 ('My kingdom is not of this world') runs like a refrain through nonconformist writing. It is especially pronounced in Quaker texts: 'my Weapons are *Spiritual, and not Carnal,* and with Carnal Weapons I do not fight; and my *Kingdom is not of this* World saith Christ... and I witnesse against all *Murtherous plots*, and such as would *imbrew the Nation in Blood*' replied Fox to the charge that he plotted insurrection. He fought only in 'the Lamb's War'. He was consistently to preach, and to practise, not only quietism but pacificism: 'All bloody principles and practices, we... do utterly deny, with all outward wars and strife and fightings with outward weapons, for any end or under any pretence whatsoever. And this is our testimony to the whole world.'[53] There is a similar strain in Bunyan's writing. From prison in 1661 he protested that he had no intention 'to disturb the peace of the nation', that he abhorred Fifth Monarchist insurrection, and

> I look upon it as my duty to behave myself under the King's government, both as becomes a man and a christian; and if occasion was offered me, I should willingly manifest my loyalty to my Prince, both by word and deed.

Twenty years later, he characterized himself as 'one of the old-fashion Professors, that covet to fear God and honour the King'. He holds that 'it is amiable and pleasant to God, when Christians keep their Rank, Relation and Station, doing all as become their Quality and Calling' and he admonishes his readers that they are 'to give thanks to God for all men, for Kings, and for all that are in authority' and not to 'mock at men in Place and Power'. 'It becomes all godly men to study to be quiet.' He writes directly against those 'of an unquiet, and troublesome spirit' who seek redress and revenge: 'A Christian must be a harmless Man, and, to that end, must imbrace nothing but harmless Principles'.[54] Just so, in *Paradise Regained* the Son of God refuses to adopt the 'politic maxims, or that cumbersome / Luggage of war' recommended by Satan to establish the Messiah's kingdom and in *Paradise Lost* Milton relegates political and military expedients to the frustrated fallen angels in Hell, reserving for his epic subject the 'better fortitude / Of patience and heroic martyrdom', the victory not of retaliation but of 'suffering for truth's sake'.[55]

This was not a counsel of despair or defeatism. Events may have conspired to make nonconformists spectators only of public affairs, but their quietism was neither compliant nor self-interestedly expedient. Its constituted a positive model of Christian commitment, actively sought, a deliberate alternative to the dominant culture. Their marginalization is constructed not as an imposed ostracism but a chosen separatism, for their political quietism was not matched by moral or religious submissiveness to the Restoration. Overwhelmingly, the Restoration world is depicted in nonconformist texts as an epitome of all that is to be rejected, resisted. Bunyan was inclined, if only in general terms, to assume that it was kings and courts which were 'drawn into [the] lewdness' of 'the *Mother of Harlots*', becoming so 'entangled with her Beauty, and with her Fornication, that they have been adulterated from God and their own Salvation', and so to associate them with the opulent decadence which Roman Catholicism and the baroque suggested to his Puritan sensibility. At Vanity Fair, 'the Ware of *Rome* and her Merchandize is greatly promoted'.[56] And if the social and legal systems of Vanity are uncomfortably like those of Restoration England, and if Lord Hategood is disturbingly reminiscent of Sir John Kelyng, then whose in England is the role of the Beelzebub who is the 'chief Lord', 'King' and 'noble Prince' of Vanity and its Fair? On this 'Prince of this Town, with all the Rablement his Attendants', Faithful's judgement is that they 'are more fit for a being in Hell, then in this Town or Countrey'. It is hence no wonder that 'God sometimes visits Prisons more / Than lordly Palaces'.[57]

Men and women impressed by this prince and the culture which flows from his court do not fare well in Bunyan. Indeed, to delight in the Restoration *beau monde*, to ape noble and courtly superiors, to be preoccupied with forms of civility and etiquette, with status and hierarchy, with fashion, dress and manners, is for Bunyan a definitive sign of moral turpitude, and especially of superficiality, mendacity and avarice. By-ends is a figure of hypocrisy and time-serving, but the form of his hypocrisy is culturally specific: he is monied and mannered, socially accomplished, and his wife is of high breeding. He is from '*Fair-speech*', 'a *Wealthy place*', where *fair* suggests *polite* and *elegant*, as well as *pleasing* and *specious*. The formalism recommended to Christian by Worldly-Wiseman may be learned not only from that 'very judicious man' Legality but also from that '*pretty young man*' his son, Civility, '*that can do it . . . as well as the old*

*Gentleman himself*'. Mercie's suitor Mr Brisk, a 'man of some breeding' who 'pretended to Religion' but who proves merely mercenary, is a kind of fop, an aspiring Restoration rake.[58] In the later *Mr Badman* (1680), what Mr Badman calls his 'Neatness, handsomness, comeliness, cleanliness . . . following of fashion' is construed, and condemned, by Mr Wiseman as pride. To pride, Restoration female fashions add shamelessness and licentiousness. 'Their Bulls-foretops, with their naked shoulders, and Paps hanging out like a Cows bag' outrage Mr Wiseman as 'the Attire of an Harlot' (Proverbs 10.7), enticing to 'the sin of uncleanness, by the spangling shew of fine cloaths'.[59] A very similar aesthetic and moral sense finds in the nakedness of Adam and Eve 'Simplicity and spotless innocence'. In *Samson Agonistes* the tempting and deceiving Dalila is 'so bedecked, ornate, and gay' that, 'Like a stately ship', she approaches 'With all her bravery on, and tackle trim', like, that is to say, a fashionable seventeenth-century lady.[60]

These are the manners and dress of gentlefolk. Christopher Hill has observed that the gentles come out of Bunyan rather badly, that he 'spoke for the poor against the rich',[61] and so he does. Bunyan finds it readily understandable that in the parable of Dives and Lazarus 'the ungodly [are] held forth under the notion of a rich man', for are they not 'most ready to be puft up with pride, stoutness, care of this world, in which things they spend most of their time, in lusts, drunkenness, wantonness, idleness'? By contrast, God's own 'are commonly of the poorer sort'; 'The Saints of God are a poor, contemptible people', 'a despised, afflicted, tempted, persecuted people'.[62] We are not, Bunyan insists, to be unduly impressed by social status, bearing or class, and this at a time when the notion of *quality* as a social signifier, and the phrase *person of quality*, are gaining currency through the heightened social sensitivity consequent upon the comparative novelty of a royal court, and a Frenchified court, as the centre of taste and patronage.[63] It is precisely their alert sense of their own quality, their snobbery and sensitivity to social slur and insult, which signals the moral standing of the natives of Vanity. Their hostility to Christian and Faithful reproduces that fundamental biblical opposition whose metaphorical vehicles structure *The Pilgrim's Progress*: it illustrates the enmity between the serpent's seed and the woman's (Genesis 3.15), the rejection of those who are strangers and pilgrims in the earth (Hebrews 11.13), the plight of the children of light walking in darkness (1 Thessalonians 5.4–5). Bunyan's attention to social detail, however, transforms the inhabitants of Vanity from general types of unregenerate hostility to the saints into culturally specific 'rulers of the darkness of this world' (Ephesians 6.12). The case against Christian and Faithful (both poor men) is pressed by 'the Gentry of our Town', allegedly 'bespattered' by Faithful. The prosecution witnesses are 'worthy Gentlemen' and gentlemen, of course, make up the jury. The 'laudable doings' which these 'gentlemen' would defend against the challenge of the pilgrims are represented in the 'trade' at Vanity Fair, where 'Houses, Lands,

Trades, Places, Honours, Preferments, Titles, Countries, Kingdoms, Lusts, Pleasures, and Delights of all sorts' are for sale.[64] 'Places, honours, preferments' were in the gift of the court.[65] 'Lusts, Pleasures and Delights of all sorts' is a terse summary of one view of the court culture epitomized in, let us say, Rochester. Though he would not care to be named in the same sentence, Bunyan is as convinced as the William Penn of *No Cross, No Crown*, that such a culture is a general pollutant.[66] Just such behaviour is to be found among the Philistines of Milton's *Samson Agonistes*: the ungodliness of Restoration culture is epitomized in their idolatrous paganism ('The Philistians understand me not' observes Bunyan), the temper of its nobility represented in the drunken, gluttonous and exulting Philistine lords, its treatment of nonconformists in their humiliation of Samson. This is hardly the image the restored regime had of itself, nor, in this representation, can 1660 any longer be claimed to signify divine approval. That number now marks not vindication and victory but nemesis and destruction, for it is at line 1660 that the Chorus begins its celebration of Samson's 'dearly-bought revenge, yet glorious' upon the Philistine 'Lords, ladies, captains, counsellors, or priests, / Their choicest nobility and flower' in the midst of their revels and their triumph, 'While their hearts were jocund and sublime, / Drunk with idolatry, drunk with wine'.[67]

Withdrawing from this corrupt world, the nonconformist attends less to public affairs than to the private self, less to courts than to conscience. Interiority and subjectivity are keys to nonconformist culture. Its characteristic productions are autobiographical – *Grace Abounding*, Baxter's *Reliquiae*, Fox's *Journal*, even *Samson Agonistes*. *The Mischiefs of Self-Ignorance* was the title given by Baxter to a series of Restoration sermons (1662). The 'upright heart and pure' preferred by the God invoked at the opening of *Paradise Lost*, the 'paradise within' to which the epic tends, the 'Christ within' preached by the Quakers, these are characteristic formulations. It is precisely his want of inner spirituality which damns poor Ignorance, for all his worthiness and good intentions. To Hopeful's query 'if ever he had Christ revealed to him from Heaven' he retorts with the sound common sense of the prevailing Restoration ideology, 'What! you are a man for revelations! I believe that what both you, and all the rest of you say about that matter, is but the fruit of distracted braines'. What Hopeful and Christian try to impress upon him is the need for an experiential religion, *experimental* or *heart religion* in contemporary terminology, for inwardness, inspiration and commitment. It was this which more sober and restrained tempers regarded, like Ignorance, as a worrying survival of Interregnum enthusiasm. 'I preached what I felt, what I smartingly did feel', said Bunyan.[68] This emphasis results in a conception of the Christian life which is intimate, personal and private (though emphatic in its public witness). Herein lies the key to the psychological accuracy of Bunyan's characterizations, as to the realism of his settings. Nonconformist culture is concerned with actual – that is, everyday – experience. Its texts therefore present a world far removed from the exoticism, and from the remoteness from common experience, of contemporary heroic drama or romance. Penn had no patience at all with the characteristic cultural productions of Restoration society – with 'stories fetched from . . . romances; some strange adventures, some passionate amours . . . wonderful surprises, unexpected encounters, castles surprised, imprisoned lovers rescued, and meetings of supposed dead ones; bloody duels, languishing voices echoing from solitary groves, overheard mournful complaints, deep-fetched sighs sent from wild deserts, intrigues managed with unheard-of subtlety . . . things that never were, nor are, nor ever shall or can be'. Milton is similarly scornful of the paraphernalia of Renaissance epic and romance. These have nothing to do with the 'better fortitude / Of patience of heroic martyrdom'. Rather than deal in absurdities and impossibilities, the nonconformist constructed an heroic ideal attainable by every person.[69]

## 4 The Licensing Act and the Press

The survival of this alternative and oppositional culture depended crucially upon communication: the struggle over nonconformity thus became a struggle over control of the press. When, on 19 May 1662, Charles assented to the Act of Uniformity he assented also to its twin, the Licensing Act (14 Car.II. c.33).[70] The restored regime sought to secure itself not only by controlling the gatherings and movement of people, their public meetings and worship, but also their access to information. This was by no means a new initiative. Like the Act of Uniformity, the Licensing Act looked back to Elizabethan notions and formulations, and, indeed, beyond. It re-enacted and refined the various measures by which, since Henry VIII, successive regimes had sought to control the press and to suppress publications unwelcome to the government. The *Act for Preventing the Frequent Abuses in Printing Seditious, Treasonable and Unlicensed Books and Pamphlets, and for Regulating of Printing and Printing Presses* reintroduced and extended the measures introduced under Mary, confirmed under Elizabeth and enforced under Charles I by the prerogative Court of Star Chamber. Its purpose was 'ideological containment'.[71]

The Act had two aims: first, to limit the capacity of the press to produce books; secondly, to ensure that what was printed had been officially sanctioned. It sought to achieve its first aim by restricting the number of master printers to twenty and of master letter founders to four, and by limiting each master printer to two presses and two apprentices (save that Masters and former Masters of the Stationers' Company were permitted three presses). Printing was confined to three locations: London, Oxford and Cambridge. No press was to be set up without its being registered with the Stationers' Company, and no carpenter was allowed to construct a press nor ironmonger to found type without first notifying the Company. It was also through the

Stationers' Company that the Act, like earlier legislation, sought to achieve its second aim of establishing a system of pre-publication censorship. This it did by appealing to the Company's self-interest. By its charter the Company was granted a monopoly of printing and the right both to search for unregistered presses and books and to proceed against offenders. In order to safeguard this monopoly and its members' interests, no book could be printed which had not been 'licensed', 'allowed' or 'tolerated' by one of the Wardens of the Company and (for a fee) 'entered' in the Company's register. This register was hence a record of copyright (vested then in the owner of the copy, and not in the author) and of authorization to print. However, the Wardens were empowered to allow in this way only manuscripts which had previously been 'licensed' by authority, that is, by the licensers (or censors) designated in the Act: the Lord Chancellor (for books on law), the Secretaries of State (for books on history and affairs of state), the Earl Marshal or Kings of Arms (for books on heraldry), the Chancellors or Vice-Chancellors of Oxford or Cambridge (for books printed at the university presses), and for all other books, 'whether of Divinity Phisick Philosophy or whatsoever other Science or Art', the Archbishop of Canterbury or the Bishop of London or their appointees. In practice, this meant that most books passed under the scrutiny of one of the Bishop of London's chaplains. A legitimately published book was thus one which had been first licensed and secondly entered in the Stationers' register. Since, then, an unentered book would be an unlicensed book, in seeking out the former to protect its own interest the Stationers' Company searchers at the same time sought out the latter in the government's interest. The Act reaffirmed the right of the Company's agents to undertake searches, and it empowered the Secretaries of State to issue general search warrants. The Act further required that its licence should be printed at the beginning of each book, that the author's and printer's name should appear on the title page, and it prohibited false imprints.[72]

Work submitted to the censor in accordance with the law seems to have been treated both very rigorously and yet very casually. On the one hand, the likelihood of finding a sympathetic licenser was slim, since the chaplains would not have held their posts were they not good party men. Thomas Grigg, then chaplain to Humphrey Henchman, Bishop of London, told Baxter that his manuscripts would be turned down even if from an unexceptionable author the same material would have been licensed. The prejudice of Baxter's name was sufficient to lend a sinister implication to whatever he should seek to publish. Baxter had to omit from *The Divine Life* (1664) 'the quantity of one Sermon . . . wherein I shewed what a mercy it is to one that hath walked with God, to be taken from this World; because it is a dark, a wicked, a malicious, and implacable, a treacherous deceitful World, &c. All which the Bishop's chaplain must have expunged, because men would think it was all spoken of them.'[73] It is no surprise that the Samuel Parker who appeared in print as an uncompromising defender of the supreme magistrate's absolute authority over private consciences and as a remorseless advocate of persecution to enforce conformity should, when Sheldon's chaplain, have refused Baxter's *Cure of Church Divisions* a licence. The partisan licensing policy of Parker and his fellow chaplain Thomas Tomkins, like Parker a polemicist against nonconformists in general and Baxter in particular, was to be one of Marvell's targets in the second part of *The Rehearsal Transpros'd* (1673). When 'all Theology must ask License' of these 'two Say-masters of Orthodoxy' the result is but 'a more authoriz'd way of libelling', while those libelled are denied the chance to reply.[74] On the other hand, however, precisely because the system depended upon individual judgement, it was inconsistent and unpredictable. The book Grigg refused subsequently appeared as *Directions for Weak Distempered Christians* (1669), duly licensed. The *Cure* which Parker rejected was authorized by Robert Grove when chaplain to Henchman, and published in 1670.[75] And, of course, licensers were subject to pressure from above. John Owen in 1669 acknowledged that it was 'through the countenance of [the] Favour' of Secretary Morice that his works were licensed. Morice's successor, Sir John Trevor, may similarly have acted on Owen's behalf. It was also commonly believed that a bribe would succeed, even with L'Estrange himself. And, besides, the mass of material presented for publication was far greater than the available censors could possibly deal with attentively: this may explain why Tomkins seems to have made only token objection to *Paradise Lost*, and then to a passage in Book I.[76]

The Licensing Act was, however, only one of the means by which the restored regime sought to control the press. Judicial censorship and suppression had as great a part to play. Indeed, booksellers, printers and authors were more likely to find themselves indicted at common law, or under other statutes, for these rendered all those involved in the production of illicit material liable to prosecution, whereas the Licensing Act permitted prosecution only of the printers of unlicensed books. The very vagueness of the law on defamation, slander, libel and sedition was in this respect very much to the authorities' advantage, for it cast a wide net. Restoration courts continued to act on the old principle that any adverse reflection upon the sovereign, government or established church was malicious and culpable since it fostered discontent, if not subversion and sedition. When in 1664 the stationer Thomas Brewster, the printer Simon Dover and the bookbinder Nathan Brooks were tried for seditious publication, they were indicted at common law, not charged under the Licensing Act. In his summing up, Chief Justice Sir Robert Hyde was in no doubt that 'by the course of the common law before this new act was made, for a printer or any other . . . to publish that which is a reproach to the king, to the state, to the church, nay to a particular person, it is a misdemeanour'. He refused to accept the defence submission that publication was Brewster's trade and that no bookseller could be expected to know, or be held responsible for, every page of his stock.[77] And in the background there was the far more threatening charge of treason: the Treason Act had quite expressly brought texts within its compass. Hyde told Brewster that he was lucky not to be tried capitally.[78] The printer John Twyn was not so lucky. His house was under surveillance and in October 1663 he was surprised at 4 a.m. printing an incitement to rebellion entitled *A Treatise of the Execution of Justice.* He also admitted having printed *Mene Tekel: or the Downfall of Monarchy* (1663), a tract in favour of elective rather than hereditary monarchy. He was hanged, drawn and quartered.[79]

In all such cases, it was the judge, not the jury, who determined whether or no the material in question was indeed scandalous, malicious or seditious. The discretion of the jury was confined to determining the responsibility for publication (and even then they might be subject to the judge's direction, if not intimidation). When in 1664 the Baptist Benjamin Keach sought to address the court on his doctrine and the particulars of his indictment (which he had had only an hour to read), Hyde cut him short: 'You shall not speak here, except to the matter of fact: that is to say, whether you writ this book or not'. Hyde's own instruction to the jury that Keach's catechetical *The Child's Delight: or Instructions for Children* was contrary to the Prayer Book and to the doctrine and practice of the Church of England was not to be challenged. The jury's misgivings that the quotations in the indictment did not correspond with the printed text were overruled, and a guilty verdict duly returned: Keach was pilloried, fined £20 and imprisoned until payment of sureties for good behaviour. The fact that conviction and sentence depended upon the judge's interpretation of the defendant's meaning and intention in a published text explains the scorn, derision, unsubstantiated allegations and browbeatings which might be delivered from the bench. These tirades were not purposeless or merely splenetic: to attribute to the defendant the worst possible character and record established malicious or seditious intent. For Hyde to assert, before any verdict had been brought in on Keach, 'you are a Fifth Monarchy man; and you can preach, as well as write books; and you will preach here, if I would let you: but I shall take such order as you shall do no more mischief' was to prepare for the appropriate sentence when the inevitable verdict of guilty of the fact of publication was eventually delivered.[80]

What especially animated the campaign against the press during the 1660s was the zeal of one man, Roger L'Estrange. Following the Restoration he had issued a series of immoderate pamphlets, culminating in *Toleration Discuss'd* (1663), which hammered at the points he would reiterate with tireless polemical indignation for the next twenty-five years: that the Restoration was not due to Presbyterian support; that the nonconformists were factious and schismatic; that they were responsible for the Civil War and the 1640s showed what was really in their minds; and that nothing less than their complete suppression would secure the realm. Essential to this suppression, so L'Estrange insisted, was the denial to them of the press. Convinced that 'Libels were not only the *Fore-runners*, but in a high Degree, the *Causes* of our late *Troubles*', he was in 1662 dismayed to find that 'this Kingdom, at this Instant labouring under the same Distempers; the Press as *busie* and as *bold*; Sermons as *factious*; pamphlets as *seditious* . . . scandalous *Reports* against the *King* and *State* . . . as currant now as they were twenty years ago'.[81] The press threatened the very survival of Restoration England: that same year he warned the Privy Council that 'upon a *Modest Calculation* . . . not so few as *Two-Hundred-Thousand* Seditious Copies have been Printed, since the blessed Return of his Sacred Majesty . . . to these may be added divers *Millions* of the *Old Stock*'. The next year his campaign reached its culmination in *Considerations and Proposals in Order to the Regulation of the Press*, which repeated his demand for more effective press control on the grounds that 'there have been *Printed*, and *Reprinted*' since the Restoration 'not so few as a *Hundred Schismatical Pamphlets*' of which 'the *Instruments*' are '*Ejected Ministers, Booksellers* and *Printers*', together with 'near *Thirty Thousand Copies of Farewel-Sermons*' and accounts of the trials and scaffold speeches of the regicides which present them as saints, martyrs and patriots. There was, L'Estrange alleged, a well-organized publishing underground which corresponded in code and was in touch with exiles abroad. To deal with this threat the Stationers' Company was inadequate, for seditious printing not only often had its members' sympathy but on occasions was actually produced by them: 'Diverse of the very *Instruments*, who are *Entrusted* with the *Care* of the Press' are in fact 'both *Privy*, and *Tacitly Consenting* to the *Corruptions* of it'.[82] An independent authority was needed to oversee the trade: on 15 August 1663 a warrant was issued establishing the office of Surveyor of the Press and appointing L'Estrange Surveyor, with power to search for unlicensed books, illegal presses and all involved in the production of illicit material.[83]

It was the determination of L'Estrange, rather than the Licensing Act, courts or Stationers' Company, which made press control during the 1660s so much more vindictive and partisan than anything experienced before. He harried nonconformist authors and printers relentlessly. He worked by secrecy, operating a network of spies; by surprise, breaking into suspected premises (it was L'Estrange who surprised Twyn at four in the morning); and by intimidation: when he learned that Baxter was planning a controversial piece against Bishop John Bramhall his threat to Baxter's bookseller, Neville Simmons that 'he would ruin him and me, and perhaps my Life should be brought in question', persuaded Baxter to give it over, for 'I perceived the Bookseller durst not Print it'.[84] L'Estrange offered rewards to encourage informers, including even the promise of a recommendation to the first vacancy to appear in the statutory quota of printers. His Surveyorship carried with it a monopoly to print licensed news, which was a lucrative but, for some one of L'Estrange's censorious temper, uncongenial privilege: the first number (13 August 1663) of his paper *The Intelligencer* carried the editorial disclaimer that 'a Publique mercury should never have my vote, because I think it makes the multitude too familiar with the actions and counsels of their superiors'. That same issue offered rewards of 40s. to any informer of a secret press, £5 for information about libels in the process of printing, 10s. for unlicensed books being printed and 5s. for the discovery of hawkers or sellers of seditious books.[85] When a suspect was apprehended, he or she was usually interrogated by L'Estrange, or by one of the Secretaries of State. Trial might follow, but more often months of imprisonment, ended either by the detainee's payment of a substantial bond for good behaviour or agreement to inform on illicit printing activities. 'It is something strange, that to publish a good Book is a sin, and an ill one a vertue' Marvell was to remark in (the anonymous and unlicensed) *Mr Smirke* (1676), ironically expressing the view of those who fell foul of this press regime: 'we seem to have got an Expurgatory Press, though not an Index; and the most Religious Truth must be expung'd'.[86]

Various expedients were adopted to circumvent these obstacles to the publication of dissenting, radical or revolutionary opinions.[87] Those opinions might be expressed cautiously, obliquely or implicitly; historical and biblical subjects were particularly serviceable in this respect. Fictional worlds could also safeguard authors: Milton's Satan is the Devil, not Charles I, however regal his trappings; Lord Hategood is not Sir John Kelynge, though he may berate Faithful much as Bunyan was berated at his trial. When the views expressed were too radical, works might remain in manuscript: Milton's heterodox *De doctrina Christiana* is a conspicuous example.[88] The ejected minister Charles Morton, who was to run the principal congregational academy in London at Newington Green, is known to have written a republican utopia entitled *Eutaxia* which was never printed and has not survived. This was by no means an infallible safeguard: the Secretary of State's agents regularly intercepted and opened mail – as both Baxter and Marvell, for example, very well knew – and illicit manuscript material might be seized even though it was held privately. (It was partly for this reason that diarists often used code or, like the ejected minister Philip Henry, were 'cautious' about what they recorded.)[89] The authorities were interested because the confining of a text to manuscript did not necessarily deny it readers. Copying and circulation of manuscripts was an established Renaissance form of publication which continued into the Restoration, in the case, particularly, of satires, but it was adopted too for such oppositional works as Marvell's *Account of the Growth of Popery*. It was on the grounds that they were places where not only printed but transcribed libels were read and copied that proclamations were issued to close and control coffee-houses in December and January 1675–6.[90]

*The Growth of Popery* did find its way into print (1678), but in an unlicensed edition. This was much the commonest way to put critical or dissident material before readers. Authorial anonymity and a failure to disclose the identity of the printer or bookseller commonly signal the unlicensed status of such publications. Erroneous imprints may be less easily detectable, though on occasions they deliberately advertised their fabrication. Marvell's *Rehearsal Transpros'd* (1672) was initially printed 'for the assigns of John Calvin and Theodore Beza' and Ralph Wallis's *More News from Rome* (1666) was 'Imprinted at London for the Author, for the only benefit of his Wife and Children'. As a rule, the Presbyterians were the least likely nonconformists to adopt such expedients, and the least likely to have need of them since their more conservative views had readier access to licences than the more radical opinions of Independents, Baptists and Quakers, among whom the incidence of anonymous and unlicensed printing, with the accompanying false or defective imprints, greatly increases. Baxter was very rarely anonymous; Owen oftener; Keach frequently; Fox habitually.

Most persistent in their evasion of the curbs on the press, and most thoroughly organized as a group, were the Quakers, whose publications were very rarely licensed. Quakers did not recognize the state's right to silence the printed, any more than the spoken, word: 'our mouths were not opened by, nor can they be shut in the will of man', wrote Edward Billing. William Penn affords a nice example of the Quaker's blithe insouciance: committed to the Tower for the unlicensed *The Sandy Foundation Shaken* (1668) he there promptly wrote *No Cross, No Crown*, which appeared, unlicensed, in 1669. Determined to continue their mission, the Quakers established a press organization and a print culture wholly independent of the state. In the 1650s Quakers had been accustomed to consult George Fox before having a work printed. With the increasingly frequent imprisonment of Fox and other Quaker leaders after 1660 this became less easy, and in 1672 the Yearly Meeting appointed ten Friends to oversee and authorize all Quaker books. The following year, the Second-day's Morning Meeting was instituted to supervise and authorize all Quaker publications and to ensure that copies were kept of every Quaker and every anti-Quaker text. This organization was less to circumvent the law than to ensure the integrity of the Quaker message: it was, in Fox's words, 'to see that young Friends' books that was sent to be printed might be stood by'.[91]

## 5 Radicals, Republicans and Plotters

L'Estrange was energetic. He succeeded in generating a general atmosphere of apprehension and fear, and he had his successes. Indeed, a chief reason for his appointment to the Surveyorship of the Press was probably his detection and detainment in 1661–3 of the group of underground printers he dubbed 'the Confederate Stationers': Giles Calvert, a prolific publisher of Quaker tracts, Thomas Brewster, and Livewell Chapman, in the 1650s a noted publisher of

Fifth Monarchist pieces. The three of them had been responsible for issuing the regicides' *Speeches and Prayers* (1660). To this commemoration of the restored regime's most prominent enemies as victims and martyrs the trio added a riposte to the public burning of the Covenant in *A Phenix: or the Solemn League and Covenant*... (1661), which publicized Charles II's acutely embarrassing acceptance of the Covenant at his Scottish coronation in 1650. Its imprint gave Edinburgh as the place of publication, but it was in fact printed in London by Simon Dover and Thomas Creake. The same group also produced a book of portents intended to refute royalist interpretations of recent providences, *Mirabilis Annus: or the Year of Prodigies* (1661; sequels appeared in 1662).[92] From October 1660, L'Estrange steadily rounded them up.[93] He was to keep up his efforts throughout the decade – in 1668 Elizabeth Poole was committed to the Gatehouse for keeping a private press for unlicensed printing[94] – but he never came anywhere remotely near controlling the press.[95] Francis Smith, an associate of the Confederates, pursued a vigorous career of radical publishing through a bewildering succession of arrests, examinations, imprisonments and pursuits by L'Estrange and his spies.[96] The widows Elizabeth Calvert and Ann Brewster (their husbands died in 1663 and 1664 respectively) not only continued to be active in the printing trade but remained committed to radical publication. They consequently found themselves repeatedly the subject of L'Estrange's attentions, but to little avail.[97] Indeed, L'Estrange was taunted by his opponents with his inability to silence them. For four years between 1664 and 1669 the anti-clerical satirist Ralph Wallis, the 'Cobbler of Gloucester', made merry with the Surveyor's incapacity to catch him or to track down the press producing his tracts.[98] Early in *The Rehearsal Transpros'd* Marvell mocks the inefficiency of the licensing system and L'Estrange's inability to exercise his surveyorship effectively, ironically representing his point of view in the exclamation that ''twas an happy time when all Learning was in Manuscript, and some little Officer like our Author [Samuel Parker] did keep the Keys of the Library... *O Printing*! how hast thou disturb'd the Peace of Mankind!'[99]

There was an honourable precedent for such activities. A tradition of surreptitious radical Protestant printing, either on secret presses or secretly on registered presses, both in England and on the Continent, stretched back through the Leveller John Lilburne in the 1630s and Martin Marprelate in the 1580s to John Bale and William Tyndale in the early years of the English Reformation.[100] This tradition clearly remained vital, but the actual amount of unlicensed printing in the 1660s is impossible to compute since the requirement that its licence be printed in every authorized book was rarely followed even in books which had, in fact, been licensed, nor was every licensed book recorded in the Stationers' register.[101] What is clear is that to enter the world of the secret printers is to enter an underground culture bound together by marital, familial, political and religious loyalties far more than by merely professional ties. A sense of a community, almost an enclave, is conveyed by the report of one of L'Estrange's spies who in 1668 was searching for a secret press run by John Darby, his wife Joan, and Ann Brewster ('a couple of the craftiest and most obstinate in the trade' was L'Estrange's view of Ann Brewster and Joan Darby). The spy was confident it was in 'one of five houses in Blue Anchor Alley; but by reason of so many back doors, bye-holes, and passages, and the sectarians so swarming thereabouts, I have been afraid of being discovered in scouting'.[102]

These printers and booksellers were part of a more extensive underground network composed of former Cromwellian officers (Thomas Blood conspicuous among them) and republicans, millenarians and Fifth Monarchists, Baptists (notably Paul Hobson) and some Congregationalists.[103] Throughout the decade, they schemed the overthrow of the restored regime, less dangerously and less often than the regime itself feared, but sufficiently to pose a significant threat to law and order. In the earlier 1660s these conspirators planned, and in part effected, a succession of risings: Venner's Fifth Monarchist uprising in 1661; the Tong Plot to seize Windsor Castle in 1662 as the catalyst to risings throughout the country to establish a republic (so-called after one of the plotters, Thomas Tong); in 1663, an attempt led by Blood to seize Dublin Castle in May and a series of risings in northern counties in the autumn (variously referred to as the Derwentdale, Kaber Rigg, Yorkshire or Northern plot); and the Rathbone plot (named after the chief conspirator, John Rathbone) to take the Tower of London, burn the city and execute the King on 3 September 1665, the anniversary of Cromwell's victories at Dunbar and Worcester.[104] None of these was either sufficiently well organized or sufficiently secure in its support to pose any real threat to the restored regime, which, through informants and spies, was commonly aware of the plotters' activities at an early stage of their preparations. It was able to intervene to prevent the execution of the Tong and Rathbone plots and the others fell apart in the confusion of their implementation. Nevertheless, they provided alarming evidence of disaffection. Venner's Rising, in particular, coming so soon after the Restoration and occurring in London, provoked ferociously fierce condemnation and there were numerous arrests.[105] Thereafter, the decade never quite recovered its nerve nor, although sectarian groups took steps to dissociate themselves from Venner,[106] did it overcome its suspicion of dissent. These conspiracies thus served to keep the restored regime in a state of nervous apprehension and to make the Secretary of State constantly susceptible to tales of plots, however far-fetched or improbable, such as the Presbyterian uprising of 1661 in the West Midlands, supposedly involving Baxter, known as the Yarrington (after one of the alleged conspirators, Andrew Yarrington) or Packington (after its 'discoverer', Sir John Packington) plot.[107] They consequently achieved the opposite of their aim: rather than overthrowing the regime they encouraged its repressive and persecutory tendencies.

These plots, inspired by religious radicalism rather than coherent political theory, had very little sense of purpose beyond the overthrow of the present authorities. Committed and thoughtful republicanism, and the searching constitutional thinking which had been undertaken – and in part enacted – in the previous 20 years did not, however, simply vanish in 1660. In the revised second edition of *The Readie & Easie Way* (April 1660) Milton's enlargements of 'those great set pieces that condemned monarchy'[108] were in no doubt what the consequences of the Restoration would be: a reactionary tyranny of decadent indulgence. 'The old encroachments' would come on 'by little and little upon our consciences', exacerbated by the anxiety of 'kings to com, never forgetting thir former ejection', 'to fortifie and arm themselves sufficiently for the future against all such attempts hereafter from the people: who shall then be so narrowly watched and kept so low' that they can anticipate only a kind of ignoble slavery. In contrast to the equitable freedom of a commonwealth, 'wherin they who are greatest . . . are not elevated above thir brethren; live soberly in thir families, walk the streets as other men, may be spoken to freely, familiarly, friendly, without adoration', there will be a culture of servile deference to a king who 'must be ador'd like a Demigod, with a dissolute and haughtie court about him, of vast expence and luxurie, masks and revels, to the debaushings of our prime gentry both male and female', and who has 'little els to do, but to bestow the eating and drinking of excessive dainties, to set a pompous face upon the superficial actings of State, to pageant himself up and down in progress among the perpetual bowings and cringings of an abject people, on either side defying and adoring him for nothing don than can deserve it'.[109]

Milton would never again be able to express such impassioned sentiments so openly, but contempt for monarchy and for court culture still informs his depictions of evil in the 1660s. In *Paradise Lost* it is with the ascendancy of the tyrant Nimrod, 'from heaven claiming second sovereignty' in good Stuart style, that the period of pastoral simplicity succeeding the Flood is brought to an end and human history enters another swift decline. Satan is the devil who would be king, for whom it is 'Better to reign in hell, than serve in heaven'. The motor of the Fall is his 'monarchical pride' and it is in a kind of nightmare presence chamber that the 'great Sultan' Satan, 'High on a throne of a royal state', displays the tyrannical barbarism of regal rule.[110] Courts in *Paradise Lost* are the locus of loveless, contrived and exploitative amours, the antithesis of prelapsarian sexual love, as they had been for Milton ever since, in his 'stately palace', Comus had exhorted the Lady in the words of many a libertine Cavalier lyric to 'be not coy, and be not cozened / With that same vaunted name virginity, / Beauty is Nature's coin, must not be hoarded, / But must be current'. The 'tedious pomp that waits / On princes' can never recover the native dignity of Adam. It is their obsession with the pageantry and paraphernalia of courts that is one reason for Milton's antipathy to chivalric epic and Renaissance romance.[111]

Such expressions of contempt do not in themselves demonstrate republicanism. Many nonconformist sermons and tracts which never question monarchy *per se* disclose a settled bias against the appurtenances and indulgence of monarchy. Politically quietist though he may have been, Bunyan, for example, can characterize Satan as a tyrannical king and for him, no less than for Milton, Nimrod's pursuit of 'Absolute Monarchy' and his 'cruel and barbarous' persecution of his people are uncomfortably reminiscent of Stuart rule.[112] David Norbrook, however, has recently demonstrated that republicanism in *Paradise Lost* goes far beyond such particular remarks; it imbues the poem's 'overall intellectual and generic structures', particularly evident in its adoption of a body of classical references (especially to Lucan) which had characterized the English republican tradition.[113] The epic articulates a republican discourse. It is thus important evidence that there was, indeed, continuity between those otherwise apparently isolated moments when republicanism emerged on to the public stage – after 1649, during the Exclusion Crisis and at the 'Glorious Revolution'. Further evidence is afforded by Algernon Sidney's then unpublished 'Court Maxims', written in 1664–5 when he was in exile in the Netherlands. The premise of the book is that discontent with the restored regime is now widespread in England and its purpose is to explain how such high expectations as were entertained in 1660 could so quickly be disappointed. It repudiates patriarchal theories of royalism and discountenances claims that absolute, hereditary monarchy is of divine institution, seeing it rather as a perversion of true government which breeds injustice, ill-will and discontent as it pursues self-interest at the expense of the public good:

> The felicity of the Israelites could as little be inferred from the riches of their kings, as any man can truly say the people of England is now happy because the Stuart family, with their creature and parasites, live in the height of splendour and luxury. The contrary may be most rightly concluded. For as the riches of the thief is the poverty of the passenger robbed by him, the plenty of the king, who has nothing but what he tears from the subject, is their want and misery.[114]

# 7

# *'Luxury with Charles Restor'd'? The Temper of the Times*

## 1 'A yeare of prodigies' (1665–1666)

The mid-decade had to endure not only military and political calamities, but natural disasters as well. The year 1666, wrote Evelyn in his diary, was 'a yeare of nothing but prodigies in this Nation: Plage, War, fire, raines, Tempest: Comets'.[1] The first of these, bubonic plague, held a peculiar terror for the grotesqueness of its symptoms, the agony and swiftness with which it brought death and the virulence with which it could kill huge numbers. It manifested itself in a high fever, blotched skin and buboes, swellings of the lymphatic glands under the arms and in the groin, which burst into suppurating sores. Pain and fever resulted often in delirium and derangement. Spread by rats which were infested with the fleas which carried the bacillus, it was at its most virulent during the warm months of summer and autumn, abating in the winter when the fleas hibernated.[2] In the autumn of 1663 it was known to be in Holland – 'got to Amsterdam, brought by a ship from Argier' says Pepys in October 1663 – and quarantine measures were introduced in the port of London in November.[3] That month it was reported in Yarmouth and the next spring there were cases in London. Pepys first mentions 'Great fears of the Sickenesse here in the City' on 30 April 1665. By early June, it had spread from the outer parishes and suburbs into the City itself. On 15 June, Pepys noted a rise in the number of plague deaths in the previous week from 43 to 112.[4] Two weeks later, plague deaths had reached nearly 300 per week. By mid-July, they had reached over 1,000 a week, by late July nearly 2,000, by mid-August over 3,000, and at the end of the month, by 'a great enrease ... beyond all expectation, of almost 2000', 6,000.[5] A week later, they were given as 6,988, certainly an underestimate: when, at the end of August, the mortality bill had recorded 7,496 deaths, of which 6,102 were said to be from the plague, Pepys thought the true figure nearer 10,000.[6] All who could afford to do so left the capital: at Cripplegate on 21 June, Pepys found 'all the town almost going out of town, the coaches and waggons being full of people going into the country'. At end of that month, the government also left. The King went first to Hampton Court, then Salisbury, and in September to Oxford, whither he summoned parliament in October. Albemarle, with a force quartered in Hyde Park, was put in command of the capital, to secure law and order and to prevent any insurrection from religious or republican dissidents who, it was feared, might take advantage of the authorities' preoccupation with the plague and of the breakdown of social cohesion.[7] The death toll began to decline with the onset of winter. The first decrease in the weekly mortality bills occurred in the second week of September, but in the third week they recorded their highest total of plague deaths, over 7,000, which, wrote Pepys in dismay, 'is quite contrary to all our hopes and expectations from the coldness of the late season'. At the end of the month, however, there was again a fall, to 5,500 plague deaths, and in October – save for an uncomfortable moment in November – a steady decline at last set in.[8] By the end of that month the city was beginning to fill up and there were signs that business and commercial activities were being resumed. At the end of December, Pepys could report that 'the town fills apace, and shops begin to be open again'. By late January 1666 the City was 'almost as full again of people as ever it was', though Covent Garden and 'all that end of the town' was still 'infinitely naked' of people. Charles himself was back in Whitehall on 1 January. Not until 9 November 1666, however, was a day of thanksgiving proclaimed for the final cessation of the plague, and the theatres reopened – though even then, reports Pepys, 'the town doth say that it is hastened before the plague is quite over, there dying some people still'. By then, somewhere in the region of 100,000 of the city's inhabitants – between a quarter and a third of the total – had died, 'reckoning the *Quakers,* and others, that were never put in the Bills of Mortality', with 'the greatest Blow [falling] on the Poor'.[9]

Understandably, the exodus from London was resisted by provincial communities. Although the plague's means of transmission was not understood, it was recognized that it could be carried by infected persons or by persons or objects which had been in contact with the diseased. Every effort was therefore made to secure disease-free towns and villages from contact with people from afflicted communities. Fear and self-interest prompted a determined enforcement of such exclusion, with a watch being kept upon roads, rivers and coastlines and travellers attempting entry being forcibly driven off. When, in July 1665, Pepys visited Dagenham in Essex, he exclaimed at people's reaction to visitors from London, 'Lord, to see in what fear all the people here do live would make one mad'. 'How fearful People were', recalled Baxter, 'thirty or forty, if not an hundred Miles from *London*, of any thing that they bought from any Mercer's, or Draper's Shop; or of any Goods that were brought to them; or of any Person that came to their Houses. How they would shut their Doors against their Friends; and if a Man passed over the fields, how one would avoid another, as we did in the time of Wars; and how every Man was a Terrour to another!'[10]

Similarly, within the capital the main expedient adopted to prevent the spread of the disease was isolation, achieved either by conveying the infected to pest houses, forcibly if necessary, or, more commonly, by sealing up houses where there was known to be infection, incarcerating the diseased and uninfected residents together. Houses were shut with padlocks, chains and nails and those without admonished by a red cross and 'Lord Have Mercy Upon Us' painted on the front door. Pepys was greatly sobered when he first saw this, on 7 June 1665 in Drury Lane; by late June, it was a common sight. Often, an armed watchman was posted to prevent any escape, 'the plague', remarked Pepys, 'making us cruel as dogs one to another'. Searchers, commonly old women, were employed by parishes to enter houses to search for plague victims in case, to prevent their being shut in, their families had failed to report them, and to inspect corpses to determine the cause of death, lest this be hidden from the authorities for the same reason. They carried a distinctive white stick so that they might be avoided. The period of confinement was forty days, which meant that any survivors among those shut in had often to wait until long after the last fatality before the house was opened up. During this time, victims and survivors alike were dependent upon friends and charity for provision, though parish and municipal resources took such steps as they could to provide relief.[11] For protection against infection, reliance was placed upon various scents, nosegays and unguents – tobacco was a favourite, and the preventative Pepys first reached for – and upon fumigation with sulphur to ward off infection. Fires were kept smoking in the streets for the same reason. And all contact with infected persons, or objects which had come near them, was shunned. Hackney coaches which had carried plague victims had to be aired for five or six days before being used again. Pepys could not bring himself to travel in one until late November, and then 'with great pain . . . for fear'. He was afraid to wear a new periwig bought in Westminster when the plague was there, and wondered what would come of the fashion since 'nobody will dare to buy any haire for fear of the infection – that it had been cut off of the heads of people dead of the plague'.[12]

To cope with the fatalities the City parishes employed carters to make rounds to collect corpses for burial and convey them to a burial ground. They worked at night, accompanied by a warning bell, to reduce the risk of infection and to keep their gruesome work out of sight, though by mid-August 'the people die so, that now it seems they are fain to carry the dead to be buried by daylight, the nights not sufficing to do it in'. They cleared not only houses but the streets, where many victims had died where they fell: one night in August Pepys stumbled over a corpse in a dark alley. By October he had so often encountered men transporting plague corpses 'that I am come almost to <think> nothing of it'.[13] As the death toll increased churchyards became nightmare places, stinking and swelling many feet above their usual level and spilling corpses and coffins from their overcrowded depths. Recourse had to be made to communal burial, without coffins, in unconsecrated pits dug in the suburbs – 'in the Commons' – without mourners or ceremony, often at night. Even when the burial was in a churchyard, funeral processions and gatherings of mourners were forbidden.[14] Eye-witness accounts speak graphically of the horrors of London's deserted streets. On 7 September Evelyn walked 'all along the Citty & suburbs from *Kent streete* to *St James's*, a dismal passage & dangerous, to see so many Cofines exposd in the streetes & the streete thin of people, the shops shut up, & all in mournefull silence, as not knowing whose turne might be next'. 'But Lord, how empty the streets are, and melancholy, so many poor sick people in the streets, full of sores, and so many sad stories overheard as I walk, everybody talking of this dead, and that man sick.'[15]

There could be no certainty that the plague would not return with the warm weather of late summer and autumn 1666, and many provincial towns and ports did suffer again, some more grievously than in 1665.[16] In London, however, it was quite another visitation which came in September 1666. Very early on Sunday 2 September, that 'fatal night', a bakery in Pudding Lane, just north of the river, caught fire and, fanned by an exceptionally strong easterly wind, it spread first to neighbouring houses, then to warehouses of tallow, oil and hemp, and then, for three days, from street to street, crossing above the narrow lanes by jumping from overhanging storey to overhanging storey, westward across the City and into the suburbs. On the first day the fire moved the short distance south to the river and consumed the houses on the north end of London Bridge. It spread westwards along the north bank of the river nearly the length of Thames Street, and northwards into Eastcheap. On the Monday, from the Southwark bank, Evelyn saw 'the whole South part of the Citty burning from Cheape side to the Thames, & all along Cornehill (for it likewise kindled back against the Wind, as well <as> forward)'. The fire now took in most of the area to the north of London Bridge, including the Poultry, Fenchurch Street and Gracechurch Street. To the west, it was now close to St Paul's, which it reached on Tuesday, 'the Easter <n> Wind still more impetuously driving the flames forewards', reducing the cathedral and its environs in northwest London – Watling Street, Cheapside, Ludgate Hill, Fleet Street, Old Bailey, Newgate – to ashes; 'the stones of *Paules* flew like granados, the Lead melting downe the streetes in a streame, & the very pavements of them glowing with fiery rednesse, so as nor horse nor man was able to tread on them'. At Whitehall there was now consternation that the fire would reach Westminster and preparations were made to evacuate government offices. It burned in Cripplegate and threatened the Tower, 'where the Magazines of Powder lay' which, had they taken fire, would not only have 'beaten downe & destroyed all the bridge, but sunke & torne all the vessels in the river, & rendred the demolition beyond all expression . . . at many miles distance', but on Wednesday 5

September the wind finally eased and the fire began to abate. It halted its westward march at Fetter Lane and the Temple, on the very edge of the West End.[17]

Burnet was astonished that he 'never heard of any one person that was either burnt or trode to death', for the scale of the destruction was awesome. Most of the city, three of its markets, St Paul's, Guildhall, the Royal Exchange, nearly 90 churches, over 50 company halls, and over 13,000 houses were destroyed. Nearly 450 acres were laid waste – 'almost all the City within the Walls' – and some 100,000 people made homeless. The very contours of the city, centuries in the making, had vanished so completely in 72 hours that when he walked the ruined streets on 7 September Evelyn found himself 'frequently mistaking where I was'. To material loss was added financial, for there was no fire insurance. Contemporary estimates put the damage to property in the region of £10,000,000, while business, commerce and the professions were crippled by the loss of goods, records and premises. Leases became unenforceable, with consequent loss of rent income. When on 8 September Pepys attended Gresham College, which, by proclamation of 6 September, was to serve as the Royal Exchange, he 'met with many people undone, and more that have extraordinary great losses'. Among the most severely hit was the book trade, for the stocks which had been carried for safety into St Faith's, the parish church in the crypt of St Paul's, were completely destroyed when the collapsing roof of the cathedral broke through the floor; the books continued to burn for a week. Their burnt leaves blew as far as Windsor Forest and Acton in Middlesex.[18] No such scene of devastation had before been witnessed by the capital (nor would be again until the 1940s):

> O the miserable calamitous spectacle, such as happly the whole world had not seene the like since the foundation of it, nor to be out don, 'til the universal Conflagration of it, all the skie were of a fiery aspect, like the top of a burning Oven, & the light seene above 40 miles round about for many nights: God grant mine eyes may never behold the like, who now saw above ten thousand houses all in one flame, the noise & crakling & thunder of the impetuous flames, the shreeking of Women & children, the hurry of people, the fall of towers, houses & churches was like an hideous storme, & the aire all about so hot & inflam'd that at the last one was not able to approch it, so as they were force'd <to> stand still, and let the flames consume on which they did for neere two whole mile<s> in length and one in bredth: The Clowds also of Smoke were dismall, & reached upon computation neere 50 miles in length.[19]

Charles and the government came rather well out of this episode. The King and his brother, in particular, were much applauded for their ready and prompt efforts in directing efforts to fight the fire, and for their willingness themselves to work alongside others.[20]

There was a popular view that the fire was the work of conspirators, either French and Catholic, perhaps Dutch, perhaps sectarian, perhaps

Commonwealthsmen, and there were scares and fears of fireraising throughout the country during the following months. On 5 September Pepys had already heard that 'the French had done it' and the next day an outbreak of fire at Bishop's Gate, 'where no fire had yet been near', convinced him that fireraisers were indeed at work. Later, his attention was called to the proximity of its outbreak to the talismanic date 3 September and the consequent likelihood of quite other culprits. A Parliamentary Committee of Enquiry into the causes of the fire was set up on 25 September. Its report, presented on 22 January 1667, found evidence that French Catholics and Jesuits were responsible for the fire, but neither Charles nor Clarendon were persuaded it was deliberately caused.[21] A French watchmaker from Rouen, Robert Hubert, did confess to starting the fire, and on 27 October was executed for starting the blaze, but his confession was 'so senseless' and so entirely lacking in corroboration that the government did not take him seriously and there seems little doubt that he was deranged.[22]

## 2 'Things going to wrack'

The events of 1665–6 were a shock to the nation, but it is not the immediacy of their horror alone which explains the reaction to these catastrophes. They derived their significance for contemporaries from their intensification of a sense of unease and disillusionment which had been steadily deepening since the first two or three heady years following the Restoration. With the signal exception of having achieved the Restoration and secured the quiescence, if not the acquiescence, of Puritan and republican opinion, the decade's political record was dismal. After the initial two years, its legislation was all either repressive or short term, or both, while the impression that the government, and especially the King, was not much interested in governing gained ground. The regime bungled its war and sacrificed its first minister. Seldom can circumstances have reduced a governing elite which came to power to such acclaim and celebration so quickly to contempt, nor a mood of relief and rejoicing to one of disenchantment and disillusionment. To view the contemporary scene in mid-decade was to descry disaster in every direction – military, political and natural. National humiliation at the hands of the Dutch, rumours of plots and insurrections, Clarendon's unpopularity and impending impeachment, all gave the impression of a government rudderless, and, what was worse, a government not much bothered by the sorry state of public affairs. The calamities of Plague and Fire were a terrible confirmation that the times were out of joint.

To minds habituated to providential explanations for natural phenomena and excited by the apocalyptic year 1666, this succession of catastrophes was inescapably portentous. It was as though the Four Horsemen were riding, just as publications throughout the century had prophesied that they would. The year 1666 had for long attracted millenarian attention,[23] and in the mid-century it had been a focus of Fifth Monarchist expectations.[24] Such speculation intensified after the Restoration. In his *Ecchoes from the Sixth Trumpet* (1666), whose title page called attention to the significance of the date with the words *Imprinted in the Year Chronogrammatically Expressed in this Seasonable Prayer LorD haVe MerCIe Vpon Vs*, George Wither drew from the Fire the eschatological inference that 'The *Saints* last *Purgatory* is now commencing'.[25] To this cast of mind the fact that MDCLXVI uniquely includes every Roman numeral once and in sequence was momentous. In Revelation 13.18 there is no connection made between the number of the beast and chronology, nor is there any straightforward connection between that number, 666, and 1666, but a great deal of exegetical, numerological and historical effort had been expended in forging such connections (and, less often, in denying them). Among those intent upon fathoming the mysteries of biblical prophecy, 1666 was anticipated as a key date in the drama of the Last Things, perhaps the year of the conversion of the Jews, of the destruction of Antichrist, perhaps of the Second Coming. Such speculations were politically charged: the collections of portents and prodigies which appeared at the Restoration in the three *Mirabilis Annus* pamphlets belittled official propaganda in their assertion that an apocalyptic purpose was being played out through the events of the Restoration. These connected dire events with the royalist and episcopal ascendancy, seeking to persuade their readers 'that upon us the ends of the world are come, and that God is now making hast *to consummate* his *whole* work in the earth, and prepare the way for his *Son to take unto himself his great power and reign*'.[26] As the year 1666 approached, apprehension and anticipation palpably increased. In February, Pepys called into his booksellers 'for a book, writ about twenty years ago in prophecy of this year coming on, 1666', namely Francis Potter's *An Interpretation of the Number 666* (1642), with which he was occupied throughout the year, finding it, whether right or wrong, 'mighty ingenious'.[27]

Not everyone was persuaded by this millenarian interpretation of prodigious events. Many were dismayed both by what it revealed of 'the over-fervent spirits of some Fanaticks' and by its seditious import.[28] Pepys was not convinced, but, as his case indicates, even those whose religion was of a very unexcited and worldly kind were subject to a kind of appalled fascination as the disasters of the decade succeeded each other. It was Baxter who regretted those 'over-fervent' fanatic spirits, but the Plague led even him to exclaim:

> Every Man is a terrour to his Neighbour and himself: for God for our Sins is a Terrour to us all. O how is *London*, the place which God hath honoured with his Gospel above all Places of the Earth, laid low in Horrours, and wasted almost to Desolation, by the Wrath of God, whom *England* hath contemned; and a

> God-hating Generation are consumed in their Sins, and the righteous are also reflect on the taken away as from greater Evil yet to come.[29]

This view that the Plague and Fire were divine punishment was developed most forcefully in *God's Terrible Voice in the City . . . where you have a catalogue of Londons sins . . . [and] an enumeration of the duties God calls for by this terrible voice* (1667) by the ejected Presbyterian divine Thomas Vincent.

This association of disaster with the nation's dissolute ways was not peculiar to nonconformist divines. To Evelyn the destruction wrought by the Fire appeared 'a resemblance of Sodome' from which, like Lot, he was preserved, or of the fires of hell, and it brought into his mind Hebrews 13.14. During the Plague, on 6 July 1665, a monthly fast day was proclaimed to express national repentance and to seek reconciliation with God, but in many quarters it was believed that the government itself had most need of repentance. Dissatisfaction came to be articulated especially through dismay at what was taken to be its preference for hedonistic indulgence over duty. Seldom is the government condemned for its ineptitude but it is also condemned for its idleness, profanity and self-indulgence. It was a constant theme among rising bureaucrats and businessmen. In 1665 Pepys records 'Talking of the ill-government of our Kingdom' with his friend the hemp merchant George Cocke, with 'nobody setting to heart the business of the Kingdom, but everybody minding their perticular profit or pleasures, the King himself minding nothing but his ease – and so we let things go to wrack'.[30] For their part, Church of England divines were no less convinced than Puritan that the disasters of the 1660s were a succession of divine admonitions to the nation to mend its ways. The rejoicing of the sermons of 1660–2 gave way, within two or three years, to sermons appalled by the profligacy and moral degeneration of the nation despite its having enjoyed the great mercy of the Restoration.[31] London sermons on national fast days inveighed against the corruption of manners, the fashion for shameless licence and the affected superciliousness of men of wit with especial fervour, as the responsive Evelyn testifies:

> This day [10 October 1666] was indicted a Generall fast through the nation, to humble us, upon the late dreadfull Conflagration, added to the Plage & Warr, the most dismall judgements could be inflicted, & indeede but what we highly deserved for our prodigious ingratitude, burning Lusts, disolute Court, profane & abominable lives, under such dispensations of Gods continued favour, in restoring Church, Prince, & people from our late intestine calamities.[32]

On 29 July 1667 the lamentable state of a nation which was 'never in so troubled a condition in this world as now' prompted one of the longest entries in Pepys's diary. The sorry conduct of the war and the humiliating peace with the Dutch demonstrate that 'in all things . . . the Dutch have the best of us, and do end the war with victory on their side'; 'Nobody [is] pleased with the peace'. That day, only four days after it met, parliament was prorogued until 20 October, to the 'general great distaste' of MPs, when 'the nation [is] in certain condition of ruin' and the King 'is only governed by his lust and women and rogues about him... They do all give up the kingdom for lost.'[33] There was a general apprehension that Charles meant to abandon parliamentary governance for rule by means of a standing Army.[34] Ten days later, Evelyn told Pepys 'that wise men do prepare to remove abroad what they have, for that we must be ruined – our case being past relief, the Kingdom so much in debt, and the King minding nothing but his lust'. Ominously, Oliver's time began to be recalled admiringly. During the second half of 1667, Pepys several times reports the opinion

> that of necessity this Kingdom will fall back again to a commonwealth... this family doing all that silly men can do to make themselfs unable to support their Kingdom – minding their lust and their pleasure, and making their government so chargeable, that people do well remember better things were done, and better managed and with much less charge, under a commonwealth then they have been by this King.[35]

The fall of Clarendon only exacerbated these fears. On 27 November, during the parliamentary debates on Clarendon's future, Pepys heard from James Pearse, Surgeon-General to the Navy,

> how the King is now fallen in and become a slave to the Duke of Buckingham, led by none but him... He doth say, and I think with right, that the King doth in this do the most ungrateful part of a maister to a servant that was ever done, in this carriage of his to my Lord Chancellor. That it may be the Chancellor may have faults, but none such as these they speak of. That he doth now really fear that all is going to ruin...[36]

In the second half of the decade this growing disquiet and discontent subjected the court and government to a sustained hostile literary assault in which the shape of the cultural and political opposition of the next 20 years can first be discerned. The years 1660–5 comprised but a pause in the nation's continuing internecine discord which, though not resumed on the battlefield (at least, not until the 1680s), had not been resolved. From 1666 the monarchical and episcopalian establishment again found itself under threat: satirical mockery and denunciation would henceforth be a feature of Charles's reign. The immediate occasion was the rhetorical extravagance of Edmund Waller's *Instructions to a Painter, for the Drawing of the Posture and Progress of his Majesties Forces at Sea, under the Command of His Highness Royal, together with the Battel and Victory obtained over the Dutch, June 3, 1665* (1666), that is the English naval victory over the Dutch at Lowestoft. The poem, an encomiastic exercise in heroic diction celebrating the Duke of York's command, was quickly overtaken by events,[37] but its extravagant celebration of the administration's achievements provoked a sustained satirical scrutiny of the government.[38] In the succeeding parodies, a prospect is painted of negligence and incompetence in preparation for the war, panic and confusion in the face of the Dutch navy (and especially in the poems which follow the English humiliations of the summer of 1667), disloyalty and cowardice in the face of the enemy, and venality and corruption in the conduct of public affairs. Coventry, bestowing naval offices in return for money, 'sells the whole Fleet away'; 'none's rewarded but the Sycophant'; 'Death picks the Valiant out, the Cow'rds survive'.[39] Ministerial grotesques parade through these satires: 'Men? nay rather Monsters', such as Clarendon with his 'transcendent Paunch'. Farmed by corrupt officials, shamed by its military incapacity, England is in such a parlous state in the summer of 1667 that, to prevent further incursions by the Dutch and the fall of its capital, it must resort to self-destruction, sinking its own ships to block the Thames as, the year before, it had destroyed houses to halt the Fire. For Marvell, those responsible are a 'race of Drunkards, Pimps, and Fools', 'Gross Bodies, grosser Minds, and grossest Cheats'. Clarendon, seeking to finance the war through taxes and loans, is depicted with 'His minion Imps that, in his secret part, / Lye nuzz'ling at the *Sacramental* wart; / Horse-leeches circling at the Hem'roid Vein; / He sucks the King, they him, he them again'.[40] This contempt is counterpointed by Marvell's admiration for the Monck to whom, despite its resentment of him, the regime turns in every emergency and, still more, by the image of true loyalty and heroism presented in the figure of Captain Archibald Douglas who refused to abandon ship and died when it was set ablaze by Dutch fireships in the Thames.[41] To praise Monck is to come uncomfortably close to recalling the military supremacy of Cromwell. When the *Third Advice*, with a similarly high regard for Monck, 'himself alone a Fleet', puts into the voice of the Duchess of Albemarle its disdain for the conduct of the restored regime, it ominously links the opposition politics of the Restoration with the aspiration of the Interregnum in its suggestion that what once sent the Stuarts overseas might do so again: 'Nor better grown, nor wiser all this while' they 'Renew the causes of their first Exile'.[42]

## 3 The Cabal (1667–1670)

On 2 September 1667, after Clarendon's flight, Pepys wrote that 'Some people, and myself among them, are of good hope from this change that things are reforming',[43] but the ministry which succeeded Clarendon's did nothing to relieve the nation's sense of unease and disillusionment; rather the contrary. For the five years following his fall and exile, the court interest was led by a group popularly stigmatized as the Cabal.[44] The Cabal, however, hardly constituted a government. It was not a coherent group of politicians working to an agreed objective, nor even a conspiratorial gathering of dubious characters out for their own ends, which was the contemporary satirical and 'Country' view of their activities. They had been brought together solely by their opposition to Clarendon and had little in common as individuals: 'they do not in their hearts trust one another, but do drive several ways, all of them'.[45] Sir Thomas Clifford, Comptroller and Treasurer of the royal household, was a closet Roman Catholic. Lord Ashley, afterwards Earl of Shaftesbury, had been, as Antony Ashley Cooper, a Cromwellian who, in the later 1650s, came to oppose the Protectorate. Raised to the peerage in 1661 for his contribution to bringing about the Restoration, he that year became Chancellor of the Exchequer. Like George Villiers, 2nd Duke of Buckingham, the son of Charles I's murdered favourite, he had Presbyterian connections. Buckingham had married Mary, Thomas Lord Fairfax's daughter, and had beside Leveller and republican associations and was, at least at stages in his career, the champion of the dissenters. He was, though, never formally a minister, unlike Henry Bennet, Earl of Arlington, Chief Secretary of State 1662–74.[46] Arlington was a Catholic sympathizer but the fifth member of the group, John Maitland, Duke of Lauderdale, was a Scot (now Secretary for Scotland), a Presbyterian, and the friend of Baxter, but a close associate of the King to whom his dissolute ways recommended him. If, however, the sinister Cabal was a contemporary myth,[47] it is not difficult to see how the myth developed. With the exile of Clarendon the tone of politics changed drastically. The Cabal worked in the Court interest and served the royal prerogative without any of Clarendon's restraint, his respect for the law, his moderate view of the constitution or his critical view of royal behaviour. Bribery became a standard means of parliamentary management[48] and self-seeking deviousness characteristic of the dealings of the Cabal's members with each other as they strove for the King's favour, the bitterest rivals being Buckingham, with the higher profile, and Arlington, with the greater political weight.[49]

There was, though, one policy objective which the members of the Cabal did share: toleration.[50] This might be expected from a group who between them either represented or had connections with the full range of possible, and proscribed, Christian opinion in the 1660s, but it remains the one feature of the Cabal with a claim upon respect. It was also their undoing, for it combined disturbingly with a growing inclination in Charles towards an assertion of the royal prerogative. Buffeted by his dealings with parliament and bothered by inadequate finances, he increasingly found attractive the despotic model of the reign of his cousin Louis XIV. Charles had returned from exile with a passion for French taste and fashion;[51] by the late 1660s, if not earlier, he had, too, an admiration for its politics and for authoritarian kingship. He was much attracted to the ideal of a constitution in which royal power was dominant and parliament subordinate, with adequate resources (including, perhaps, military resources) available to the monarch and the church (Church of England or Roman Catholic perhaps hardly mattered) devoted to sustaining the monarchy. The Whiggish Burnet reports that Charles 'had made such observations on the French government, that he thought a king who might be checked, or have his ministers called to an account by a parliament, was but a king in name'. When 'the carelessness and luxury of the court came to be so much exposed' by the 1669 report of the Commission of Public Accounts, 'All the flatterers about him magnified foreign governments, where the princes were absolute, that in France more particularly', as a model for Charles, who 'loved the project in general, but would not give himself the trouble of laying or managing it'.[52]

In the final years of the decade this inclination in Charles and the Cabal's interest in toleration became embrangled with foreign policy. Early in 1668 England joined in a Triple Alliance with the Protestant United Provinces and Sweden aimed at curtailing Louis XIV's Catholic power,[53] though it is probable that from Charles's point of view this was less a decision to weigh England in the balance against France than a means to secure the goodwill (that is, good financial will) of the Cavalier Parliament.[54] A year later, however, secret negotiations were underway to secure an alliance with France. On the French side, Charles's sister, Henriette, since 1661 wife of Louis XIV's brother Philippe, Duc d'Orleans, played a major part. On the English side, clandestine negotiations were conducted by Henry Jermyn, Earl of St Albans, Henry Lord Arundell, and Sir Richard Bellings, while Buckingham and the French ambassador Colbert de Croissy pursued a commercial treaty in ignorance of the secret negotiations. Only James, Duke of York, and Clifford participated in the final negotiations at Dover, and only Arlington was afterwards informed of the full text of the treaty. In the secret clauses of the Treaty of Dover, concluded on 22 May 1670,[55] Charles acknowledged the truth of Roman Catholicism and undertook to be publicly reconciled with Rome as soon as the affairs of his kingdom allowed, in respect of which he received 2 million *livres* as a token of French support, and a promise of additional funds and 6,000 troops (paid by France) should they be required (that is, presumably, should the announcement of Catholicism provoke a rebellion in England). The two monarchs further agreed that all previous treaties with the United Provinces were void and that they would declare war on the United Provinces at a date of Louis's choosing. Charles was to receive an annual subsidy of 3 million *livres* to defray the cost of his participation in the war on Holland. Charles could not become a king such as he would be without becoming (or without promising to become) a Roman Catholic.[56]

Charles could hardly hope for the nation's conversion over a century after the Reformation: a renewed attempt at toleration was consequently an essential part of this policy. However, when, on 15 March 1672, Charles issued his second *Declaration of Indulgence*, a much more determined and comprehensive assertion of the royal prerogative right to suspend the execution of all penal religious legislation than in 1662, he encountered even firmer opposition than he had then. Nonconformists (though they did take out licences to preach in significant numbers) were opposed to the extension of toleration to Roman Catholics, while parliament was jealous of its prerogative. When, after a 21-month prorogation, it reassembled in February 1673, its first debates attacked the royal suspending power. A resolution was passed that 'penal statutes in matters ecclesiastical, cannot be suspended but by Act of Parliament', a direct challenge to the scope of the royal prerogative. Charles submitted and on 7 March withdrew the *Declaration*, but parliament followed through on its success with the first Test Act which required all holders of public office, civil and military, to take the sacrament by the Church of England rite and to disavow transubstantiation.[57] This broke the Cabal: Ashley, though he favoured toleration for Protestant dissenters, came to support the Test Act as an anti-Catholic measure, and by the end of 1673 had moved to opposing the court; the Act's provisions led to Clifford's resignation as Treasurer; in the collapse of the royal policy Buckingham was dismissed. Arlington resigned. The episode served to enflame anti-papist feeling, the more so since James, Duke of York, heir to the throne, resigned as Lord High Admiral. His failure to take the sacrament at Easter 1673 was the first public affirmation of his faith. With his marriage in September to the Catholic Mary of Modena (Anne Hyde had died in 1671), the succession begins to emerge as the burning issue of politics around which disputes coalesce. This would be the making, and the breaking, of Ashley, by then 1st Earl of Shaftesbury and a much greater political figure than any other of the Cabal's members.

## 4 Porno-politics

If the Cabal was thought to be politically devious, a group of intriguing and self-interested rivals, so too it was generally held to be morally dissolute. Political corruption is inextricably bound up with sexual corruption in the satirical caricatures of the court and the Cabal. In one way, this was nothing new. Satire has always found courts corrupt. However, what lent these caricatures their satirical force was their foothold in fact. Burlesques they may be, but not fictions. The sexual promiscuity of Charles and his court, its applause of the sexually voracious male, its attraction of sexually available women and its contempt for marital fidelity in men or women, were both distinctive and new in English culture. A feature of Renaissance culture had been the status accorded to, and the patronage wielded by, courtesans. The word itself, which entered English from Italian in the early sixteenth century, at once registered this elevation and denoted the only means by which a position analogous to that of the male courtier was customarily attainable by a woman. Successive rule by a queen, a misogynist and homosexual, a faithfully married monarch and a Puritan protector, had in their various ways denied the figure any great play at the English court for a hundred years, but Charles II's court, in libertine reaction against what it took to be the kill-joy hypocrisy of Puritanism, gave a new lease of life to the role of courtesan. The ennoblement of Charles II's own mistresses set her at the apex of English society. 'His love of pleasure and his vast expense with his women, together with the great influence they have had in all his affairs both at home and abroad, is the chief load that will lay on him', wrote Burnet; 'for not only the women themselves have great power, but his court is full of pimps and bawds, and all matters in which one desires to succeed must be put in their hands'.[58]

The Restoration had announced itself as initiating a period of prodigality and plenty. Re-invigoration and liberality, registered through images of fecundity and sexual potency, had been a feature of the eulogies and panegyrics, and of the iconography, of 1660. Dryden's celebration of the coronation in 'To His Sacred Majesty' closes by associating the King's sexual fertility with the commercial and political well-being of the nation: there is a sense in which the ripeness of future promise depends upon Charles's loins.[59] More generally, the celebrations of that year, heralding a time of pleasure and plenty, had a Bacchanalian air, offensively so to those of a Puritan disposition.[60] Those Restoration hopes had, as in Dryden's panegyric, anticipated Charles's fruitful marriage, and understandably so: the future of the throne depended upon an heir. The constitutional significance of the royal bed would become pressing during the next two decades as it became clear that Charles, 'the most potent Prince in Christendom', would have no legitimate heir.[61] That anxiety was already present in the 1660s – witness the hostile interpretation of the marriage of Anne Hyde to the Duke of York.[62] It was matched by a growing anxiety about the frequency with which Charles, 'The easiest prince and best bred man alive', was to be found in other beds. As Ailesbury delicately put it, Charles was 'of an amorous disposition'. Rochester's couplets were less delicate: 'Restless he rolls about from whore to whore / A merry monarch, scandalous and poor'.[63] On 29 July 1667 Pepys heard of 'the strange bold sermon of Dr. Creeton yesterday before the King; how he preach against the sins of the Court, and perticularly against adultery, over and over instancing how for that single sin in David, the whole nation was undone'. In 1667–8, Allestree preached at Whitehall before Charles against sensuality and lust.[64] Such homiletic admonitions quite failed of their mark. 'The ruin of his reign, and of all his affairs, was occasioned chiefly by his delivering himself up at his first coming over to a mad range of pleasure', wrote Burnet, of which the chief was 'his passion' for Castlemaine, 'the prerogative whore', 'a woman of great beauty, but most enormously vicious and ravenous, foolish but imperious, ever uneasy to the king, carrying on intrigues with other men'. Burnet's censoriousness may have been immune to the attraction which so besotted Pepys (though he 'knew well enough she is a whore'), and his judgement that the sway of this 'imperious mistress' over the 'amorous king' 'did so disorder him, that often he was not master of himself, nor capable of minding business' recalls the political resentment of Clarendon at her influence, but it remains uncomfortably true that no man was better suited than Charles to represent a culture of indulgence and licence.[65]

The example of Charles's libertinism encouraged his court to strive to avoid the 'dull shore of lazy temperance' as strenuously as himself.[66] The frenetic sexual circus at the apex of English society is finely caught in Pepys's account of a quarrel between Charles and Castlemaine when, in the summer of 1667, the King refused to acknowledge as his the child she was carrying:

> the bottom of the quarrel is this: she is fallen in love with young Jermin, who hath of late lain with her oftener then the King and is now going to marry my Lady Falmouth. The King, he is mad at her entertaining Jermin, and she is mad at Jermin going to marry from her, so they are all mad; and thus the kingdom is governed.[67]

The Henry Jermyn to whom Pepys there refers was the nephew of Henry Jermyn, Earl of St Albans. Both are generously present in contemporary gossip and rumour which reached beyond Charles to embrace the whole of the royal family. It was widely believed that St Albans, 'The new Courts pattern, Stallion of the old', was the lover of the Queen Mother, Henrietta Maria,[68] while the marriage of Anne Hyde generated extravagant depictions of her quest for sexual gratification, pursuing 'forbidden Arts' to satisfy her 'triumphant taile'. She was said to have been the lover of the younger Jermyn, the Duke of York's Master of the Horse; of her own Master of Horse, Henry Sidney, afterwards Earl of Romney; and of Henry Savile, brother of the future Marquis of Halifax; and she was rumoured to have murdered one of the Duke of York's mistresses, Lady Denham, wife of Sir John Denham.[69] Castlemaine's appetite was popularly reported to extend beyond Jermyn to all sorts and conditions of men, from the King to the rope dancer and tumbler Jacob Hall.[70] In 1662 Henry Jermyn was injured, and his second Giles Rawlins killed, in a duel on 17 August with Thomas Howard, brother of the Earl of Carlisle, over the Countess of Shrewsbury, Anna Maria Talbot (née Brudenell). She had married Francis Talbot, 14th Earl of Shrewsbury, in 1659 at the age of 16, and had since been so generously disposed that it came to be believed that, 'As no person could boast of being the only one in her favour, so no person could complain of having been ill received'. Her lovers were said to include not only Jermyn and Howard, but Richard Butler, Earl of Arran, and Henry Killigrew.[71] In 1666 she became the mistress of Buckingham, whose interest had been excited, according to Hamilton, by Killigrew's 'luxurious descriptions' of her 'most secret charms and beauties, which above half the court were as well acquainted with as himself'. She is, wrote Pepys in January 1668, 'a whore and is at this time, and hath for a great while been, a whore to the Duke of Buckingham'. Provoked by this liaison to challenge Buckingham, her husband was seriously wounded in a duel on 16 January 1668, and died two months later, perhaps as a result of his injuries. After his death, the Countess and Buckingham lived openly together, the Duke's wife, Mary Fairfax, daughter of the parliamentarian commander Thomas Lord Fairfax, and in the 1650s Marvell's pupil, retiring to her father's house. Having been won, 'this famous Helen' continued Buckingham's mistress until 1674: 'no amour in England ever continued so long' opined Hamilton.[72]

To read Anthony Hamilton's *Memoirs of the Count Grammont* is to enter this world of endless sexual pursuit and intrigue. In exile in St Germain after the flight of James II, the Roman Catholic Hamilton wrote, in French, the *Memoirs* of his brother-in-law, Philibert, Comte de Grammont, who, disgraced for his attentions to a mistress of Louis XIV, came to London in 1662 where, before returning to France in 1664, he married Hamilton's sister, Elizabeth. The young Hamilton, not yet 20 years old, had himself then been at Charles's court, and so could lay claim to first-hand knowledge, but how much of what he records is factually true is of less consequence than what the management of the narrative reveals about the notions of subjectivity and identity, of masculinity and femininity, of status and value, which appealed to, and to a large degree controlled, the behaviour of the circle around Charles. Romance conventions control this text, biographical in some sense though it is; but those are precisely the conventions which shaped not only the writer's and Grammont's own subjectivity, but also the sense of itself which dominated the public behaviour of the court. Women are characterized and assessed exclusively by their physical attributes; men by their dexterity in achieving sexual gratification. Hamilton celebrates the beauty of Castlemaine; Elizabeth Stanhope (née Butler), Countess of Chesterfield; Anna, Countess of Shrewsbury; Jane Middleton, wife of Charles Middleton; Lady Anne Hamilton, daughter of the 2nd Duke of Hamilton and afterwards the wife of Robert Carnegie, 2nd Earl of Southesk; Frances Stuart, who in 1667 eluded Charles by marrying Charles Stuart, 3rd Duke of Richmond, 'the beautifullest creature that ever I saw in my life', judged Pepys, of whom Hamilton less kindly opined that 'it was hardly possible for a woman to have less wit, or more beauty'; Frances Jennings, sister of Sarah, afterwards Duchess of Marlborough, in 1665 wife of Sir George Hamilton and, in 1679, of Richard Talbot, Earl of Tyrconnel; Anne Temple, who in 1666 became the second wife of Sir Charles Lyttleton.[73] And it is with their sexual affairs that he is preoccupied, as they circulate among male courtiers, the Duke of York prominent among them, and not even Sheldon, 'as very a wencher as can be', it was said, excluded from the circle.[74] They participate knowingly and willingly, complicit in, and often instigators of, the intrigues which are the motor of the narrative, and not only in Hamilton's *Memoirs*. He tells of Castlemaine's favouring of Frances Stuart, the two of them sleeping in the same bed, and showing no displeasure at Charles's inclination towards 'la belle Stuart'. Pepys has a story to similar effect:

> Another story was how my Lady Castlemayne, a few days since, had Mrs. Stuart to an entertainment, and at night begun a frolique that they two must be married; and married they were, with ring and all other ceremonies of church service, and ribbands and a sack-posset in bed and flinging the stocking. But in the close, it is said that my Lady Castlemayne, who was the bridegroom, rose, and the King came and took her place with pretty Mrs. Stuart. This is said to be very true.[75]

This is undoubtedly the kind of story Pepys would like to believe true, and it is also the kind of story the court liked to believe of itself; but, beyond that, it is a story both of a strategy for female survival in a powerfully masculinist court, and also, perhaps, of a kind of emancipation: after all, that burlesque wedding cuts at the very root of established social values. There is a kind of liberty here, as well as a sad kind of constraint and compulsion. Compared to these women and such behaviour, Catherine of Braganza, 'with a short fat body', like the abandoned Mary, Duchess of Buckingham, and 'accompanied by six frights, who called themselves maids of honour, and a duenna, another monster', and, like Mary again, 'a most virtuous and pious lady, in a vicious age and court', 'gave but little additional brilliancy to the court' and, within Hamilton's text, commands no authority at all.[76] While Hamilton's memoir of Grammont recognizes that there is a kingdom being governed, no textual time is expended on such matters. The beaux and beauties are quite otherwise preoccupied.

Charles pardoned Buckingham and Shrewsbury and, though his private life was judged scandalous, Buckingham's standing was in no serious jeopardy. Upon this moral laxity and indifference critics of the King and his court seized. In the satires and lampoons of the second half of the decade, that fecund cluster of Restoration images no longer promises a positive culture of pleasure but is perverted to the degrading pursuit of self-gratification: liberality becomes libertine licence, fecundity fecklessness and prodigality profligacy. What had been construed as a welcome emancipation from political and religious tyranny has now become an abnegation of all moral restraint which threatens the governance of the state. Uncontrollable sexual appetite and perverse sexual practice is both a central charge against, and one of the rhetorical means by which is registered the degradation of, the court in Marvell's 'Last Instructions to a Painter' (1667). Far from a world of liberty and promise, the poem depicts a world of degeneration, deformity and crudity, reading from the degraded human body to the degraded body politic.[77]

Castlemaine's inordinate sexual appetite is both a symptom and a cause of the court's political failures: to conjecture Castlemaine uncontrollably aroused by the sight of her footman is to humiliate Charles.[78]

The satirists were correct to perceive that what was at stake was less sexual gratification than the exercise of power. A sensibility like the Duke of York's assumed rights of possession over any woman who held a position in his household, or was maid of honour to his wife. Charles may have been less gross, but hardly presumed less. We may consequently suppose that the pleasure which controls Hamilton's figures was not the sole, and hardly the primary, incentive in these affairs. If, as Reresby heard Charles say, 'the woemen seemd to be the aggressours, and . . . did sometimes offer themselves to his imbraces', it will have been neither from selfless affection nor from sexual voraciousness.[79] Pressure to secure patronage and status for family and friends will have impelled some, anxiety to secure their own place and income others. In this 'eroticized court culture', as Lawrence Stone has called it, the erotic was a means, not an end. Our witnesses are male, and we may, as John Morrill has noted, rather suspect sexual harassment (and worse) than the willing compliance of such fancies as Hamilton's, or, indeed, Pepys's, who entertained himself with the thought that Castlemaine performed 'all the ticks of Aretin'.[80] The King's entry into Pepys's story of her 'marriage' to Frances Stuart asserts a power structure to which she, too, is subject: her fondness for Frances Stuart was as much politic as affectionate. And, of course, there will have been ambition. In the 1670s in Rochester's satires, to rouse a sexually flagging monarch is to assume his power: the King's 'sceptre and his prick are of a length; / And she that plays with one may wield the other'.[81] For this reason, Burnet's belief that Castlemaine wielded more power over Charles than any minister was widely shared.[82] It was further commonly supposed that this was also the way to loosen the strings of the public purse. 'The court delivered itself up to vice', as Burnet put it, 'so the house of commons lost all respect in the nation, for they gave still all the money that was asked'.[83]

## 5 À la mode

'A sad, vicious and negligent Court, all sober men there fearful of the ruin of the whole Kingdom', was Pepys's verdict at the end of 1666, but it was not sober men who had the ear of Charles, nor their fears which he heard recounted. What Hamilton called 'the whole band of wits' formed his intimate company, of whom the 'three most eminent' were John Wilmot, 2nd Earl of Rochester, aged 13 at the Restoration, 'without contradiction, the most witty man in all England; but . . . likewise the most unprincipled', who 'gave himself up to all sorts of extravagance, and to the wildest frolicks that a wanton wit could devise'; Charles Sackville, Lord Buckhurst, afterwards Earl of Middlesex and 6th Earl of Dorset, aged 15 at the Restoration, who kept a 'merry house' with Nell Gwyn, 'the indiscreetest and wildest creature that ever was in a court'; and Sir Charles Sedley, aged 21 at the Restoration, 'one of the lewdest fellows of the age', 'a debauchee, [who] set up for a satyrical wit, a comedian, poet, and courtier of ladies'.[84] Buckingham was their veteran, aged 32 at the Restoration, 'a man of a noble presence' says Burnet, 'full of wit and vivacity', 'wholly turned to mirth and pleasure', 'the finest gentleman of person and witt I thinke I ever see, but could not be long serious or mind business', says Reresby. 'It cannot be imagined', wrote the exiled Clarendon in some incomprehension,

> considering the loose life he led (which was a life more by night than by day) in all the liberties that nature could desire or wit invent, how great an interest he had in both houses of parliament... His quality and condescensions, the pleasantness of his humour and conversation, the extravagance and sharpness of his wit, unrestrained by any modesty or religion, drew persons of all affections and inclinations to like his company.

Buckingham was chosen to lead the Treaty of Dover negotiations because, reports Wood, he was 'then accounted the most vain and fantastical person of any nobleman in the nation to please that great prince'.[85]

Presided over by Charles, 'inferior to none either in shape or air' and himself aged only 30 at the Restoration, they constituted a court which 'was an entire scene of gallantry and amusements, with all the politeness and magnificence, which the inclinations of a prince, naturally addicted to tenderness and pleasure, could suggest'. 'Bestial, predatory and violent' is perhaps closer to the mark,[86] for theirs was often the 'wild rout' with its 'savage clamour' and 'barbarous dissonance / Of Bacchus and his revellers' from which Milton turned in such disdain to his 'fit audience'.[87] Neither women nor inferiors were safe when they took to the streets. Sedley had the actor Edward Kynaston assaulted and beaten for impersonating him, 'so as he is mightily bruised and forced to keep his bed'; in February 1662 Buckhurst and his brother Edward Sackville were apprehended 'for killing and robbing a Tanner' but were acquitted after, in Pepys's view, making 'a very good tale, that they were in pursuit of thiefs and that they took this man for one of them'. In July 1663, at Oxford Kate's, a cook's house in Covent Garden, Sedley came

> in open day into the Balcone and showed his nakedness – acting all the postures of lust and buggery that could be imagined, and abusing of scripture and, as it were, from thence preaching a Mountebanke sermon from that pulpitt, saying that there he hath to sell such a pouder as should make all the cunts in town run after him – a thousand people standing underneath to see and hear him.
>
> And that being done, he took a glass of wine and washed his prick in it and then drank it off; and then took another and drank the King's health.[88]

Five years later he and Buckhurst were still to be caught 'running up and down all the night with their arses bare through the streets, and at last fighting and being beat by the watch and clapped up all night' (for which the constable was afterwards 'chid and imprisoned for his pains') and all with Charles's connivance, who thoroughly enjoyed reports of their goings-on: 'there was no man in England', Pepys reports the Keeper of the Privy Purse, Baptist May, saying of this episode, 'had heads to lose, durst do what they do every day with the King'. During a royal progress through East Anglia they and Charles had 'the fiddlers of Thetford . . . sing them all the bawdy songs they could think of'.[89] When, in 1665, the court removed to Oxford to avoid the plague, though 'they were neat and gay in their apparell', yet, reports Wood, 'they were very nasty and beastly, leaving at their departure their excrements in every corner, in chimneys, studies, colehouses, cellars. Rude, rough, whoremongers; vaine, empty, carelesse.' Evelyn was as much offended by Charles's habit of allowing his spaniels to 'lie in his bed-Chamber, where often times he suffered the bitches to puppy & give suck, which rendred it very offensive, & indeede made the whole Court nasty & stinking'.[90]

Offensive such behaviour certainly was. By this date, the civil notions of propriety and privacy so assiduously fostered by della Casa and other Renaissance conduct books, expected 'private parts' (the phrase is a seventeenth-century coinage) and bodily functions to remain hidden in the public domain.[91] There is, though, more than outrageous indecency here. The key to Sedley's balcony scene lies in the element of parody: his mock sermon is subversive. This is an uninhibited counter-culture unimpressed by those constraints which bear on less daring lives. Its libertinism betokens a kind of free-thinking libertarianism: as Rochester put it, 'Such natural freedoms are but just: / There's something generous in mere lust'. Rochester was reported 'a perfect Hobbist' and a Wood says he heard Buckhurst 'talking blasphemy and atheism'.[92] A largeness of mind could accompany such licence. Buckingham, like Charles, was a supporter of toleration, so enabling Baxter, otherwise improbably, to salute him, though 'a Man of no Religion, but notoriously and professedly lustful', as 'a defender of the Priviledges of Humanity', 'of greater wit and parts, and sounder Principles as to the interest of Humanity and the Common good, than most Lords in the Court'.[93] In its literary manifestation, it continued that vein of ironic, subversive and satirical interrogation of cultural values which Donne had so strikingly introduced into English poetry 70 years before: Buckingham 'had a great liveliness of wit, and a peculiar faculty of turning all things into ridicule, with bold figures and natural descriptions'; Buckhust's poems were 'a sort of epigrams. Wit was his talent.'[94] In Rochester's 'A Ramble in St James's Park' (*ante* 1673) this disaffection became a powerfully satirical, even nihilistic, critique of the grosser side of London and court life, and in 'A Satyr against Mankind' (*c.*1674) of human aspiration more generally.

Restoration wit differed, however, in one signal respect from Metaphysical wit. For those whom Pope later disdained as a 'Mob of Gentlemen who wrote with Ease'[95] the ease was essential. The erudite allusiveness of Metaphysical wit delighted to perplex; it was demonstratively worked-up and wilfully obscure. Restoration wit is urbane. For the Restoration gallant, linguistic wit, denoting a capacity dexterously to turn any occasion to advantage, was, though startling and original, felicitous, poised and articulate. Here, literary style touches a larger cultural shift in manner which begins to manifest itself in the decade following the Restoration. Evelyn, no sympathetic witness, credits Charles with having 'brought in a politer way of living' (even though it 'passed to Luxurie & intollerable expense in due course').[96] It is at this time that notions of *quality* as a social signifier, and the phrase *person of quality*, are gaining currency through the heightened social sensitivity consequent upon the comparative novelty of a royal court, and a court which returned to England with distinctive manners. In the sense of *nobility, high birth or rank, good social position*, the terms enter English in the late sixteenth century, but their vogue, and the sense of socially accomplished manners and of acquired or demonstrable status independent of birth, belong to the late seventeenth and eighteenth centuries.[97] In the 1660s this took a distinctive turn. Reresby recalled that under 'the custome and manners' of the Commonwealth, Londoners 'could scarce endure the sight of a gentleman, soe that the common salutation to a man well dressed was "French dog", or the like'. Charles, however, had spent his exile in the orbit of the French court, in Paris, at Fontainebleau, and mostly at St Germain-en-Laye just outside Paris, and he returned to England in 1660, as the disillusioned republican Ludlow remarked in disdain, 'altogether Frenchyfied (not only being so by birth of the surer die, but also by education and inclynation)'. Within a few months of the Restoration he caused some offence by silencing the court musicians in order to have a French group play.[98] His inclination promoted French taste and manners as a mark of the new age, and he had the style to carry it off: Burnet may have thought Tiberius a type for Charles, but he also saw in the King 'certainly the best bred man of the age'.[99] Style was similarly what marked out Buckingham. It was said to have been 'impossible for you not to follow him with your eyes as he went along – he moved so gracefully'. Indeed, Louis XIV was said to have judged him the finest, indeed only, English gentleman he had met. In a letter to Pepys, Evelyn regretted that 'avowed luxurie & prophaness . . . *a la mode de France*' had succeeded the old English style of manners. When Grammont came to London from Paris in 1662 'he found so little difference in the manners and conversation of those with whom he chiefly associated, that he could scarcely believe he was out of his own country', as if 'the court of France had quitted [France] to accompany him in his exile'.[100]

This increased attentiveness to self-presentation and performance was not confined to the higher reaches of society. While there is no evidence that the sexual licence of the court extended beyond its confines (it after all required a greater expenditure of funds and time than most could afford), society more generally does now begin to heed a notion of refinement in manners and to aspire, self-consciously, to an ideal of politeness governing public engagements and discourse, a civility which obliged men no less than women.[101] Gentlemanliness, consisting in decorous control of the body and its utterances before a social audience, had, of course, been a Renaissance ideal, but the polite, civil and decent are now replacing the courtly as a more general expectation. The outrageousness of Sedley's behaviour depends for its effect upon the notion of propriety and respectable manners which Allestree's *The Gentleman's Calling* (1660) did so much to establish. For Allestree, the gentleman shuns all immoderation and grossness. His behaviour is 'affable and civil, not insolent & imperious', his language 'temperate and decent', avoiding 'immodest and obscene talk'. In a world where men who so 'hunt after' 'Variety' that, 'might they have the *Turk's Seraglio*, they would not stick to take his *Mahometanism* withal', the true gentleman is temperate, faithful and discreet.[102]

A measure of this preoccupation is the store increasingly set by fashion in clothes. In his *Advice to a Son* (1656) Francis Osborne had recommended attention to dress and appearance: 'spare all other waies, rather then prove defective in this'.[103] Self-construction and self-promotion through clothes are recurrent concerns of Pepys's diary. A rising man, he was very sensitive to the impression he was making. In October 1660 he exchanged his 'long black Cloake for a short one', 'long cloaks being now quite out', but in February 1661 he discarded his cloak and first wore a coat and sword in the French fashion 'as the manner now among gentlemen is'.[104] In this renewed attention to masculine attire lay the germ of the fop in the Restoration sense of that term; that is, a man obsessed by his appearance, addicted to the ornamental and flamboyant in style, and preoccupied with fashion. The distinction between Dorimant, the protagonist of Sir George Etherege's *The Man of Mode* (1676), reportedly based upon Rochester, and the comic character of the title, Sir Fopling Flutter, turns on a 'manly' continence in self-presentation (entirely compatible with sexual incontinence) and an 'effeminate' self-absorption (incompatible with a human relationship of any kind). The fop had attracted the scorn of Evelyn's *Tyrannus: or the Mode*... as early as 1661.[105] And a notable step of another kind was taken in defining English taste and manners when, on 25 September 1660, Pepys took 'a Cupp of Tea (a China drink) of which I never had drank before'.[106]

There were two arenas in which the town conspicuously admired itself: the theatre and the park. Drama quickly established itself as the definitive genre of the new age, in part for good patriotic reasons: this form of public entertainment had been proscribed since 1642 (though not therefore entirely moribund, as Davenant's career shows); its reintroduction was yet another affirmation that the Puritan past was past. Evelyn first saw a play 'after divers years' when on 16 January 1661 he attended a performance of Beaumont and Fletcher's *Scornful Lady* by Thomas Killigrew's King's Company at 'a new *Theater* in *Lincoln-in-fields*', that is the Theatre Royal opened in Vere Street on 8 November 1660. Pepys had been there within a fortnight of its opening, judging it 'the finest play-house, I believe, that ever was in England'. It was in a performance there of Massinger and Fletcher's *The Beggar's Bush* that on 3 January 1661 he first saw 'Women come upon the stage'. Two days later he thought the boy actor Edward Kynaston 'the prettiest woman in the whole house' in Jonson's *The Silent Woman*, but when he returned on 12 February to find a woman taking the part of Epicoene it made 'the play appear much better then ever it did to me'. Pepys had seen his first play since the Restoration on 18 August, at the Cockpit, Drury Lane, and there had been productions at the Red Bull, Clerkenwell (including one of *The Silent Woman*, attended by the King's brothers, the dukes of York and Gloucester) since the early summer of 1660. At the Cockpit in Whitehall plays were being performed before the court from the autumn of 1660.[107] By November 1661 an 'old playe' like *Hamlet* began 'to disgust this refined age'. Ten years later, Dryden was confidently distinguishing from such Elizabethan dramatists as Jonson the products of 'an age more gallant than the last' in which 'Wit's now arrived to a more high degree, / Our native language more refined and free'.[108]

In the developing comedy of manners (and its satiric and comic exaggeration is, of course, only possible once an elaborate code of manners is accepted) the *beau monde* admired its sophistication, its cultivated poise and its liberation from disabling emotional attachments and from moral constraints in deftly turned aphorisms: 'A mistress should be like a little country retreat near the town, not to dwell in constantly, but only for a night and away, to taste the town the better when a man returns'. The names Freeman and Courtall in Etherege's *She Would If She Could* (1668) strike the note. The description of these two in the list of *dramatis personae* as 'two honest gentlemen' refers not to any such integrity as Bunyan represented in his Mr Honest but to social position and, more particularly, to a social adroitness which is never wrong-footed. It is Courtall who, discovered in a deceit, extricates himself with the exclamation 'fie, fie, the keeping of one's word is a thing below the honour of a gentleman', an apt retort from a man about the town dominated by a monarch 'Whose promise none relies on, / Who never said a foolish thing, / Nor ever did a wise one'.[109]

Plays took their place in a more general economy of leisure. It had been early Stuart policy to politicize play, to encourage sports and pastimes as statements of loyal opposition to Puritan dissent, religious and political,[110] and in the reaction of the 1660s they assumed, without the need for such declarations as the Books of Sports of 1618 and 1633, this declarative and affirmative role. Partying signified a return to the prewar condition. Those 1660 Maypoles had been as much emblematic as functional; only disloyal spirits would decline such outward manifestations of joy at the happy revolution in the state's affairs. It was 'very much observed' when at a Lord Mayor's banquet in 1661 William Bates (a moderate Presbyterian) did not join in the drinking of toasts.[111] Charles showed the way. Dining with Charles could be demanding: in November 1673 Edward, 3rd Viscount Conway, with Buckingham, Lady Shrewsbury, the Speaker Edward Seymour, Nell Gwyn and the King went to Supper 'about three a clock in the morning . . . were very merry, and drank smartly'. This had been Charles's habit since his return: in June 1660, Sandwich did not get to bed until 5 in the morning after dining with the King. As a result, the Earl understandably 'lay a-bed till 11 a-clock', but Charles remained all his life an early riser: the King, observed Pepys in August 1660, 'doth tire all his people that are about him with early rising since he came'.[112] And not only with his early rising. He had scarcely set foot in England before he was off hunting at break of day, and he was throughout his reign a great sportsman, whose energy and stamina could quickly exhaust any courtier. His enterprise extended to the new activity of yachting, introduced (like the word) from the Netherlands. In October 1661 Evelyn sailed 'with his *Majestie* <on> one of his Yaachts (or Pleasure boates) Vessells newly known amongst us', 'his Majestie sometimes steering himselfe'.[113]

For those who found tennis too energetic, there were the parks in which to walk (though Charles would outpace any who accompanied him). Hyde Park, the old royal hunting park opened to the public by James I, quickly became an arena for display after 1660, on foot or by coach around the 'Ring': on 3 July 1660 Evelyn 'went to *Hide-park* where was his *Majestie* & aboundance of Gallantrie' promenading and parading the new state of things. In the autumn of 1660 the construction of the Mall and the landscaping of St James's Park made for another 'very fine place' for promenading and 'for his Majesty to play in, beeinge a very princly play'. Henrietta Maria employed the French architect André Millet to redesign the previously marshy and wild St James's Park, draining and embellishing it with a 'canal' (that is, a straight sheet of water), an island, walks and lines of trees. The innovations included 'A snow house and an Iice [*sic*] house . . . as the mode is in some parts of France and Iteily and other hot countryes, for to coole wine and other drinks for the sumer season'. In the 1660s, London society defined and reassured itself through conspicuous leisure.[114]

# 8

# 'Male and Female Created He Them'

## 1 Men and Women

Addressing the problem of infertility in his *The Ladies Companion, or the English Midwife* (1671), William Sermon, physician to Charles II, proposed a number of remedies. These included bathing the woman in a hot bath, sitting her on an open stool over a pot of boiling potion in order to receive 'the fume up into her privy parts' and having the man anoint his penis with civet, musk or ambergris.[1] Sermon is dealing in reputable medical science, seeking to warm the womb in the conviction that a hot womb is a necessary prerequisite for conception. This idea had been abroad for the best part of two thousand years before being taken up by Sermon. The practice and findings of experimental anatomy constituted the most significant sixteenth-century advances in physiology, but these discoveries made little impact upon professional thinking until very late in the seventeenth century, and they hardly affected the popular idea of the functioning of the body until the eighteenth.[2] In biology and physiology, the 1660s invoked not such moderns as Andreas Vesalius or Gabriel Harvey, but Aristotle and the ancient physicians Hippocrates and Galen, deferring to them with as much reverence as had the Middle Ages.[3]

On their authority, the decade continued to construe the operation of the human body in terms of the combinations and superfluities of its four constituent 'humours'. Humoral physiology valued heat over coldness, dryness over moisture, and this led it to understand female identity in terms not of its difference from the male but of its insufficiency, the degree to which it failed to attain to male characteristics. It explained woman's inferiority by pointing to the debilitating moistness and coldness of the female body,[4] a consequence of the disadvantageous circumstances of the conception and generation of females. The Aristotelian idea that fully developed foetuses issued in male children was still current; females were thought of as the product of incomplete development caused by insufficient generative heat in the womb: women were regarded biologically as 'failed males'. Evidence of this imperfect development was to be found not only in woman's want of physical strength but in such signs of incomplete development as her internal genital organs which the coldness and moistness of the womb had prevented from developing and extending without the body, like a man's.[5] In medicinal and gynaecological texts woman is hence analogically related to man, represented through her imperfect imaging of the male body. Physical organs peculiar to her were presented in terms of male organs and were often supposed to perform the same functions: 'The womb is like to a mans Cod, turned inside outward...'; 'the neck of the womb... resembleth a Yard [penis] turned inwards'; the clitoris 'answers to a Man's Yard in shape, situation, substance, repletion with spirits and erection, and differs from it only in length and bigness'.[6]

To these notions were added age-old prejudices against the sinister or left side and preferences for the higher over the lower. On the authority of Hippocrates, Sermon asserted that males were the product of hot sperm from the right testicle deposited on the right (hotter) side of the womb, where the foetus was carried. Females, on the other hand, were produced by cold sperm from the inferior left testicle and were carried on the left side. Furthermore, a male child 'lieth high above the navel by reason of its heat. The female at the bottom of the belly by reason of its coldness and ponderosity'. In texts by both men and women these signs, circumstantially developed, are taken to indicate the sex of an unborn child, even though application to women's own experience would promptly have shown them to be erroneous: a male child,

> when it is come to some perfection in the womb, the right eye of the mother would to appearance move swifter, and sparkle more than the other. The right pap rise and swell more than the left, and become harder, the nipple sooner changing colour... when she goes, though she regard it not, she commonly sets her right leg first... Contrary are the symptoms of the females.[7]

As this suggests, the process of conception and generation was imperfectly understood. In his *Anatomy of Humane Bodies Epitomized* (1682), the physician Thomas Gibson judiciously avoided all discussion of conception as 'too philosophical' for his anatomical treatise. In Aristotelian thought, woman contributes nothing to generation save the sustaining context of the womb. In Galen, conception is the product of the combination of male and female seed. The latter is the commoner view, but, whatever the particular line taken, the characteristic emphasis is that the male contribution is hot, and therefore active and dynamic, the female cold, and so passive and receptive; the man is 'agent', the woman 'patient'.[8] The microscope allowed the existence of spermatozoa to be demonstrated by Anton van Leeuwenhoek in the 1670s and the hypothesis of the ovum was at the same time convincingly argued by Regnier de Graaf, but not until two centuries later, when ovulation and fertilization began to be understood, did the purpose and causes of menstruation become apparent. In the 1660s menstruation continued to be explained as the voiding of unused seed (*menstruum*), or of *menses* (the matter from which, in some Aristotelian accounts, the foetus is formed by the animating effect of the male seed), and of excess blood which the woman's cold nature fails to absorb. It was associated with the curse of Genesis 3.16, as were gynaecological complaints generally and the suffering of childbirth in particular, and it retained something of the sense of pollution and uncleanness evident in the Levitical taboos.[9]

If the female body was considered but a poor imitation of a man's, so, too, was the female mind. Aristotelian tradition and humoral biology provides the starting-point for Margaret Cavendish's *apologia* in the preface to her *Worlds Olio* (1655):

> It cannot be expected that I should write so wisely or wittily as Men, being of the Effeminate Sex, whose Brains Nature hath mix'd with the coldest and softest Elements... there is a great difference betwixt the Masculine Brain and the Feminine, the Masculine Strength and the Feminine; For could we choose out of the World two of the ablest Brain and strongest Body of each Sex, there would be great difference in the Understanding and Strength; for Nature hath made Mans Body more able to endure Labour, and Mans Brain more clear to understand and contrive than Womans; and as great a difference there is between them, as there is between the longest and strongest Willow, compared to the strongest and largest Oak.

The conviction that, because of what Baxter called the 'natural imbecility' of the female sex, it is impossible for women to aspire to intellectual equality with men, was sufficiently strong to hold sway even over such a highly educated and intellectually able woman as Lucy Hutchinson, who cautioned that

> as our sex, through ignorance and weakness of judgement (which in the most knowing women is inferior to the masculine understanding of men), are apt to entertain fancies, and [be] pertinacious in them, so we ought to watch ourselves, in such a day as this, and to embrace nothing rashly; but as our own imbecility is made known to us, to take heed of presumption in ourselves, and to lean by faith upon the strength of the Lord.[10]

While such hierarchical notions could appeal to the ancients and to classical culture their primary authority was biblical and Christian: Eve was never far distant when sexual relations were under discussion. Like their patristic and medieval predecessors, seventeenth-century commentators preferred the second, more discriminatory, creation story in Genesis (2.4b – 3.24) to the first (1.1 – 2.4a), paying far more attention to the subsequent creation of Eve from Adam's rib in the latter than they did to the simultaneous creation of male and female in the former ('male and female created he *them*') which grants apparently equal authority to man and to woman ('let *them* have dominion over the fish of the sea . . .'). Read with a strong Pauline gloss,[11] this narrative provided evidence of woman's secondary status ('created after man, for man's good and out of man's side'); in the creation from Adam's rib, grounds to dispute in what sense she was formed in the image of God; in the rib itself, a symbol of her crooked nature ('The fatal Rib was crooked and unev'n / From whence they have their Crab-like Nature giv'n', as one satire put it);[12] in Adam's naming of the beasts before Eve's creation, evidence of her intellectual inferiority; in the story of the Fall, reason to blame her for all the ills of humankind; and in the curse placed upon her, confirmation of her subordination to man. Indeed, even before the Fall Adam and Eve, as the narrator has it in *Paradise Lost*, were

> Not equal, as their sex not equal seemed;
> For contemplation he and valour formed,
> For softness she and sweet attractive grace,
> He for God only, she for God in him:
> His fair large front and eye sublime declared
> Absolute rule . . .[13]

## 2 The Weaker Vessel

To woman's mental and physical incapacity such readings of Genesis added moral inferiority: 'Because they are weaker built, and because the Devil doth easier fasten with them than with Men, therefore they are more prone to Vanity and all mis-orders', wrote Bunyan in his (unpublished) *An Exposition on the First Ten Chapters of Genesis*. 'The fallen Angel knew what he did when he made his Assault upon the Woman. His subtilty told him that the Woman was the weaker Vessel [1 Peter 3.7]' was his entirely typical reading of the temptation in the Garden of Eden. For Bunyan, Adam was the all but innocent victim of a 'woeful tragedy' occasioned by Eve's refusal to accept the limitations of her 'weak and simple Sex' and by her temerity in engaging 'so mighty an Adversary' as the Devil 'when her Husband, who was more able than she, was at hand'. Stepping 'out of her place' she 'so failed there-about, that at one clap she overthrew not only . . . the reputation of Women for ever, but her Soul, her Husband, and the whole World besides'. This bore directly upon the lives of Restoration women: because ''Twas the *Woman* that at the first the *Serpent* made use of, and by whom he then overthrew the World . . . the *Woman*, to the Worlds end, must wear tokens of her *Underlingship*':

> Women therefore, when-ever they would perk it and lord it over their husbands, ought to remember, that both by Creation and Transgression they are made to be in Subjection to their own Husbands.[14]

Bunyan is so insistent on female submissiveness because women's weakness was construed in physical and intellectual terms, as want of strength and judgement, not in psychological, as want of character. She might be weak-willed, but temperamentally, she is more than a match for any man. It was precisely because their 'natural imbecility' was believed to be wedded to a passionately determined nature that the century echoes with excoriations of their vices and reiterations of their duty to submit their wills to masculine guidance. Seventeenth-century stereotypes of woman are energetic and robust. The figures of the virago and the Amazon, the whore and the witch, the shrew and the scold, presented in a great variety of genres, both fascinated and appalled since in them woman's nature is writ large. What meets us in seventeenth-century texts is not any fragile or pallid image of woman but rather a horrified fascination with her over-powering wilfulness, stubbornness, irrationality, pride and licentiousness. In that weak frame there pulse frightening urges and desires.

In part, this was again biologically explicable. The one organ allowed to be distinctively and peculiarly the woman's was the womb. This was thought of almost as a separate organism within the woman's body, with a will, if not quite a life, of its own, upon which depended the woman's psychological and physical health. To the womb and its humoral complexion were attributed a whole series not only of physical ills but of mental aberrations and temperamental defects, particularly those quintessentially female complaints, irrationality, uncontrollable passion and 'the mother' or hysteria (that is, etymologically, 'womb disease'). It was held responsible also for woman's pronounced sexual appetite. Believing that the womb desired conception, opening to suck in male seed, closing to retain it, medical treatises suppose the female to be at the mercy of biologically determined desires: 'We see that there is in women so great a longing to conceive with child, that ofttimes for want of it the womb falls into convulsions and distracts the whole body' warned the midwife Jane Sharp. Woman was consequently credited with a much greater sexual appetite than the male. It was accepted that the womb's voraciousness and insatiability could lead to nymphomania.[15] Sexual desire is thus intrinsic to female nature. Satisfaction of the womb's desire to breed is a biological necessity which, denied, can lead to physical and psychological disorder, to dementia and depression. The common remedy for this complaint in young women was that prescribed early in the century by Robert Burton: marriage, 'to give them content in their desires'.[16]

This conviction that woman is a sexual being, and that sexual intercourse is essential to her health, drew support from Galenic ideas about generation. If conception requires discharge of female as well as of male seed, then sexual excitement and orgasm are as necessary for its release in the woman as in the man; simultaneous orgasm yields the greatest chance of conception.[17] The clitoris, first described in the medical literature of Western Europe in 1559, was consequently assigned an important, indeed, essential role in generation since without sexual excitement there could be no conception. The French physician Ambroise Paré, whose works (translated into English in 1634, with a second edition in 1665) were the most frequently cited modern medical authority, advised that 'When the husband commeth into his wives chamber, he must entertain her with all kinde of dalliance, wanton behaviour, and allurement to Venery' in order to excite the womb to 'wax fervent with a desire of casting forth its seed'.[18] Consequently, barrenness could be attributed to lack of sexual pleasure, and particularly to a husband's failure to stimulate his wife. No heed is paid in medical texts to the contrary evidence of women's own experience. On these grounds, for example, Sharp explains that 'women seldom or never conceive when they are ravished'.[19]

These views happily chimed with English Protestantism's rejection of the ascetic and monastic tradition of Roman Catholicism. Protestantism generally, and Puritanism in particular, were a good deal less anxious about, and more realistically sympathetic towards, sexual desire than the medieval celibate tradition of Rome. Despite the notable exceptions of Augustine and Aquinas, who held that concupiscence and lust, not sexuality itself, were the result of the Fall, the Church Fathers and medieval schoolmen had in general been hostile to the idea that sexual relations were part of God's conception of unfallen humanity. In contrast, Protestant treatises characteristically present sexuality not as innately evil, nor as a consequence of the Fall, but as part of the divine scheme and according to the will of God. The most signal instance in our period is Milton, who in *Paradise Lost* goes out of his way to insist on (marital) sexual relations in Eden, and to distinguish his image of prelapsarian bliss from both courtly libertinism and indulgence on the one hand and from the Roman (monastic) ascetic tradition on the other; it is the latter which he explicitly damns as Satanic: 'who bids abstain / But our destroyer, foe to God and man?' In *Paradise Lost* it is the 'sum of earthly bliss' to make love within the nuptual bower.[20]

This positive image of sexual relations is, however, constantly under threat from a contrary thrust. Though sermons and guides to godliness are as ready as the medical treatises to admit female sexuality as right and proper, they are also sensitive to the dangers of concupiscence. As the archangel Raphael admonishes Adam, 'In loving thou dost well, in passion not'.[21] The weight of tradition stretching from the Old Testament prophets and wisdom literature left no doubt where lay the likeliest temptation to deviate from this ideal of moderation. Indeed, the homiletic literature and anti-feminist satire, drawing on the powerful Old Testament diatribes against harlots and seductive women, can range misogynistically far beyond woman's susceptibility to libidinous desire. Her innate wilfulness, deceitfulness, loquacity, pride, selfishness, inconstancy and cunning, as well as her lasciviousness, were as proverbial in the 1660s as throughout the early modern period. From the energetic multiplication of insults by Joseph Swetnam's enthusiastically adopted persona of woman-hater in *The Arraignment of Lewde, Idle, Froward and Unconstant Women* (1615), to Robert Gould's *Love Given O're: or, a satyr against the pride, lust, and inconstancy &c. of woman* (1682), the refrain is the same. Taking their cue from 1 Timothy 2.9, diatribes against provocative dress and the use of 'paint' or cosmetics betray something of an obsession with women's lascivious vanity which readily appropriates the phrasing of the characterization of the whore in Proverbs 7 and in Ecclesiasticus 25 and 26. These themes had been ingeniously developed by Alexis Trousset's (alias Jacques Olivier) *Alphabet de l'imperfection et malice des femmes*, a relentless collection of classical dicta, patristic sayings and biblical exempla to the detriment of women, derived from medieval models, first published in Paris in 1617. Ingeniously contriving a female vice for each letter of the alphabet, it proved very much to seventeenth-century taste, going into an English translation in 1662.

In this parlous state, disabled by their own female natures and helpless before the force of their own passions, women were often said to be incapable of managing themselves:

> Except it be very few that are patient and manlike, women are commonly of potent *fantasies*, and tender *passionate* impatient spirits, easily cast into anger, or jealousie, or discontent: and of weak understandings, and therefore unable to reform themselves. They are betwixt a *man* and a *child*: Some few have *more* of the *man*, and many have more of the *child*; but most are but in a middle state.[22]

They consequently stand in need of masculine guidance. As it was men's duty to provide firm patriarchal direction, so it was women's duty to heed it:

> And as a Will . . . resign'd to Reason and just Autority, is a felicity all rational natures should aspire to; so especially the feminine Sex, whose passions being naturally the more impetuous, ought to be the more strictly guarded and kept under the severe discipline of Reason; for where 'tis otherwise, where a woman has no guide but her Will, and her Will is nothing but her Humor, the event is sure to be fatal to her self, and often to others also.[23]

From this compliant submissiveness flow the virtues held to be distinctively feminine: silence, reticence, patience, discretion, piety, modesty and chastity. These forms of behaviour are recommended in Richard Allestree's anonymous *The Ladies Calling* (1673) quite as firmly as they had been in Richard Braithwait's *The English Gentlewoman* (1631) or William Gouge's *Of Domesticall Duties* (1622).

There is, however, a new bias detectable in Allestree: an increasing emphasis upon modesty and passivity. After the Restoration, and in reaction against the radical sexual politics of the Interregnum, the traditional distinction of gender roles is ever more inclined to infer from the softness of women's bodies the softness (that is, sensitivity and compassion) of their natures. Allestree was in no doubt that there are 'Virtues... universally necessary to Women in all Ages' which are distinct from those appropriate to a man. A woman who fails to exemplify his ideal of submissive and docile femininity is frustrating her own nature: meekness is 'particularly enjoin'd to women as a peculiar accomplishment of their sex'; modesty is 'a thing so essential and natural to the sex, that every the least declination from it, is a proportionable seceding from Womanhood'. Immodest behaviour in a woman is consequently shocking in a way it is not in a man because, in her, it is monstrous, a perversion of nature:

> Such a degenerous age do we now live in, that everything seems inverted, even Sexes; whilst men fall to the Effeminacy and Niceness of women, and women take up the Confidence, the Boldness of men, and this too under the Notion of good Breeding. A blush (tho formerly reputed the color of Virtue) is accounted worse manners than those things which ought to occasion it, and such as nothing but the simplicity of a Country Girl can excuse. But the infirmity for the most part proves very corrigible; a few weeks of the Town Discipline wears off that piece of Rusticity and advances them to a Modish assurance. Nor is that design'd to terminate in itself, but it is to carry them on, till they arise to a perfect Metamorphosis, their Gesture, their Language, nay somtimes their Habit too being affectedly masculine... there are women who think they have not made a sufficient escape from their sex, 'till they have assumed the Vices of men too. A sober modest Dialect is too effeminate for them; a blustring ranting style is taken up... 'Tis true indeed an Oath sounds gratingly out of whatever mouth, but out of a womans it hath such an uncouth harshness, that there is no noise on this side Hell can be more amazingly odious.[24]

Allestree is here developing an essentialist notion of sexual difference which will lead to the construction of that infantile, pallid, almost diaphanously insubstantial image which was to characterize the heroine of the age of sensibility.[25] There are in Allestree the first signs of discomfort at thinking of woman as physical and sexual, of the idea that there is something unfeminine about female desire, and of the view that it is indecorous and impolite to mention bodily matters in female company. By the end of the century the entry on *Conception* in *The Ladies Dictionary* (1694) expects female sensibilities to blush at references to generation and cannot bring itself to mention the most obvious sign of conception, cessation of menstruation. Its designation of its readers as 'ladies', or the 'fair sex', signals the notion of sexual difference to which it now subscribes. Allestree's stress on gracefulness and passivity has become distinctive of, and supposedly inherent in, female nature.[26]

## 3 'An honourable estate'

It is the overriding assumption of the conduct books and guides to godliness current in the 1660s that it is woman's lot to become a wife and that her self-fulfilment is to be found in the faithful and obedient performance of that role. Eve was created not only a woman but a wife; unlike Adam, she had never known a single state. From Genesis 2.18 ('It is not good that the man should be alone') the Protestant tradition inferred that celibacy is undesirable. Marriage, as the marriage service of the 1662 Book of Common Prayer had it, is 'an honourable estate, instituted of God in the time of man's innocency'. A Puritan sensibility might go further: Lucy Hutchinson derided Edward the Confessor's claim to sanctity on the grounds of his celibacy, describing him as that 'superstitious prince, who was sainted for his ungodly chastity'.[27] In the Roman Catholic tradition celibate monasticism might offer women a possible, and highly esteemed, alternative to the role of wife and mother; no such alternative existed in Protestant England. A widow enjoyed some status, and some independence, being vested in common law with dower, a third of her husband's estate, until this was abolished by statute in 1692, but an unmarried woman was an anomaly with no defined role or position. 'Old maid' was a name of 'scorn', and a spinster 'looked on as the most calamitous creature in Nature', as was noted by Allestree, who rather regretted the abolition of the monasteries at the Reformation.[28] And it was assumed that any wife desired children. Through childbirth the curse on Eve (and woman) is reversed, for the pains of labour issue in the blessing of children through which salvation becomes possible (1 Timothy 2.15). It follows from this emphasis upon the wifely and maternal roles that the woman's sphere was domestic: 'the primary provision of maintenance belongeth most to the Husband, so the secondary provision of maintenance within doors belongeth specially to the wife'.[29] Keeping *within doors* was the mark not merely of the good housewife but of the virtuous woman. 'Now is she without, now in the streets, and lieth in wait at every corner' (Proverbs 7.12): our period continued to maintain the link between wandering outdoors and an immoral life forged by this Old Testament characterization of the harlot . Following Proverbs 31, the assumption is that the good woman is a virtuous wife, and that her virtue is manifest in concern for her husband's well-being and reputation and for the welfare of her children. Her skills and duties are those belonging to efficient household management. 'Nothing lovelier can be found / In woman, than to study household good' remarks Milton's Adam, in this faithfully reflecting the belief of his author's age.[30]

With marriage conceived as women's proper and 'natural' destiny,[31] their character, education and behaviour were discussed almost exclusively in relation to it. Their recommended demeanour in this sphere continued to be what the Puritan William Whately had declared it to be early in the century: 'The whole duty of the wife is referred to two heads: the first is, to acknowledge her inferiority; the next, to carry her selfe as inferiour'.[32] In the model family of the conduct books the man is the head of a little commonwealth or church, responsible for, and in a governing position over, the other members of the household, namely, wife, children and servants. His duties towards each are carefully distinguished and delineated.[33] The wife is accorded a position next to the husband in this hierarchy, and supplies his place if ever he is away, but she is certainly not his equal. Her very nearness, however, together with her female nature and the husband's duty of love towards her, make her much the most difficult member of the family to govern successfully. Commonly, far more space is devoted to her than to any other member of the family. The husband is reassured that he must exert his authority; the wife is admonished that it is her duty to obey with a tirelessly reiterated array of such biblical proof-texts as Genesis 3.16, 1 Corinthians 11.5–11, 1 Timothy 2.9–15, Ephesians 5.22–3 and 1 Peter 3.7. 'Under this phrase (*submit yourselves*)' in Paul's admonition in Ephesians 5. 22 ('Wives submit yourselves unto your own husbands as unto the Lord') is comprised 'all the duties which a wife oweth to her husband' Gouge had written in *Of Domesticall Duties*. 1 Corinthians 11.3 left no doubt that 'the head of the woman is the man': the notion that husband and wife are equal is 'a fond conceit', and, no matter how far he may be socially or intellectually her inferior, a wife can never be her husband's superior. The only qualification is that wives should not 'fear their husbands more than they fear God'. The best service the husband can render his wife is to recognize that she is the 'weaker vessel' (1 Peter 3.7). The promise of spiritual equality to male and female in Galatians 3.28 is not permitted by Gouge to compromise this dominion.[34] The Restoration did not demur. Bunyan was saying exactly the same thing in the 1660s: 'It is an unseemly thing to see a *woman* so much as once in all her life-time, to offer to over-top her husband; she ought in every thing to be in subjection to him'. And no more than Gouge could he tolerate women assuming to themselves a masculine authority.[35]

All the commentators agreed on how to recognize proper wifely submissiveness. It issued in a reverential attitude and an 'awfull respect . . . in her heart of her husband'; in a submissive, quiet, soberly dressed and retiring manner, avoiding gaudy clothes and loud gestures; 'a comely, grave and gracious carriage'; in '*sobriety, mildnesse, courtesie* and *modestie*'; in meekness, moderation and restraint in her requests and expectations, restraining her tongue and her passions; in a 'cheerful contentedness with your condition', taking heed of 'an impatient, murmuring spirit'; in a pious and modest habit of mind; and in a hard-working and diligent management of household affairs.[36] And there was imposed upon the wife particularly the duty of sexual fidelity. While, like other divines, Gouge refused to grant the husband greater sexual licence than the wife, he cannot but acknowledge that 'more inconueniences may follow vpon the womans default then vpon the mans' since a 'man cannot so well know which be his owne children, as the woman'. The consequence in practice was the 'double standard' which required women to be virgin at marriage and to continue sexually faithful as wives while it tolerated men coming to marriage sexually experienced and their infidelity thereafter.[37]

There is, however, also a contrary trend in the literature. The thesis that during the early modern period the 'open lineage' (or extended) family was replaced by the nuclear family and that, correspondingly, the notion of marriage as a matter of duty and parental arrangement yielded to a marital ideal of loving companionship,[38] has attracted much criticism,[39] but the weight of medieval tradition unquestionably preferred celibacy and virginity to marriage and sexual fulfilment; an air of concession and regret consequently hangs over marriage counsels, of suspicion and disquiet over discussions of sexual love. That disquiet is much less evident in Protestant manuals: while they continued to hold that marriage was instituted for the procreation of children and as a remedy for lust, they present marriage as the norm to which Christians should aspire and devote their homiletic and expository energies to the joys of its loving fellowship. Procreation may be 'one end of marriage, yet it is not the only end'. This recognition of the need for 'mutual liking' in spouses and for 'a true entire conjugal love' in marriage was prepared to grant the woman the right to refuse marriage to a man she could not like. Though marriages contracted without parental approval or advice were not likely to win approval, neither were forced marriages. Hence, although daughters could not expect easily to marry against their parents' wishes, by the end of the century conduct literature allowed them to dissent from a parental marriage choice.[40] The romantic love which medieval literature had found it so hard to accommodate within marriage was in the 1660s becoming essential to its representation: witness the marital love lyrics of Anne Bradstreet or memoirs such as Margaret Cavendish's or Lucy Hutchinson's of their husband's lives.

There is, consequently, a tension between two marital models in the conduct books of the period which, for all their insistence on wifely obedience, insist also upon the mutual duty of love within marriage. Just so, despite the narrator's firm hierarchical pronouncements in *Paradise Lost* ('He for God only, she for God in him'), the poem's dramatic and imaginative commitment is to equal relations between Adam and Eve. The solitary Adam is, after all, lonely in Eden, as the Father knew he would be; the creation of Eve is the perfection of paradise. What Satan finds intolerable, what is to him 'sight hateful, sight tormenting', is the prospect of Adam and Eve 'Imparadised in one another's arms, / The happier Eden'. It is in their mutual embrace ('one another's arms') that the essence of prelapsarian bliss is located ('the happier Eden').[41]

## 4 A Woman's Place

The education of daughters typically consisted of preparation for married life. In 1652 Sir Ralph Verney wrote to his god-daughter that

> I did not think you had beene guilty of soe much learning as I see you are; and yet it seems you rest unsatisfied or else you would not threaten Lattin, Greeke and Hebrew too. Good sweet-hart bee not soe covitous; beleeve me, a Bible (with the Common prayer) and a goode plain cattichisme in your Mother Tongue being well read and practised, is well worth all the rest and much more sutable to your sex; I know your Father thinks this false doctrine, but bee confident your husband will bee of my oppinion. In French you cannot bee too cunning for that language affords many admirable bookes fit for you, as Romances, Plays, Poetry, Stories of illustrious (not learned) Woemen, receipts for preserving, making creames and all sorts of cookeryes, ordring your gardens, and in Breif all manner of good housewifery.[42]

Ann, Lady Fanshawe's education by her mother consisted in 'working allsorts of fine works with my needle, and learning French, singing, lute, the virginals, and dancing'. Margaret Cavendish, afterwards Duchess of Newcastle, had the benefit of tutors, but, in an autobiographical essay first published in her *Natures Pictures Drawn by Fancies Pencil to the Life* (1656), she describes the same course of instruction in 'all sorts of virtues', that is 'singing, dancing, playing on music, readings, writing, [needle-]working and the like'. Of her brothers' education she can say nothing, for 'the breeding of men were after different manner of ways from those of women'.[43] Exceptionally, a girl's education could be more extensive, even if, as in the case of Lucy Hutchinson, at the price of the 'emulation' of her brothers and without her mother's approval, who 'would have been contented I had not so wholly addicted myself' to books as 'to neglect my other qualities', including the needlework which her daughter 'absolutely hated'.[44] Her mother shared the prevailing view that 'Man is made to govern Common-Wealths, and Women their privat Families'. Those are Margaret Cavendish's words.[45] Women of evident learning and attainments themselves accepted this divorce between the private (feminine) and public (masculine) spheres and shared the age's dismay at the prospect of female involvement in public affairs. For Lucy Hutchinson the key to the cause of the Civil War lay not in Charles I's arbitrary exercise of patriarchal authority but in his unmanly submission to a woman who usurped a power which did not belong to her, namely

> the Queen [Henrietta Maria], who, grown out of her childhood, began to turn her mind from those vain extravagances she lived in at first, to that which did less become her, and was more fatal to the kingdom, which never is in any place

> happy where the hands that are made only for distaffs affect the management of sceptres. If any one object the fresh example of Queen Elizabeth, let them remember that the felicity of her reign was the effect of her submission to her masculine and wise counsellors; but wherever male princes are so effeminate to suffer women of foreign birth and different religion to intermeddle with the affairs of state, it is always found to produce sad desolations.[46]

In similar vein, Margaret Cavendish ascribes the Civil War in large part to the unruliness and insubordination of women. She argues that those 'ambitious to be State-Ladies' are misguided on the grounds that, while women 'are full of Designs and Plots', their lack of political wisdom only causes disarray in public affairs; 'witness our late Civil war, wherein Women were great, although not good actors': 'Temperance and Quietness are strangers to our sex'.[47]

And yet within a few pages of her discountenancing of those ambitious to be 'state ladies', Margaret Cavendish can propound a radically different, and potentially seditious, view of women's political and social position, stressing their marginalization and exclusion: 'the truth is, we are no subjects' of the state since women

> are not tied, nor bound to State or Crown; we are free, not Sworn to Allegiance, nor do we take the Oath of Supremacy; we are not made Citizens of the Commonwealth, we hold no Offices, nor bear we any Authority therein; we are accounted neither Useful in Peace, nor Serviceable in War; and if we be not Citizens in the Commonwealth, I know no reason we should be Subjects to the Commonwealth.[48]

Her own writings are in fact fascinated by the prospect of a woman's exercise of power, most notably in her creation for herself of the fictional role of empress of *The New Blazing World* (1666): 'though I cannot be *Henry* the Fifth or *Charles* the Second, yet I endeavour to be *Margaret* the *First*' by making a fictional 'world of my own' to rule.[49] In her 'True Relation of My Birth' she presents herself as a bashful and submissive wife, unwilling to intercede on her exiled husband's behalf during a visit to England in 1652–3, yet on that very same visit she ensured that her voice might nevertheless be publicly heard on her own behalf by arranging to have her first publication printed.[50]

On the Puritan side, women's public engagement had in the recent past received positive encouragement. In the early years of the Civil War the eminent Independent divine Jeremiah Burroughes had exhorted women to put aside 'womanish fears' and to assume the valiant spirit of Deborah and Jael. The preacher and prophetess Katherine Chidley, arguing in the Independent manner for toleration of divergencies in religious belief and practice, had denied the husband authority over his wife's conscience as she denied the state authority over the subject's conscience.[51] The incidence of female petitioners of parliament during the years 1642–53 and in 1659 is a clear and specific example of the Civil War enabling women to forgo their customary womanly silence for an 'Amazonian' or 'masculine spirit'; the activities of prophetesses is another.[52] Evidence of this radical tradition can be found after the Restoration. In a work anonymously published in 1666 the Quaker Margaret Fell refuted the received interpretation of the Pauline texts forbidding women a voice in church assemblies (and, by extension, in public debate). She distinguishes between the unregenerate (who should keep silent) and those regenerate women, illuminated by the Spirit, who enjoy spiritual equality with men. In an entirely salutary way, she calls attention to the significant part played by women in the gospels, to Jesus's acceptance of them as messengers of his Word, and to the biblical fondness for personifying the church as a woman.[53] Hers, however, was a lonely voice. Nonconformists in general retreated from the Interregnum's radical sexual politics. The Baptist Anne Wentworth, attempting to fulfil the prophetic role in the 1660s and 1670s and to exercise 'liberty of conscience' despite her husband's opposition to the publication of her opinions, encountered nothing but hostility.[54] Although apparently liberating Christiana and Mercy to roam outdoors and become the protagonists of their own narratives in Part II of *The Pilgrim's Progress* (1684), Bunyan in fact inculcates wifely domesticity as their proper role and through them warns that women who stray out of doors bring their misfortunes upon themselves. When women in his congregation began to hold their own separate meetings in the Quaker manner, he would not tolerate this usurpation of the masculine role and 'laboured to keep them in their place'.[55]

The dominant ideology was no more sympathetic to female aspiration. Allestree, that spokesman for the genteel taste of the Restoration period, decried the 'great indecency of Loquacity in Women' and rebuked as reprehensible boldness any female pretensions to speak or teach in public.[56] Though prevalent, however, this was not quite the only view. Pointing out in her *Essay to Revive the Antient Education of Gentlewomen* (1673) that 'Custom, when it is inveterate, hath a mighty influence: it hath the force of Nature itself', Bathsua Makin, much influenced by the Utrecht scholar Anna Marie van Schurman whose *De ingenii muliebris* was translated into English in 1659 as *The Learned Maid*, argued that women's supposed mental incapacity was merely the product of educational neglect and social expectation:

> The barbarous custom to breed women low is grown general amongst us, and hath prevailed to far, that it is verily believed (especially amongst a sort of debauched sots) that women are not endued with such reason as men, nor capable of that improvement by education as they are. It is looked upon as a monstrous thing to pretend to the contrary.[57]

Henry More knew the contrary. In his correspondence with Lady Anne Conway, wife of Edward, 3rd Viscount Conway, which began in the early

1650s and continued until her death in 1679, a wide range of current philosophical, religious and scientific issues – Cartesianism, Familism, Quakerism (in 1677 she herself became a Quaker), Cabbalism, Copernican cosmology – are discussed by both correspondents on the basis of first-hand knowledge of the primary sources. It is an exchange between intellectual equals, with no assumption of intellectual superiority on More's side. On the contrary, he publicly acknowledged that he had 'scarce ever met with any Person, Man or Woman, of better Natural parts' and that 'in the knowledge of all things as well Natural as Divine, you have not onely outgone all of your own Sex, but even of that other also'.[58] There was, however, no cultural or institutional context in which a woman could devote herself to the life of the mind. Anne Conway's commitment to study was only possible because her circumstances contrived to isolate her from all other demands. For 20 years she lived a life of retirement in Ragley Hall in Warwickshire, much of the time confined to her darkened room, where she suffered repeatedly from severe and prolonged headaches. Her family were inclined to attribute her ill-health to the overtaxing of her female brain in study, but not so More. When he expresses the fear that 'you increase your disease by over much meditation' it is not because of her vulnerability as a woman but from his own experience that 'intension of thoughts, and anxious consyderations of thinges, will extremely heat a mans spiritts, and call them up into the head', with the inference that those, male or female, who are 'lyable to the head-ache . . . must needs encrease that maladie, by over much intending their braine'.[59]

While social and religious institutions could not conceive of women apart from men, poetic and romance genres might construct independent female roles and delight in female societies (as did Cavendish in her play *The Convent of Pleasure* (1668)). The pastoral tradition was particularly serviceable here: as in Renaissance pastoral the male lover had retreated to idyllic scenes for emotional solace after disappointment by women, so now this retreat offered a refuge to women oppressed by men and the promise of an exclusively female space. Celibacy and the attractions of female company and friendship become marked literary themes from the 1650s onward, allowing the contemplation of an alternative emotional and social order. By the early eighteenth century a tradition of romantic female friendship was a fact of higher-class life as well as of letters.[60] The key figure in establishing this tradition of Platonic affection was Katherine Philips, 'the matchless Orinda', both through her 'Society of Friendship', a literary coterie of royalists who in the 1650s continued the ideals of Platonic love, honour and elaborate manners fostered at court by Henrietta Maria, and, more influentially, through the celebration of female friendship in her poetry. Her *Poems* of 1664, and the enlarged posthumous folio collection of 1667, explicitly prefer women's companionship to heterosexual love, celibacy to marriage. Her lyrics find in the 'happy quiet' of female friendship a security and emotional fulfilment which the changing and inconstant patriarchal world cannot provide. The experience of this friendship is presented as 'Calme as a Virgin', but the ardent intensity with which, in the manner of the seventeenth-century heterosexual love lyric (often echoing Donne), Philips can address women suggests a lesbian sensibility in a culture which barely had a word for sexual relations between women.[61]

There was one way in the 1660s for a woman to take centre stage. At the Restoration, women were for the first time permitted to perform publicly in plays, but their roles were frequently in 'breeches parts' which offered a titillating spectacle to a society taught that 'The woman shall not wear that which pertaineth unto a man, neither shall a man put on a woman's garment: for all that do so are abominations unto the Lord thy God' (Deuteronomy 22.5).[62] Actresses were commonly supposed to be prostitutes, and a similar charge was made against that other form of public performance, publication. 'Whore is scarce a more reproachful name, / Than poetess', declared Rochester. In Lovelace's phrase (perhaps with reference to Margaret Cavendish), a woman who publishes 'prostitutes' herself in 'publick Aire'.[63] Domestic and religious subjects might be unexceptionable, but women who in print attempted other subjects or genres commonly anticipated hostility and sought to minimize it through some form of prefatory apology for their transgressive behaviour.[64] 'I am', acknowledges Anne Bradstreet, 'obnoxious to each carping tongue / Who says my hand a needle better fits, / A poet's pen all scorn I should thus wrong; / For such despite they cast on female wits.' She seeks to win a hearing by judiciously conceding (but with a hint of irony?) the inevitable superiority of male achievement: 'Men can do best and women know it well. / Pre-eminence in all and each is yours; / Yet grant some small acknowledgement of ours'.[65] Cavendish is bolder: though she presents herself as a traditionally compliant and retiring wife who finds happiness only in her husband's company, she also acknowledges that she delights 'in singularity', that she is 'what the vulgar call proud' and that she is 'very ambitious'. Only in fiction can she resolve this tension between aspiration and subservience. In *The New Blazing World* she empowers herself as an author not only through the scheme of a narrative in which the Duchess herself assumes and exercises supreme political power, but also in the imaginative freedom with which she 'makes a world of my own creating' within the text and in the absolute authority the epilogue grants her as 'Authoress of a whole world'.[66]

## 5 Men of the World

Margaret Cavendish was not much regarded by her own age, save as an idiosyncratic oddity, unusually preposterous even for a woman, with her 'antique dress' and 'deportment so unordinary' sought out as one of the sights of the capital (by, among others, Pepys). Her indecorum extended to speculations in natural philosophy, where atomism especially intrigued her. She was, it seems on her own initiative, invited to a meeting of the Royal Society in May 1667. Whether or not Pepys was correct in his report that during her visit she did not say 'anything that was worth hearing, but . . . she was full of admiration, all admiration',[67] the Duchess showed shrewd judgement for here she penetrated what would become a temple of the masculinist intellect. It grew out of informal Interregnum meetings of like-minded men, notably a group meeting in London from 1645. John Wilkins, afterwards Bishop of Chester, was a member of this 'Philosophical College' and when, in 1648, he became Warden of Wadham College, Oxford, a similar group formed there, while the weekly London meetings continued. In 1660 members of both groups began to meet in London each week after Christopher Wren's astronomy lecture at Gresham College. In November 1660 they formed themselves into a society under Wilkins's chairmanship, keeping minutes of their meetings, and on 15 July 1662 Charles II granted it a charter as the Royal Society 'for the Improvement of naturall knowledge by Experiment'.[68] Its founding fellows were men who shared a Baconian belief in the superiority of observation, experimentation and induction over *a priori* argument. They shared, too, a Cartesian scepticism about received knowledge: in 1661 Robert Boyle published the pointedly titled *The Sceptical Chymist.* This is written in the form of a dialogue between, in the main, on the one hand the 'hermetic philosopher' Themistius, for whom 'it is much more high and philosophical to discover things *a priore* than *a posteriore*' and who finds the harmony and comprehensiveness of the Aristotelian system far more persuasive than the findings of any particular experiment; and on the other, the sceptic of the title, Carneades, who, insisting on observation before generalization, seeks, in the words of Boyle's preface, to draw 'the chymists' doctrine out of their dark and smokie laboratories' of alchemical practice and 'into the open light' by revealing 'the weakness of their proofs'.[69] The book thus epitomizes a crucial stage in the development of the modern scientific tradition from the Aristotelianism, providentialism, occultism and various kinds of allegorical *emblemata* and mystical *arcana* which had hitherto shaped thinking about the natural world. The founding of the Society in 1662 gave institutional authority to this empirical, analytical and rational way of understanding the world. Experimental science accorded the human mind an interpretative and analytical capacity in natural philosophy which it had not hitherto enjoyed, and increasingly it attributed to the natural world a self-contained coherence as a self-functioning system which, though it might retain God as the Creator and First Cause, allowed him no other causal, still less interventionist, role in his creation. What they construed as the pretentiousness of this enterprise dismayed those of conservative mind, such as the divine Robert South, formerly Clarendon's chaplain, who ridiculed the Society in an oration at the dedication of the Sheldonian Theatre in Oxford in 1669, prompting a *Defence* of the new science by John Wallis (1678).

While their shared scientific bias (as it would now be called, thought the term *science* had not yet is modern sense)[70] caused dismay in such quarters as potentially irreligious, the earliest members of the Society shared something else hardly less momentous. Among them were represented a range of political and religious commitments, but fellows were characteristically of a moderate and latitudinarian temper, like Samuel Hartlib's associate, the indefatigable ecumenist John Dury, or Wilkins himself, an advocate of comprehension after the Restoration. In his *Essay Towards a Real Character* (1667), Wilkins extended Dury's project by aspiring to universal concord and world peace through the adoption of a scientific language which would harmonize the discord of Babel. This emphasis on consensus and reasonableness was the burden of Thomas Sprat's *History of the Royal Society* (1667), 'as much a confession of faith as a factual record' of the Society's formative years.[71] His *History* located the Interregnum origins of the Society in men seeking 'the satisfaction of breathing a freer air, and of conversing in quiet one with another, without being ingag'd in the passions, and madness of that dismal Age', men who were 'invincibly arm'd against all the inchantments of *Enthusiasm*'. The design of the Society was to redeem intellectual enquiry 'from the Artifice, and Humors, and Passions of Sects', and so it 'freely admitted Men of different Religions, Countries, and Professions of Life'. Like the libertinism for which *free* was also a talismanic term, the Society was another, though very different, attempt to liberate the 1660s from the past.[72]

That this model of co-operation and joint enterprise succeeded in the divisively partisan 1660s is the more important because the degree to which the early Society actually fostered scientific advance and discovery is debated.[73] While it undoubtedly numbered among its founding members men of extraordinary ability – Robert Boyle, say, or Christopher Wren – it also included, for example, Pepys and Evelyn, whose interest in experimentation had an altogether more dilettante character. They demonstrate the kind of fashionable curiosity about natural phenomena expected of a Restoration gentleman. Sprat notes that 'the farr greater Number' of its members were 'Gentlemen' and Evelyn described the Society as 'an Assembly of many honourable Gentlemen, who meete inoffensively together under his Majesty's Royal Cognizance; and to entertain themselves ingenuously, whilst their other domestique avocations or publique businesse deprives them of being allwayes in the company of learned men and that they cannot dwell forever in the Universities'.[74] A third of its members were from the aristocracy and landed gentry, a third from the professions (including many episcopal divines, such as Sprat himself, Stillingfleet, Wilkins and two future archbishops of Canterbury, Tillotson and Tenison). Of the remainder the majority were connected with the court or government.[75] It thus represented the coming together of the higher echelons of London society rather than of men committed to advancing the new science. In the 1660s the Society did seek funding to establish itself on a secure basis, with its own premises and a permanent staff, as a recognized academic centre of scientific research, but these efforts came to nothing. It met in Gresham College in Bishopsgate Street. After the Fire, when the College was used for civic functions, it was granted the use of rooms in Arundell House in the Strand by Henry Howard, afterwards 6th Duke of Norfolk, who was elected a fellow in November 1666. It returned to Gresham in 1673.[76]

In this respect the Society continued the tradition of the *virtuosi* and its members demonstrated the Renaissance cast of mind which had been, and continued to be, fascinated by the cabinets of curiosities which featured in so many noble London and provincial houses. These collections of intrinsically striking objects were not brought together to serve any larger project or to illustrate any overarching theory. It was not their categorization or orderliness but the arbitrariness and startling juxtapositions in the cabinets – their very lack of coherence or design – which was their attraction, to which wonder and surprise (such as the Duchess of Newcastle expressed, by Pepys's account) was the appropriate response.[77] Evelyn displays something of the virtuoso attitude in his diary, commenting on what was extraordinary or marvellous in the Society's experiments. He had been one of the original 40 fellows proposed at the establishment of 'the *Philosophic Society*' in November 1660 and he was duly elected in January 1661. Thereafter, he regularly records its meetings in his diary. Within 18 months he has marvelled at 'the famous *Queene-pine* [pine-apple] from *Barbados*', 'a Bird of *Paradise* or *Manucodiata*', the embryos of two puppies 'no bigger than the top of ons fingers, perfectly shaped both within and without: which were preserved in Spirit of Wine' and a sample of '*Hippomanes*', a supposed aphrodisiac secreted by a mare in heat or foaling; he had been intrigued by the working of poisons, antidotes and 'strange cures', by a '*Vernish* that should resist all Weathers, & preserve yron from rust', by a powder that 'corroded the thickest glass'; and he was struck by reports of a woman 'who sweate so excessively, that a quart of water, might at any time be taken out of the Palmes of her hands, not smelling ill'.[78] He was similarly impressed, during a visit to the College of Physicians in October 1662, by 'divers natural Curiosities' in its Library, including a brainless '*Devil* Fish', the thigh bone of an ostrich and 'divers *skelletons*'.[79] And he remarks the donation of 'a piece of *Elephant* skin, which was about inch-thick' for the Society's own 'Repository'.[80] There is an intellectual generosity in this wide-ranging responsiveness, but Eveyln does not record what he made of these observations. These amateur collectors and enthusiasts became a sufficiently marked feature of London society to attract satirical attention in Thomas Shadwell's play *The Virtuoso* (1676). Three years later, the Ashmolean Musem in Oxford would be founded upon just such a 'Closet of Rarities', that collected by the Tradescant family.[81]

The reputation of the Society in Britain and abroad grew rapidly, especially as a result of its journal, the *Philosophical Transactions*, which from its inception in 1665 immediately established itself as the primary organ for the dissemination of new discoveries, not only by fellows of the Society but by other experimenters and observers throughout Europe. As established by the Society's first secretary Henry Oldenberg, the *Transactions* took a comprehensive and inclusive view of its readership and its mission. It addressed a wide public (permitting a kind of intellectual curiosity in natural philosophy impossible in the area of public affairs, where L'Estrange's *London Gazette* narrowly drew the lines of permissible speculation). It was particularly anxious to solicit information from those whose lives brought them into immediate contact with kinds of evidence not available in Britain, or who in their work grappled with the technological consequences of imperfect scientific knowledge. Mariners, for example, were encouraged to participate in a worldwide data collecting exercise. It was in this spirit of technological utility that Evelyn presented to the Society his *Sculptura: or, the History, and Art of Chalcography and Engraving in Copper* (1662, dedicated to Boyle) and his *Sylva, or a Discourse of Forest Trees, and the Propagation of Timber*, the first book to be printed at the Society's order by its own printer (1664).[82] Similarly, it is a digression concerning the very practical matter of 'shipping and navigation' in his *Annus Mirabilis* which leads Dryden to apostrophize the Society as the source of invention, and through invention, progress, for, strikingly, the digression takes an evolutionary view of technological development.[83] In this, it is one of the earliest English examples of a cast of mind which will become characteristic of European modernity.

As this suggests, the speculations and theories of the Society's members were expected to issue in practical applications. In a famous passage, Sprat writes that the Society rejected all 'amplifications, digressions and swellings of style' in order to

> return back to the primitive purity, and shortness, when men deliver'd so many *things*, almost in an equal number of *words*. They have exacted from all their members, a close, naked, natural way of speaking; positive expressions; clear senses; a native easiness: bringing all things as near the Mathematical plainness, as they can: and preferring the language of Artizans, Countrymen, and Merchants, before that, of Wits, or Scholars.

This preference for the language of artisans was partly to avoid slip-shod vagueness, but it was also to enable the Society to communicate its findings to artisans. Despite its overwhelmingly gentlemanly membership, this was an emphatically utilitarian venture: as 'an Instrument, whereby Mankind may obtain a Dominion over *Things*', the Society would advance '*Manual Trade*', '*Mechanick Arts*' and '*Manufacture*'.[84] Defending the new science in *Plus Ultra* (1667), Joseph Glanvill stressed its practicality and utility, its benefit to society. He sets out, in the words of his subtitle, *to encourage Philosophical endeavours* by giving *an Account of some of the most remarkable late improvements of Practical Useful Learning*. (In this respect, Charles, 'a great lover of mechanics' with a technological bent, was fitting patron.)[85] This utility was above all championed in the context of trade. Through the Privy Council Committee of Trade and Plantations, the Council of Trade and the Council for Foreign Plantations, the restored regime put a good deal of effort into promoting overseas trade.[86] So, too, did the Society. In his *History*, Sprat saw the Royal Society and the Royal Company of Adventurers Trading into Africa as 'Twin Sisters': new science and improved trade go hand in hand. In his *Observations* (1665) he anticipated the English being 'Masters of the Trade of the World',[87] much as Dryden does in his *Annus Mirabilis*. It is the extraordinary achievement of this poem, composed in the second half of 1666 and published early in 1667,[88] to produce a positive and optimistic account of national affairs, and to celebrate the King and court in the midst of the crisis of the mid-1660s. It contrives to render the division of the fleet under Monck and Rupert and the Four Days Battle of 3–6 June 1666 in victorious and heroic terms, recalling Rome's rivalry with Carthage. In an ambitious evocation of national destiny it constructs a present marked by unity, order, harmony and security from which will emerge a glorious future. In that future, the poem foresees not the fulfilment of the eschatalogical portents of the radical *Mirabilis Annus* pamphlets of 1661 and 1662, to which its very title is a retort, but English dominion of the seas and imperial glory. The connection between this future and the Dutch war which is the poem's immediate occasion lies in trade. In rivalry for limited resources lies the inevitability of war with the Dutch, and by no means only in Dryden's view. Pepys, for example, reports in 1664 the hemp merchant George Cocke opining that 'the trade of the world is too little for us two, therefore one must down' and 'discoursing well of the good effects in some kind of a Dutch war and conquest'. On 21 April that year Clifford, the chair of the Committee of Trade, reported to the Commons that the activities of the United Provinces were the greatest single obstruction to England's foreign trade.[89] And so *Annus Mirabilis* expends a good deal of imaginative energy on the celebration of trade, for therein lies the justification for this war and the key to England's future, a future in which 'the venturous merchant' 'Shall here unlade him and depart no more', England 'From all the world shall vindicate [i.e. defend] her trade' and 'A constant trade-wind will securely blow, / And gently lay us on the spicy shore'.[90] The 1660s had opened by announcing an expansionist and imperialist ideology on those triumphal arches at Charles's coronation procession; Dryden reaffirms confidence in an imperialist future, despite the catastrophes of the Plague and Fire, political ineptitude and national humiliation in war.

London is central to this vision. Sprat, after the Plague and Fire, was excited by the prospect that 'A *New City* is to be built, on the most advantageous Seat of all *Europe*, for Trade, and command'. At the time of the Fire, London was a city of some 400,000 inhabitants, the largest city in Europe save for Paris and by far the largest conurbation in the country; Norwich and Bristol, at

20–30,000 inhabitants each, were next largest, and hardly any other town had more than 1,000 inhabitants.[91] Something of the disruption caused by the Fire to this huge metropolis can be inferred from the pages of the *London Gazette* for the last four months of 1666, which give notice of relocated businesses, food relief, temporary food markets, redirection of mail, building regulations and measures against escalating crime. In the destruction, however, lay an opportunity. Within days Evelyn, who had already shown his concern for the capital in his *Fumifugium* (1661), a plea for the regulation of smoke pollution, produced his own plan and written proposals for *Londinum Redivivum, or London Restored not to its Pristine, but to Far Greater Beauty Commmodiousness and Magnificence.* This envisages a city regularly laid out, with 'handsome architecture, in form of triumphal arches, adorned with Statues, Relievos, and apposite Inscriptions' at its entry gates, and within its walls wide thoroughfares and paved streets lined by 'substantially built' brick or stone buildings which 'exactly respect uniformity', interspersed by 'Spaces for ample Courts, Yards, and Gardens', and 'enlargements into piazzas at competent distances, which ought to be built exactly uniform, strong, and with beautiful fronts'. This is a neo-classical city, a new Rome. The plan was presented to the King on 13 September, who, with the Duke of York, spoke to Evelyn for an hour about it, 'seeming to be extreamly pleasd' with the scheme; and on 22 December Evelyn sent a copy of it to the Royal Society's Secretary, Oldenberg. Wren presented a still more ambitious and radical plan, with wide arterial roads, the noisome River Fleet transformed into a canal, the Thames provided with new embankments and quays, and all noisy or smelly trades and sites removed beyond the city limits.[92]

A week after the Fire, Charles issued proclamations promising orderly rebuilding and prohibiting unlawful acquisition or occupation of land, but the pressing need for the resumption of normal business and the complexities and obligations of land titles prevented any new city from being constructed *ab initio*. In February 1667 parliament passed two acts: one to set up fire courts to determine disputes; the second a rebuilidng act which imposed a set of building rules. These required all external walls to be of brick or stone (the destroyed city had been built predominantly of wood) and they specified the proportions of newly built houses according to their location: the 'least sort' of property, situated in 'By lanes', were to be of two storeys (with cellar and garret); the second class, in 'Streets and Lanes of note', of three storeys; and the third, in 'high and principall Streetes', of four storeys. No house, even those of 'persons of extraordinary quality', could exceed these dimensions, and all buildings were now to be flat-fronted (that is, without overhanging upper storeys).[93] The City's Common Council had classified streets accordingly by late the next month: there were six 'principal' streets, 214 'of note' and the rest were 'by lanes'.[94] One new street – King Street, from Guildhall to Cheapside – was created; otherwise, the old medieval plan was followed, with slight modifications. Building began in April and continued under the eye of

Wren, appointed Surveyor General of the Royal Works in 1669. By 1671 nearly 7,000 houses had been built. A total of 87 city churches were destroyed by the Fire: 52 of these were rebuilt to designs by Wren. The foundation stone of St Paul's was laid in 1675 and, with Wren attending as the sole survivor of those who had been present in 1675, the cathedral was completed in 1711. The Monument was erected in 1677 (its inscription blaming the Fire on 'the popish faction'). It records 13,200 homes destroyed.[95]

None of this, of course, gets into Dryden's poem. As he turns the engagements of the Dutch war to heroic purpose, so he turns the catastrophe of the Fire to national advantage. Charles's behaviour allows Dryden a complimentary opportunity entirely to the monarch's credit, but beyond that, through alchemical imagery, the figure of the phoenix and glances at the golden age of Elizabeth and at imperial Rome, Dryden imagines an imperial capital rising to enjoy hegemony over the entire earth:

> Methinks already from this chymic flame
> I see a city of more precious mould:
> Rich as the town which gives the Indies name,
> With silver paved, and all divine with gold...
>
> More great than human, now, and more August,
> New deified she from her fires does rise:
> Her widening streets on new foundations trust,
> And opening, into larger parts she flies...
>
> Now like a maiden queen she will behold
> From her high turrets hourly suitors come:
> The east with incense and the west with gold
> Will stand like suppliants to receive her doom.[96]

# *Afterword*

Writing in exile at the decade's end Clarendon found the course of the 1660s all but incomprehensible. Those who had witnessed the 'wonderful change and exclamation of all degrees of men' at the King's return in May 1660 could not but suppose that

> there must be some wonderful miscarriages in the state, or some unheard of defect of understanding in those who were trusted by the king in the administration of his affairs; that there could in so short a time be a new revolution in the general affections of the people, that they grew even weary of that happiness they were possessed of and had so much valued, and fell into the same discontents and murmurings which had naturally accompanied them in the worst of times.[1]

Clarendon may be forgiven the ironic implication that public disaffection (and his own downfall in 1667) were inexplicable, but reasons for the general decline in regard for the government are not far to seek: in public affairs the record of the 1660s was dismal. The decade which had begun in such optimistic public ceremonial descended so swiftly into dismay and discontent at the mendacity, venality and incompetence of its rulers that Clarendon may well be right to detect here yet another of the many seventeenth-century revolutions. In 1670 the restored monarchy had not yet endured for as long as the period of non-monarchical government which had preceded it and, though it may have survived the decade, it had by no means secured its future. Public confidence in its enduring stability was markedly less in 1670 than in 1660. Persecution and repression had contained dissent, and the memory of the anarchic collapse of the Republic was still sufficiently fresh to disincline the majority of the English again to try that experiment, but before the decade's end an imaginatively rich and politically committed literature was both invoking the Cromwellian past and raising serious questions about monarchy's prospects. Here were the seeds of another revolution, one which within twenty years would remodel the Restoration itself. However, while the political record is a sorry one (the Cavalier Parliament enacted no enduringly significant legislation during the 1660s), a decade which can lay claim in literature to, among others, Bunyan, Butler, Cavendish, Clarendon himself, Dryden, Hutchinson, Milton and Philips; to Evelyn and Pepys, unrivalled diarists; in fine art and architecture to Lely and Wren; to Boyle, Hooke and the founding of the Royal Society; in law to Hale and in economics and statistics to the pioneering work of Petty; and to the developing trade of the great mercantile companies; such a decade is as creatively diverse as any in our cultural history. Setting out determined to speak with one voice, it proved to be vociferously multivocal. If, perhaps in consequence, political instability was its legacy to the 1670s, so, too, was a vitality which refused to rest content with compliant acceptance or unquestioning iteration in any field of human endeavour.[2]

# Notes

## INTRODUCTION

1 Pepys, i. 122 (2 May 1660).
2 Hutton *R*, p. 1.
3 Evelyn, iii.296 (29 May 1660).
4 Milton *SA*, l. 695.
5 This is discussed below, pp. 50–3.
6 Sir Philip Warwick, *Memoires* (1703), pp. 390, 399.
7 See their comments quoted below, p. 47.
8 Marchamont Nedham, *Interest Will Not Lie* (1659), p. 20.
9 Pepys, ix. 299 (4 September 1668), 399 (25 December 1668).
10 Bunyan *GA*, §276.

## 1 THE RETURN OF THE KING (1658–1660)

1 For fuller accounts of events briefly treated in this section see: Davies, pp. 3–85; Hutton *R*, pp. 21–41; Austin Woolrych, 'Introducution' to Milton *CPW*, vii.4–71; and on both them and Richard Cromwell's career in general, see Earl M. Hause, *Tumble-Down Dick* (New York, 1972).
2 Baxter *RB*, I.100, §145; Clarendon *HR*, vi.98 (XVI.§1); David Underdown, *Royalist Conspiracy in England, 1649–1660* (1960), pp. 230–1; Paul Hardacre, *The Royalists during the Puritan Revolution* (The Hague, 1956), p. 132.
3 Burnet *OT*, i.147; Thomas Birch (ed.), *Collection of State Papers of John Thurloe*, 7 vols (1742), vii.374, quoted in Davies, p. 7.
4 Baxter *RB*, I.100, §145; Baker, pp. 652–4; Thurloe, *State Papers*, vii.372–3, 375, 377–8, 415; Whitelocke, pp. 675, 676; *Mercurius Politicus*, 432 (2–9 September 1658), pp. 803–4.
5 Hutchinson, pp. 257, 261. Hutton *R*, p. 41, thinks this reputation undeserved.
6 Thurloe, *State Papers*, vii.375; *Mercurius Politicus*, 434 (16–23 September 1658), pp. 844–74 [*recte* 47]; Godfrey Davies, 'The Army and the Downfall of Richard Cromwell', *HLB*, vii (1935), 135–6; The address is printed in *Old Parl. Hist.*, xxi.233–6.

7 Thurloe, *State Papers*, vii.436, 447–9, 490–1, 497–8, 500; Davies, 'Army and the Downfall of Richard Cromwell', 136–43.

8 *CJ*, vii.593–4, 596, 601–5; Baker, p. 659, quoted in Austin Woolrych, 'Last Quests for Settlement, 1657–1660', in G. E. Aylmer (ed.), *The Interregnum: The Quest for Settlement, 1646–1660* (1972), p. 191; K. H. D. Haley, *The First Earl of Shaftesbury* (Oxford, 1968), pp. 97–9. For the composition and proceedings of this parliament see: *Old. Parl. Hist.*, xxi.281–90; Godfrey Davies, 'The Election of Richard Cromwell's Parliament', *EHR*, lxiii (1948), 489–501; G. B. Nourse, 'Richard Cromwell's House of Commons', *BJRL*, lx (1977–8), 95–113; Ivan Roots, 'The Tactics of the Commonwealthsmen in Richard Cromwell's Parliament', in Donald Pennington and Keith Thomas (ed.), *Puritans and Revolutionaries* (Oxford, 1978), pp. 283–309.

9 *CJ*, vii.589–92, 605–12; Thurloe, *State Papers*, vii.615; Whitelocke, p. 677; C. H. Firth, *The Last Years of the Protectorate, 1656–8*, 2 vols (Oxford, 1909), ii.16–41; Haley, *Shaftesbury*, pp. 100–5.

10 *CJ*, vii.604; Austin Woolrych, 'The Good Old Cause and the Fall of the Protectorate', *CHJ*, xiii (1957), 138–44, which gives the titles of relevant tracts.

11 Baxter *RB*, I.100, §145.

12 Whitelocke, p. 678; Baxter *RB*, I.101, 102, §§145, 147 (cf. I.74–6, §119); *CJ*, vii.632; *Mercurius Politicus*, 561 (31 March–7 April 1659), p. 352. The petition is printed in *Old Parl. Hist.*, xxi.340–5.

13 *CJ*, vii. 641; *Mercurius Politicus*, 564 (21–28 April 1659), p. 391.

14 Whitelocke, p. 678.

15 *CJ*, vii. 644–5; Whitelocke, pp. 678–9; *Mercurius Politicus*, 566 (5–12 May 1659), pp. 423–4. The Army's declaration is printed in Baker, p. 661, and in *Old Parl. Hist.*, xxi.367–8.

16 For fuller accounts of events briefly treated in this section see: Davies, pp. 86–143; Hutton *R*, pp. 43–55, 62–6; Woolrych in Milton *CPW*, vii.96–112.

17 *CJ*, vii.653. The 42, with William Lenthall as Speaker, are listed in *Old Parl. Hist.*, xxi.370–1, from [Arthur Annesley], *England's Confusion: or, A Just and Impartial Relation of the Late Traverses of State in England... Written by One of the Few English Men that are Left in England* (1659), pp. 10–11. This is, of course, a hostile record: 'Pedantick *Thomas Scot*... Hastily rich *Cornelius Holland*, Single-hearted, preaching Sir *Henry Vane*... Smiling Sir *James Harrington*...'.

18 For this earlier history, see David Underdown, *Pride's Purge: Politics in the Puritan Revolution* (Oxford, 1971); A. B. Worden, *The Rump Parliament 1648–1653* (Cambridge, 1974); G. E. Aylmer, *The State's Servants: The Civil Service of the English Republic, 1649–1660* (1973).

19 Abernathy, pp. 27–8, 37; William Lamont, *Marginal Prynne* (1963), pp. 191–3. From Prynne's *Conscientious, Serious, Theological and Legal Queries Propounded to the... Westminster Juncto* (1659), *Old Parl. Hist.*, xxi.372–5, lists 213 surviving secluded members of the Commons.

20 Woolrych, 'Last Quests', p. 196, citing Sir Archibald Johnston of Wariston, *Diary*, 3 vols (Edinburgh, 1911–40), iii.124, and James Harrington, *A Discourse, Shewing that the Spirit of Parliament* (1659), p. 5.

21 *CJ*, vii.651; Woolrych in Milton *CPW*, vii.71–2. The petition is printed in Baker, pp. 662–4, and in *Old Parl. Hist.*, xxi.400–5.

22 Pepys, x.253; M. Coate (ed.), *The Letter-Book of John, Viscount Mordaunt*, Camden Soc. 3rd ser. lxix (1945), pp. 33–4; Hutchinson, p. 263; Baxter *CCRB*, Letter 581, with its headnote (and cf. Letter 535, with its headnote).

23 Underdown, *Royalist Conspiracy*, pp. 234–85; Mordaunt, *Letter-Book*, pp. 13–36; William H. Dawson, *Cromwell's Understudy* (1938); pp. 327–34; John Morrill, *Cheshire, 1630–1660* (Oxford, 1974), pp. 300–33.

24 For the Sealed Knot and Great Trust see Underdown, *Royalist Conspiracy*, chapters 5 and 11, and index.

25 Abernathy, pp. 32–3.

26 From the title of a mock romance (1661) satirizing the collapse of the Republic, published under the pseudonym Montelion, usually attributed to Thomas Flatman. For fuller accounts of events briefly treated in this section see: Davies, pp. 144–89; Hutton *R*, pp. 66–84; Woolrych in Milton *CPW*, vii.112–17, 131–55; Dawson, *Cromwell's Understudy*, pp. 349–80.

27 Thurloe, *State Papers*, vii.679–80; Hutchinson, pp. 257, 265. For Lambert's earlier career, see: Dawson, *Cromwell's Understudy*; Maurice Ashley, *Cromwell's Generals* (1954), pp. 99–113, 168–97; Austin Woolrych, *Commonwealth to Protectorate* (1982; rptd. 2000), pp. 72–4, 352–61 and passim.

28 *CJ*, vii.784–5, 792; Whitelocke, pp. 685–6; Mordaunt, *Letter-Book*, p. 54. The September petition is printed in Baker, p. 677; the October petition is in Baker, pp. 679–81, and in *Old Parl. Hist.*, xxi.460–5.

29 *CJ*, vii.794–7; *Mercurius Politicus*, 590–1 (6–20 October 1659), pp. 792–3, 803; Whitelocke, p. 686; Baker, pp. 681–2; Mordaunt, *Letter-Book*, pp. 55 (cf. p. 65), 59, 60.

30 Evelyn, iii.234 (16 October 1659); Mordaunt, *Letter-Book*, p. 61; *Mercurius Politicus*, 592 (20–27 October 1659), pp. 819, 827–8; *A Declaration of the General Council of the Officers* ([October] 1659), printed in *Mercurius Politicus*, 592 [*sic*] (27 October–3 November 1659), pp. 883–4; Whitelocke, p. 687; John Price, *The Mystery and Method of his Majesty's Happy Restauration* (1686), p. 43; Thomas Gumble, *The Life of General Monck* (1671), p. 168.

31 Hutchinson, pp. 272–3; Mordaunt, *Letter-Book*, pp. 43, 65–6, 69, 116.

32 Baker, pp. 672–5; Price, *Mystery and Method*, pp. 4–29; Gumble, *Monck*, pp. 103–9; Clarendon *HR*, vi.154 (XVI.§98); Mordaunt, *Letter-Book*, pp. 59 (cf. pp. 69, 115), 110.

33 George Monck, *Observations upon Military & Political Affairs* (1671), p. 2; Thurloe, *State Papers*, vii. 623, 666, 669–70; C. H. Firth (ed.), *Clarke Papers*, 4 vols (1891–1901), iv.22–3 (quoted by Davies, p. 110, by Maurice Ashley, *General Monck* (1977), pp. 154–5, and by Woolrych in Milton, *CPW*, vii.134). Cf. Whitelocke, pp. 679–80.

34 *A Letter from a Person of Quality in Edinburgh* (1659); *Mercurius Politicus*, 592 (27 October–3 November 1659), pp. 834–5; Whitelocke, p. 687; Baker, pp. 685–7; Price, *Mystery and Method*, pp. 49–50; Gumble, *Monck*, pp. 113, 137v–8; Ashley, *Monck*, pp. 166–8. Monck's letters are printed in *Old Parl. Hist.*, xxii.4–7.

35 Baxter *RB*, II.214, §67; Mordaunt, *Letter-Book*, pp. 80, 118; Whitelocke, pp. 687–90; Baker, pp. 687–9; Price, *Mystery and Method*, pp. 50–60, 63–4; Gumble, *Monck*, pp. 139–69; *Old Parl. Hist.*, xxii.7–21; Ashley, *Monck*, pp. 169–79; Haley, *Shaftesbury*, pp. 113–16.

36 Mordaunt, *Letter-Book*, p. 136; *Mercurius Politicus*, 597 (1–8 December 1659), p. 939; Reginald R. Sharpe, *London and the Kingdom: A History*, 3 vols (1894), ii.358–9. The

apprentices' 5 December petition was printed as *To ... the Lord Mayor, Aldermen and Commonalty ... the Most Humble Petition and Address of Divers Young Men* (1659). See further S. R. Smith, 'Almost Revolutionaries: The London Apprentices during the Civil Wars', *HLQ*, xlii (1978–9), 313–28.

37 *Two Letters from Vice-Admiral John Lawson* (1659); *A Letter from Sir Arthur Hesilrige in Portsmouth* (1659); *Memoirs of the Civil War: The Fairfax Correspondence* (1859), ii.151–71; *Mercurius Politicus*, 600 (22–29 December 1659), pp. 675–7; Whitelocke, pp. 691–2; Baker, pp. 690, 695–6, 698; Price, *Mystery and Method*, pp. 68–9; Haley, *Shaftesbury*, pp. 116–22.

38 Whitelocke, p. 692 (repr. in *Old Parl. Hist.*, xxii.26–8); *CJ*, vii.797; *Mercurius Politicus*, 600 (22–29 December 1659), pp. 678–9; Firth (ed.), *Clarke Papers*, iv.220 (quoted by Woolrych in Milton, *CPW*, vii.154).

39 *CJ*, vii.806, 812; Mordaunt, *Letter-Book*, pp. 118, 147; Monck, *Observations*, pp. 12–13, 16; Gumble, *Monck*, p. 174; Ashley, *Monck*, pp. 183–5. Lambert was still at large in mid-February (*CJ*, vii.837, 841). Refusing to give security to live quietly in his country house at Wimbledon he was committed to the Tower on 6 March (*CJ*, vii.864).

40 For fuller accounts of events briefly treated in this section see: Davies, pp. 256–306; Hutton *R*, pp. 85–107; Woolrych in Milton *CPW*, vii.156–76; Ashley, *Monck*, pp. 180–203.

41 Gumble, *Monck*, p. 166; Evelyn, iii.241 (3 January 1660). For summaries of Monck's possible motives and intentions, see: Ashley, *Monck*, pp. 180–2, 247–51; Hutton *R*, pp. 70–1, 90; and cf. Davies, p. 216.

42 Baker, p. 688; Price, *Mystery and Method*, sig. A4, pp. 29, 153; Gumble, *Monck*, pp. 116–17, 123.

43 Mordaunt, *Letter-Book*, pp. 118, 119, 155, 160, 162, 166; Pepys, i.22 (18 January 1660), 87 (4 March 1660), 125 (4 May 1660); Rugg, p. 60; cf. Burnet *OT*, i.151–2; Davies, pp. 307–8.

44 Sir Gyles Isham (ed.), *The Correspondence of Bishop Brian Duppa and Sir Justinian Isham, 1650–1660*, Northants. Record Soc. Pubs. xvii (Lamport, Northants, [1956]), pp. 177, 181; Mordaunt, *Letter-Book*, p. 165; Price, *Mystery and Method*, p. 85; *Old Parl. Hist.*, xxii.68–70.

45 Pepys, i.40 (2 February 1660), 58 (17 February 1660), 75, 76 (3 March 1660); cf. i.33 (30 January 1660); Ludlow, p. 92. Pepys thought at least Richard Cromwell's return impossible (i.76).

46 *Parliamentary Intelligencer*, 15 (2–9 April 1660), pp. 229–30; Ludlow, pp. 92, 117; Evelyn, iii.237–8 (10 January 1660); Pepys, i.86 (13 March 1660); Mordaunt, *Letter-Book*, pp. 157, 174. For Monck's contact with Charles in March, see below, p. 28.

47 *CJ*, vii.802–6, 808, 812–13, 828, 841; Whitelocke, pp. 693, 694; Baker, pp. 699–700.

48 *CJ*, vii.803, 806–7.

49 *CJ*, vii.819; Mordaunt, *Letter-Book*, p. 147; Pepys, i.5 (2 January 1660), 27 (24 January 1660), quoted in Davies, p. 262; Rugg, p. 27. The declaration is printed in *Old Parl. Hist.*, xxii.58–62.

50 Mordaunt, *Letter-Book*, pp. 126, 147 (cf. p. 177); Sharpe, *London and the Kingdom*, ii.359–60, 364, 366; Lamont, *Prynne*, pp. 192–5; Ethyn W. Kirby, *Prynne* (1931),

pp. 202–5. Prynne's titles included *The Case of the Old Secured, Secluded and now Excluded Members*, 'one of the best of his many pamphlets' (Davies, p. 259).

51 Hutton *R*, p. 88, finds the earliest use of the term *Rump* by a royalist in May 1659. E. S. de Beer, in Evelyn, iii.242 n.2, also notes that it becomes frequent in pamphlets from November 1659, but cites its use (as does *OED*) by 'Theodorus Verax' (i.e. the Presbyterian Clement Walker), *Anarchia Anglicana: or, The History of Independency. The Second Part* (1648–9), p. 32, of the MPs remaining after Pride's Purge: 'this Rump of a Parliament with corrupt Maggots in it'.

52 *CJ*, vii.834–5; Baker, pp. 701–6; Price, *Mystery and Method*, pp. 85, 91–3; Gumble, *Monck*, pp. 229–34; Whitelocke, p. 696. Monck's speech is in Baker, pp. 705–6, Gumble, *Monck*, pp. 229–34, and in *Old Parl. Hist.*, xxii.88–90.

53 *CJ*, vii.837–8; Whitelocke, p. 697; *Mercurius Politicus*, 607 (9–16 February 1660), pp. 1096, 1098; Baker, p. 706; Sharpe, *London and the Kingdom*, ii.360–1, 366–7.

54 Rugg, pp. 38–9; Pepys, i.49 (10 February 1660); Baker, p. 706.

55 *CJ*, vii.841; *Mercurius Politicus*, 607 (9–16 February 1660), pp. 1101–2; Baker, pp. 706–9; Price, *Mystery and Method*, pp. 95–103; Gumble, *Monck*, pp. 234–45. Pepys, who heard the Speaker (Lenthall) read the letter to the House, and afterwards talked with Monck's secretary Matthew Lock, summarizes its contents under 11 February 1660 (i.51). Monck's letter is in *Old Parl. Hist.*, xxii.98–103, which also prints *The Representation and Address of the Well-affected Persons Inhabitants of the Cities of London and Westminster* on pp. 94–7.

56 Gumble, *Monck*, p. 244; Pepys, i.50, 52 (11 February 1660); Roger L'Estrange, *L'Estrange His Apology* (1660), pp. 71–2; Rugg, p. 39; Sharpe, *London and the Kingdom*, ii.368–9.

57 *CJ*, vii.842–6; *Mercurius Politicus*, 608 (16–23 February 1660), pp. 1121–2; Whitelocke, pp. 698–700; Baker, pp. 709–10; Price, *Mystery and Method*, pp. 103, 109–14; Gumble, *Monck*, pp. 260–3; Abernathy, pp. 39–40.

58 *The Speech and Declaration of his Excellency the Lord General Monck* (1660), printed in *Old Parl. Hist.*, xxii.140–3; Evelyn, iii.242 (11 February 1660); Rugg, p. 34 (cf. 42); Pepys, i.63 (21 February 1660).

59 Davies, p. 293; Hutton *R*, p. 101.

60 Ludlow, pp. 94–5, 96, 100; Price, *Mystery and Method*, pp. 116–18; Gumble, *Monck*, pp. 263–4; Davies, p. 290. The text of the letter is in *Mercurius Politicus*, 608 (16–23 February 1660), pp. 1119–20, and in Baker, pp. 710–11.

61 Thurloe, *State Papers*, vii.687; *CJ*, vii.646, 846–8, 852, 860, 872, 878; *Mercurius Politicus*, 608 (16–23 February 1660), pp. 1123–6; Whitelocke, pp. 698–700; Burnet *OT*, i.157; Sharpe, *London and the Kingdom*, ii.371. For the appreciation of the Common Council, see *Mercurius Politicus*, 609 (23 February–1 March 1660), pp. 1128–30.

62 *CJ*, vii.847–8, 855, 856, 858, 862, 874, 880; Price, *Mystery and Method*, p. 131; Burnet *OT*, i.154; Baker, p. 712; C. H. Firth and R. S. Rait (ed.), *Acts and Ordinances of the Interregnum*, 2 vols (1911), ii.1418 (Council of State), 1459–62, 1465–9 (Presbyterian legislation).

63 Milton *CPW*, vii.340–88, 396–463; Pepys, i.61 (20 February 1660), 74 (2 March 1660); Evelyn, iii, 235 (7 November 1659), 243 (17 February– 5 April 1660). Pepys's editors identify the 'pamphlet' he read as probably [Roger L'Estrange?], *A Plea for Limited Monarchy, as it was established in this nation, before the late war*; Evelyn's pamphlet

was *The Late News or Message from Bruxels Unmasked, and his Majesty Vindicated, from the base calumny and scandal therein*, which Baker (pp. 741–2) applauded for 'dexterously' cutting off the 'Hydra' of Nedham's mischief and winning many to the royalist cause. It and *New from Brussels* are summarized in Davies, pp. 315–16; *The Armies' Plea* and Evelyn's *Apology* are summarized on pp. 164–7. See also below, pp. 58–9.

64 Pepys, i.75 (2 March 1660), 77, 79 (6 March 1660), 89 (16 March 1660), 92 (19 March 1660), 103 (4 April 1660), 113 (21 April 1660); Rugg, pp. 44, 60, 67, 73; *CJ*, vii.857, 880; Firth and Rait, *Acts and Ordinances*, ii.1469–70.

65 For fuller accounts of events briefly treated in this section see: Davies, pp. 307–54; Hutton *R*, pp. 102–18.

66 Matthew Griffith, *The Fear of God and the King* (1660), sigs. a3v–A4, p. 910 (*recte* 106); Milton *CPW*, vii.464–5, 482; *CSPD 1659–60*, p. 572.

67 *Mercurius Politicus*, 615 (5–12 April 1660), pp. 1216 (*recte* 1253)–4; *Mercurius Publicus*, 17 (19–26 April 1660), pp. 269–71; Whitelocke, p. 701; Baker, pp. 720–1; Gumble, *Monck*, pp. 279–86; Ludlow, pp. 109, 111 (for attempts to involve him in the uprising, see pp. 111–14); Dawson, *Cromwell's Understudy*, pp. 387–92.

68 Whitelocke, p. 701; Pepys, i.110–13 (18–21 April 1660).

69 Baker, pp. 673, 717–18; Price, *Mystery and Method*, pp. 4–10, 41, 133–8; Gumble, *Monck*, pp. 103–8, 275–8; Clarendon *HR*, vi.191–5, 196–7 (XVI.§§159–68, 171–2); Underdown, *Royalist Conspiracy*, pp. 300, 313; Ashley, *Monck*, pp. 160–3, 206–8; M. Coate, 'William Morice and the Restoration of Charles II', *EHR*, xxxiii (1918), 368–73. Monck finally wrote to Charles on 5 May (Baker, p. 731).

70 Abernathy, pp. 34, 48–9.

71 Clarendon *HR*, vi.191 (XVI.§159); Price, *Mystery and Method*, pp. 138–42; Mordaunt, *Letter-Book*, pp. 95 (cf. p. 23), 82, 111, 148, 169; Underdown, *Royalist Conspiracy*, pp. 307–8.

72 *CJ*, vii.867–8, 880; Firth and Rait, *Acts and Ordinances*, ii.1469–72; Steele, 3171; *Mercurius Politicus*, 611 (8–15 March 1660), p. 1171, and 612 (15–22 March 1660), pp. 1179–81; Ludlow, p. 97; Clarendon *HR*, vi.193 (XVI.§163).

73 Price, *Mystery and Method*, p. 132; Burnet *OT*, i.158; Godfrey Davies, 'The General Election of 1660', *HLQ*, xv (1951–2), 211–35; Louise F. Brown, 'Religious Factors in the Convention Parliament', *EHR*, xxii (1907), 52–5; J. R. Jones, 'Political Groups and Tactics in the Convention of 1660', *HJ*, vi (1962–3), 160; Henning, i.27, 31–2. Commons members of the Convention are listed in *Old Parl. Hist.*, xxii.210–25, and (though not as a distinct group) with biographies, in Henning, i–ii passim.

74 *CJ*, viii.35–6, 56, 60, 61; Ludlow, pp. 106–7, 110, 119–20, 151–2; Hutchinson, pp. 276–8, 280–1; Baker, p. 735; Henning, ii.623 (Hutchinson), 633 (Ingoldsby), 711 (Lascelles), 780 (Ludlow), iii.661 (Wallop).

75 Clarendon *HR*, vi.193 (XVI.§163); Ludlow, pp. 108, 118, 162. Ludlow held that the Long Parliament had been dissolved by an inquorate House, and, anyway, by the *Act against the Inconveniences which may Happen by . . . Dissolving this Present Parliament* of 1641 (17 Car. I, cap. 7; *Statutes*, v.103; Gardiner (ed.), *Constitutional Documents*, pp. 158–9), it could be dissolved only by act of parliament, that is, with the consent of King, Lords and Commons. It was a curious argument for a republican.

76 *CJ*, viii.1; Hutchinson, p. 280; Abernathy, pp. 54–5; Jones, 'Political Groupings', pp. 162–71; Henning, i.27, 32.

77 Pepys, i.116 (26 April 1660); Burnet *OT*, i.160–1; Andrew Marvell, *The Rehearsal Transpro'd*, ed. D. I. B. Smith (Oxford, 1971), p. 43.

78 Hutchinson, p. 280; Clarendon *HR*, vi.215 (XVI.§§212–13); *CJ*, viii.4–8; *LJ*, xi.6–9; Steele, 3177a–c; Whitelocke, p. 702; Price, *Mystery and Method*, pp. 155–8; Maurice F. Bond (ed.), *The Diaries and Papers of Sir Edward Dering* (1976), pp. 35–7; *Parliamentary Intelligencer*, 19 (30 April–7 May 1660), pp. 289–93; Pepys, i.122 (2 May 1660). The texts are in *CJ* and *LJ* loc. cit., Baker, pp. 723–9, Clarendon *HR*, vi.202–10 (XVI.§§181–203), and in *Old Parl. Hist.*, xxii.237–48, which also prints (pp. 263–7) the Commons' letter in reply; the Lords' letter in reply is in *LJ*, xi.12–13.

## 2 THE RESTORATION YEAR (1660–1661)

1 Evelyn, iiii.246 (29 May 1660).

2 *The Letter-Book of John, Viscount Mordaunt, 1658–1660*, ed. Mary Coate, Camden Soc. 3rd ser. lxix (1945), p. 178; John Price, *The Mystery and Method of His Majesty's Happy Restauration* (1686); *CJ*, viii.6

3 Clarendon *HR*, vi.234 (XVI.§247); Baxter *RB*, I.100, §145; Abraham Cowley, *The Essays and Other Prose Writings*, ed. Alfred B. Gough (1915), p. 46; George [Morley], *Sermon Preached at the . . . Coronation of . . . Charles the IId* (1661), p. 60.

4 Baxter *RB*, II.214, §67 (cf. I.101, §146); [Morley], *Coronation Sermon*, p. 57; Gilbert Sheldon, *David's Deliverance and Thanksgiving* (1660), p. 17.

5 Price, *Mystery and Method*, p. 161; Sir Giles Isham (ed.), *Correspondence of Bishop Brian Duppa and Sir Justinian Isham, 1650–1660*, Northants. Record Soc. Publ. xvii (1956), p. 180.

6 Milton *SA*, ll.667–70.

7 Reresby, p. 27.

8 Marjorie Hope Nicolson (ed.), *The Conway Letters*, revd Sarah Hutton, 2nd edn (Oxford, 1992), p. 161; Isham, *Correspondence of Duppa and Isham*, pp. 176–7, 178, 179, 180.

9 Clarendon *HR*, vi.98–9, 105, 109, 122, 163, 177 (XVI. §§2, 13, 20, 45, 113, 114, 137); Pepys, i.180 (21 June 1660).

10 Clarendon *HR*, vi.142–3 (XVI.§77).

11 Baker, sig. A4; Rugg, p. 87; Reresby, p. 31; Abraham Cowley, 'Upon his Majesty's Restoration and Return', ll.143–4, in G. A. E. Parfitt (ed.), *Silver Poets of the Seventeenth Century* (1974), p. 228.

12 Philip Henry, *Diaries and Letters*, ed. Matthew Henry Lee (1882), p. 12.

13 Burnet *OT*, i.86–7.

14 Ludlow, pp. 100, 122; Patricia Crawford, 'Charles Stuart: "Man of Blood" ', *JBS*, xvi (1977), 41–61; Christopher Hill, *The English Bible and the Seventeenth-Century Revolution* (Harmondsworth, 1994), pp. 324–31.

15 Andrew Marvell, 'An Horatian Ode upon Cromwell's Return from Ireland', l. 53, in *P&L*, i.92; C. V. Wedgwood, *The Trial of Charles I* (1964; rptd 1967), pp. 150, 151, 156. Contemporary accounts of the trial are reprinted in *State Trials*, iv.990–1154.

16 For reproductions of this frontispiece, and discussions of the rhetorical strategy of *Eikon Basilike*, see: Laura Lunger Knoppers, *Historicizing Milton: Spectacle, Power and Poetry in Restoration England* (Athens, GA, 1994), pp. 17–21; Thomas N. Corns,

*Uncloistered Virtue: English Political Literature, 1640–1660* (Oxford, 1992), pp. 80–91, 208–20; Lois Potter, *Secret Rites and Secret Writing: Royalist Literature, 1641–1660* (Cambridge, 1989), pp. 160–3, 170–84; Ernest Gilmore, *Iconoclasm and Poetry* (Chicago, 1986), pp. 154–8; Elizabeth Skerpan Wheeler, '*Eikon Basilike* and the Rhetoric of Self-Representation', in Thomas N. Corns (ed.), *The Royal Image: Representations of Charles I* (Cambridge, 1999), pp. 122–40.

17 *Eikon Basilike: The Pourtraicture of his Sacred Maiestie in his Solitudes and Sufferings* (1649), pp. 32, 55, 172, 194, 221, 222 (quotations are from issue no. 9 in Francis F. Madan, *A New Bibliography of the Eikon Basilike of King Charles the First* (Oxford, 1950)).

18 Madan, *Bibliography*, pp. 1–79; Potter, *Secret Rites*, pp. 171–2.

19 *LJ*, xi.235; *Statutes*, v.288 (the anniversary was enacted in the Act for the Attainder of the Regicides, 12 Car.II c.30); Steele, 3283; Evelyn, iii.269 (30 January 1661); Isham, *Correspondence of Duppa and Isham*, pp. xxxi, 179n.; Thomas Reeve, *A Dead Man Speaking* (1661), sigs. *2, *2v; B. S. Stuart, 'The Cult of the Royal Martyr', *CH*, xxxviii (1969), 175–81; and Helen W. Randall, 'The Rise and Fall of a Martyrology: Sermons on Charles I', *HLQ*, x (1946–7), 135–67.

20 *LJ*, xi.11, 12, 16; Potter, *Secret Rites*, p. 161.

21 John Ogilby, *The Entertainment of His Most Excellent Majestie Charles II in his Passage through the City of London to his Coronation*, facs. edn, intro. by Ronald Knowles (Binghampton, NY, 1988), p. 15 and illustration facing p. 13 of text (and see further Roy Strong, *Van Dyck: Charles I on Horseback* (1972)); John Fitzwilliam and Joseph Ailmer, untitled poems in *Britannia Rediviva* (Oxford, 1660), sigs. 2B3, 2E1v.

22 Baker, p. 762; Potter, *Secret Rites*, p. 160; Cowley, 'Upon His Majesty's Restoration', ll.174–81, in Parfitt, *Silver Poets*, p. 229.

23 Bulstrode, p. 225; Alexander Brome, *A Congratulatory Poem on the Miraculous and Glorious Return of that Unparallel'd King Charls the II* (1660), p. 5 (quoted in Knoppers, *Historicizing Milton*, p. 33).

24 G. S., *The Dignity of Kingship Asserted in answer to Mr Milton's Ready and Easie Way to Establish a Free Commonwealth* (1660), sig. A1. Probably not by Gilbert Sheldon (to whom it is attributed in Wing), but George Starkey (see the facsimile edition, ed. William R. Parker (New York, 1942), pp. x–xxi).

25 *LJ*, xi.239; J[ames] R[amsey], *Moses Returned from Midian: or, Gods Kindnesse to a Banished King* (Edinburgh, 1660); Gilbert Sheldon, *Davids Deliverance and Thanksgiving* (1660); Arthur Brett, *The Restauration* (1660); Robert Mossom, *England's Gratulation for the King and His Subjects Happy Union* (1660).

26 Richard Allestree, *Sermon Preached at Hampton-Court on ... the Anniversary of His Sacred Majesty's Most Happy Return* (1662), pp. 34–5.

27 Steven Zwicker, *Dryden's Political Poetry: The Typology of King and Nation* (Providence, RI, 1972), pp. 61–77.

28 Evelyn, iii.250 records this ceremony in the Banqueting House at Whitehall under 6 July 1660, unreliably, as his editor points out on p. 251, n. 1.

29 As noted by Knoppers, *Historicizing Milton*, p. 33.

30 *LJ*, xi.18–19; Whitelocke, p. 703; Steele, 3188; Pepys, i.131 (8 May 1660); Baker, pp. 730–1; Clarendon *HR*, vi.221 (XVI.221); Rugg, pp. 79–80; *Parliamentary Intelligencer*, 20 (7–14 May 1660), pp. 308–10. The proclamation is printed in *LJ*, xi.18–19, and in *Old Parl. Hist.*, xxii.275–6.

31 For examples, see *Mercurius Publicus*, 19–21 (3–24 May 1660), pp. 300–2, 305–7, 313–14, 316–18, 322–5. Rugg, pp. 95–6, reports similar festivities in Edinburgh.

32 Pepys, i.117 (27 April 1660); Ludlow, p. 118; Clarendon *HR*, vi.226, 227 (XVI.232, 234); Katherine Philips, 'On the numerous accesse of the English to waite upon the King in Holland', ll.1–2, 9–10, 13–14, in *The Collected Works*, vol. 1: *The Poems*, ed. Patrick Thomas (Stump Cross, Essex, 1990), p. 70. Cf. *Mercurius Politicus*, 615 (5–12 April 1660), p. 1139.

33 Baker, pp. 731–2; *LJ*, xi.12; *CJ*, viii.11, 15; Clarendon *HR*, vi. 228–33 (XVI.§§236–45); Pepys, i.123–7 (3 and 4 May 1660), i.133 and n. 2 (10 May 1660), i.140 (15 May 1660), 148 (19 May 1660), i.151 (20 May 1660), i.152 (22 May 1660), i.154 (23 May 1660), i.156 (24 May 1660); *Parliamentary Intelligencer*, 20 (7–14 May 1660), p. 306; *Mercurius Publicus*, 19 (3–10 May 1660), pp. 302–3.

34 Rugg, pp. 86, 88; Baker, p. 733; Clarendon *HR*, vi.233 (XVI. §246); Thomas Gumble, *The Life of General Monck* (1671), pp. 382–7; Pepys, i.158 (25 May 1660).

35 Evelyn, iii.246 (29 May 1660). The section heading is from Evelyn, iii.285 (1 May 1661).

36 Peter Mundy, *The Travels of Peter Mundy in Europe and Asia*, ed. Richard C. Temple and Lavinia May Anstey, vol. 5 (1936), p. 118 (quoted in Knoppers, *Historicizing Milton*, p. 72); Rugg, pp. 85, 89–90; *Parliamentary Intelligencer*, 23 (28 May–4 June 1660), p. 360. For further acounts of the entry and festivities see: Baker, p. 734; Gumble, *Monck*, pp. 387–93; Ludlow, pp. 156–7; Whitelocke, pp. 703–4; Clarendon *LC*, i.278–80 (§14); *Mercurius Publicus*, 22 (24–31 May 1660), pp. 341–2; *England's Joy: or, a Relation of the Most Remarkable Passages from His Majesty's Arrival at Dover to his Entrance at White-Hall* (1660); *A True Relation of the Reception of His Majesty, and Conducting Him through the City of London, by the Right Honourable Thomas Allen, Lord Mayor...* (1660); *A Short History of His Royal Majesty King Charles the Second, Ending with his Royal Entry into the City of London* (1660).

37 Rugg, pp. 98–9, 113; Baker, p. 736; Evelyn, iii.250 (5 July 1660), 259 (29 October 1660); *Parliamentary Intelligencer*, 28 (2–9 July 1660), pp. 445–6, and 45 (29 October–5 November 1660), p. 716; Pepys, i.193 (5 July 1660), 277 (29 October 1660), 283 (5 November 1660); John Tatham, *London's Glory* (1660; the Lord Mayor's Feast) and *The Royale Oake, with other various and delightfull scenes presented... in honour of... Sir Richard Brown* (1660; the Lord Mayor's Show); Steele, 3206, 3217, 3231, 3242; Hutton *R*, p. 126.

38 Pepys, i.121 (1 May 1660); Eric Halfpenny, '"The Citie's Loyalty Display'd" (A Literary and Documentary Causerie of Charles II's Coronation "Entertainment")', *The Guildhall Miscellany*, i (1952), pp. 25–6; cf. Rugg, pp. 175–6. See further David Underdown, *Revel, Riot and Rebellion: Popular Politics and Culture in England, 1603–1660* (Oxford, 1985), pp. 271–91.

39 Knoppers, *Historicizing Milton*, p. 1. See further Paula Backscheider, *Spectacular Politics: Theatrical Power and Mass Communication in Early Modern Europe* (Baltimore, MD, 1993), pp. 3–11.

40 Reresby, p. 38; Nicolson, *Conway Letters*, p. 187.

41 Pepys, ii.37 (14 February 1661); cf. ii.39 (21 February 1661).

42 For an account of these works, and their circumstances of publication, see Halfpenny, '"The Citie's Loyalty Display'd"', pp. 19–35. For Ogilby, see Katherine S. Van Eerde, *John Ogilby and the Taste of His Times* (Folkestone, 1976).

43 *Kingdomes Intelligencer*, 16 (22–29 April 1661), pp. 249–54. Ogilby's *Entertainment* begins with a ten folio-page engraving of the cavalcade by Wencelaus Hollar. Members of the procession are enumerated in Baker, p. 759.

44 *The Cities Loyalty Display'd or the four famous and renowned fabricks in the city of London exactly described in their several representations, with their private meanings* (1661); engravings of the arches are in Ogilby, *Entertainment*, facing pp. 13, 43, 111, 139, and their classical precedents explored on pp. 1–12. See further Gerard Reedy, 'Mystical Politics: The Imagery of Charles II's Coronation', in Paul J. Korshin (ed.), *Studies in Change and Revolution* (Menston, 1972), pp. 19–41; Knoppers, *Historicizing Milton*, pp. 97–105; Backscheider, *Spectacular Politics*, pp. 13–31. For the earlier tradition see Roy Strong, *Art and Power: Renaissance Festivals, 1450–1650* (Berkeley, CA, 1984).

45 Ogilby, *Entertainment*, pp. 40–2, 104–20, 135–7, 165; Nicolson, *Conway Letters*, p. 187.

46 Sir Edward Walker, 'The Preparations for his Majesties Coronation', quoted from Halfpenny, '"The Citie's Loyalty Display'd"', pp. 24–5. For other accounts, see: Rugg, pp. 173–5; Evelyn, iii.276–8 (22 April 1660).

47 James Heath, *The Glories and Magnificent Triumphs* (1662), p. 208; Evelyn, iii.276 (22 April 1660); Rugg, p. 176; Pepys, ii.82, 83, 88 (22 and 23 April 1661). The coronation ceremony is described in: Sir Edward Walker, *A Circumstantial Account of the Preparations for the Coronation of His Majesty King Charles II* (1820), pp. 66–78; Evelyn, iii.278–84 (23 April 1661); *Kingdomes Intelligencer*, 16 (29 April 1661), pp. 254–6; and, with the feast, Baker, pp. 760–71. For examples of provincial coronation celebrations see *Mercurius Publicus*, 16–18 (18 April–9 May 1661), pp. 241–4, 257–70, 281–4.

48 Milton, *PL*, v.350–7.

49 This is the burden of Jonathan Sawday, 'Re-writing a Revolution: History, Symbol and Text in the Restoration', *The Seventeenth Century*, vii (1992), 171–99.

50 Bulstrode, p. 222; Baker, p. 736; Margaret Cavendish, *Memoirs of the Duke of Newcastle*, ed. C. H. Firth (1906), p. 136; Hamilton, i.90.

51 Harris, p. 30. Christopher Hill is particularly sceptical of 'the universality and spontaneity of rejoicing at Charles II's return', pointing to its encouragement by 'the men of property' and privileged patrons (*Some Intellectual Consequences of the English Revolution* (1980), pp. 10–12; *The World Turned Upside Down* (Harmondsworth, 1975), p. 354).

52 Ludlow, pp. 118, 149. For exemplary punishment and repressive measures, see pp. 55–7, 75–6, 91–3, 138–44.

53 Clarendon *LC*, i.279 (§14); Clarendon *HR*, vi.215, 216 (XVI.§§213, 214), vi.220 (XVI.§220), vi.234 (XVI. §246); Hutchinson, p. 278.

54 John Milton, *Readie and Easie Way*, 2nd edn (April 1660), in *CPW*, vii.463; Ludlow, pp. 109–10, 149, 284, 287; Rugg, p. 55; Pepys, i.78–9 (6 March 1660); Hutchinson, p. 274; M. H. Lee (ed.), *Diaries and Letters of Philip Henry* (1882), p. 84, quoted in Hutton *R*, p. 154.

55 Ludlow, pp. 283, 285–6; Pepys, ii.57 (20 March 1661), ii.58–9 (23 March 1661); cf. *CSPD 1660–61*, pp. 536–9, 546. The four City members were Thomas Fowlke, John Jones, William Love and William Thompson.

56 *CJ*, viii.259; *LJ*, xi.260; *Pepys*, ii.109 (28 May 1660), 167 (31 August 1661); Nicolson, *Conway Letters*, p. 193.

57 Hutton *R*, pp. 5, 89; E. A. Wrigley and R. S. Schofield, *The Population History of England, 1541–1871: A Reconstruction* (1981), pp. 531–4.

58 *Mercurius Politicus*, 613 (22–29 March 1660), pp. 1197–8; Baker, pp. 719–20; Steele, 3160, 3166, 3174; Davies, pp. 314–15; Hutton *R*, pp. 109–10, 114. Clarges

was afterwards knighted and was Edward Phillips's chief informant for his continuation of Baker's *Chronicle*.

59 Ludlow, pp. 156, 176, 184, 196, 197; Burnet, *OT*, i.281; Hutton *R*, pp. 138–9. For the legislative process, see below, pp. 79–80.

60 Browning, p. 58; Whitelocke, iv.406; Rugg, p. 132; Steele, 3270 (repeated in April 1661, 3296); *CJ*, viii.155; *CSPD 1660–61*, p. 567; *Statutes*, v.241–2 (12 Car.II c.16); Pepys, i.256 (1 October 1660); Hutton *R*, p. 139.

61 Pepys, i.99–100 (29 March 1660; cf. i.107 (11 April 1660)), 101 (1 April 1660), 110 (17 April 1660; cf.i.109 (15 April 1660)), 125 (3 May 1660), 141 (15 May 1660).

62 Pepys, i.109 (15 April 1660), 115 (24 April 1660); Rugg, p. 88; Isham, *Correspondence of Duppa and Isham*, pp. 181, 187.

63 Ludlow, p. 279; Pepys, ii.10–11 (10 January 1661). See further below, pp. 156–7.

64 Bulstrode, p. 223; Thomas Hobbes, *Behemoth, or the Long Parliament*, ed. Ferdinand Tonnies (Chicago, 1990), p. 196.

65 Scott, p. 6.

66 See above, pp. 19, 23.

67 Nicholas Jose, *Ideas of the Restoration in English Literature, 1660–71* (Cambridge, MA, 1984), pp. 6, 10–12.

68 In 'The Word "Revolution"' in his *A Nation of Change and Novelty* (1990), pp. 100–20, Christopher Hill collects examples of contemporary usage to argue that the modern sense of the word, signifying an abrupt break or radical innovation, rather than a recursion or circular movement, was coming into being at this time. See also Ilan Rachum, 'The Meaning of "Revolution" in the English Revolution', *JHI*, lvi (1995), 195–215; Vernon Snow, 'The Concept of Revolution in Seventeenth-Century England', *HJ*, v (1962), 167–74.

69 Sir Philip Warwick, *Memoires* (1703), pp. 390, 399 (quoted in Jose, *Ideas of the Restoration*, p. 9); Baxter *RB*, II.214, §67; Isham, *Correspondence of Duppa and Isham*, p. 180; Rugg, p. 1; Ludlow, p. 120.

70 *OED*, s.v. 'restauration', sense 1c; 'restoration', senses 1a, 2a; 'revolution', sense 8a.

71 Browning, p. 57; *CJ*, viii.49; Clarendon *HC*, vi.216 (XVI.§214); Evelyn, iii.246; Reresby, p. 31; Cowley, 'Upon his Majesty's Restoration and Return', in G. A. Parfitt (ed.), *Silver Poets of the Seventeenth Century* (1974), p. 225.

72 Hutchinson, p. 278; Ludlow, pp. 200, 210, 276; Andrew Marvell, *The Rehearsal Transpros'd*, ed. D. I. B. Smith (Oxford, 1971), p. 312. *Restoration* is not recorded in either Laurence Sterne and Harold H. Kollmeier (ed.), *A Concordance to the English Prose of John Milton* (Binghampton, NY, 1985) or in William Ingram and Kathleen Swaim (eds), *A Concordance to Milton's English Poetry* (Oxford, 1972).

73 Browning, p. 58; Clarendon, *HR*, vi.180 (XVI.§142); [Anon.], *The New Key to the Rehearsal* (1717), p. vi.

74 Baker, p. 771.

75 Baker, p. 733; Gumble, *Monck*, p. 387; *Statutes*, v.237; *LJ*, xi.147; *CJ*, viii.49; *Mercurius Publicus*, 20 (16–23 May 1661), p. 320; Knowles, in Ogilby, *Entertainment*, pp. 13–14 (quoting the statute). A form of prayer for this 'state holy-day' was published in May and appeared in the revised 1662 Prayer Book. For a description of the celebrations in London on 29 May 1662, see William Schellinks, *Journal of... Travels in England, 1661–1663*, ed. Maurice Exman and H. L. Lehmann, Camden Soc. 5th ser. i (1993), pp. 89–90.

76 J. N., *A Perfect Catalogue of all the Knights of the Most Noble Order of the Garter* (1661); *Kingdomes Intelligencer*, 16 (22–29 April 1661), pp. 242–7; Knowles in Ogilby, *Entertainment*, pp. 14, 15 and illustration facing p. 13 of text. Evidence that the coronation day was changed is provided by Walker, *Circumstantial Account*, p. 28. Rugg, pp. 165–9, 172, lists those created knights, and describes the attendant ceremonies.

77 Baxter *RB*, II.303, §169; Ogilby, *Entertainment*, pp. 190, 191; cf. Pepys, ii.86 (23 April 1661); Ludlow, pp. 286–7. The anonymous 'Narrative' was by Elias Ashmole (Knowles, in introduction to Ogilby, *Entertainment*, p. 16).

78 Sawday, 'Re-writing a Revolution', p. 175, which gives many of the following details.

79 Rugg, p. 60; Pepys, i.89 (16 March 1660). Cf. *Mercurius Politicus*, 612 (15–22 March 1660), p. 1182; Roger L'Estrange, *L'Estrange His Apology* (1660), p. 119.

80 Pepys, i.99 (29 March 1660), 113 (21 April 1660; cf. i.106 (11 April 1660), 113 (22 April 1660)); *CJ*, viii.17, 18, 19; *LJ*, xi.12, 20; *Mercurius Politicus*, 19 (3–10 May 1660), p. 303; *Parliamentary Intelligencer*, 20 (7–14 May 1660), p. 307; Whitelocke, p. 703.

81 Pepys, i.133–4 (11 May 1660), 136–7 (13 May 1660; cf. *CSPD 1659–60*, pp. 431–2), 154 (23 May 1660); Baker, p. 733; Calarendon *HR*, vi.233 (XVI. §245); Dryden, *Astraea Redux*, 11.230–1, in Dryden, p. 49; Rugg, pp. 90, 92, 109; Ludlow, p. 156.

82 *Parliamentary Intelligencer*, 22 (21–28 May 1660), p. 340, cited in Knoppers, *Historicizing Milton*, p. 73.

83 Rugg, pp. 66–7, 73; Pepys, i.45 (7 February 1660). The contributions to *The Rump: or an exact collection of the choycest Poems and Songs relating to the late times* (1662) are indexed and often identified in H. F. Brooks, 'Rump Songs: An Index with Notes', *Oxford Bibliographical Society: Proceedings and Papers*, v (1936–7), pp. 281–304.

84 *State Trials*, v.947–1302. The ten executed were Thomas Harrison (13 October); John Carew (15th); John Cooke and Hugh Peters at Charing Cross (16th); Thomas Scot, Gregory Clement, Adrian Scroope and John Jones at Charing Cross (17th); Daniel Axtell and Francis Hacker at Tyburn (19th). For the relevant legislation, see below pp. 70–6.

85 Evelyn, iii.259 (17 October 1660); Mundy, *Travels*, pp. 125–6; Ludlow, p. 237; Pepys, i.265 (14 October 1660) 280 (1 November 1660). See also *Old Parl. Hist.*, xxii.388–92.

86 *CJ*, viii.52, 56, 61, 70, 140; Schellinks, *Travels*, p. 48; Pepys, i.266 (15 October 1660); *CSPD 1660–1*, pp. 316, 339, 494 .

87 Pepys, i.269 (20 October 1660).

88 *Mercurius Publicus*, 3 (17–24 January 1661), pp. 33–9; *Kingdomes Intelligencer*, 3–4 (14–28 January 1661), pp. 41–6, 57–8; Rugg, p. 144; Schellinks, *Travels*, pp. 82–3. The Fifth Monarchists executed were, in addition to Venner and Hodgkin: Joanas Allen, Stephen Fall, John Gowler, John Butler, Will Ashton, John Tod, John Elson, John Smith, Thomas Oxman, William Corbett, Thomas Harris, John Gardiner, George Hancock. See further pp. 50, 75, 156.

89 *CJ*, viii.197; *LJ*, xi.202; Browning, p. 62; *Mercurius Publicus*, 5 (31 January–7 February 1661), p. 80.

90 Rugg, pp. 143, 145, 146; *Kingdomes Intelligencer*, 5 (28 January–4 February 1661), p. 72; *Mercurius Publicus*, 4 (24–31 January 1661), p. 64. The body of Pride, the only one of the designated four not to be buried in Westminster Abbey, escaped this treatment (Ludlow, p. 272). For discussion of the representation and import of these events, see Sawday, 'Re-writing a Revolution', pp. 187–93; Knoppers, *Historicizing Milton*, pp. 51–3.

91 Evelyn, iii.269 (30 January 1661). Characteristically, Pepys was less impressed and felt uncomfortable that 'a man of so great courage' as Cromwell 'should have that dishonour' done to him (Pepys, i.309 (4 December 1660)).

## 3 GREAT ZERUBBABEL: CHARLES AND THE CONVENTION (1660)

1 Evelyn, iii.247 (4 June 1660).

2 [Marchamont Nedham], *News from Brussels. In a Letter from a Neer Attendant on His Majesties Person* (1660), in *Somers Tracts*, vii.390–1.

3 Nedham, *Interest Will Not Lie: or, A View of England's True Interest* (1659), p. 45.

4 [John Evelyn], *The Late News or Message from Bruxels Unmasked* (1660), pp. 1, 3, 4–5.

5 [Sir Edmond Peirce], *Vox Vere Anglorum* (1659), p. 8; [Evelyn], *An Apology for the Royal Party* (1659), pp. 9–11; Roger L'Estrange, *A Sober Answer to a Jugling Pamphlet*, in *L'Estrange His Apology* (1660), p. 109.

6 [Samuel Tuke], *A Character of Charles the Second, written ... for information of the people* (1660), pp. 4, 5, 6–7, 9, 10; George [Morley], *A Sermon ... at the ... Coronation of ... Charles the IId* (1661), pp. 39, 44; Thomas Reeve, *England's Restitution* (1661), p. 160.

7 Hutton *CII*, p. 447. This is now the standard biography. See also: J. R. Jones, *Charles II: Royal Politician* (1987); K. H. D. Haley, *Charles II* (1966); Antonia Fraser; *King Charles II* (1979); John Miller, *Charles II* (1991). For a summary account of the seventeenth-century characterizations, see Richard Ollard, *The Image of the King: Charles I and Charles II* (1979), pp. 162–75.

8 Ailesbury, i.93; George Savile, Marquess of Halifax, *A Character of King Charles the Second*, in J. P. Kenyon (ed.), *Complete Works* (Harmondsworth, 1969), p. 257. Burnet has similar (and more pointed) remarks in *OT*, i.167, ii.469, and in *SOT*, p. 48.

9 Burnet *OT*, i.166, 167; Halifax, *Character*, pp. 257–60.

10 Scott, p. 169; Burnet, *OT*, i.167. For these early experiences see Hester Chapman, *The Tragedy of Charles II in the Years 1630–1660* (1964; rptd Bath, 1974). John Miller, 'The Later Stuart Monarchy' in J. R. Jones (ed.), *The Restored Monarchy, 1660–1688* (1979), pp. 33–5, argues that the experiences of the 1650s made survival Charles's overriding priority.

11 See below, pp. 82–4, 103–4, 156.

12 Halifax, *Character*, pp. 255, 265, 266; Ailesbury, i.20, 96; Burnet *OT*, i.295.

13 See further p. 182 below

14 Pepys, vi.210 (3 September 1665); Hamilton, i.92; Burnet *OT*, i.167, 168, 493 (cf. Burnet *SOT*, p. 50); Halifax, *Character*, pp. 262, 265.

15 [Tuke], *Character*, pp. 11–12; [Evelyn], *News from Bruxels Unmasked*, p. 5; [William Walwyn], *A Character of His Most Sacred Majesty King Charles the IId* (1660 (*sic*)), p. 24.

16 W. D. Macray (ed.), *Notes which Passed at Meetings of the Privy Council between Charles II and the Earl of Clarendon* (1896), p. 65.

17 On theses episodes see Chapman, *Charles II*, pp. 68–9, 91–100, 133–6, 140–1, 220–8. The intended bride was Anne-Marie-Louise de Montpensier, 'La Grande Mademoiselle', Henrietta Maria's niece and the cousin of Louis XIV and of Charles.

18 Pepys, ii.38 (18 February 1661); Thomas Carte, *An History of the Life of James, Duke of Ormonde*, 4 vols (1851), iii.651, iv.108–9, 112; Burnet *OT*, i.133–4, ii.472; Halifax, *Character*, pp. 247–8, 249.

19 Evelyn, iv.476 (2 October 1685). Two papers, in Charles's hand, with corrections and interlinings, rehearsing Roman aguments against the Church of England, which James II published (*Copies of Two Papers Written by the Late King Charles II* (1686)) struck neither Ormonde, to whom James showed them, nor Evelyn, who was shown them by Pepys, nor Tenison, to whom Pepys also showed them, nor Halifax, who saw them in print, as authentically confessional: 'Though neither his temper nor education made him very fit to be an author, yet in this case – a known topic so very often repeated – he might write it all himself and yet not one word of it his own' (Halifax, *Complete Works*, p. 250); 'they were not drawn up by the King who was too lazy to spend any time in that way' (Carte, *Ormonde*, iv.111); 'so well penn'd as to the discourse, as did by no means seeme to me, to have ben put together by the Late King' (Evelyn, iv.477 (2 October 1685)); 'he never composed them: for he never read the Scriptures, nor laid things together further than to turn them to a just or some lively expression' (Tenison's view, reported in Burnet *OT*, ii.472; cf. Burnet *SOT*, pp. 170–1).

20 Davies, p. 316; Baxter *CCRB*, letter 641, with its headnote.

21 Carte, *Ormonde*, iv.111 (quoted in Ollard, pp. 107–8); Burnet *OT*, i.166–7.

22 W. Portman, untitled poem in *Britannia Rediviva* (Oxford, 1660), sig. [2]A2.

23 [Bulstrode Whitelocke], *Monarchy Asserted to be the Best, Most Ancient and Legall form of Government* (1660), p. 10; Burnet *OT*, i.122–3.

24 Alexander Scrougie, *Mirabilia Dei* (Edinburgh, 1660), p. 10; *Plea for a Limited Monarchy*, in *Harl. Misc.*, i.15. The *Plea* is usually attributed to L'Estrange. If it is his, its uncharacteristic moderation is perhaps explicable by its date; see below, p. 67.

25 Reeve, *England's Restitution*, pp. 64–5, 77; Robert Sheringham, *The King's Supremacy Asserted* (1660), p. 4; [James Ramsey], *Moses Returned from Midian* (Edinburgh, 1660), p. 10; [Sir Edmond Peirce], *Vox Vere Anglorum: or, Englands Loud Cry to their King* (1659), p. 6; Morley, *Coronation Sermon*, p. 33; Sir Robert Filmer, *Patriarcha*, ed. Johann P. Sommerville (Cambridge, 1991), pp. 1, 7, 9. Some of these are among the works discussed in Carolyn A. Edie, 'The Popular Idea of Monarchy on the Eve of the Stuart Restoration', *HLQ*, xxxix (1975–6), 344–63.

26 *L'Estrange His Apology* (1660), p. 55; G. S., *The Dignity of Kingship Asserted* (1660), pp. 36, 56, 64–5, 125–6.

27 Gilbert Sheldon, *Davids Deliverance and Thanksgiving* (1660), p. 32; *Plea for Limited Monarchy*, in *Harl. Misc.*, i.15, 16, 17. This tract is summarized in Edie, 'Popular Idea of Monarchy', pp. 366–72.

28 Morley, *Coronation Sermon*, p. 36; G. S., *Dignity of Kingship*, pp. 34–5.

29 [Roger L'Estrange], *No Blinde Guides* (1660), p. 5; *L'Estrange His Apology* (1660), p. 103; *A Caveat to the Cavaliers* (1661), p. 28.

30 Thomas Reeve, *A Dead Man Speaking* (1661), sig. 4v; *England's Restitution* (1660), pp. 10, 66, 100; Matthew Griffith, *The Fear of God and the King* (1660), p. 1.

31 Thomas Reeve, *England's Beauty in Seeing King Charles the Second Restored to Majesty* (1660), pp. 22, 50 (quoted in Edie, 'Popular Idea of Monarchy', p. 357); [Elias Ashmole], *Sol in Ascendente* (1660), pp. 4–5.

32 For a summary of seventeenth-century ideas of kingship see J. P. Sommeville, 'Absolutism and Royalism', in J. H. Burns and Mark Goldie (eds), *The Cambridge History of Political Thought, 1450–1700* (Cambridge, 1991), pp. 347–73, and for

discussion more at large, C. C. Weston and J. R. Greenberg, *Subjects and Sovereigns: The Grand Controversy over Legal Sovereignty in Stuart England* (Cambridge, 1981).

33 Browning, pp. 57–8.

34 For summary accounts of the Restoration political settlement see: Hutton *R*, pp. 125–54; Holmes, pp. 27–43; Ogg, pp. 148–88; and, more at large, Seaward, pp. 103–214.

35 *LJ*, xi.236; *CJ*, viii.19, 24; Baker, p. 756. Charles's speech is in *Old Parl. Hist.*, xxiii.88–90.

36 *CJ*, viii.66–7, 86, 94; *LJ*, xi.87, 99, 108–9; Ludlow, pp. 181, 188, 292. Baker, pp. 737–9, prints both the message and the speech; the speech is in *Old Parl. Hist.*, xxii.397–400.

37 Excerpt in Browning, pp. 164–5; full text in *Statutes*, v.226–34. The act is summarized in Baker, pp. 742–4. That same day Charles also signed *An Act for Confirmation of Judiciall Proceedings* (12 Car. II cap. 12) which, confirming all judicial decisions made since 1642, had had to concede the efficacy and durability of at least some of the events of the last 20 years (see p. 78 below).

38 *LJ*, xi.108–9. Monck's speech introducing the bill is given in Lister, iii.500–3. For the subsequent debates see *CJ*, viii.19, 24, 26, 43, 46, 51–68, 76–94, 115, 117–18, 125–47; *LJ*, vii.87, 89, 92, 95, 99–148; Maurice F. Bond (ed.), *The Diaries of... Sir Edward Dering* (1976), pp. 41–3; Ludlow, pp. 153–4, 158–9, 163–7, 170, 172–81, 183–6; Hutchinson, pp. 278–80; Baker, pp. 735–40; *Old Parl. Hist.*, xxii.337–455 passim; Hutton *R*, pp. 132–6.

39 The 33 wholly excepted consisted of the original seven (John Barkstead, Thomas Harrison, Cornelius Holland, John Jones, John Lisle, William Say, Thomas Scott,) and Daniel Axtell, Daniel Blagrave, Andrew Broughton, John Carew, William Cawley, Thomas Challoner, Gregory Clement, John Cooke, Miles Corbet, Edward Dendy, John Dixwell, William Goffe, Francis Hacker, William Hewlett, John Hewson, Sir Michael Livesey, Nicholas Love, Edmund Ludlow, Henry Marten, John Okey, Hugh Peters, Adrian Scroope, Valentine Walton, Edward Whalley, and 'those two persons... disguised by Frocks and Vizards [who] did appeare on the Scaffeld', that is, the executioner and his assistant. Not included in this list were John Hutchinson who, though a regicide, was only prevented from holding public office, and Ingoldsby who, though a regicide, was not excepted from the act (see below, pp. 73, 74 ). For the additional two cases of Vane and Lambert, see below, pp. 75–6.

40 These were those who surrendered; see below, pp. 75 with n. 51.

41 The five who had been nominated as judges were James Challoner, Sir James Harrington, Sir Henry Mildmay, William, Lord Monson, and Robert Wallop. Haslerig and Challoner died before the *Act for Declaring the Pains, Penalties, and Forfeitures imposed... upon... Offenders, excepted out of the Act of... Oblivion* (13 Car.II c.15) received the royal assent in July 1661 (*LJ*, xi.330; *Statutes*, v.317–19). For this act see also below, pp. 75, 90.

42 Hutchinson, pp. 234–5; Baker, p. 735. The list comprised: John Blackwell, William Burton, Ralph Cobbet, Richard Creed, Richard Deane, John Desborough, Charles Fleetwood, John Goodwin, John Hutchinson, John Ireton, Richard Keeble, Francis Lascelles, William Lenthall, Thomas Lister, Philip Nye, Christopher Pack, Sir Gilbert Pickering, John Pyne, Oliver St John, William Sydenham. For the case of Hutchinson, see below, p. 73.

43 *CJ*, viii.61, 63, 65, 118, 126, 132, 135, 137 (Haslerig, Lambert and Vane), 118–19, 132, 137 (lords); *LJ*, xi.114, 136, 143 (Haslerig, Lambert and Vane), 156, 163 (petition), 119, 136 (1649 lords); Baker, p. 739; Violet A. Rowe, *Sir Henry Vane the Younger* (1970), p. 232.

44 Ludlow, pp. 124–5, 160; Hutchinson, p. 278; Henning, iii.295–6, which judges that Prynne, named to 132 committees and making some 90 recorded speeches, was 'probably the most active Member of the Convention'.

45 *CJ*, viii.60, 63–4 (Hutchinson); *LJ*, xi.318 and Baker, pp. 739–40 (Haslerig); Hutchinson, pp. 279–82; Ruth Spalding, *The Improbable Puritan* (1975), pp. 225–9; Ludlow, p. 161.

46 *CJ*, viii.24, 26, 27, 32–3, 59, 111, 118; *LJ*, xi.100, 101, 104, 113; Henning, iii.295; Hutchinson, p. 282. Unreliable lists of judges were circulated, and appeared in print, necessitating public advertisements to set the record straight by those wrongly included: see e.g. *Mercurius Politicus*, 613 (22–29 March 1660), p. 1199, and *Mercurius Publicus*, 21 (17–24 May 1660), p. 332.

47 *CJ*, viii.60, 117–19 (Pickering); *LJ*, xi.103, 113–14 (Thomlinson), 118 (Lister and Pickering); Pepys, i. 178 n. 4 (Pickering); Baker, p. 735 (Ingoldsby); Hutchinson, p. 279 (Ingoldsby); Henning, ii.633 (Ingoldsby).

48 *CJ*, viii.62, 65, 118 (Keeble), 60–1, 68, 118, 139 (Scroope); Hutchinson, p. 284.

49 Steele, 3224 (naming 44 men); *LJ*, xi.52–3, 101–2, 136; *CJ*, viii.51–3, 55, 133, 137; Ludlow, pp. 159, 163, 176, 179–80. On 14 May the Convention had ordered that all regicides should be secured (*LJ*, xi.33; *CJ*, viii.25–6).

50 Ludlow, pp. 154, 160–6, 169, 172, 182–4, 186–96; Hutchinson, pp. 280–1.

51 *LJ*, xi.143. Those who surrendered were John Bourchier (who died in the summer of 1660), John Downes, George Fleetwood, Augustine Garland, Edmund Harvey, William Heveningham, Robert Lilburne, Henry Marten, Simon Mayne, Gilbert Millington, Isaac Penington Snr., Vincent Potter, Owen Row, Adrian Scroope, Henry Smith, James Temple, Peter Temple, Robert Tichborne, Thomas Waite, Sir Hardress Waller, Thomas Wogan. Ludlow's list of 19 who surrendered omits Bourchier and Wogan (Ludlow, p. 186). For the bill for their execution, introduced in the summer of 1661 but never passed into law, see below, pp. 75, 90.

52 These were Daniel Axtell, John Carew, Gregory Clement, John Cooke, Francis Hacker, Thomas Harrison, John Jones, Hugh Peters, Thomas Scot.

53 *CJ*, viii.177–9, 185, 201, 207–8; *LJ*, xi.203–12, 234–5; *Old Parl. Hist.*, xxiii.16–58; *Statutes*, v.288–90. The act named 19 regicides who had fled. In addition to the six named above in the text, these were John Barkstead, Daniel Blagrave, Andrew Broughton, William Cawley, Thomas Challoner, Miles Corbet, Edward Dendy, John Dixwell, John Lisle, Sir Michael Livesey, Nicholas Love, John Okey, William Say.

54 Ludlow, pp. 297–303; C. H., *A True Narrative . . . of the Apprehension of . . . Thomas Scot* (1660); *State Trials*, v.1302–35; *The Speeches . . . of . . . Barkstead . . . Okey, and . . . Corbet . . . with an account of . . . their taking in Holland* (1662). In 1685 Lisle's 70-year-old widow, Alice, was executed for sheltering a supporter of Monmouth (Scott, p. 48).

55 *CJ*, viii.280–7, 297, 301–14 (pains and penalties), 287, 317, 319–20, 342, 349, 355–6 (execution); *LJ*, xi.316–30 (pains and penalties), 372–81 (execution), 380 (Marten); Ludlow, pp. 292–3, 294–5. For the inscription, see also above, p. 54.

56 *CJ*, viii.287, 308, 317, 368; *The Tryal of Sir Henry Vane at the King's Bench, Westminster* (1662); Rowe, *Vane*, pp. 234–42; William H. Dawson, *Cromwell's Understudy* (1938), pp. 404–5; Hutton *R*, pp. 162–3.

57 Hutchinson, pp. 297–305, 318–19, 327–32; Dawson, *Cromwell's Understudy*, pp. 413–44; Ludlow, p. 17; Edmund Ludlow, *The Memoirs*, ed. C. H. Firth, 2 vols (1894), ii.509–11; Earl M. Hause, *Tumble-Down Dick* (New York, 1972), passim.

58 *LJ*, xi.147–8. Charles's speech is also in Baker, p. 740.

59 Pepys, i.79 (6 March 1660); Clarendon *LC*, i.272 (§9).

60 Halifax, *Political Thoughts and Reflections*, in Kenyon (ed.), *Complete Works*, p. 203.

61 Harris, pp. 14–17; Cynthia Herrup, 'The Counties and the Country', in Geoffrey Eley and William Hunt (eds), *Reviving the English Revolution* (1988), pp. 290–5; Anthony Fletcher, *Reform in the Provinces: The Government of Stuart England* (New Haven, CT, 1986), passim; C. G. F. Forster, 'Government in Provincial England under the Later Stuarts', *TRHS*, xxxiii (1983), 29–48; A. M. Coleby, *Central Government and the Localities: Hampshire, 1649–1689* (Cambridge, 1987), pp. 89–103.

62 *CJ*, viii.11; *LJ*, xi.20, 51; *Statutes*, v.179.

63 *CJ*, viii.8, 26; *LJ*, xi.48, 51; *Statutes*, v.180–1.

64 *CJ*, viii.19; *LJ*, xi.87, 147; *Statutes*, v.234–6.

65 *Statutes*, v.296 (12 Car.II c.33).

66 *CJ*, viii.11; *LJ*, xi.212, 225–6; *Statutes*, v.259–66 (12 Car.II. c.24).

67 *CJ*, viii.7, 47; *LJ*, xi.51; *Statutes*, v.179–80 (12 Car.II c.2).

68 *CJ*, viii.107, 150 (committee), 156, 233 (supply bills); *LJ*, xi. 171, 231, 235; *Statutes*, v.252 (2nd supply bill: 12 Car.II c.21), 282–7 (3rd supply bill: 12 Car.II c.29).

69 *CJ*, viii.110–16, 184–8, 193, 207; *LJ*, xi. 214, 225–6; *Statutes*, v.255–9 (12 Car.II c.23). The authoritative account of these matters is C. D. Chandaman, *The English Public Revenue, 1660–1688* (1975), pp. 11–15, 36–40, 196–202; see also Hutton *R*, pp. 148–9, and p. 104 below.

70 See below, pp. 103–5.

71 Evelyn iii.258 (6 October 1660); *CJ*, viii.38, 62–126 (1st poll bill), 161–9 (2nd poll bill), 176–234 (3rd poll bill); *LJ*, xi. 91–147 (1st poll bill), 169–71 (2nd poll bill), 215–35 (3rd poll bill); *Statutes*, v.207–25 (1st poll bill, 12 Car.II c.9), 225–6 (2nd poll bill, 12 Car.II c.10), 277–82 (3rd poll bill, 12 Car.II c.28). There were also two further supply bills for disbanding the Army, for £140,000 (12 Car.II c.20; *Statutes*, v.250–1) and £420,000 (12 Car.II c.27; *Statutes*, v.269–77). See also *CTB*, vol. 1, pp. viii–xv and Hutton *R*, p. 138.

72 *CJ*, viii.143–71 passim (disbanding bill), 176–7, 189–91, 196–7 (reports on disbandment); *LJ*, xi.159–71; *Statutes*, v.238–41 (12 Car.II c.15); Lois Schwoerer, *No Standing Armies!* (Baltimore, MD, 1974), pp. 72–9.

73 See below, pp. 109–24.

74 *CJ*, viii.19; *LJ*, xi.171; *Statutes*, v.242–6 (12 Car.II c.17). For debates surrounding the Act, see Bosher, pp. 171–9. As a result of this Act, nearly 700 men were ejected from their positions (A. G. Matthews (ed.), *Calamy Revised* (Oxford, 1934), p. xiii).

75 *CJ*, viii.11, 41, 86, 112–14, 167, 178, 179, 184–6, 205; *LJ*, xi.93. For discussion of these issues see: H. Egerton Chesney, 'The Transference of Lands in England 1640–1660', *TRHS*, 4th ser. xv (1932), 181–210; Hutton *R*, pp. 140–2; Ian Gentles, 'The Sale of Crown Lands during the English Revolution', *Ec.HR*, 2nd ser. xxvi (1973), 614–35, and 'The Sale of Bishops' Lands', *EHR*, xcv (1980), 573–96; H. J.

Habbakuk, 'The Land Settlement and the Restoration of Charles II', *TRHS*, 5th ser. xxviii (1978), 201–22, and 'Landowners and the Civil War', *Ec.HR*, 2nd ser. xviii (1965), 130–51, and 'Public Finance and the Sale of Confiscated Property during the Interregnum', *Ec.HR*, 2nd ser. xv (1962–3), 70–88; Joan Thirsk, 'The Restoration Land Settlement', *Journal of Modern History*, xxvi (1954), 315–28, and 'The Sales of Royalist Land during the Interregnum', *Ec.HR*, 2nd ser. v (1952), 188–207.

76 Ailesbury, i.6; Ogg, p. 163; Hutton *R*, p. 142; Holmes, pp. 35–7. See further the articles cited in the previous note. On the development of parties see further below, pp. 85–9.

77 Roger L'Estrange, *A Caveat to the Cavaliers* (1661), pp. 12, 19–20, 28. This was an answer to James Howell, *A Cordial for the Cavaliers* (1661), which was more reassuring. The debate continued in [Howell]'s *Som Sober Inspections Made into those Ingredients that Went into the Composition of a Late Cordial* (1661) and L'Estrange's *A Modest Plea both for the Caveat and the Author thereof* (1662).

78 Notably Hyde (created Earl of Clarendon in 1661); James Butler, Marquess of Ormonde (created Duke in 1661); Thomas Wriothesley, 4th Earl of Southampton; and Sir Edward Nicholas.

79 Notably Monck (created Duke of Albemarle in 1660); Antony Ashley Cooper, Lord Ashley (created Earl of Shaftesbury in 1672); and Edward Mountague, created Earl of Sandwich in 1660.

80 Notably Arthur Annesley (created Earl of Anglesey in 1661); Edward Montagu, 2nd Earl of Manchester; Algernon Percy, 10th earl of Northumberland; John, Lord Robartes (created Earl of Radnor in 1679); Denzil, Lord Holles;and Sir William Morice. See further Edward R. Turner, *The Privy Council of England in the Seventeenth and Eighteenth Centuries*, 2 vols (Baltimore, MD, 1927–8), ii.375–7.

81 Hutton *R*, pp. 127, 128–30; Baker, p. 734.

82 Bulstrode, p. 226; Lister, ii.33–42; Clarendon *LC*, i.309 (§§40–1); Burnet *OT*, i.176, 288–9 (cf. Burnet *SOT*, pp. 55–6). For the Cavalier Parliament's discussion of the Act of Oblivion, see above, pp. 70–4, and for resentment of Clarendon, pp. 95–101.

83 *An Humble Representation of the Sad Condition of Many of the King's Party, who since his majesty's happy restauration have no relief, and but languishing hopes* (1661), in *Somers Tracts*, vii.516–20; Burnet *OT*, i.289; L'Estrange, *Caveat*, p. 35. Cf. Charles Hammond, *Truth's Discovery: or, the Cavaliers Cases Stated by Conscience and Plain-dealing* (1664), in *Somers Tracts*, vii.557–67.

84 Pepys, iii.42–3 (7 March 1662), vi.303 (19 December 1665), 329–30 (15 December 1665).

## 4 ROYAL SERVANTS: CLARENDON AND THE CAVALIER PARLIAMENT (1661–1667)

1 For this reason Hutton *R*, pp. 125, 154, argues that we should properly speak not of the 'Restoration Settlement' but of two, quite separate, settlements.

2 Lacey, p. 30 and appendix iii; Henning, i.31–2; Hutton *R*, pp. 152–3.

3 Burnet *OT*, i.317. For this parliament and its business see: Seaward; Derek Witcombe, *Charles II and the Cavalier House of Commons, 1663–1674* (Manchester, 1966); D. Hirst, 'The Conciliatoriness of the Cavalier Commons Reconsidered', *Parliamentary History*, vi (1987), 221–35; K. H. D. Haley, *Politics in the Reign of Charles II* (1985).

4 Burnet *OT*, i.162. Cf Holmes, p. 107: 'The possibilities of future trouble in Charles II's reign were latent from the very start in the indeterminate constitutional boundaries of 1660'.

5 Pepys, v.56, 60 (22 February 1664). The men named are Lauderdale, Buckingham, Hamilton (probably Anthony, author of the *Memoires de la Vie du Comte de Grammont*), Berkeley, Edward Projer (a groom of the bedchamber) and Bennet.

6 *State Trials*. v.1030, quoted in Harris, p. 37.

7 Burnet *OT*, i.276–7, 451.

8 On these men see Lacy, appendix ii. See further below, pp. 167–8.

9 John Miller, 'Charles II and his Parliaments', *TRHS*, 5th ser. xxxii (1982), 1–23; Andrew Browning, 'Parties and Party Organization in the Reign of Charles II', *TRHS*, 4th ser. xxx (1948), 21–36. For the Lords see Richard Davis, 'The "Presbyterian" Opposition and the Emergence of Party in the House of Lords in the Reign of Charles II', in Clyve Jones (ed.), *Party and Management in Parliament, 1660–1784* (Leicester, 1984), pp. 1–35.

10 Pepys, ix.490 (20 March 1669).

11 See above, p. 82–4.

12 Henning, i.27, 36, and passim.

13 W. D. Macray (ed.), *Notes which Passed at Meetings of the Privy Council between Charles II and the Earl of Clarendon*, Roxburghe Club (1896), p. 55; *To My Lord Chancellor, presented on New-years-day* (1662), ll.67, 70, in Dryden, p. 65.

14 Clarendon's career and exile are discussed below, pp. 95–101, 105–8, and the Cabal on pp. 168–71.

15 Quoted by Holmes, p. 112 from Add. MSS. 369165, fol. 166 (newsletter to Sir Willoughby Aston of 19 February 1670).

16 Burnet *OT*, i. 180, 402; Pepys, viii.185 (26 April 1667).

17 E.g. by Holmes, p. 112. For a full account of factionalism and the Clarendon/Arlington rivalry see Seaward, pp. 77–99, 217–35.

18 Burnet *SOT*, p. 68; [Anon.], *A Lively Pourtraict of our New-Cavaliers, Commonly Called Presbyterians* (1661); Marvel, *P&L*, ii.341.

19 Pepys, vii.356 (5 November 1666), viii.483 (17 October 1667); Marvell, *LI*, ll.107–8, 287–90, 827–36, in *P&L*, i.150, 154, 168; Burnet *OT*, i.489. *OED* is clearly astray in not recording *Country party* before 1735, nor illustrating *party* in a political sense before the early eighteenth century (senses 6, 19).

20 Harris, pp. 1 (referring to Sir Thomas Meres, in a debate in February 1673 (Henning, i.29)), 64; J. R. Jones, 'Green Ribbon Club', *Durham University Journal*, xlix (1956), 17–20. See also K.H. D. Haley, *The First Earl of Shaftesbury* (Oxford, 1968), pp. 349–52.

21 Harris, p. 8, cites from David Underdown, *Revel, Riot and Rebellion: Popular Politics and Culture in England, 1603–1660* (Oxford, 1985), p. 289, a Somerset use of *Tory* for *Cavalier* in 1655. *Whig*, according to Burnet (*OT*, i.72–3), derived from *whiggamor*, used of Scottish Covenanter insurgents, while *Tory* referred to Irish Catholic outlaws. See further: Robert Williams, 'The Origins of "Whig" and "Tory" in English Political Language', *HJ*, xvii (1974), 247–64; J. R. Jones, 'Parties and Parliament', in J. R. Jones (ed.), *The Restored Monarchy, 1660–1680* (1979), pp. 48–70; and the contributions to, and exchanges in, *Albion*, xxv (1993) by and between Tim Harris, Richard L. Greaves, Jonathan Scott and Gary S. De Krey.

22 [Earl of Shaftesbury], *A Letter from a Person of Quality to his Friend in the Country* (1675), p. 1, and [Edmund Bohun], *An Address to the Free-Men and Free-Holders of the Nation* (1682), p. 23 (quoted in Harris, pp. 8, 74).
23 [Daniel Defoe], *A New Test of the Church of England's Loyalty* (1702), p. 4.
24 *LJ*, xi.240–1.
25 *LJ*, xi.302.
26 *CJ*, viii.248, 272, 278; *LJ*, xi.300, 303; *Statutes*, v.309–10 (13 Car.II stat.i c.7).
27 Macray, *Notes Passed at the Privy Council*, p. 29.
28 Evelyn, iii.288–9; *LJ*, xi.260; *CJ*, viii.254, 259; *Mercurius Publicus*, 20 (16–23 May 1661), pp. 317, 320.
29 Steele, 3239 (13 August 1660); *CJ*, viii.66. Milton was not taken into custody until November, and then quickly released the next month (William Riley Parker, *Milton: A Biography*, 2 vols (Oxford, 1968), i.567–76; J. Milton French (ed.), *The Life Records of John Milton*, 5 vols (1956; rptd New York, 1966), iv.322–3, 339–40, 349–50).
30 *Statutes*, v.424 (14 Car.II c.29).
31 *CJ*, viii.261–75; *LJ*, xi.329; *Statutes*, v.306 (13 Car.II stat.i c.2); Browning, p. 208.
32 *CJ*, viii.247. On 3 July 22 absentees were reported, of whom William Love was suspended until he could produce his certificate (*CJ*, viii.289; Henning, ii.760).
33 For its religious legislation, see below, pp. 115–24.
34 *CJ*, viii.247–68; *LJ*, xi.261–76, 330; *Statutes*, v.304–6 (13 Car.II stat.i c.1); Browning, pp. 63–5.
35 *CJ*, viii.260–97; *LJ*, xi.252–308, 330; *Statutes*, v.308 (13 Car.II stat.i c.5); Browning, p. 66.
36 This received the royal assent on 19 May 1662 (*LJ*, xi.472). See below, pp. 148–54.
37 *CJ*, viii.252–305, 353–6, 376; *LJ*, xi.316–38, 353–72, 388–97, 431; *Statutes*, v.350–1 (14 Car.II c.1).
38 *CJ*, viii.345–66, 429–35; *LJ*, xi.387–90, 404–39, 465–71; *Statutes*, v.401–5 (14 Car. II. c.12).
39 *CJ*, viii.275–340; *LJ*, xi.308–58; *Statutes*, v.321–3 (13 Car.II stat.ii c.1); Browning, pp. 375–6; Hutton *R*, pp. 158–61.
40 *CJ*, viii.260–78, 325–41; *LJ*, xi.376.
41 See below, pp. 115–24.
42 *Statutes*, v.304–6 (13 Car.II stat.i c.1); Browning, pp. 63–5.
43 *CJ*, viii.447, 534–40; *LJ*, xi.588–90, 593; *Statutes*, v.513 (16 Car.II c.1); Browning, pp. 153–4. The earlier act was 16 Car.I c.1 (*Statutes*, v.54–7).
44 *CJ*, viii.249–314; *LJ*, xi.313–23, 330; *Statutes*, v.308–9 (13 Car.II stat.i c.6); Browning, p. 793. Cf. *Statutes*, v.358–64 (14 Car.II. c.3); Browning, pp. 793–5.
45 John Childs, *The Army of Charles II* (1976), pp. 15–18; Lois Schwoerer, *No Standing Armies!* (Baltimore, MD, 1974), pp. 79–89. For Venner's rising, see above, p. 50.
46 The Convention passed 35 public acts and the Cavalier Parliament 52 in 1661–2, far more than in any other comparable period of the 1660s. The seven remaining years of the decade added 72 acts to these 87.
47 *CJ*, viii.254; Pepys, ii.111 (30 May 1661).
48 *To My Lord Chancellor, Presented on New-years-day* (1662), ll.27–30, in Dryden, p. 64.
49 Burnet *OT*, i.160, 169.
50 Cf. Hutton *R*, p. 192: Clarendon 'was not a natural companion to Charles, and was accordingly vulnerable to those who were'.

51 'Second Advice to a Painter', l.150, and 'Third Advice', ll.249–50, in Marvell *CP*, pp. 123, 138.

52 Clarendon *LC*, i.316–18, 320–6 (§§48, 52–5); Lister, ii.68–75; Burnet *OT*, i.294–5, 298–9 with n. 2; Hutton *R*, pp. 149–50.

53 For the negotiations surrounding this alliance, see: Clarendon *LC*, i.416–51 (§§151–87); Keith Feiling, *British Foreign Policy, 1660–1672* (1930), pp. 31–52; G. Belcher, 'Spain and the Anglo-Portuguese Alliance of 1661', *JBS*, xv (1975), 67–88; Hutton *CII*, pp. 158–60.

54 Burnet *OT*, i.308; Hamilton, i.96; Lillias Campbell Davidson, *Catherine of Braganza* (1908), pp. 10–17.

55 Burnet *OT*, i.307; Lister, iii.196; Arthur Bryant (ed.), *Letters of Charles II* (1935), p. 127.

56 Burnet *OT*, i.451, 459; Burnet *SOT*, p. 54; Ailesbury, i.7.

57 Pepys, i.199 (13 July 1660), ii.80 (20 April 1661), 229 (7 December 1661), iii.147 (27 July 1662), 302 (31 December 1662); Brian Masters, *The Mistresses of Charles II* (1979), pp. 43–57; Elizabeth Hamilton, *The Illustrious Lady* (1980), pp. 1–42.

58 Pepys, iii.87 (21 May 1662), 82 (14 May 1662), 147 (26 July 1662), 289 (23 December 1662), iv.1 (1 January 1663); Clarendon *LC*, i.582–608 (§§358–92); Lister, iii.202–3, 222; Campbell Davidson, *Catherine*, pp. 119–44; Hamilton, *Illustrious Lady*, pp. 43–52; Masters, *Mistresses*, pp. 58–65.

59 Pepys, iv.1 (1 January 1663), 30 (1 February 1663), 112 (25 April 1663).

60 Burnet *OT*, i.287–8, 309, and *SOT*, p. 65, adding (p. 66) that, in view of what was at stake, Clarendon's 'firmness in that matter was truly heroical'.

61 Pepys, iii.227 (17 October 1662), 282 (15 December 1662), iv.238 (22 July 1663). On the Castlemaine–Clarendon rivalry, see Hamilton, *Illustrious Lady*, pp. 53–68.

62 Pepys, iv.136–7 (15 May 1663). Cf. *CSPD 1661–62*, p. 371; Burnet *OT*, i.182, for whom the Castlemaine and Clarendon groups are composed respectively of vicious and virtuous ministers.

63 Clarendon *LC*, i.589 (§366); Burnet *OT*, i.445. For Buckingham see further, pp. 169, 173–4, 177–8 below, and Hesther Chapman, *Great Villiers* (1949).

64 Burnet *OT*, i.181; Burnet *SOT*, p. 65; Pepys, vi.71 (31 March 1665). For Berkeley see further Cyril Hughes Hartmann, *The King's Friend* (1951).

65 Clarendon *LC*, ii. 92 (§581). For Ashley, see further p. 99 above and below, p. 169, and K. H. D. Haley, *The First Earl of Shaftesbury* (Oxford, 1968).

66 Clarendon *LC*, i.636 (§438). For Nicholas, see Donald Nicholas, *Mr Secretary Nicholas* (1955).

67 Pepys, iii.227 (17 October 1662), 290 (24 December 1662), iv.224 (10 July 1663); Clarendon *LC*, ii.92 (§582); Hutton *R*, pp. 192–3. For Arlington, see further pp. 88, 99–100 above and p. 169 below, and Violet Barbour, *Henry Bennet, Earl of Arlington* (1914).

68 Pepys, iv.115 (29 April 1663).

69 Clarendon, *LC*, ii.10–18 (§§455–65); Lister, ii.166–77; Burnet *OT*, i.303–5; Pepys, iii.229 (19 October 1662), and editors' note; Feiling, *Foreign Policy*, pp. 57–63; Hutton *R*, pp. 190–1, and *CII*, pp. 184–5. The articles are given in *LJ*, xi.555–7. Pepys, iv.223–4 (10 July 1663) gives an inaccurate list which reflects the charges to which Clarendon was popularly liable.

70 *LJ*, xi.559; Pepys, iv.229 (13 July 1663); J. R. Jones, 'The Bristol Affair', *Journal of Religious History*, v (1968–9), 16–30; Hutton *R*, pp. 202–3, and *CII*, p. 203.

71 Burnet *OT*, i.445–6; Pepys, vi.39 (20 February 1665), viii.269 (14 June 1667); Marvell, *P&L*, i.143–6; Lister, ii.386–8. The point of the jibe about Tangier was that it was held to be a useless and costly acquisition (see Lister, ii.166; Feiling, *Foreign Policy*, p. 59).

72 Pepys, iv.230 (13 July 1663), viii.184 (26 April 1667); cf. Hamilton, i.106.

73 Pepys, iv.37–8 (8 February 1663), 142 (18 May 1663), 174 (4 June 1663), viii.183–4 (26 April 1667). Hamilton, i.136, presents this as simple-minded naivety; Cyril Hughes Hartmann, *La Belle Stuart* (1924), pp .60–1, ascribes it rather to moral integrity; Hutton *CII*, p. 204, judges 'the evidence unclear'.

74 Rumours circulating about the various schemes proposed at this time to release Charles from Catherine and secure a legitimate Protestant heir included acknowledgement of a marriage to Lucy Walters (the mother of the Duke of Monmouth), polygamy, Catherine's entering a nunnery – even, it was said by Buckingham, abducting her to a plantation and alleging her desertion of the King, which Charles reportedly rejected with the observation that 'it was a wicked thing to make a poor lady miserable, only because she was his wife, and had no children by him, which was no fault of hers' (Burnet *OT*, i.469–74).

75 Pepys, viii.145 (3 April 1667), 183 (26 April 1667), 343 (17 July 1667), 414–15 (2 September 1667); Bryant, *Letters*, pp. 203–4; Burnet *OT*, i.451–3; Hartmann, *La Belle Stuart*, pp. 100–30; Hutton *CII*, pp. 250–1.

76 Pepys, v.352 (22 February 1665); Feiling, *Foreign Policy*, pp. 127–8; Hutton *R*, pp. 214–19. On these matters see K. G. Davies, *The Royal African Company* (1957) and George F. Zook, *The Company of Royal Adventurers Trading into Africa* (Lancaster, PA, 1919).

77 C. H. Firth and R. S. Rait (eds), *Acts and Ordinances of the Interregnum, 1642–1660*, 2 vols (1911), ii.559–62. The 1651 act was confirmed by the 1660 Navigation Act (12 Car. II c.18; *Statutes*, v.246–50; Browning, pp. 533–7). See further L. A. Harper, *The English Navigation Laws* (New York, 1939), pp. 38–58; Ralph Davis, *The Rise of the English Shipping Industry* (1972), pp. 303–7.

78 For accounts of the course of the war see: Hutton *R*, pp. 220–5, 240–5, 257–9, 268–70; C. R. Boxer, *The Second Dutch War* (1967); Feiling, *Foreign Policy*, pp. 83–201; P. G. Rogers, *The Dutch in the Medway* (1970). Much the fullest and most persuasive account of its cultural and political context is now Steven C. A. Pincus, *Protestantism and Patriotism: Ideologies and the Making of English Foreign Policy, 1650–1688* (Cambridge, 1996).

79 See further below, pp. 164–6.

80 *CJ*, viii.659, 661, 662; Milward, p. 56, Clarendon *LC*, ii.321 (§949). The initial attempt was frustrated by the Court party, but the Commission was set up in October 1667 (*CJ*, ix.3, 29; *LJ*, xii.175–9; Milward, pp. 87, 89; *Statutes*, v.624–7 (19 & 20 Car. II c.1)). Its report, presented on 26 October 1669, found a deficit of £1,500,000. On this report, and the membership and work of the Commission,, see *CTB*, II.xxxiv–lxxxvii.

81 Burnet *OT*, i.485, ii.3; Pepys, vii.399 (8 December 1666).

82 See above, p. 79.

83 *Statutes*, v.306–8, 325–48, 390–3; *CJ*, viii.257–314, 317–25; *LJ*, xi.352–85, 408–11, 474–5; Browning, pp. 307–8, 330–3; C. D. Chandaman, *The English Public Revenue, 1660–88* (Oxford, 1975), pp. 77, 200–4; *CTB*, I.xv–xxiv.

84 Pepys, iii.127 (end of June 1662); Chandaman, *Public Revenue*, pp. 81–97.

85 *CTB*, I.xxiv–xxxvii; *Old Parl. Hist.*, xxiii.10–22; Holmes, pp. 88–9; Chandaman, *Public Revenue*, pp. 197–200, 205–13.

86 Browning, p. 879; Hutton *CII*, pp. 242, 249.

87 Clarendon *LC*, ii.410 (§1083); Chandaman, *Public Revenue*, pp. 213–14; Hutton *CII*, p. 244. For the Commission and its work see: Chandaman, *Public Revenue*, pp. 214–21; Henry Roseveare, *The Treasury 1660–1870* (1973), pp. 17–45; Stephen Baxter, *The Development of the Treasury, 1660–1702* (1957), pp. 11, 39–41, 43–4, 50–2.

88 See further below, pp. 170–1.

89 Burnet *OT*, i.278 (cf. i.451); Clarendon *LC*, ii.7 (§450); Bryant, *Letters*, p. 205.

90 Pepys, viii.401 (26 August 1667), 404 (27 August 1667); Bryant, *Letters*, pp. 204, 205; Clarendon *LC*, ii.451, 453 (§§1143, 1147); Burnet *OT*, i.461, ii.471; Lister, ii.383–414. For Charles and his sister, and their correspondence, see Cyril Hughes Hartmann, *Charles II and Madame* (1934).

91 *LJ*, xii.119; *CJ*, ix.4; Clarendon, *LC*, ii.430 (§1114), 454 (§1148), 459–61 (§§1155–8); Pepys, viii.360–1 (29 July 1667), 482 (16 October 1667); Milward, pp. 84, 88.

92 *CJ*, ix.18; Pepys, viii.526 (12 November 1667); Milward, pp. 95, 99–103, 111–27; Burnet, *OT*, i.456–60. Cf. Pepys viii.502 (25 October 1667), 505–6 (28 October 1667), 518 (4 November 1667), 522–3 (8–9 November 1667), 525 (11 November 1667). On the causes and process of this impeachment, see Clayton Roberts, *The Growth of Responsible Government in Stuart England* (Cambridge, 1966), pp. 155–73.

93 Pepys, viii.401 (26 August 1667), 415 (2 September 1667). The 17 articles of impeachment are in Clarendon *LC*, ii.467–9 (§1166) with Clarendon's answers in ii.522–82 (§§1245–1350).

94 *LJ*, xii.137, 141–2; *CJ*, ix.22; Pepys, viii.541–2 (21 November 1667), 544 (22 November 1667); Milward, p. 148; Burnet, *OT*, i.458, 459.

95 *LJ*, xii.152; *CJ*, ix.29; Milward, pp. 128–52; Clarendon *LC*, ii.475–85 (§§1177–91). Burnet *OT*, i.460–2; Pepys, viii.527 (13 November 1667), 529 (15 November 1667), 532–4 (16 November 1667), 557–8, 559 (2 December 1667), 561 (3 December 1667), 568 (6 December 1667).

96 *CJ*, ix.32; Clarendon, *LC*, ii.495–7 (§§1198–1201); Milward, pp. 153–5; Pepys, viii.563 (4 December 1667), 566 (6 December 1667). Clarendon's *Humble Petition and Address* is in *LJ*, xii.154–6, and in *LC*, ii.488–95 (§§1196–7).

97 *LJ*, xii.159, 162, 163, 177; *CJ*, ix.37, 42; *Statutes*, v.628 (19 & 20 Car. II c.2); Clarendon *LC*, ii.500–2 (§§1208–9); Milward, p. 176; Pepys, viii.565–6 (6 December 1667), 578 (13 December 1667).

98 Clarendon *LC*, ii. 471 (§1170); Evelyn, iii.493 (27 August 1667).

## 5 FATHERS IN GOD: THE CHURCH OF ENGLAND

1 Baxter *RB*, II.229, §87; for the *Declaration*, see above pp. 68–70.

2 See below, p. 138.

3 Baxter *RB*, III.217, §76 and III.218, §80 (and cf. I.62, §93(2)); Abernathy, pp. 44–6; Bosher, pp. 120–1; I. M. Green, *The Re-Establishment of the Church of England* (Oxford, 1978), pp. 13–16. Baxter prints the *Reduction of Episcopacy unto the Form of Synodical Government received in the Ancient Church, proposed in the year 1641* in *RB*, II.238–40. It had been published in 1656 and was reissued in 1660.

4 Baxter *RB*, II.269, §106 (2) and *RB*, II.217, 218, §§76, 80. Baxter refers to a meeting with Ussher in 1654/55 (*RB*, II.206, §61). His sermon was printed as *A Sermon of Repentance* (1660).
5 Baxter *CCRB*, headnote to letter 309.
6 Baxter *RB*, II.218, §81; Bosher, pp. 105–14, citing (pp. 113–14) Peter Barwick, *The Life of John Barwick* (1724), p. 525; Abernathy, pp. 46–7, 54–5.
7 Baxter *RB*, II.229, §88. They were: Simeon Ashe; William Bates; Richard Baxter; Edmund Calamy; Thomas Case; Thomas Manton; Edward Reynolds; William Spurstowe: 'But never any of them was called to Preach at Court, saving Mr *Calamy*, Dr. *Reynolds*, my Self, and Dr. *Spurstow*, each of us once' (ibid.).
8 Baxter *RB*, II.229, 230–1, §§87, 90–1.
9 Baxter *RB*, II.232–58, §§92–101, which prints the papers (quotations from p. 231, §92, p. 232, §96, p. 235, §96, 2(2)); cf. II.278, §113. For the names of those involved in the discussions, see II.229, §§87–8, and II.232, §§95–6.
10 For further discussion of these notions, see below, pp. 125, 129.
11 Baxter *RB*, II.241, §101, II.243, §101 (§8), II.245,§101 (§20), II.246, §101 (§§24, 26).
12 *CJ*, viii.149; Bosher, p. 177. See above, p. 80.
13 *CJ*, viii.95; *LJ*, xi.175–6; Bosher, p. 169.
14 For the Worcester House negotiations, those present, and attendant papers (including the draft *Declaration*), see Baxter *RB*, II.259–79, §§105–14; Bosher, pp. 184–8; Abernathy, pp. 65–77.
15 Baxter *RB*, II.279, §§114–15. The final version of the *Declaration* is printed in Browning, pp. 365–70.
16 Spurr, p. 35. The nine surviving bishops were: Brian Duppa of Salisbury (1641, translated to Winchester in 1660); Accepted Frewen of Coventry and Lichfield (1643, elevated to York in 1660); William Juxon of London (1633, elevated to Canterbury in 1660); Henry King of Chichester (1642); William Piers, successively of Peterborough (1630) and Bath and Wells (1632); William Roberts of Bangor (1637); Robert Skinner, successively of Bristol (1636) and Oxford (1641); John Warner of Rochester (1637); Matthew Wren, successively of Norwich (1635) and Ely (1638).
17 Baxter *RB*, II.281–4, §§118–27; Bosher, pp. 193–4; Green, *Re-Establishment*, pp. 83–7.
18 The consecrations were, on 4 October 1660: George Griffith (St Asaph), Humfrey Henchman (Salisbury), George Morley (Worcester, translated to Winchester in 1662), Robert Sanderson (Lincoln) and Gilbert Sheldon (London, elevated to Canterbury in 1663); in December 1660: John Cosin (Durham), John Gauden (Exeter), Benjamin Laney (Peterborough, translated to Lincoln in 1663 and Ely in 1667), Hugh Lloyd (Llandaff), William Lucy (St Davids), Richard Sterne (Carlisle, elevated to York in 1664) and Brian Walton (Chester, succeeded by Henry Ferne in 1662, George Hall in 1663 and John Wilkins in 1668); and in January 1661: Gilbert Ironside (Bristol), Nicholas Monck (Hereford), William Nicolson (Gloucester), Edward Reynolds (Norwich). John Hacket became Bishop of Coventry and Lichfield in December 1661 and Isaac Barrow took the vacant see of Sodor and Man in 1663.
19 Bosher, pp. 179–84; Norman Sykes, *From Sheldon to Secker* (1959), pp. 6–8; Green, *Re-Establishment*, pp. 28–30, 82–90, 89–98, 255 and appendix vi; Spurr, p. 35.

20 Baxter *RB*, II.284–5, §§128–9 (which prints the address of thanks, dated 16 November 1660), II.379–80, §263, II.430, §419.
21 Baxter *RB*, II.277, §110; Bosher, pp. 187–90; Keeble, p. 27.
22 See above, pp. 92–3.
23 Clement Barksdale, *The King's Return* (1660), p. 16, cited in Spurr, pp. 36–7; Evelyn, iii.214 (23 May 1659), 251–2 (8 July 1660); Pepys, i.190 (1 July 1660), 215 (5 August 1660), 282 (4 November 1660), 289 (11 November 1660).
24 Clarendon *HR*, vi.232 (xvi.244); Pepys, i.176 with n. 1 (17 June 1660), 195 (8 July 1660), 283 (4 November 1660), 324 (30 December 1660), ii.70 (10 April 1661), 135–6 (15 July 1660); Evelyn, iii.231 (29 May 1659).
25 Green, *Re-Establishment*, pp. 61–71; Pepys, i.259 (4 October 1660); John Sudbury, *A Sermon Preached at the Consecration of the . . . Bishop . . . of London . . . Sarum . . . Worcester . . . Lincolne . . . St Asaph* (1660), pp. 2–9.
26 *CJ*, viii.194; Lacey, pp. 12–13; Bosher, pp. 195–9; Marvell *P&L*, ii.6; *Third Advice to a Painter*, ll.239–40, in Marvell *CP*, p. 137.
27 Baxter *RB*, II.281, §121, II.287, §143; Burnet *SOT*, p. 69. For different interpretations of the episcopalian strategy see Bosher, pp. 176–7, 180, 190; Anne Whiteman, 'The Restoration of the Church of England', in Geoffrey F. Nuttall and Owen Chadwick (eds), *From Uniformity to Unity* (1962), pp. 71–2; Spurr, pp. 34–8.
28 See above, p. 85.
29 Reresby, p. 36. For Venner's Rising, see above, p. 50, and Richard L. Greaves, *Deliver Us From Evil: The Radical Underground in Britain, 1660–1663* (New York, 1986), pp. 50–7.
30 E.g. *The Humble Apology of Some Commonly Called Anabaptists* (1661); *To the King . . . the Humble Representation of . . . Anabaptists* (1661); *A Declaration from the Harmles & Innocent People of God called Quakers* (1660[/61]); *Renunciation . . . of the Congregational Churches* (1661). For Bunyan's forceful repudiation of such means as Venner's, see below, pp. 144–5.
31 Norman Penney (ed.), *Extracts from State Papers relating to Friends, 1654 to 1672* (1913), pp. 117–27; Steele, 3278; Greaves, *Deliver Us From Evil*, pp. 57–60.
32 See above, pp. 43–6.
33 See above, p. 91.
34 Bosher, pp. 213–15, 222–3, 230–1; Seaward, pp. 165–6; Spurr, pp. 39, 40.
35 For the proceedings at the Savoy see: Baxter *RB*, II. 303–72, §§170–241; Edward Cardwell, *A History of Conferences . . . connected with the Revision of the Book of Common Prayer* (1840), pp. 257–368; E. C. Ratcliffe, 'The Savoy Conference', in Nuttall and Chadwick, *Uniformity to Unity*, pp. 89–146; Bosher, pp. 226–30; Horton Davies, *Worship and Theology in England from Andrewes to Baxter and Fox* (Princeton, NJ, 1975), pp. 365–73; Spurr, pp. 38–9; Keeble, p. 30 (which is drawn on in this paragraph).
36 Baxter *RB*, II.336, §192, II.364–5, §237, II.368, §240; [George Morley], *The Bishop of Worcester's Letter to a Friend* (1662), p. 13; Izaak Walton, *The Lives*, World's Classics (1927; rptd 1966), pp. 403–4.
37 Baxter *RB*, II.384, §276; The Book of Common Prayer (1662), pref., sig. b6; Bosher, pp. 244–9; Davies, *Worship and Theology*, pp. 373–89; Spurr, pp. 40–1.
38 *CJ*, viii.279; Bosher, p. 223; Seaward, pp. 166–8; Spurr, p. 39.
39 *CJ*, viii.296, 300; *Statutes*, v.315–16 (13 Car.II c. 12).

40 Pepys, iii.97 (31 May 1662). For the parliamentary history of the Act see: Bosher, pp. 224–5, 239–44, 249–54, 274–7; Lacey, pp. 36–7, 48–50; Seaward, pp. 166–8, 188–9.

41 *Statutes*, v.364–70.

42 Richard Allestree, *Sermon Preached at Hampton-Court on . . . the Anniversary of His Sacred Majesty's Most Happy Return* (1662), pp. 16–17.

43 For the established church's earlier views on orders see Norman Sykes, *Old Priest and New Presbyter* (1957), and for the 'outstanding innovation' of the 1662 'unvarying requirement of episcopal ordination', ibid., pp. 118–41.

44 *CSPD 1661–62*, pp. 418, 428, 488; Pepys, iii.117 (22 June 1662), 127 (30 June 1662), 169 (17 August 1662), 178 (24 August 1662), 183 (31 August 1662), 186 (3 September 1662), 210 (30 September 1662); A. G. Matthews, *Mr Pepys and Nonconformity* (1954), pp. 141–3; Keeble, p. 32 (from which this paragraph derives).

45 See below, pp. 138–41.

46 Alan MacFarlane (ed.), *The Diary of Ralph Josselin* (1976), pp. 490–3, 498, 508, 511, 535, 548, 549, 556, 587, 593, 614, 615, 627–8; Alan MacFarlane, *The Family Life of Ralph Josselin* (1970), pp. 27–30; Harold Smith, *The Ecclesiastical History of Essex* (1932), pp. 223–4; Spurr, pp. 188–9.

47 Spurr, pp. 185–95, discusses the inefficiency of the church's structure and hierarchy and the persistence of only partial conformity among its clergy.

48 Seaward, pp. 175–80; Spurr, pp. 41–2; Abernathy, pp. 81–6; Lacey, pp. 48–50; Bosher, pp. 250–3; Keith Feiling, 'Clarendon and the Act of Uniformity', *EHR*, xliv (1929), 289–91.

49 Bodleian Library MS Carte 45, fo. 151, quoted in Spurr, p. 47.

50 See the comments from his correspondence quoted by Spurr, pp. 57, 58.

51 For Sheldon's activities and discussion of this point see: Spurr, pp. 49–50; Seaward, pp. 62, 67, 193–5, 328; Paul Seaward, 'Gilbert Sheldon, the London Vestries and the Defence of the Church', in Tim Harris, Paul Seaward and Mark Goldie (eds), *The Politics of Religion in Restoration England* (Oxford, 1990), pp. 49–73; Hutton *R*, pp. 168–9, 174.

52 *Statutes*, v.516–50. For the plot, see below, p. 156.

53 E[dward] B[illing], *A Faithful Testimony for God* (1664), p. 9; Norman Penney (ed.), *Extracts from State Papers Relating to Friends 1654 to 1672* (1913), pp. 221, 230–1; William C. Braithwaite, *The Second Period of Quakerism*, 2nd edn, revd Henry J Cadbury (1961; rptd York, 1979), pp. 40–52.

54 *Statutes*, v.575; Spurr, p. 52.

55 *Statutes*, v.648–51. For the debates surrounding this Act, its implementation, and resistance to it, see Gary De Krey, 'The First Restoration Crisis: Conscience and Coercion in London, 1667–73', *Albion*, xxv (1993), 565–80.

56 Norman Penney (ed.), '*The First Publishers of Truth*' (1907), p. 101; Penney, *Extracts*, pp. 299–201; Marvell *P&L*, ii.314; Lacey, pp. 61–2.

57 Steele, 3301, 3367; John L. Nickalls (ed.), *The Journal of George Fox* (1952; rpt York 1975), pp. 411–12, 423, 557–8; Penney, *Extracts*, pp. 132–3, 150; Lacey, p. 100.

58 Browning, p. 373.

59 Browning, p. 373; Baxter *RB*, II.429–30, §§417–18; Seaward, pp. 181–5; Green, *Re-Establishment*, pp. 219–26; John Miller, *Popery and Politics in England, 1660–1688*

(Cambridge, 1973), pp. 100–3; Spurr, pp. 50–1; Lacey, pp. 50–3; Bosher, pp. 258–66 (p. 261 prints the Presbyterian reply); George Abernathy, 'Clarendon and the Declaration of Indulgence', *JEH*, xi (1960), 55–73.

60 Burnet *OT*, i.465, which (n. 2) refers to Pepys, viii.584–5 (21 December 1667), here quoted.

61 Spurr, p. 57.

62 Keeble, pp. 72–3.

63 For these negotiations, with papers, see Baxter *RB*, III.23–36, §§62–81; Baxter *CCRB*, letters 794, 795; Roger Thomas, 'Comprehension and Indulgence', in Nuttall and Chadwick, *Uniformity to Unity*, pp. 196 –203.

64 *CJ*, ix.44; Baxter *RB*, III.36, §81; Steele, 3514; Pepys, ix.60 (10 February 1668).

65 Baxter *CCRB*, letters 757, 760; Baxter *RB*, III.36–9, §§85–6, III.74, §169.

66 Burnet *OT*, i.466–7; Baxter *RB*, III.38, §86.

67 For tracts putting the contrary case, and discussion of their arguments, see Gary De Krey, 'Rethinking the Restoration: Dissenting Cases for Conscience, 1667–1672', *HJ*, xxxviii (1995), 53–83.

68 John W. Packer, *The Transformation of Anglicanism 1643–60, with Special Reference to Henry Hammond* (Manchester, 1969), pp. 46–7; Bosher, pp. 25–7, 89–99; Green, *Re-establishment*, pp. 81–2; D. E. Underdown, *Royalist Conspiracy in England, 1649–1660* (New Haven, CT, 1960), pp. 181–3, 236; Peter King, 'The Episcopate during the Civil Wars', *EHR*, lxxxiii (1968), 533–4.

69 Spurr, pp. 10–11, 138–43; Packer, *Transformation*, pp. 104–71; Isabel Rivers, 'Prayer-book Devotion: The Literature of the Proscribed Episcopal Church', in N. H. Keeble (ed.), *Cambridge Companion to Writing of the English Revolution* (Cambridge, 2001), pp. 198–214.

70 Baxter *RB*, I.97, §140; II.149, §29; Baxter *CCRB*, letter 130 and ensuing correspondence (and cf. letters 517, 520); N. H. Keeble, *Richard Baxter: Puritan Man of Letters* (Oxford, 1982), pp. 117–18 with n. 6. Spurr, pp. 132–63, surveys views of episcopacy in the Restoration church with a wealth of evidence.

71 Although Spurr, p. 163, holds that 'there is no reason for thinking that the "new episcopalianism" of Hammond and his friends was responsible for the political decision in 1662 to make episcopacy a touchstone of the church, whatever it may have later contributed to the enhancement and elaboration of that decision', the conception episcopacy's definitive status embodied in the Act would hardly have been available without their work.

72 Spurr, pp. 122–32 rehearses the arguments.

73 For summary accounts see: Isabel Rivers, *Reason, Grace and Sentiment: A Study of the Language of Religion and Ethics in England, 1660–1780*, vol.i: *Whichcote to Wesley* (Cambridge, 1991), pp. 25–80; Irène Simon, *Three Restoration Divines: Barrow, South, Tillotson*, 2 vols (Paris, 1967–76); John Spurr, '"Latitudinarianism" and the Restoration Church', *HJ*, xxxi (1988), 61–82; John Spurr, '"Rational Religion" in Restoration England', *JHI*, xlix (1988), 1–23.

74 S[imon] P[atrick?], *A Brief Account of the New Sect of Latitude-Men* (1662), ed. T. A. Birrell (Los Angeles, CA, 1963), p. 5; Baxter *RB*, III.386, §284 (2); Burnet *OT*, i.334 (quoted in Rivers, *Reason, Grace and Sentiment*, p. 28). See further Edward Fowler, *The Principles and Practices, of Certain Moderate Divines of the Church of England* (1670).

75 Rivers, *Reason, Grace and Sentiment*, p. 26, judges that in the 1660s 'the number of the latitude-men was relatively small and their influence restricted, though increasing; by the 1690s the latitudinarians . . . were the dominant, though not the majority, party in the Church of England'.

76 By 12 Car.II c.30 and 12 Car.II c.14; see above, pp. 37, 53.

77 Thomas Pierce, *A Collection of Sermons* (Oxford, 1671), p. 22, quoted in Spurr, p. 240; see Spurr, pp. 238–44, for further examples of such sentiments.

78 Spurr, pp. 10–11, 138–43; C. J. Stranks, *The Life and Writings of Jeremy Taylor* (1952), pp. 104–8.

79 Robert South, *The Sermons*, 5 vols (Oxford, 1842), ii.145, quoted in Spurr, p. 284.

80 P. Elmen, 'Richard Allestree and *The Whole Duty of Man*', *The Library*, 5th ser. vi (1951–2), 19–27.

81 See Spurr, pp. 281–6; C. J. Stranks, *Anglican Devotion* (1952), pp. 123–48.

82 Spurr, pp. 296–330, argues this charge is misplaced; for the contrary view, see: C. F. Allison, *The Rise of Moralism: The Proclamation of the Gospel from Hooker to Baxter* (1966); J. S. McGee, *The Godly Man in Stuart England* (New Haven, CT, 1976), esp. pp. 59–63, 94–5, 208–34, 251–3.

83 In *A Defence of the Doctrine of Justification by Faith* (1672), in *MW*, iv.1–130.

84 Spurr, pp. 173–7; John Pruett, *The Parish Clergy under the Later Stuarts: The Leicestershire Experience* (Urbana, IL, 1978), pp. 81–114; R. O'Day, 'Anatomy of a Profession: The Clergy of the Church of England', in W. Prest (ed.), *The Professions in Early Modern England* (1987), pp. 50–8.

85 Pierce, *Sermons*, p. 53, quoted in Spurr, p. 244.

86 John Tillotson, preface to John Wilkins, *Of the Principles and Duties of Natural Religion* (1675), sig. A5v, quoted in Rivers, *Reason, Grace and Sentiment*, p. 25. This theme is developed in ibid., pp. 81–7, and in Rivers, 'Grace, Holiness, and the Pursuit of Happiness: Bunyan and Restoration Latitudinarianism', in N. H. Keeble (ed.), *John Bunyan: Conventicle and Parnassus – Tercentenary Essays* (Oxford, 1988), pp. 45–69.

87 See above, p. 125.

88 Christopher Hill, *Antichrist in Seventeenth-century England*, revd edn (1990), pp. 146–54 (mentioning More on pp. 148–9, Hammond and Sheldon on pp. 152–3).

89 Baxter *RB*, III.38, §86 (11); cf. I.113, §170 (15); II.280, §117. The books by Thorndike are: *An Epilogue to the Tragedy of the Church of England* (1659); *The Due Way of Composing the Differences on Foot* (1660); and *Just Weights and Measures* (1662).

90 See above, p. 63. Clarendon *LC*, i.532–9 (§§291–8), discusses the 'ground' of Charles's 'graciousness' towards his Roman Catholic subjects, locating it in the experiences of his exile.

91 *His Majesties Gracious Speech . . . 18 February* (1663); *LJ*, xi.478; Steele, 3381; Clarendon *LC*, ii.92–3 (§§583–91); Pepys, iv.224 (10 July 1663). For the *Declaration*, see above, pp. 122–3, and for Bristol's accusations, p. 100.

92 Pepys, ii.38 (18 February 1661).

93 Lister, iii.443.

94 See below, pp. 170–1.

95 William Lamont argues that Marvell is, indeed, a Baxterian, in 'The Religion of Andrew Marvell: Locating the "Bloody Horse"', in Conal Condren and A. D. Cousins (eds), *The Political Identity of Andrew Marvell* (Aldershot, 1990), pp. 135–56.

96 Pepys, vii.358, 360, 363, 369–70 (5, 7, 9, 10 November 1666). On the Fire of London, see pp. 162–4 below.

97 *CSPD 1666–67*, p. 242; Burnet *OT*, i. 416.

98 Part of the title of *A True and Faithfull Account of the Several Informations Exhibited to the Honourable Committee Appointed by the Parliament to Inquire into the Late Dreadful Burning of the City* (1667). Publishers spotted the opportunity to issue during the next two years lurid accounts of the roll-call of papist atrocities: the Fires of Smithfield, the St Bartholomew's Day Massacre, the Spanish Armada, the Gunpowder Plot and the Irish Massacre.

99 Steele, 3479; see below, p. 164.

100 Pepys, viii.269–70 (14 June 1667); cf. viii. 264 (13 June 1667); Miller, *Popery and Politics*, p. 105.

## 6 'THE PATIENCE OF HEROIC FORTITUDE': NONCONFORMITY, SEDITION AND DISSENT

1 Although *Paradise Lost* was begun before the Restoration and *The Pilgrim's Progress* not published until 1678, the composition of each belongs in the main to the 1660s: see Milton *PJM*, pp. 422–3; Bunyan *PP*, pp. xxix–xxxv.

2 Milton is associated with radical Puritanism most tellingly in Christopher Hill, *Milton and the English Revolution* (1977) and both Milton and Bunyan are discussed in radical terms in Hill's *The World Turned Upside Down* (1972; Harmondsworth, 1975), pp. 44–9, and his *The English Bible and the Seventeenth-century Revolution* (Hardmondsworth, 1994), pp. 371–91.

3 Bunyan *MW*, ii.16; Milton *SA*, l.1659 (John Carey's note in *PJM*, p. 398, points out that this detail is a Miltonic addition to the biblical account); *PL*, vii.31; Milton *CPW*, vii.368–75.

4 Bunyan *GA*, §318 and pp. 105–6; William Riley Parker, *Milton: A Biography*, 2 vols (Oxford, 1968), i. 567–76 (and above, p. 91).

5 J. Milton French (ed.), *The Life Records of John Milton*, 5 vols (1956; rptd New York, 1966), iv. 349–50, 352–3, 390; Andrew Marvell, *The Rehearsal Transpros'd*, ed. D. I. B. Smith (Oxford, 1971), p. 312; Thomas Ellwood, *The History of his Life* (1714), p. 131.

6 For two, rather different, accounts of this disappointment and its effect upon the Puritan temper, see Christopher Hill, *The Experience of Defeat: Milton and Some Contemporaries* (1984), and Keeble, passim.

7 For the contrary argument that they remain very different, see Thomas N. Corns, 'Bunyan, Milton and the Diversity of Radical Protestant Writing', in N. H. Keeble (ed.), *John Bunyan: Reading Dissenting Writing* (Bern, forthcoming).

8 Bunyan *MW*, iii.5, 62; *GA*, p. xliv, 113; *PP*, p. 8.

9 Milton *PL*, vii.24–8.

10 *Seriatim* George Bate, Richard Perrinchief, Henry Foulis, John Taylor (?), Robert South and Roger L'Estrange, as cited in French, *Records*, iv. 359, 365, 366, 379, 315.

11 Hill, *Milton*, p. 365 (cf. pp. 238, 404–5); Michael Wilding, *Dragons Teeth: Literature in the English Revolution* (Oxford, 1987), p. 237.

12 Milton *PL*, vi.29–37, 143–8.
13 Milton *PL*, v.902, vii.24. Cf. Hill, *Milton*, pp. 370–1, 391.
14 Bunyan, *The Resurrection of the Dead* (1665), in *MW*, iii.204.
15 Bunyan *MW*, ii.240, 253, 266, 284.
16 Milton *PL*, vii.30–5, xii.521–2, 531–8.
17 Bunyan *PP*, pp. 87 (alluding to Acts 14.22), 92–8; *GA*, pp. 113–19.
18 Milton *PL*, xi.798–804, xii.537–8.
19 For final demonstration that this is a late text, post-dating the Restoration, see Blair Worden, 'Milton, *Samson Agonistes* and the Restoration', in Gerald MacLean (ed.), *Culture and Society in the Stuart Restoration* (Cambridge, 1995), pp. 111–36.
20 Milton *SA*, ll.7–9, 641–2, 693–5.
21 This theme is developed in N. H. Keeble, 'Wilderness Exercises: Adversity, Temptation and Trial in *Paradise Regained*', *Milton Studies* (forthcoming).
22 See above, pp. 127–9.
23 Bunyan *MW*, x.95; Milton *PR*, iii.194–5; Bunyan *GA*, §§311–12; William Penn, *No Cross, No Crown*, ed. Norman Penney (1930; rptd York, 1981), p. 105. Penn's title derives from Luke 19.23; his book was reissued in greatly expanded form in 1682.
24 Bunyan, *The Resurrection of the Dead* (1665), in *MW*, iii.237, 238–9.
25 Bunyan, *The Holy City* (1665), in *MW*, iii.134, 154. For this Foxean tradition, see J. R. Knott, *Discourses of Martyrdom in English Literature, 1563–1694* (Cambridge, 1993), and for this emphasis in nonconformist culture, Keeble, pp. 187–91.
26 Bunyan, *Christian Behaviour* (1663), in *MW*, iii.18.
27 Bunyan *PP*, p. 96.
28 N. H. Keeble, *Richard Baxter: Puritan Man of Letters* (Oxford, 1982), pp. 23–8 and references there given. For the Reconcilers see Roger Thomas, 'The Rise of the Reconcilers' in C. F. Bolam et al., *The English Presbyterians* (1968), pp. 46–72, and E. W. Kirby, 'The Reconcilers and the Restoration (1660–62)', in *Essays in . . . Honor of Wilbur Cortez Abbott* (Cambridge, MA, 1941), pp. 46–79.
29 [Andrew Marvell], *Mr Smirke: or, the Divine in Mode* (1676), pp. 53, 62, 74, 75.
30 Baxter, *The Cure of Church-Divisions* (1670), p. 296, and *The True Catholick* (1660), p. 165; Edmund Calamy, *Memoirs of John Howe* (1724), pp. 31–2.
31 Calamy, *Memoirs*, p. 39.
32 Burnet *OT*, i.328; Baxter, *An Answer to Mr Dodwell and Dr. Sherlock* (1682), p. 178.
33 Edmund Calamy, *An Historical Account of my Own Life*, ed. J. T. Rutt, 2 vols (1829), i.473.
34 Calamy, *Memoirs*, p. 213.
35 The phrases are George Fox's in *The Pearle Found in England* (1658), p. 11, but they were part of a standard discourse.
36 Baxter *RB*, III.43, §98.
37 Baxter *RB*, III.43, §96.
38 On this, see Keeble, pp. 40–4: 'it is the idea of willing choice, with no desire for reunion, which informs "dissenter"; of unwilling, and if possible temporary, necessity which informs "nonconformist" '.
39 A. C. Underwood, *A History of the English Baptists*, 2nd edn (1956), p. 98.
40 [William Penn and William Mead], *The People's Antient and Just Liberties Asserted* (1670). For a general survey of this legislation as it related to Quakers, see William

Charles Braithwaite's appendix to Norman Penney (ed.), *The First Publishers of Truth* (1907), pp. 343–63.

41 For these acts, see above, pp. 120–2. For their implementation and effects upon nonconformists in general see: G. R. Cragg, *Puritanism in the Period of the Great Persecution* (Cambridge, 1957); Michael Watts, *The Dissenters: From the Reformation to the French Revolution* (Oxford, 1978), pp. 221–43; Keeble, pp. 45–55 and passim; for Baptists, see: Underwood, *English Baptists*, pp. 89–115; for Congregationalists, see: R. Tudur Jones, *Congregationalism in England, 1662–1962* (1962), pp. 63–89; for Quakers, William C. Braithwaite, *The Second Period of Quakerism*, 2nd edn, revd Henry J. Cadbury (1961; rptd York, 1979), pp. 21–54, 75–81, 100–15.

42 A. G. Matthews, *Calamy Revised* (Oxford, 1934), pp. xii–xv; Watts, *Dissenters*, pp. 153, 159–64, 219, 229. There were also 120 ejections in Wales. There were also men who were not put out simply because at the time they did not hold a benefice (including such notable figures as John Owen, Peter Sterry and Increase Mather).

43 See Keeble, pp. 137–8, for a survey of the evidence, and the references there cited. For national population figures see E. A. Wrigley and R. S. Schofield, *The Population History of England, 1541–1871* (1981), pp. 528–9, 532–3, 540, 563–76.

44 See above, p. 120.

45 Hutton *R*, p. 208.

46 For these and other such expedients, with details, see Keeble, pp. 48–9.

47 E[dward] B[illing], *A Faithful Testimony for God & My Country* (1664), pp. 3–4.

48 Baxter *RB*, II.436, §431; Pepys, v.235 (7 August 1664).

49 Sir William Holdsworth, *A History of English Law*, 17 vols (1903–72; vols. i–iii, 3rd edn, 1922–3), iii.616–20, iv.531, 535–6; Alfred W. Braithwaite, '"Errors in the Indictment" and Pardons', *Journal of the Friends' Historical Society*, xlix (1959), 24–30, and his *Thomas Rudyard, Journal of the Friends Historical Society* supplement xxvii (1956).

50 Baxter *RB*, III.47, §107; Bunyan *GA*, pp. 114–19, 125–9.

51 [Anon.], *Another Cry of the Innocent & Oppressed for Justice* (1665), pp. 3–4; Billing, *Faithful Testimony*, p. 8; [Thomas Rudyerd], *The Second Part of the Peoples Antient and Just Liberties Asserted* (1670); Baxter *RB*, III.87, §190; *State Trials*, vi.999–1026.

52 Baxter *RB*, I.132–3, §213 (28).

53 George Fox, *The Summ of Such Particulars as are Charged against George Fox* (1660), p. 3; *A Declaration from the Harmless and Innocent People of God, called Quakers, against All Plotters and Fighters in the World* (1661), in John Nickalls (ed.), *The Journal of George Fox* (1975), p. 399.

54 Bunyan *GA*, p. 120; *Of Antichrist and His Ruine*, in *MW*, xiii.489; *Christian Behaviour* (1663), in *MW*, iii.10; *Seasonable Counsel* (1684), in *MW*, x.5, 35, 39, 75, 99–104. On pacificism and quietism in nonconformist writing at this time, see Keeble, pp. 19–20, 23–4, 191–214.

55 Milton *PR*, iii.400–1; *PL*, ix.31–2 and xii.569. For discussion of this strain in Bunyan and Milton, see Laura K. Knoppers, *Historicizing Milton: Spectacle, Power and Poetry in Restoration England* (Athens, GA, 1994), pp. 13–41, 123–41; Knott, *Discourses of Martyrdom*, esp. pp. 168–78, 181–5; David Loewenstein, *Representing Revolution in Milton and his Contemporaries* (Cambridge, 2001), pp. 242–68; and works cited in these pieces.

56 Bunyan, *The Holy City* (1665), in *MW*, iii.149; *PP*, p. 89. See further below, pp. 176–82.

57 Bunyan *PP*, pp. 93, 94, 95; *Prison Meditations* (1665), st. 27, in *MW*, vi.46.

58 Bunyan *PP*, pp. 98, 99, 19, 226.
59 John Bunyan, *The Life and Death of Mr Badman*, ed. James Forrest and Roger Sharrock (Oxford, 1988), pp. 121–2, 125.
60 Milton *PL*, iv.318, and *SA*, ll.714–17; Nicholas Jose, *Ideas of the Restoration in English Literature, 1660–71* (Cambridge, MA, 1984), p. 162.
61 Christopher Hill, *A Turbulent, Seditious and Factious People: John Bunyan and his Church* (Oxford, 1988), pp. 125–30, 212–15.
62 Bunyan, *A Few Sighs from Hell* (1658), in *MW*, i.253–4, 255, 256.
63 See further below, p. 179.
64 Bunyan *PP*, pp. 88, 93, 95, 96.
65 As noted by Hill, *Turbulent People*, p. 224.
66 For discussion of this aspect of Penn, and of nonconformist writing, see Keeble, pp. 215–29.
67 Bunyan *GA*, p. 1; Milton *SA*, ll.1653–4, 1660, 1669–70; Jose, *Ideas of the Restoration*, pp. 155, 160. For such a reading of *SA* see Jose's whole chapter (pp. 142–63), the essay by Blair Worden cited above, n. 19, and Hill, *Milton*, pp. 428–48.
68 Bunyan *PP*, p. 148; *GA*, §276.
69 Penn, *No Cross, No Crown*, pp. 252–3; Milton *PL*, ix.27–41. For further discussion of these matters, see Keeble, pp. 220–35.
70 *Statutes*, v.428–33, excerpted in Browning, pp. 67–9
71 Scott, p. 422. For this earlier history of censorship and control of the press, see: Frederick S. Siebert, *Freedom of the Press in England, 1476–1776* (Urbana, IL, 1952), pp. 21–51; Cyprian Blagden, *The Stationers' Company: A History, 1403–1959* (1960); Holdsworth, *English Law*, iv.305–6, vi.303, 311–12, 360–79. It is summarized in Keeble, pp. 93–6.
72 For this act and the Company, see Blagden, *Stationers' Company*, pp. 130, 148, 153–9, 164; J. Walker, 'The Censorship of the Press in the Reign of Charles II', *History*, n.s. xxxv (1950), 219–38.
73 Baxter *RB*, I.123, §211 (2) and I.120, §206.
74 Baxter *RB*, III.61, §140; Marvell, *Rehearsal Transpros'd*, pp. 205, 166 (and cf. pp. 196–8).
75 Baxter *RB*, I.123, §211 (3), III.61, §§137, 140, III.86, §186.
76 John Owen, *Exercitations on the Epistle to the Hebrews* (1668), sig. A2; Peter Toon, *God's Statesman: The Life of John Owen* (1971), p. 127; George Kitchin, *Sir Roger L'Estrange* (1913), pp. 200–3; Parker, *Milton*, i.600–1, 613–14.
77 *State Trials*, vi.548, 552, 558, 564, quoted in Walker, 'Censorship of the Press', p. 228, and in Keeble, p. 98. For the law in this respect, see Holdsworth, *English Law*, v.208–9, viii.333–78; Siebert, *Freedom of the Press*, pp. 116–26, 269–75.
78 *State Trials*, vi.549. For the Treason Act, see above, p. 92. The law of treason is discussed in Holdsworth, *English Law*, viii.314–16; in Siebert, *Freedom of the Press*, pp. 265–9; and by Jennifer Carter in J. R. Jones (ed.), *The Restored Monarchy* (1979), pp. 81–3.
79 *State Trials*, vi.514–17, 519–34. To Secretary Bennet the author of *Mene Tekel* was later reported to be Roger Jones (*CSPD 1664–65*, p. 6), whose authorship is accepted as 'probable' by Richard L. Greaves in his account of the episode in *Deliver Us From Evil: The Radical Underground in Britain, 1660–1663* (New York, 1986), pp. 222–3, 224.

80 *State Trials*, vi.707–10.

81 Roger L'Estrange, *A Memento* (1662; rptd 1682), pp. 6–7; cf. *A Modest Plea* (1661), *Apology to Clarendon* (1661), *Truth and Loyalty Vindicated* (1662).

82 Roger L'Estrange, *Truth and Loyalty Vindicated* (1662), sig. A2v, and *Considerations and Proposals* (1663), sigs, A3–A3v, A4v, pp. 1, 6, 24–5.

83 *CSPD 1663–4*, p. 240 (and cf. *CSPD 1661–2*, pp. 282–3); Kitchin, *L'Estrange*, pp. 105–7, 126–30.

84 Baxter *RB*, III.102, §221.

85 Kitchin, *L'Estrange*, pp. 142–4; cf. L'Estrange, *Considerations*, pp. 2, 5, 30–1.

86 [Marvell], *Mr Smirke*, p. 10.

87 For the following, and other, examples, see Christopher Hill, 'Censorship and English Literature', *Writing and Revolution in 17th Century England* (Brighton, 1985), pp. 32–71, and Keeble, pp. 110–20.

88 For the current state of the question of Milton's authorship of this work, see Gordon Campbell et al., 'The Provenance of *De Doctrina Christiana*', *Milton Quarterly*, xvii (1997), 67–121.

89 Milton *CPW*, vi.23–35; A. G. Matthews, *Calamy Revised* (Oxford, 1934), *s.vv.* Morrice, Morton; N. H. Keeble, '"I would not tell you any tales": Marvell's Constituency Letters', in Conal Condren and A. D. Cousins (eds), *The Political Identity of Andrew Marvell* (Aldershot, 1990), pp. 111–15; Philip Henry, *Diaries*, ed. M. H. Lee (1882), p. 173.

90 Steel, 3622, 3623, 3625.

91 E[dward] B[illing], *A Faithful Testimony for God* (1664), p. 4; William C. Braithwaite, *The Second Period of Quakerism*, 2nd edn, revd Henry Cadbury (1961; rptd York, 1979), pp. 279–81; Russell S. Mortimer, 'The First Century of Quaker Printers, Part I', *Journal of the Friends' Historical Society*, xi (1948), 38–9; Luella Wright, *The Literary Life of the Early Friends* (Columbia, MS, 1932), pp. 95–109; Fox, *Journal*, pp. 732–3.

92 *CSPD 1654*, pp. 378, 389; *CSPD 1659–60*, pp. 572, 575; *CSPD 1661–2*, pp. 23, 173; Walker, 'Censorship', pp. 226–36; Leona Rostenberg, *Literary, Politic, Scientific... Printing and Bookselling, 1551–1700*, 2 vols (New York, 1965), i.203–36 (esp. pp. 230–4); Greaves, *Deliver Us from Evil*, pp. 212–15. See further below, pp. 165, 203.

93 Greaves, *Deliver Us from Evil*, pp. 216–25; Keeble, pp. 121–2, and references there given.

94 *CSPD 1667–68*, pp. 363, 369.

95 For L'Estrange's continuing efforts, and the continuing productivity of the radical press, see Richard L. Greaves *Enemies Under His Feet: Radicals and Nonconformists in Britain, 1664–67* (Stanford, CA, 1990), pp. 167–84.

96 See the account in *State Trials*, vii.937–60.

97 Greaves, *Enemies Under His Feet*, pp. 174–5, 178, 182; Keeble, pp. 122–3.

98 The contest is described in detail in Greaves, *Enemies Under His Feet*, pp. 170–1, 178; Keeble, pp. 106–8.

99 Marvell, *Rehearsal Transpros'd*, pp. 4–5.

100 John N. King, *English Reformation Literature* (Princeton, NJ, 1982), pp. 21, 72, 418; Leona Rostenberg, *The Minority Press* (New York, 1971), pp. 170–86, 190–8; Siebert, *Freedom of the Press*, pp. 96–100; Watts, *Dissenters*, pp. 68–9.

101 For discussion, see Keeble, pp. 111–17.

102 *CSPD 1667–68*, pp. 319, 360, 378.

103 In *Deliver Us from Evil*, Greaves exhaustively documents the activities of this underground, their plottings and suspected plots, to argue that, though 'the large majority of Nonconformist churches were not engaged in plotting' (ibid.: p. 7) and 'a large majority of nonconformists posed no violent political threat to the Stuart regime' (*Enemies Under His Feet*, p. 121), yet elements in nonconformity were far more militant and subversively active than has been appreciated.

104 See on these, successively, Greaves, *Deliver Us from Evil*, pp. 49–65, 112–29, 138–57, 165–206; Greaves, *Enemies Under His Feet*, pp. 34–5; for Venner, see above, pp. 50, 116. On the decade's fear of plots and factionalism see also McKeown, pp. 79–98.

105 E.g. Ephraim Pagitt, *Heresiography*, 6th edn, enlarged (1662), pp. 285–6, 291, 292; John Clarke, *Plotters Unmasked, Murderers No Saints* (1661); Thomas Marriot, *Rebellion Unmasked... wherein is opened the resemblance between rebellion and the sins of idolatry and withchcraft* (1661).

106 See above, p. 116.

107 Greaves, *Deliver Us from Evil*, pp. 72–7.

108 The phrase is Austin Woolrych's in Milton *CPW*, vii.207.

109 Milton *CPW*, vii.423, 425, 426, 449.

110 Milton *PL*, i.263, 348, ii.1–6, 428, xii.13–62. Cf. Hill, *Milton*, pp. 366, 382.

111 Milton *PL*, iv.765–9, v.350–8, ix.29–41; 'A Masque Presented at Ludlow Castle', ll.736–9.

112 Bunyan, *Seasonable Counsel* (1684), in *MW*, x.13–14; *An Exposition on the Ten First Chapters of Genesis*, in *MW*, xii.267–8. Nimrod was commonly taken to represent not merely oppressive monarchy but (by their opponents) Charles I and Charles II: see Hill, *Turbulent People*, pp. 326–7; Tindall, *John Bunyan, Mechanick Preacher*, pp. 141–2.

113 David Norbrook, *Writing the English Republic: Poetry, Rhetoric and Politics, 1627–1660* (Cambridge, 1999), p. 437, where see pp. 433–95 for demonstration of the point.

114 Algernon Sidney, *Court Maxims*, ed. Hans W. Blom, Eco Haitsma Mulier and Ronald Janse (Cambridge, 1996), p. 196. On this text, Sidney and the republican tradition, see: Jonathan Scott, *Algernon Sidney and the English Republic, 1623–1677* (Cambridge, 1988) and *Algernon Sidney and the Restoration Crisis, 1677–1683* (Cambridge, 1991); Blair Worden, 'English Republicanism', in J. H. Burns and Mark Goldie (eds), *The Cambridge History of Political Thought, 1450–1750* (Cambridge, 1991), pp. 443–75.

## 7 'LUXURY WITH CHARLES RESTOR'D'? THE TEMPER OF THE TIMES

1 Evelyn, iii.477 (12 March 1667).

2 On the incidence of the plague in general see J. F. D. Shrewsbury, *A History of Bubonic Plague in the British Isles* (Cambridge, 1970); more particularly, Walter George Bell, *The Great Plague in London in 1665*, 2nd edn (1951).

3 Pepys, iv.340 (19 October 1663). He notes its increase in the Netherlands during 1664 in iv.399 (26 November 1663), v.142 (4 May 1664), 186 (22 June 1664), 220 (25 July 1664), 231 (3 August 1664), 279 (24 September 1664).

4 Pepys, vi.93 (30 April 1665), 124 (10 June 1665), 128 (15 June 1665).

5 Pepys, vi.142 (29 June 1665), 157 (13 July 1665), 163 (20 July 1665), 173 with n. 3 (27 July 1665), 178 (31 July 1665), 187 with n. 2 (10 August 1665), 191 with n. 2 (14 August 1665), 207–8 (31 August 1665).

6 Pepys, vi.208 (31 August 1665), 214 with n. 2 (7 September 1665). The weekly mortality bills, prepared and printed by the Parish Clerks' Company, listed the total number of deaths in the capital from Tuesday to Tuesday, arranged under their causes and in parishes. Those for 1665 were collected in *London's Dreadfull Visitation* (1665). On their unreliability, see Shrewsbury, *History of the Bubonic Plague*, pp. 454–63. Pepys records an admission of a false return by a parish clerk (vi.207 (30 August 1665)). The bills were the subject of a pioneering work of statistical analysis, John Graunt's *Natural and Political Observations . . . made upon the bills of mortality* (1662), which went through revised third and fourth editions in the plague year.

7 Pepys, vi.133 (21 June 1665), 141–2 (29 and 30 June 1665), 189 (12 August 1665); Evelyn, iii.423 with n. 7 (27 November 1666); Hutton *R*, pp. 230–1.

8 Pepys, vi.224–5 with n. 1 (14 September 1665), 234 with n. 1 (20 September 1665), 243 with n. 3 (27 September 1665), 253 (5 October 1665), 295 (9 November 1665).

9 Pepys, vi.278 (26 October 1665), 328 (13 December 1665), 342 (31 December 1665), vii.3 (5 January 1666), 18 (19 January 1666), 376–7 with n. 2 (20 November 1666); Evelyn, iii.428 with n. 6, 429 with n. 1 (29 January and 2 February 1666); Baxter *RB*, III.1, §§2–3; Shrewsbury, *History of Bubonic Plague*, p. 454.

10 Pepys, vi.173 (28 July 1665); Baxter *RB*, III.2, §4. Nevertheless there were, inevitably, outbreaks in the provinces, particularly severe in Southampton and Yarmouth: see Hutton *R*, p. 229 with n. 42.

11 Pepys, vi.120 (7 June 1665), 140 (26 June 1665), 141 (28 June 1665), 150 (6 July 1665), 181 (3 August 1665), 212 (3 and 4 Septmeber 1665), 283 with n. 4 (31 October 1665); Bell, *Plague*, pp. 112–13, 132–3, 197–8, 214. *The Shutting Up Infected Houses . . . Soberly Debated* (1665) realized that this expedient was ineffectual.

12 Pepys, vi.120 (7 June 1665), 210 (3 Septmeber 1665), 213 with n. 5 (6 September 1665), 311 (27 November 1665); cf. vi.225 (14 September 1665); *Orders Received and Published by the Lord Mayor . . . concerning the Infection of the Plague* (1665), in *A Collection of Very Valuable and Scarce Pieces relating to the Plague* (1721), p. 9; Bell, *Great Plague*, pp. 112–13, 132–3, 197–8, 214.

13 Pepys, vi.189 (12 August 1665), 192 (15 August 1665), 256 (6 October 1665); cf. vi.187 (10 August 1665), 225 (14 September 1665).

14 Pepys, vi.162 (18 July 1665), 207 (30 August 1665), 211 with n. 5 (3 September 1665), vii.30 (30 January 1666); Bell, *Great Plague*, pp. 36, 39, 47–9, 178–9.

15 Evelyn, iii.417–18 (7 September 1665); Pepys, vi.268 (16 October 1665).

16 For examples, see Hutton *R*, pp. 246–7. Quite why this was the last epidemic is disputed. Immunity may have developed, in rats or humans, or both (though it had not done so before). See A. B. Appleby, 'The Disappearance of Plague', *EcHR*, 2nd ser. xxxiii (1980), 161–73; P. Slack, 'The Disappearance of Plague: An Alternative View', *Ec.HR*, 2nd ser. xxxiv (1981), 469–76.

17 Evelyn, iii.450–7 with nn. (2–5 September 1666), 458 (7 September 1666); Pepys, vii.267–76 (2–5 September 1666). The essential modern account is Walter George Bell, *The Great Fire of London in 1666* (1923; reprt 1994). For an excellent summary

account, see Hutton *R*, pp. 247–50. There is a map drawn by T. F. Reddaway which shows the extent of the fire in Pepys, vii.428–30 and x.632–5.

18 Burnet *OT*, i.416; Evelyn, iii.458, 459 (7 September 1666); Baxter *RB*, III.16, §31; Pepys, vii.280 (7 September 1666), 282 (8 September 1666), 286 with n. 2 (15 September 1666); Steele, 3473. For estimates of destruction and losses, see Bell, *Great Fire*, pp. 210–29.

19 Evelyn, iii.452–4 (3 September 1666). Evelyn gives a detailed eye-witness account of the destruction in his report of a walk taken through the smouldering city on 7 September (iii. 458–61). Cf. Pepys's account of his walk through the city on 5 September (vii.276–7) and Baxter *RB*, III.16–17, §§31–3. Fires continued to break out, and cellars to smoulder, for months afterwards. At the beginning of December Pepys saw a fire in Tower Street which the wind had revived in a wood cellar; he encountered smouldering ashes on 16 January 1667 and on 16 March he reports seeing smoke issuing from cellars 'from the late great Fire, now above six months since' (vii.393, viii.17, 114).

20 Evelyn, iii.457 (6 September 1666); Bell, *Great Fire*, pp. 114–15, 333–4, 349–50.

21 Pepys, vii.275 (5 September 1666), 405 with n. 3 (13 December 1666); Milward, pp. 7, 11, 68–9; *CJ*, viii.681; Clarendon *LC*, ii.288–9; Burnet *OT*, i.410–16; Bell, *Great Fire*, pp. 200–9. The government sought to prevent the publication of the unauthorized *True and Faithfull Account* (1667) of the Committee's proceedings (distributed by Elizabeth Calvert) which it took to be 'maliciously published by some Presbyterian hand' (*CSPD 1667*, pp. 290, 393, 401).

22 Clarendon *LC*, ii.289–91 (§§899–901); *State Trials*, vi.807ff.; Pepys, viii.81–2 with n. 4 (24 February 1667); Bell, *Great Fire*, pp. 191–5; Hutton *R*, p. 250.

23 See, for example, Joseph Mede, *The Key of the Revelation* (1643); Francis Potter, *An Interpretation of the Number 666* (Oxford, 1642); Henry Archer, *The Personall Reign of Christ upon Earth* (1642), which foresaw the conversion of the Jews in the 1650s, the destruction of Rome in 1666 and the Second Coming in 1700.

24 See, for example, John Canne, *A Voice from the Temple to the Higher Powers* (1653), pp. 24–5; John Rogers, *Ohel or Beth-shemesh* (1653) and *Sagrir, or Doomes-day Drawing Nigh* (1653), both cited and summarized in McKeon, pp. 198 –200; [Anon.], *A Brief Description of the Future History of Europe, from Anno 1650 to An. 1710 Treating Principally of those Grand and Famous Mutations yet Expected in the World, as the Ruine of the Popish Hierarchy . . . the Conversion of the . . . Jews . . . and the Fifth Monarchie of . . . Christ upon Earth* (1650), pp. 4, 9.

25 George Wither, *Ecchoes from the Sixth Trumpet* (1666), sig. C1v, cited in McKeon, p. 219. Other examples include [Anon.], *Christ and Antichrist: or, 666 Multiplied by 2½, whereby the True Number of Antichrists Reign is Discovered* (1662); Robert Codrington (trans.), *The Prophecies of Christopher Kotterus . . . concerning . . . the Sudden Destruction of the Papall Power* (1664).

26 *Mirabilis Annus* (1661), sig. A4v, quoted in McKeon, p. 201. This was followed by *Mirabilis Annus Secundus: or the Second Year of Prodigies* (1662) and *Mirabilis Annus Secundus: or the Second Part of the Second Year of Prodigies* (1662). For those involved in their compilation, see above, p. 155.

27 Pepys, vii.47, 355, 364 (18 February, 5 November, 10 November 1667).

28 Baxter *RB*, II.432, §424. See, for example, John Spencer, *A Discourse concerning Prodigies: wherein the Vanity of Presages by Them is Reprehended… To which is added a Short Treatise concerning Vulgar Prophecies* (1663), written to discountenance the *Mirabilis Annus* tracts.

29 Baxter *RB*, II.448, §445.

30 Evelyn, iii.415 with n. 5 (2 August 1665), 454 (3 September 1666), 457 (5 September 1666); Steele, 3426; Pepys, vi.210 (3 September 1665).

31 Richard Allestree's *The Causes of the Decay of Christian Piety* (1667) is representative. For discussion of such texts from the 1660s, see Spurr, pp. 236–8

32 Evelyn, iii.464 (10 October 1666). For other examples see Evelyn, iii.275, 295, 311–12, 415–16, 418

33 Pepys, viii.359–60, 361–2 (29 July 1667); cf. viii.353 (25 July 1667).

34 Pepys, viii.361, 366 (29 July 1667). Charles explicitly denied any such intention in his speech to the Lords when proroguing parliament (*LJ*, xii.114; Milward, p. 84).

35 Pepys, viii.377 (8 August 1667), 378 (9 August 1667). cf. viii.390–1 (19 August 1667), 556 (30 November 1667).

36 Pepys, viii.550 (27 November 1667). Cf. Pepys's end-of-year review, viii.602.

37 See above, pp. 102–3.

38 A *Second Advice to a Painter* (1667), dated April 1666, was seen by Pepys, perhaps in a manuscript copy, in December 1666 (Pepys, vii.407 (14 December 1666)); a *Third Advice*, dated 1 October 1666 and covering actions in the summer of 1666 under the command of Rupert and Albemarle, was lent to him in January 1667 (Pepys, viii.20 (20 January 1667)); he saw a *Fourth Advice*, 'upon the coming in of the Dutch to the River and the end of the war', in September 1667 (Pepys, viii.439 (16 September 1667)). A *Fifth Advice* was added when these three were published together later in 1667 as *Directions to a Painter for Describing our Naval Business*, attributed to Sir John Denham, an unlikely perpetrator of unlicensed publications whose authorship has never been accepted. Marvell has been accepted as the author of the *Last Instructions to a Painter* (first published in 1689 in the third part of *Poems on Affairs of State* but, on internal evidence, written in the late summer and autumn of 1667), and he has besides been claimed as the author of the second and third *Advices*. See further Marvell *P&L*, i.346–50; Annabel Patterson, *Marvell: The Writer in Public Life* (2000), pp. 76–9; M. T. Osborne, *Advice-to-a-Painter Poems, 1633–1856: An Annotated Finding List* (Austin, TX, 1949).

39 *Second Advice*, ll.38, 216, 218, in Marvell *CP*, pp. 119, 125.

40 *Third Advice*, l.229, and *Second Advice*, l.113, in Marvell *CP*, pp. 121, 137; Marvell *LI*, ll.12, 179, 495–8, 711–22, in *P&L*, i.147, 151, 160, 165.

41 Marvell *LI*, ll.512–18, 649–96, in *P&L*, i.160, 163–5.

42 *Third Advice*, ll.52, 233–4, in Marvell *CP*, pp. 132, 137.

43 Pepys, viii.417 (2 September 1667).

44 From the initials *C*lifford, *A*rlington, *B*uckingham, *A*shley, *L*auderdale.

45 Pepys, viii.597 (30 December 1667).

46 There were two Secretaries of State at any one time, responsible for domestic (especially intelligence) and foreign affairs, the latter divided between Northern (Russia, Scandinavia and the United Provinces) and Southern (including France) Europe. Bennet was preceded by Sir Edward Nicholas (1660–2). His fellow Secretaries were Sir William Morice (1660–8) and Sir John Trevor (1668–72).

47 On the Cabal's administration see M. Lee, Jr, *The Cabal* (Urbana, IL, 1965); K. H. D. Haley, *The First Earl of Shaftesbury* (Oxford, 1968), pp. 266–326; Ogg, pp. 326–41.

48 See above, pp. 87–8.

49 Hutton *CII*, p. 254, entitles his account of the years following Clarendon's fall 'The Ministry of Arlington'. Cf. Ogg, p. 327: 'Chief of these men was sir Henry Bennet . . .'.

50 For the 1667–8 negotiations over toleration, see above pp. 123–4.

51 See below, p. 179.

52 Burnet *OT*, i.167, 486–7 (cf. ii.468). John Miller 'The Potential for "Absolutism" in Later Stuart England', *H*, lxix (1984), 187–207, argues that Louis XIV's rule was in fact far less 'absolute' than it appeared to English observers and that Charles, whatever his inclinations, 'lacked the application or fixity of purpose to develop a systematic "absolutist" policy'. For the Commission, see above, p. 103 with n. 80.

53 The treaty is in Browning, pp. 859–63.

54 The view of Holmes, pp. 99–100. Cf. Ogg, p. 334: 'Charles' policy was a . . . well-timed bid for the support of English opinion'.

55 The secret treaty is in Browning, pp. 863–7.

56 For details of the negotiations and views of the Treaty and of Charles's motives, see: Ogg, pp. 338–50; Haley, *First Earl of Shaftesbury*, pp. 281–5; Keith Feiling, *British Foreign Policy, 1660–72* (1930), pp. 308, 313–14; John Miller, *Popery and Politics in England, 1660–1688* (Cambridge, 1973), pp. 108–20; Ronald Hutton, 'The Making of the Secret Treaty of Dover', *HJ*, xxix (1986), 297–318; Hutton *CII*, pp. 263–6, 270–4.

57 Browning, pp. 78, 81, 387–8, 389–91. On the debates surrounding the Declaration, see Lacey, pp. 54–70; Keeble, pp. 57–9.

58 Burnet *SOT*, p. 49.

59 'To His Sacred Majesty', ll.117–37, in Dryden, pp. 60–1.

60 See above, pp. 40–6.

61 Carew Reynel, *The True English Interest* (1674), sig. A6, quoted in Rochester, p. 329.

62 See above, pp. 96–7.

63 Ailesbury, i.7; 'On King Charles' (1673), ll.4, 22–3, in Rochester, p. 30.

64 Pepys, viii.362 (29 July 1667). 'Creeton' is Robert Creighton, Professor of Greek at Cambridge; his sermon seems not to have been published. Allestree's were published as *Eighteen Sermons* (1669).

65 Burnet *OT*, i.168–9, 358; Pepys, iii.139 (16 July 1662) .

66 'The Maimed Debauchee' (1675?), l.16, in Rochester, pp. 33, 87.

67 Pepys, viii.366 (29 July 1667); for a lewder account, see viii.368–9 (30 July 1667).

68 Marvell *LI*, l.30, in *P&L*, i.148. Both Pepys and Reresby (disbelievingly) record a milder version of this rumour, that Jermyn and the Queen Mother were married (Pepys, iii.263 (22 November 1662); Reresby, p. 29).

69 *Second Advice*, l.53, in Marvell *CP*, p. 199; Marvell *LI*, ll.67, 73, 75–6, in *P&L*, i.149; Pepys, vi.302 (17 November 1665), vii.8, 323, 365, 366 (9 January, 15 October, 10 and 12 November 1666); Hamilton,, i.95–6, 107–8. For the kind of gossip which circulated about the Duchess of York, see Hamilton, i.163–4.

70 Hamilton, i.108; Pepys, viii.366 (29 July 1667). Cf. 'Mistress Knight's Advice to the Duchess of Cleveland', in Rochester, p. 83.

71 Hamilton, i.108–11, ii.135; Pepys, iii.170–1 (19 August 1662).
72 Hamilton, ii.135–8; Pepys, ix.26–7 (17 January 1668), 52 (5 February 1668), 201 (15 May 1668).
73 For representative descriptions see Hamilton, i.114 (Middleton), 140 (Stanhope), 107–8 (Stuart, with Pepys, vii.383 (25 November 1666) and iv.230 (13 July 1663)), ii.43 (Jennings), 44 (Temple).
74 Pepys, viii.364 (29 July 1667); Marvell *LI*, ll.811–14, in *P&L*, i.168.
75 Hamilton, i.106–7; Pepys, iv.36–7 (8 February 1663).
76 Hamilton, i.96–7, ii.138.
77 See on this theme Steven N. Zwicker, 'Virgins and Whores: The Politics of Sexual Misconduct in the 1660s', in Conal Condren and A. D. Cousins (eds), *The Political Identity of Andrew Marvell* (Aldershot, 1990), pp. 85–110 (esp. p. 97).
78 Marvell *LI*, ll.79–86, in *P&L*, i.149.
79 Reresby, pp. 35–6.
80 Lawrence Stone, *The Family, Sex and Marraige in England, 1500–1800* (Harmondsworth, 1979), p. 335; John Morrill, *Revolution and Restoration: England in the 1650s* (1992), p. 116; Pepys, iv.136 (15 May 1663).
81 'On King Charles', ll.11–12, in Rochester, p. 30.
82 See, for example, Pepys, viii.368 (30 July 1667).
83 Burnet *OT*, i.482.
84 Hamilton, ii.2, 56 (Rochester); Burnet *OT*, i.476 (Rochester); Anthony a Wood, *Athenae Oxonienses*, ed. Philip Bliss, 3rd edn, 4 vols (1813–20), iii.1233 (Rochester); Pepys, viii.337 (14 July 1667 (Sackville)); Burnet *OT*, i.474 (Gwyn); Pepys, vii.426 (31 December 1666), viii.532–3 (16 November 1667 (Sedley)); Wood, *Athenae Oxonienses*, iv.731 (Sedley).
85 Hamilton i.93; Reresby, p. 24; Burnet *OT*, i.89–90, 182; Clarendon *LC*, ii.322; Wood, *Athenae Oxonienses*, iv.208.
86 Burnet *OT*, i.92, 174; Hesther W. Chapman, *Great Villiers* (1949), p. 142.
87 Milton *PL*, vii.30–7.
88 Pepys, iii.34 (22 February 1662), 36 (25 February 1662), iv.209 (1 July 1663), ix.435 (1 February 1669).
89 Pepys ix.335–6 (23 October 1668), 339 (26 October 1668).
90 Andrew Clark (ed.), *The Life and Times of Anthony a Wood*, abridged Llewelyn Powys (1932), p. 127; Evelyn, iv.410 (6 February 1685).
91 As noted by Anna Bryson, *From Courtesy to Civility: Changing Codes of Conduct in Early Modern England* (Oxford, 1998), p. 255. *OED*'s first citation for 'private parts' is from 1634.
92 Wood, *Athenae Oxonienses*, iii.1229; Rochester, 'A Ramble in St James' Park' (*ante* 1673), ll.97–8, in Rochester, p. 33. See on this theme Warren Chernaik, *Sexual Freedom in Restoration Literature* (Cambridge, 1995).
93 Baxter *RB*, III.21, §49.
94 Burnet *OT*, i.182; Joseph Spence, *Observations, Anecdotes, and Characters of Books and Men*, ed. James M. Osborn, 2 vols (Oxford, 1966), i.200.
95 Pope, 'The First Epistle of the Second Book of Horace Imitated', l.108.
96 Evelyn, iv.409–10 (6 February 1685).
97 *OED*, *quality* 4.

98 Reresby, p. 22; Ludlow, p. 285; Pepys, i.298 (20 November 1660).

99 Burnet *OT*, ii.469, 470.

100 Spence, *Observations*, i.276; Evelyn, iii.493 n. 6; Hamilton, i.99.

101 Elizabeth A. Foyster, *Manhood in Early Modern England: Honour, Sex and Marriage* (1999), pp. 214–15. There are relevant examples from our period in Paul Langford, *Englishness Identified: Manners and Character, 1650–1850* (Oxford, 2000).

102 [Allestree], *The Gentleman's Calling* (1664), pp. 26, 37, 86. The classic study of this process of cultural change is Norbert Elias, *The Civilizing Process*, trans. Edmund Jephcott (1939; rptd Oxford, 1994). See also Bryson, *From Courtesy to Civility*, which discusses the figure of the libertine on pp. 243–75.

103 Francis Osborne, *Advice to a Son* (1656), p. 17.

104 Pepys, i.260 (7 October 1660), ii.29 (3 February 1661). The phrases *in* and *out of fashion* are seventeenth-century coinages (*OED*, *fashion* 11) which gained in currency at the end of the century.

105 On fops, see Philip Carter, *Men and the Emergence of Polite Society in Britain, 1660–1800* (2001), pp. 137–56.

106 Pepys, i.253.

107 Evelyn, iii.268 with n. 6; Pepys, i.171 (6 June 1660), 224 (18 August 1660), 297 (20 November 1660), ii.5 (3 November 1661), 7 (7 January 1661), 35 (12 January 1661).

108 Evelyn, iii.304 (20 November 1661), which notes that Evelyn probably watched Davenant's version; Dryden, Epilogue to *The Conquest of Granada*, Part II (1671), ll.23–4, 34, in Dryden, p. 244.

109 William Wycherley, *The Country Wife*, I.i.357–8; Sir George Etherege, *She Would If She Could*, II.ii.224–5; Rochester, 'God bless our good and gracious King', in Rochester, p. 197.

110 See Leah Marcus, *The Politics of Mirth* (Chicago, 1986).

111 Pepys, ii.105 (23 May 1661).

112 Marjorie Hope Nicolson (ed.), *The Conway Letters*, revd edn, ed. Sarah Hutton (Oxford, 1992), p. 377; Pepys, i.186 (28 June 1660), 222 (15 August 1660).

113 Rugg, p. 106, 113; Eveyln, iii.296 (1 October 1661).

114 Evelyn iii.249 (2 July 1660); Pepys, ii.51 (9 March 1661); Rugg, pp. 120, 121.

## 8 'MALE AND FEMALE CREATED HE THEM'

1 William Sermon, *The Ladies Companion* (1671), pp. 7–15.

2 Ian Maclean, *The Renaissance Notion of Woman* (Cambridge, 1980), pp. 28–9. On the implications of anatomy for early modern culture, see Jonathan Sawday, *The Body Emblazoned: Dissection and the Human Body in Renaissance Culture* (1995).

3 For the durability of Galenic medicine see Nancy Siraisi, *Medieval and Early Renaissance Medicine* (Chicago, 1990), p. 84; Thomas Laqueur, *Making Sex: Body and Gender from the Greeks to Freud* (1990; rptd Cambridge, MA, 1992), pp. 151, 170, 265–6; Owsei Temkin, *Galenism: The Rise and Decline of a Medical Philosophy* (Ithaca, NY, 1973), pp. 34–92.

4 Maclean, *Renaissance Notion*, pp. 30–4; Audrey Eccles, *Obstetrics and Gynaecology in Tudor and Stuart England* (1982), p. 26. For this 'one-sex' (male) model of human

biology, see Lacqueur, *Making Sex*, pp. 1–69 and passim, and Eccles, *Obstetrics*, pp. 17–22.

5 Maclean, *Renaissance Notion*, pp. 8–9, 31–3; Laqueur, *Making Sex*, p. 4.

6 Jane Sharp, *The Midwives Book*, ed. Elaine Hobby (New York, 1999), p. 37 (but see also p. 67); [Thomas Gibson], *Anatomy of Humane Bodies Epitomized* (1682), pp. 136–44, 159.

7 Sermon, *Ladies Companion*, pp. 25–7, 183; Nicholas Culpeper, *A Directory for Midwives* (1668), p. 92; [N. H.], *The Ladies Dictionary* (1694), pp. 123–4; Sharp, *Midwives Book*, p. 83.

8 [Gibson], *Anatomy*, p. 163; Culpeper, *Directory*, p. 43; Sharp, *Midwives Book*, pp. 58, 68, 75.

9 Sharp, *Midwives Book*, p. 129; Charles T. Wood, 'The Doctor's Dilemma: Sin, Salvation and the Menstrual Cycle in Medieval Thought', *Speculum*, lvi (1981), 713, 716–17; Maclean, *Renaissance Notion*, pp. 39–40; Janice Delaney et al., *The Curse: A Cultural History of Menstruation* (New York, 1976), pp. 33–9.

10 Margaret Cavendish, *The Worlds Olio* (1655), sig. A4; Richard Baxter, *A Christian Directory* (1673), II.i.480; Lucy Hutchinson, *Principles of the Christian Religion*, ed. Julius Hutchinson (1817), pp. 5–6.

11 Margaret Olofson Thickstun, *Fictions of the Feminine: Puritan Doctrine and the Representation of Women* (Ithaca, NY, 1988), pp. 1–36.

12 [Robert Gould], *Love Given O're* (1682), p. 2.

13 Milton *PL*, iv.296–301.

14 Bunyan *MW*, iv.306–7, 325, xii.128, 147, 148. For seventeenth-century applications of Genesis to sexual relations see James Grantham Turner, *One Flesh: Paradisal Marriage and Sexual Relations in the Age of Milton* (Oxford, 1987); more generally, see John Phillips, *Eve: The History of an Idea* (San Francisco, 1984).

15 Sharp, *Midwives Book*, p. 76; Culpeper, *Directory*, p. 79; [N. H.], *Ladies Dictionary*, p. 234; Maclean, *Renaissance Notion*, pp. 40–2; Eccles, *Obstetrics*, p. 28; Laqueur, *Making Sex*, pp. 108–12.

16 Robert Burton, *Anatomy of Melancholy* (1621–51), I.iii.2 (4).

17 Sharp, *Midwives Book*, pp. 39, 103; Lacquer, *Making Sex*, pp. 43–52, 66–7.

18 Ambroise Paré, *The Workes* (1665), pp. 592–3, quoted in Anne Laurence, *Women in England, 1500–1760* (1994), p. 67; Laqueur, *Making Sex*, pp. 64–6, but see also p. 98; Eccles, *Obstetrics*, pp. 26–42.

19 Sharp, *Midwives Book*, p. 80; cf. Culpeper, *Directory*, pp. 63, 64–5.

20 Milton *PL*, iv.737–73, viii.510–22. For sexuality and sexual relations in Milton see Turner, *One Flesh*; Diane McColley, *Milton's Eve* (Urbana, IL, 1983); Julia Walker (ed.), *Milton and the Idea of Woman* (1988).

21 Milton *PL*, viii.588.

22 Baxter, *Christian Directory*, II.i.480.

23 [Richard Allestree], *The Ladies Calling* (Oxford, 1673), p. 39.

24 [Allestree], *Ladies Calling*, pp. 12–13, 29–30.

25 Janet Todd, *Sensibility: An Introduction* (1986), pp. 110–28.

26 [N. H.], *Ladies Dictionary*, *s.vv.* '*Compassion and a Merciful Disposition praiseworthy in the female sex*' ('this chiefly should reign in the lovely tender breasts of the femal sex, made for the seats of mercy and commiseration'), '*Gracefulness*' ('from a well-

tempered spirit ariseth gracefulness'), '*Meekness*' ('is not only enjoined to all as a Christian virtue but is in a more peculiar manner enjoined to women'), '*Natural Modesty*' ('is so inherent to their frame, that they cannot divest themselves of it without violence to their nature'), '*Patience, admirable in either sex*' ('The female sex especially ought to be endured with it, because they have frequent occasion to use it').

27 Hutchinson, p. 5.

28 Jane Barker, 'A Virgin Life', in *Poetical Recreations* (1688), p. 12; [Allestree], *Ladies Calling*, part II, pp. 3–5.

29 Baxter, *Christian Directory*, II.ix.532.

30 Milton *PL*, ix.232–3.

31 The records however suggest that a high proportion of women remained unmarried: see Peter Laslett, 'Mean Household Size in England since the Sixteenth Century', in Peter Laslett and R. Wall (eds), *Household and Family in Time Past* (Cambridge, 1972), p. 145 (table reproduced in Laurence, *Women in England*, p. 33).

32 [William Whately], *A Bride-Bush* (1617), p. 36.

33 For a summary of typical advice, see Ralph Houlbrooke, *The English Family, 1450–1700* (1984), pp. 96–119.

34 William Gouge, *Of Domesticall Duties* (1622), pp. 26–30, 267–73, 329–30.

35 Bunyan, *Christian Behaviour* (1663), in *MW*, iii.32.

36 Gouge, *Domesticall Duties*, pp. 274–88; Bunyan *MW*, iii.32–4.

37 Gouge, *Domesticall Duties*, p. 219; Keith Thomas, 'The Double Standard', *Journal of the History of Ideas*, xx (1959), 195–216; Lawrence Stone, *The Family, Sex and Marriage in England, 1500–1800* (1977), pp. 501–7.

38 Stone's *Family, Sex and Marriage* traces the development through the seventeenth century of the 'companionative marriage' and, in what he calls the 'decisive shift' in the later seventeenth century, the 'closed domesticated nuclear family'.

39 Stressing continuity with the past, Stone's critics dispute that marriage was transformed in the early modern period, that the nuclear family was not characteristic of medieval society, and that Protestantism introduced a more positive view of the marriage partnership: see, for example, Houlbrooke, *English Family, 1450–1700*; Margaret Ezell, *The Patriarch's Wife: Literary Evidence and the History of the Family* (Chapel Hill, NC, 1987); Peter Laslett, *The World We Have Lost Further Explored*, 3rd edn (1983), pp. 90–6; K. M. Davies, 'Continuity and Change in Literary Advice on Marriage', in R. B. Outhwaite (ed.), *Marriage and Society: Studies in the Social History of Marriage* (1981), pp. 58–80.

40 Gouge, *Domesticall Duties*, pp. 182–3, 224–7; [N. H.], *Dictionary*, *s.v.* '*Obedience, in virgins*'.

41 Milton *PL*, iv.299, 506–7, viii.364–5, 445. On this tendency to undercut the insistence on wifely subjection, see further David Leverenz, *The Language of Puritan Feeling* (New Brunswick, NJ, 1980), pp. 70–104; Edmund Morgan, *The Puritan Family* (New York, 1966), pp. 29–64; Christopher Durston, *The Family in the English Revolution* (1989), passim.

42 Frances Parthenope Verney (ed.), *Memoirs of the Verney Family*, 4 vols (1892–9), iii.73–4. On the education of women see further Dorothy Gardiner, *English Girlhood at School* (1929); Elaine Hobby, *Virtue of Necessity: English Women's Writing, 1649–88* (1988), pp. 190–8; Myra Reynolds, *The Learned Lady in England, 1650–1760* (Boston, MA, 1964).

43 John Loftis (ed.), *The Memoirs of Anne, Lady Halkett, and Ann, Lady Fanshawe* (Oxford, 1979), p. 110; Margaret Cavendish, 'A True Relation of My Birth', in her *The Life of William Cavendish Duke of Newcastle*, ed. Charles Firth (1906), pp. 157, 158.

44 Hutchinson, p. 15.

45 Cavendish, *World's Olio*, sig. A4v.

46 Hutchinson, p. 70.

47 Cavendish, *CCXI Sociable Letters* (1664), pp. 12–13.

48 Cavendish, *Sociable Letters*, p. 27.

49 *The Description of a New World, called The Blazing World*, ed. Kate Lilley (1992), p. 124.

50 Cavendish, 'True Relation', in *Life of William Cavendish,* pp . 166–8; Kathleen Jones, *A Glorious Fame: The Life of Margaret Cavendish* (1988), pp. 75–6, 89–92. For other examples of tensions between the demands of a wifely, domestic role and the exigencies of Civil War see N. H. Keeble, 'Obedient Subjects? The Loyal Self in Some Later Seventeenth-century Royalist Women's Memoirs', in Gerald Maclean (ed.), *Culture and Society in the Stuart Restoration* (Cambridge, 1995), pp. 201–18

51 Jeremiah Burroughes, *The Glorious Name of God* (1643), pp. 78–81; Katherine Chidley, *Justification of the Independent Churches of Christ* (1641), p. 26. See further Keith Thomas, 'Women and the Civil War Sects', *Past and Present*, xiii (1958), 432–62.

52 See further: Patricia Higgins, 'The Reactions of Women', in Brian Manning (ed.), *Politics, Religion and the English Civil War* (1973), pp. 179–222; Elaine Hobby, 'Prophecy, Enthusiasm and Female Pamphleteering', in N. H. Keeble (ed.), *Cambridge Companion to Writing of the English Revolution* (Cambridge, 2001), pp. 162–78; Phyllis Mack, 'Women as Prophets during the English Civil War', *Feminist Studies*, viii (1982), 19–45; Ellen McArthur, 'Women Petitioners and the Long Parliament', *EHR*, xxiv (1909), 698–709; the essays by Ann Maria McEntee and Rachel Trubowitz in James Holstun (ed.), *Pamphlet Wars: Prose in the English Revolution* (1992), pp. 92–111, 112–33.

53 [Margaret Fell], *Womens Speaking Justified* (1666), pp. 3–8.

54 Anne Wentworth, *A Vindication* (1677), extracted in Elspeth Graham et al. (eds), *Her Own Life: Autobiogrpahical Writings by Seventeenth-century Englishwomen* (1989), pp. 180–96.

55 John Bunyan, *A Case of Conscience Resolved* (1683), in *MW*, iv.291–330; N. H. Keeble, ' "Here is her glory, even to be under him": The Feminine in the Thought and Work of John Bunyan', in Anne Laurence et. al (eds), *John Bunyan and his England 1628–88* (1990), pp. 131–47 (esp. p. 142) and Thickstun, *Fictions of the Feminine*, pp. 87–104.

56 [Allestree], *Ladies Calling*, p. 8.

57 [Bathsua Makin], *An Essay to Revive the Antient Education of Gentlewomen* (1673), pp. 3–7.

58 Richard Ward, *The Life of…Henry More* (1710), p. 193; More, *Antidote against Atheism* (1652), ded. ep.; both cited in Marjorie Hope Nicholson (ed.), *The Conway Letters*, revd Sarah Hutton (Oxford, 1992), p. 46, n. 15.

59 Nicholson, *Conway Letters*, p. 76.

60 Lilian Faderman, *Surpassing the Love of Men: Romantic Friendship and Love Between Women from the Renaissance to the Present* (1985), pp. 65–143.

61 Philips, 'Friendship', l.49, in Patrick Thomas (ed.), *Collected Works*, 2 vols (Stump Cross, Essex, 1990–2), i.151 (see also 'A Retired Friendship, to Ardelia', 'To My Excellent Lucasia, on our Friendship', 'Friendship', 'A Married State' (i.97–8, 121–2, 150–1, 254)); Rudolph M. Dekker and Lotte van de Pol, *The Tradition of Female Transvestism in Early Modern Europe* (1989), pp. 55–8; Faderman, *Surpassing the Love of Men*, pp. 68–71. *OED* can find only one citation for *tribade* before the nineteenth century.

62 Jacqueline Pearson, *The Prostituted Muse: Images of Women and Women Dramatists, 1642–1737* (1988), pp. 100–18. See further Elizabeth Howe, *The First English Actresses* (Cambridge, 1992). Dekker and Van de Pol, *Female Transvestism*, argue that female transvestism nevertheless amounted almost to a tradition in Northern Europe (pp. 1, 9, 11, 54, 115 n. 3).

63 Richard Lovelace, 'On Sanazar's being Honoured with Six Hundred Duckets by the Clarissimi of Venice', *Lucasta: Posthume Poems* (1659), p. 84; Rochester, *A Letter from Artemiza in the Town to Chloe in the Country* (1679), ll.26–7, in Rochester, p. 49.

64 The standard account of the circumstances of seventeenth-century female literary production is Hobby, *Virtue of Necessity*. See also: Ezell, *The Patriarch's Wife*; Germaine Greer et al (eds), *Kissing the Rod: An Anthology of Seventeenth-century Women's Verse* (1988), pp. 1–31; Jane Spencer, *The Rise of the Woman Novelist* (Oxford, 1986), esp. pp. 3–74; Janet Todd, *The Sign of Angellica: Women, Writing and Fiction, 1660–1800* (1989), esp. pp. 13–98.

65 Anne Bradstreet, 'The Prologue', *The Tenth Muse* (1650), ll.27–32, 42–4, in Jeannine Hensley (ed.), *The Works* (Cambridge MA, 1967), p. 16. Ezell, *Patriarch's Wife*, argues that literary composition was in fact a more generally available option for women than their own printed *apologias* might suggest (see esp. pp. 62–100).

66 Cavendish, 'True Relation', in *Life of William Cavendish*, pp. 172, 175, 177; *Blazing World*, pp. 124, 224.

67 Pepys, viii.163–4 (11 April 1667),196–7 (1 May 1667), 242–3 (30 May 1667).

68 Evelyn, iii.330 (13 August 1662). On the Society's antecedents see Michael Hunter, *Science and Society in Restoration England* (1981), pp. 21–31, and references there given, especially Charles Webster, *The Great Instauration: Science, Medicine and Reform, 1629–1660* (1975). For its founding and activities in the 1660s see Thomas Birch, *The History of the Royal Society of London*, 4 vols (1756–7), vols 1–2; Sir Henry Lyons, *The Royal Society, 1660–1940* (Cambridge, 1944), pp. 19–71; Sir Harold Hartley (ed.), *The Royal Society: Its Origins and Founders* (1960).

69 Robert Boyle, *The Sceptical Chymist*, Everyman's Library (1914), pp. 6, 20.

70 *Science* carried the general sense of humanly acquired knowledge (in contrast to divinely revealed theology); *mechanical*, *natural* or *experimental philosophy* are the usual terms to distinguish science in the modern sense (*OED*).

71 Hunter, *Science and Society*, p. 29.

72 Thomas Sprat, *History of the Royal Society*, ed. Jackson Cope and Harold Jones (St Louis, MO, 1959), pp. 53, 62, 63. Sprat explicitly defends this liberal intercourse from the charge that it is injurious to the established Church of England, if not to Christianity (pp. 345–78).

73 This question is canvassed in Hunter, *Science and Society*, passim, with extensive bibliographical references.

74 Sprat, *History*, p. 67; letter from Evelyn to John Beale 27 July 1670, John Evelyn's Letterbook, Evelyn ms. 39, Christ Church, Oxford, quoted in Hunter, *Science and Society*, p. 44.

75 Hunter, *Science and Society*, p. 71; see more at large Hunter, 'The Social Basis and Changing Fortunes of an Early Scientific Institution: An Analysis of the Membership of the Royal Society, 1660–85', *Notes and Records of the Royal Society*, xxxi (1976), 9–114. The original 40 fellows are listed in Birch, *History*, i.41; Lyons, *Royal Society*, p. 22; Hartley, *Royal Society*, pp. 33–4.

76 On these efforts, see Hunter, *Science and Society*, pp. 38–43.

77 See on this tradition Hunter, *Science and Society*, pp. 66–84; W. E. Houghton, 'The English Virtuoso in the Seventeenth Century', *JHI*, iii (1942), 190–219; M. H. Nicolson, *Pepys' Diary and the New Science* (Charlottesville, VA, 1965).

78 Evelyn, iii.266 (6 January 1661), 289 (22 May 1661), 290 (19 May 1661), 293 (9 August 1661), 304 (20 November 1661), 306 (4 December 1661), 316 (19 February 1662), 317 (19 April 1662), 325 (10 June 1662), 337 (1 October 1662). This is a far from complete list of the sessions Evelyn records in these 18 months.

79 Evelyn, iii.338 (3 October 1662).

80 Evelyn, iii.334 (3 September 62), 433 with n. 3 (2 April 1666).

81 C. H. Josten (ed.), *Elias Ashmole, 1617–1692*, 5 vols (Oxford, 1966), i.126–8, 205–6, 218–19, 232–4.

82 Evelyn, iii.325 (10 June 1662), 340 (15 October 1662).

83 *Annus Mirabilis*, ll.617–64, in Dryden, pp. 168–71.

84 Sprat, *History*, pp. 62, 113, 378–9.

85 Ailesbury, i.96; cf. Sprat, *History*, p. 149; Burnet *OT*, i.167, and *SOT*, p. 49.

86 Charles Andrews, *British Committees, Commissions and Councils of Trade and Plantations, 1622–1675* (Baltimore, MD, 1908), pp. 61–95.

87 Sprat, *History*, p. 407; Sprat, *Observations on Monsieur de Sorbier's Voyage into England* (1665), p. 165.

88 Dryden, p. 106. This poem is set in its historical context in McKeon.

89 Pepys, v.35 (2 February 1664); McKeon, pp. 117–18.

90 *Annus Mirabilis*, ll.1197–1216, in Dryden, p. 200–1.

91 Roger Finlay and Beatrice Shearer, 'Population Growth and Suburban Expansion', in A. L. Beier and Roger Finlay (eds), *London, 1500–1700: The Making of the Metropolis* (1986), pp. 37–59.

92 Evelyn, *London Revived*, ed. E. S. De Beer (Oxford, 1938), pp. 2, 37, 49, 50–1; Evelyn, *Diary*, iii.462–3 (13 September 1666); Harold F. Hutchison, *Sir Christopher Wren* (1976), pp. 64–5. Evelyn apparently made use of Hollar's engraved plans of London before the Fire (*London Revived*, p. 25n.), for which, and prospects both before and after, see Arthur M. Hind, *Wenceslaus Hollar and his Views of London and Windsor in the Seventeenth Century* (1922), pp. 35–44, 49.

93 Steele, 3473, 3475, 3477; *Statutes*, v.601–3 (18 & 19 Car. II c.7, setting up the Fire Court), 603–12 (18 & 19 Car. II.c.8, the Rebuilding Act). On this legislation and the Fire Court see T. F. Reddaway, *The Rebuilding of London after the Great Fire* (1940), pp. 68–111.

94 *CSPD 1666–67*, p. 577.

95 Hutchison, *Wren*, pp. 134–5. On the whole subject of the rebuilding see Reddaway, *Rebuilding*; John Schofield, *The Building of London* (1984); W. G. Bell, *The Great Fire of London* (1923; rptd 1994), pp. 230–98.

96 Dryden, *Annus Mirabilis*, ll.1173–88, in Dryden, pp. 199–200 (in a note Dryden states that Augusta was the old name of London). For other contemporary responses see Robert Arnold Aubin (ed.), *London in Flames, London in Glory: Poems on the Fire and Rebuilding of London, 1666–1709* (New Brunswick, NJ, 1943).

## AFTERWORD

1 Clarendon *LC*, i.268–9 (§1).

2 See John Spurr, *England in the 1670s: 'This Masquerading Age'* (Oxford, 2000), for a marvellously detailed and comprehensive account of the ensuing decade.

# Index